Fodor's

PHILADELPHIA

Welcome to Philadelphia

Little did we realize that the emergence of a novel coronavirus in early 2020 would abruptly bring almost all travel to a halt. Although our Fodor's writers around the world have continued working to bring you the best of the destinations they cover, we still anticipate that more than the usual number of businesses will close permanently in the coming months, perhaps with little advance notice. We don't expect things to return to "normal" for some time. As you plan your upcoming travels to Philadelphia, please confirm that places are still open and let us know when we need to make updates by writing to us at this address: editors@fodors.com.

TOP REASONS TO GO

★ **Local Cuisine:** Cozy BYOBs, cheesesteaks, Reading Terminal Market.

★ **Iconic Landmarks:** The Rocky Steps, the *LOVE* Statue, Boathouse Row.

★ **Eclectic Neighborhoods:** Historic Society Hill, funky Fishtown, chic Rittenhouse Square.

★ **Revolutionary History:** Liberty Bell, Independence Hall, Museum of the American Revolution.

★ **Art:** World-class museums, street murals, high-end galleries, and everything in between.

★ **Bar Scene:** From lively beer gardens to chic cocktail lounges, nightlife flourishes.

Contents

MAPS

Chapter 1

EXPERIENCE PHILADELPHIA

15 ULTIMATE EXPERIENCES

Philadelphia offers terrific experiences that should be on every traveler's list. Here are Fodor's top picks for a memorable trip.

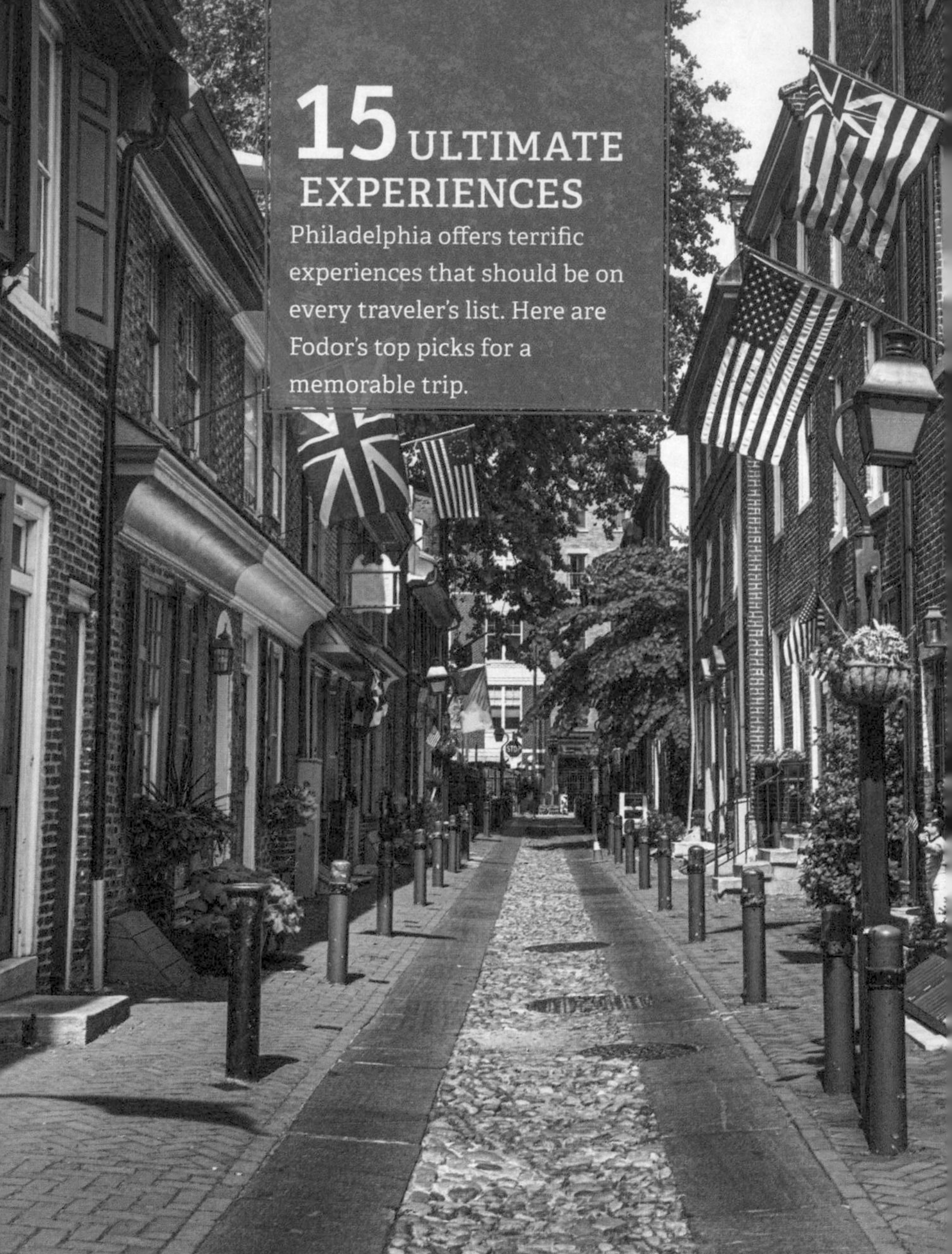

1 Explore Old City

Known for its cobblestone streets and historic sites, the city's oldest neighborhood is a mix of 18th-century charm and lively nightlife spots, galleries, and restaurants. *(Ch. 3)*

2 Cheesesteaks. Enough Said.

A trip to Philly isn't complete without trying the city's most legendary sandwich. Pat's or Geno's? Or try locals' spots like John's or Jim's. *(Ch. 8)*

3 A City of Murals

The city's wonderful Mural Arts program, begun in 1984, views every blank wall as a canvas. You can see the work of local artists showcased all around town. *(Ch. 9)*

4 Schuylkill River Bike Rides

For a fresh look at the city, rent wheels through the Indego bike share program. One place to explore is the Schuylkill Banks Boardwalk with its spectacular city views. *(Ch. 7, 11)*

5 Independence National Historical Park

The early history of the United States is recalled here, including the Liberty Bell, Congress Hall, and Independence Hall, where the Declaration of Independence was signed in 1776. *(Ch. 3)*

6 Reading Terminal Market

This historic public market is a must-visit for any food lover. Head to longtime favorite DiNic's for a famous pork sandwich, and then try Bassetts delicious ice cream. *(Ch. 5)*

7 Sports

This city is famous for its sports teams—and for its die-hard fans. Tickets to an Eagles game are almost impossible to get, but check out the Phillies, Flyers, or Sixers. *(Ch. 1, 8)*

8 Ritzy Rittenhouse Square

One of city founder William Penn's five original squares, Rittenhouse is known for its elegance and charm. Restaurants, shops, and apartments line this green refuge. *(Ch. 6)*

9 Fabulous Fairmount Park

One of the world's largest city parks, Fairmount boasts trails, bike paths, and historic mansions—as well as stunning views of Boathouse Row on the Schuylkill River. *(Ch. 7)*

10 Museum of the American Revolution

History comes alive through interactive displays at this museum. Step back and consider the stakes in the Revolutionary War for groups like Native Americans, enslaved Africans, and women. *(Ch. 3)*

11 Eastern State Penitentiary

A visit to the empty cellblocks of this semi-ruined jail is both an eerie, entertaining excursion to sites like Al Capone's cell and a thought-provoking look at criminal justice past and present. *(Ch. 7)*

12 Parkway Museums

The Parkway is home to some of the city's most famous museums including the Franklin Institute (pictured), Barnes Foundation, Rodin Museum, and Philadelphia Museum of Art. *(Ch. 7)*

13 South Street

With an unapologetically edgy vibe, this famous street combines ethnically diverse restaurants, shops, and bars into one lively area that always buzzes with activity. *(Ch. 8)*

14 Dining in Passyunk

A foodie favorite, the stretch of East Passyunk Avenue between Broad and 9th Streets lets you dine around the world on cuisine from Italy to Mexico to Asia. *(Ch. 8)*

15 Brewery Scene

Beer lovers can sip great suds at many craft breweries or brew pubs; new spots continue to pop up in funky neighborhoods like Fishtown and Northern Liberties. *(Ch. 10)*

What to Eat and Drink

WATER ICE
Known as Italian ice everywhere else, this icy, slushy treat was first created in Philadelphia in the 1930s. Today, some of the same South Philly shops—or newcomers like D'Emilio's Old World Ice Treats—are selling cups in flavors like lemon, cherry, and chocolate, using their original recipes.

CHEESESTEAKS
Other places try to replicate Philly's most quintessential food, but few get it right. Made with chopped steak, cheese—American, provolone, or Whiz—and often, fried onions, all on a chewy Italian roll. A side-by-side taste test of the original Pat's King of Steaks and Geno's is a fun rite of passage, but locals love John's Roast Pork, as well as Dalessandro's, Jim's, Angelo's, Woodrow's, Tony Luke's, and Max's.

SOFT PRETZELS
These aren't your typical mall or movie-theater snacks. The Philly version—with roots in the city's Pennsylvania Dutch culture—has an elongated shape with a soft interior and perfectly browned, salted exterior. Find them everywhere from street carts and the ubiquitous chain Philly Pretzel Factory, to independent shops like Miller's Twist inside the Reading Terminal Market.

MARKETS
Speaking of Reading Terminal Market, there might be nothing that encapsulates Philadelphia's diverse, delicious food scene better than its iconic markets. Not far from City Hall, Reading Terminal is the oldest continuously operating indoor market in the country with more than 75 food stalls that run the gamut from cheesesteaks and pretzels to Amish goodies. Philly's other famous market, the outdoor Italian Market, can be found on a lively stretch of 9th Street in South Philly. Around since the late 1800s, the market has vendors selling everything from fresh pasta and spices to meats and dry goods. There are even places to get lunch or coffee.

ZAHAV
According to the James Beard Association, Zahav is America's best restaurant right now. Reservations are tough to land, and it's not uncommon for diners to plan trips around them. Try calling to see if there are any cancellations the morning of, or visit one of the other excellent Philly eateries Solomonov runs including K'Far, Merkaz, Abe Fisher, and the newest star, Laser Wolf in Fishtown.

HOAGIES
Don't call them subs, grinders, or heroes. In Philly, sandwiches made on long Italian rolls are called hoagies, and they're pretty outstanding—head to Middle Child in Center City East for a taste. Find varieties made with turkey, ham, tuna salad, and the classic Italian version—with thinly sliced meats and cheeses, shredded lettuce, tomatoes, oil, and vinegar—in delis and restaurants all over town. If you really want to eat like a local, ask for Duke's mayo or stop by one of the many Wawa's around town...you won't be alone.

The Philly cheesesteak—pictured as "Whiz, witout" (no onions).

THE SCHMITTER
Speaking of the city's love of sandwiches, head to McNally's Tavern in Chestnut for what many locals consider to be one of the greatest bar sandwiches of all time. The Schmitter has steak, cheese, and fried onions topped with fried salami and a special sauce, all on a kaiser roll—it's as delicious as it sounds.

ROAST PORK SANDWICH
By now you may have picked up on the fact that Philadephians are serious about sandwiches. Also created in Italian-American kitchens, the roast pork sandwich is made with thinly sliced hot roasted pork, sharp (or mild) provolone cheese, and garlicky sautéed spinach or broccoli rabe. Most locals will tell you John's Roast Pork makes the best version in town—the no-frills spot won a James Beard Award for culinary excellence in 2006—and they're correct. Another deserving contender is DiNic's in the Reading Terminal Market.

ITALIAN CUISINE
The city embraces Italian food in all forms, from South Philly's simple, perfect red gravy (also known as marinara or tomato sauce) joints to restaurants that showcase handmade pasta and regional cuisine like Vetri in Center City East. We can't talk about the city's great Italian food without mentioning Termini Brothers Bakery in East Passyunk. They've been churning out Italian pastries since 1921. Stop by for their filled-to-order cannoli, as well as pizzelles, biscotti, cakes, and other traditional Italian sweet treats.

SCRAPPLE
The distinctive regional specialty—made with pork scraps, spices, flour, and cornmeal—is a Pennsylvania Dutch tradition. You can find simple, classic versions of the breakfast specialty on diner menus around the city, including Dutch Eating Place in Reading Terminal Market, and Sulimay's in Fishtown.

CRAFT BOOZE
Before Prohibition, Philadelphia was home to a high concentration of breweries and distilleries, and in the past decade, booze has been making a big comeback. Yards, in Northern Liberties, is the oldest continuously operating craft brewer in the city, while Fishtown's Philadelphia Distilling is Pennsylvania's first craft distillery since Prohibition.

Philadelphia's Best Historic Sites

INDEPENDENCE HALL
This stately redbrick building looks surprisingly low-key for a national icon and symbol of freedom, but if these walls could talk, they would tell tales of how the building that began life as the Pennsylvania State House became the site of monumental decisions and events for a new nation.

CLIVEDEN
The stately fieldstone house is quiet now, but back in the revolutionary days of 1777, Cliveden played an important role in the bloody Battle of Germantown. You can take a guided tour of the house, or check out exhibits in the Carriage House visitor center that examine the historical legacy of slavery and how it can be used to understand what the house—and freedom—mean.

MOTHER BETHEL AFRICAN METHODIST EPISCOPAL CHURCH
Former slave Richard Allen founded this church and purchased the land it still occupies in 1787; it's the country's oldest real estate continuously owned by African Americans. He and his wife, Sarah Allen, ran a station on the Underground Railroad. In the crypt, you can see their tombs, pews from the original church, and a museum.

EASTERN STATE PENITENTIARY
This massive prison in the Fairmount neighborhood takes you through the history of criminal justice reform. Peek into cells that held Al Capone, Willie Sutton, and others. Take a guided tour or the excellent audio tour narrated by Steve Buscemi to appreciate the crumbling spaces, and study displays on current issues in criminal justice.

RITTENHOUSE SQUARE
A sculpture-filled, leafy retreat beloved by locals, the square and neighborhood remain chic and expensive, though apartments, restaurants, and fancy shops have replaced the original houses right around the square. To channel the neighborhood vibe, relax on a bench or people-watch while dining alfresco.

THE BENJAMIN FRANKLIN MUSEUM
Benjamin Franklin played many critical roles in Philadelphia and in the nation's founding, and all get their due in lively exhibits at this museum in Franklin Court. Interactive displays reflect on his key qualities, and videos bring an icon to life, even for children.

MUSEUM OF THE AMERICAN REVOLUTION
Opened in 2017, the Museum of the American Revolution isn't historic in itself, but it's well worth a visit to explore engaging interactive displays and intriguing artifacts that make the struggle for independence feel far fresher than the account in your high-school history textbook.

Elfreth's Alley

PRESIDENT'S HOUSE
Just north of the Liberty Bell Center, an unassuming, open-air site with partial brick walls and window frames marks the footprint of the vanished President's House, home of Presidents George Washington and John Adams from 1790 to 1800.

ELFRETH'S ALLEY
Built from the early 1700s to 1830, the 32 modest Federal- and Georgian-style houses on the country's oldest continuously occupied residential street were not the grand mansions of Society Hill. Craftspeople from silversmiths to cabinet makers lived here, and in season you can stop by the Elfreth's Alley Museum at Nos. 124–126 to explore the former homes of a Colonial dressmaker and chair maker.

LIBERTY BELL CENTER
Famously cracked, the bronze bell has long inspired lovers of freedom. Learn its history at the Liberty Bell Center, a complex with the bell, interpretive displays, and a film. Activists groups for women's suffrage and civil rights have embraced the bell as a powerful emblem.

Best Museums in Philadelphia

The Mutter Museum

BARNES FOUNDATION
Boasting one of the most impressive collections of art in the country (81 Renoirs, 69 Cézannes, 59 Matisses, 46 Picassos, 7 van Goghs, 6 Seurats), the Barnes moved from its longtime home in the Main Line suburbs to a serene, higher-profile Parkway plot in 2012. The unusual layout of its mixed-media galleries, a hallmark of Albert Barnes's style, remains.

PHILADELPHIA MUSEUM OF ART
A pretty, new, street-level entrance off Kelly Drive lets you bypass the famous Rocky Steps (or run 'em, if you'd like) and go directly into Philly's hallowed temple of art. Inside, you'll find paintings, furniture, textiles, and more from names like Diego Rivera, Georgia O'Keeffe, Charles Eames, and Frank Gehry.

MUSEUM OF THE AMERICAN REVOLUTION
Opened in 2017, the AmRev Museum (as locals have nicknamed it) emphasizes an immersive, interactive format in its retelling of the Revolutionary War from the Boston Tea Party to the Battle of Yorktown. Fans of *Hamilton* won't want to miss the gallery of 30 artifacts related to the former treasury secretary.

African American Museum

RODIN MUSEUM
The only museum dedicated to Auguste Rodin outside France, Philly's beaux arts tribute features nearly 150 bronzes, marbles, and plasters. The lovely garden is the perfect place to contemplate alongside *The Thinker*.

ACADEMY OF THE FINE ARTS
Located just north of City Hall, the country's oldest art museum and school doesn't rest on its laurels; it regularly augments its diverse mixed-media collection with compelling exhibits throughout the year.

THE MÜTTER MUSEUM
Lovers of the medical and the macabre should not miss this fascinating and unusual collection, which is filled with skulls, organs, skeletons, and other oddities; an expansion scheduled for 2023 will double its footprint.

FRANKLIN INSTITUTE
Science is the thread stitching the various family-friendly galleries together (the giant walk-through heart is a favorite), with nationally touring exhibits often setting up shop. There's also an escape room and Center City's only IMAX theater.

MUMMERS MUSEUM
The Mummers have been part of Philly tradition for centuries, and this museum in Pennsport, the heart of Mummers culture, charts its history from its 17th-century origins to the modern New Year's Day parade, when thousands of elaborately costumed musical brigades march down Market Street.

NATIONAL MUSEUM OF AMERICAN JEWISH HISTORY
Founded in 1976 and relocated to a gleaming new home in 2010, this museum shares the experience of Jewish people in America through interactive exhibits, photographs, artifacts, and film. A Smithsonian affiliate, general admission (not including special exhibits) is free.

AFRICAN AMERICAN MUSEUM IN PHILADELPHIA
Compelling and well designed, Philly's African American museum documents the experience of the people of the African diaspora in Philadelphia and beyond. The interactive projections of important 18th-century figures in the permanent *Audacious Freedom* exhibit are especially well done.

WHAT'S WHERE

1 Old City and Historic Downtown. Given its historical importance, *everything* in Old City is a highlight including Independence National Historical Park home to the Liberty Bell and Independence Hall.

2 Society Hill and Penn's Landing. Well-preserved Society Hill is filled with cobblestone streets and hidden courtyards. Penn's Landing features a network of parks and pop-ups.

3 Center City East and Chinatown. This area encompasses everything east of City Hall including great restaurants and bars, the vibrant and diverse Chinatown, and landmarks like Reading Terminal.

4 Center City West and Rittenhouse Square. From City Hall to the Schuylkill River, this part of the city has great restaurants and bars. You'll also find Rittenhouse Square, the heart of upper-crust Philadelphia.

5 Parkway Museum District and Fairmount Park. From City Hall the Benjamin Franklin Parkway stretches northwest to the Philadelphia Museum of Art.

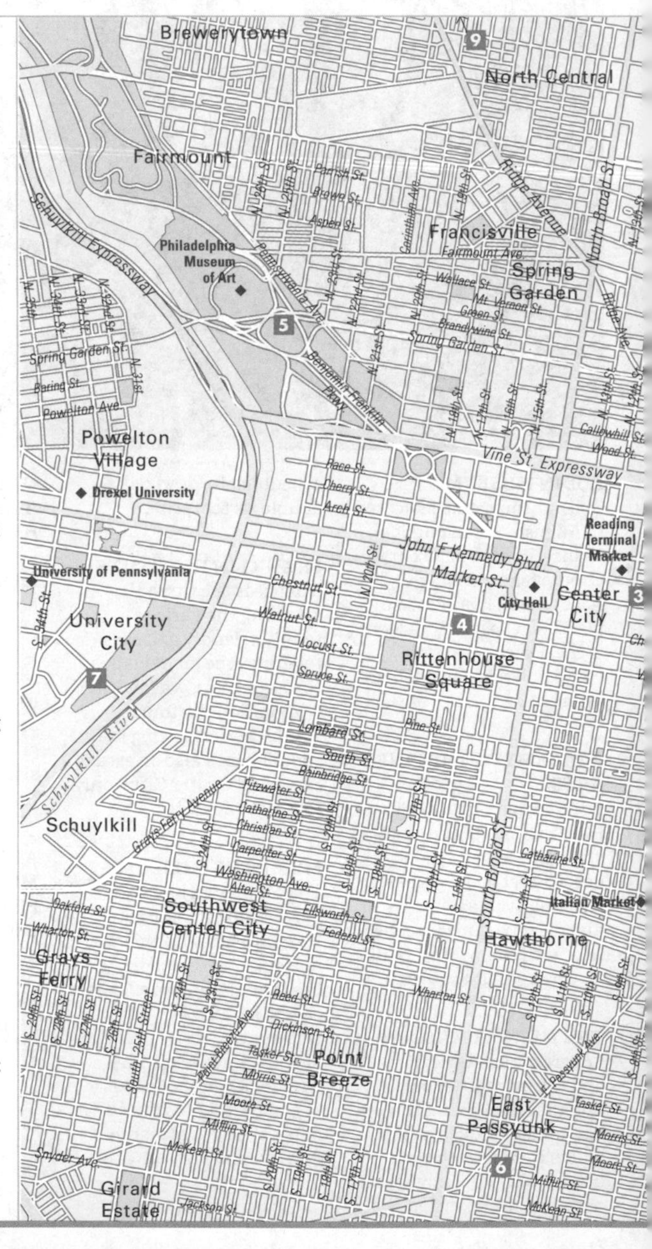

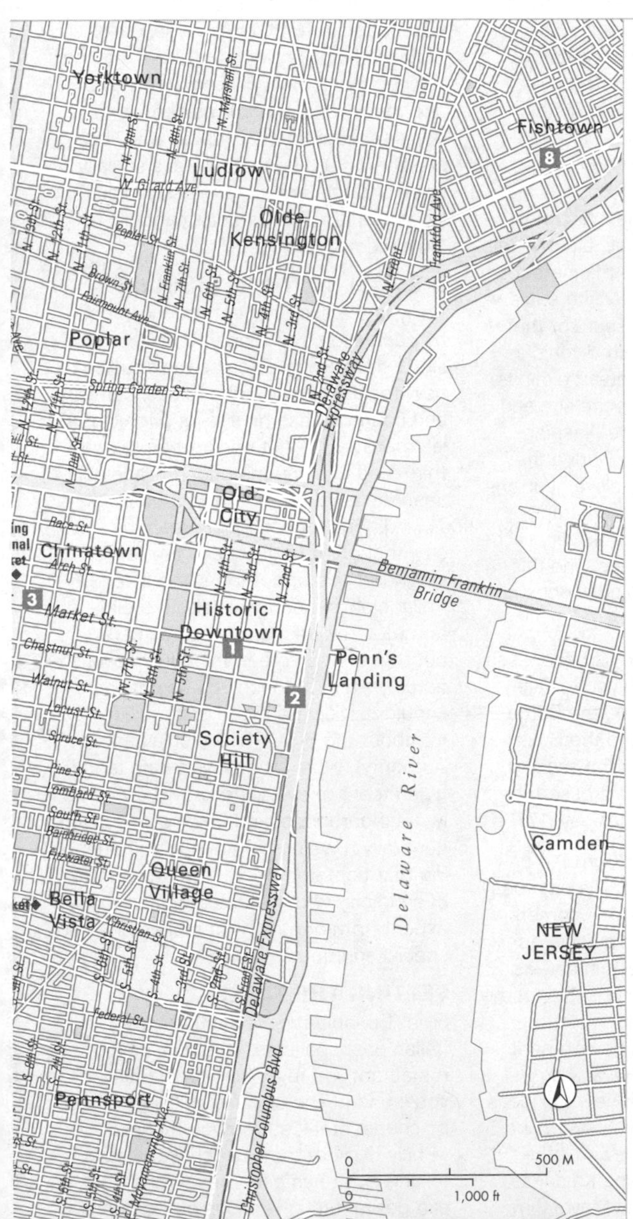

Fairmount is home to solid dining, drinking, and shopping, while 8,500-acre Fairmount Park is the world's largest landscaped city park.

6 South Philadelphia and East Passyunk. South Philadelphia gave the world Rocky Balboa and 9th Street's Italian Market. Bella Vista is home to a number of bars and restaurants, as is trendy East Passyunk.

7 University City and West Philadelphia. The University of Pennsylvania and Drexel University are the anchors of University City, the easternmost portion of West Philadelphia. Beyond is a high concentration of bars, restaurants, and cafés.

8 Northern Liberties and Fishtown. This area of North Philadelphia has come into its own in recent years and is one the city's best places for eating and drinking.

9 Manayunk, Chestnut Hill, and Germantown. Manayunk, wedged between the Schuylkill River and some steep hills, is full of restaurants and boutiques. Chestnut Hill and Mount Airy are charming residential areas, while Germantown features beautifully preserved historic homes.

Philadelphia Today

Without Philadelphia, there might not be a United States of America. The Declaration of Independence was signed here, kick-starting the American Revolution, and the city went on to become the first capital of the young USA. History is everywhere. Concentrated in the Old City, where spotting costumed reenactors (Ben Franklin, Betsy Ross) is a regular occurrence, the main historical sites like Independence Hall, Liberty Bell, and Betsy Ross House are magnets for domestic and international visitors. Newer on the scene is the Museum of the American Revolution, which chronicles the war through state-of-the-art exhibits, and the President's House, the site and partial re-creation of George Washington's presidential mansion. During the archaeological excavation, slave quarters were discovered, resulting in a frank discussion about the role of slavery in the lives of America's forefathers, one this open-air museum (refreshingly) does not shy away from exploring.

There's history outside the city, too. Less than an hour's drive brings you to Valley Forge National Historic Park, the Battlefield of the Brandywine, and the Buck County town of Washington's Crossing, where General Washington crossed the Delaware River on Christmas day, 1776.

But listen up: history is far from the only reason to visit Philadelphia. The city today looks forward—to tech, to newcomers, to cutting-edge design and cuisine, to climate advocacy, to social justice—as much as it looks back. Philly is a longtime Democratic stronghold with historic minority representation in government and a former civil rights lawyer, Larry Krasner, for its district attorney. Big ideas about the future of politics, justice, and reform are percolating here and influencing the country, including Krasner's prohibition on cash bail and Mayor Jim Kenney's soda tax, a tariff on sugary beverages that, while controversial, succeeded in funding universal pre-K. Philadelphians are not shy about sharing their opinions, political and otherwise, and there are plenty of residents that don't self-identify as card-carrying liberals. But by and large, Philly is a socially open and tolerant city. Unless you are a Cowboys fan. Then no one can help you. (Just kidding. Kinda.)

A SMALL TOWN IN DISGUISE

Philly is the sixth-largest American city by population, but it operates very much like a small town. Even as the infusion of new residents from other cities, states, and countries has hit a fever pitch in the last decade, it's not uncommon to meet third- and fourth-generation Philadelphians who have lived here all their lives. "Lived here" doesn't just mean the city, though. It might mean the same neighborhood, if not the same block. Philadelphians complain about their hometown (parking, trash, wage tax) but that doesn't mean they don't love it fiercely—and it doesn't mean outsiders should participate in the griping. Unless it's about the PPA (Philadelphia Parking Authority), which is always a safe target. It can feel like everyone knows everyone in neighborhoods, and Philadelphians are generally a welcoming bunch. Experiencing that tight knitted-ness, in the context of a big city with all the amenities you'd expect from one, is what makes Philly so special and unusual.

SETTING THE TABLE

From Ethiopian *injera* joints to luxe Italian pasta palaces, whatever kind of restaurant you're looking for in Philly, you'll find it. The city has so evolved past its cheesesteak stereotype that even the "Philly is more than just cheesesteaks" talking point has become a cliché. You can get fantastic versions of the famous sandwich, along with its cousin, the roast pork (with broccoli rabe and sharp provolone), at places like John's Roast Pork and Angelo's Pizza, both in South Philly, but to go to Philly and only eat sandwiches would mean you're missing out on a diverse and world-class dining destination. A metaphorical buffet of modern Philadelphia might include internationally renowned lamb tacos (South Philly Barbacoa), homey potato gnocchi covered in pesto (Mr. Joe's Cafe), aromatic Indonesian beef *rendang* (Hardena), and jewel-like Lebanese baklava (Manakeesh). And that's just on the inexpensive end. A trip to Philly means you can easily balance the low with the high, and no restaurants do high better than Zahav, Laurel, Royal Izakaya, and Vernick Food & Drink, all must-make reservations that have earned longtime *Philadelphia Inquirer* critic Craig Laban's coveted four-bell rating.

OUTSIDE LANDS

There's no getting around it: as a dense, gridded, East Coast city, Philly can feel like a concrete jungle. Fortunately there are plenty of opportunities close by and further afield where you can alleviate the urban crush, from William Penn's four main "Squares" (aka parks) to the botanical curiosities of Batram's Garden in West Philly and the mystical John Heinz National Wildlife Refuge out by the airport. Fairmount Park, which reaches out from the edge of the Art Museum and crosses the Schuylkill River to encompass more than 2,000 acres, is one of the largest city parks in the country. (When Will Smith rapped, "Back in Philly we be out in the Park / A place called the Plateau is where everybody go" in "Summertime," he meant Fairmount Park's Belmont Plateau, a wide grassy savanna with a killer view of the skyline.) Apple orchards and sheep farms stretch out north of the city, and beyond, the Pocono Mountains lure skiers, sledders, and holidaymakers. Cross the Delaware River and you'll soon find yourself in New Jersey's Pine Barrens, a land of cranberry bogs, quarry pools, storybook woods, and quirky characters. Keep going and you'll eventually hit the ocean, as hordes of Philadelphians do every summer. Going "down the Shore" is one Philly tradition almost everyone can agree on.

THE AFTERMATH OF COVID-19

In the spring of 2020, the United States (including Philadelphia) was gravely impacted by the COVID-19 virus. Restaurants, hotels, shops, bars, and even cultural institutions were forced to closed. Unfortunately, at the time of press, there was no clear end in sight. If you're currently planning a visit, remember to call ahead to verify open hours, and to make sure that the property is still in operation.

RACISM AND UNREST

As in many places around the U.S., Philadelphia erupted in protests in early June 2020 following the senseless death of George Floyd in Minneapolis. Citizens had had enough, and protestors filled the streets from the Center City West neighborhood along the retail corridor to Rittenhouse Square. While some businesses were looted and damaged, business owners on the whole pledged to rebuild. The City of Brotherly love is no stranger to social injustice, unfortunately, as the city experienced some of its darkest days under the hands of former police commissioner and mayor Frank Rizzo. A statue and mural of the controversial figure were finally removed following the protests.

Free in Philly

Many of Philadelphia's most historic and best-known attractions are free—or suggest a small donation for admission—every day. This lengthy list includes **Independence Hall,** the **Liberty Bell, Carpenter's Hall, Franklin Court,** and the other buildings and sites of **Independence National Historic Park** including **the President's House,** an open-air space that marks the site of the nation's first executive mansion.

MUSIC AND THEATER

Check the calendar of the **Curtis Institute of Music** (🌐 *www.curtis.edu*) to catch one of the frequent free student recitals. **The Philadelphia Orchestra** (🌐 *www.philorch.org*) also gives free neighborhood concerts. Visit **Macy's** across from City Hall; the former Wanamaker's boasts the largest pipe organ in the world, and there are daily free concerts. The Christmas show around the holidays is a definite favorite with shoppers. Check out a dress rehearsal or pay-what-you-can performance at the **Arden Theater**—they're open to the public and accept donations for admission. Local independent radio station **WXPN** offers free concerts Fridays at noon at its home base, **World Café Live** (🌐 *www.xpn.org*).

OUTDOOR FUN AND FESTIVALS

Take your pick of activities in **Fairmount Park**: hike the trails of the **Wissahickon** (🌐 *www.fow.org*), bring a picnic to **Belmont Plateau** and enjoy the view; or meander around the **Horticultural Center,** look for the scattered pieces of public art, or take the kids to **Smith Memorial Playground,** one of the country's oldest playgrounds. All summer long, multicultural festivals at **Penn's Landing** feature live music and dance instruction. Open spring through fall, **Spruce Street Harbor Park** overlooks the Delaware River creating a great (free) spot to rest, complete with hammock-lounging.

ARCHITECTURE, ART, AND LITERATURE

Take a tour of **City Hall.** See Maurice Sendak's original illustrations and James Joyce's *Ulysses* manuscript, among other treasures, at the **Rosenbach Museum and Library.** Visit the lobby of the **Curtis Center** to gawk at the giant *Dream Garden* by Maxfield Parrish. Visit the **Galleries at the Moore College of Art & Design,** the first and only women's visual arts college in the United States.

It's always fun to stroll the galleries in Old City, but it's especially fun on **"First Fridays"**—the first Friday of every month is celebrated with wine receptions, and galleries keeping later hours. The first Sunday of each month and every Wednesday night (5–8:45 pm) is "pay what you wish" at the **Philadelphia Museum of Art.** The **Institute of Contemporary Art** at the University of Pennsylvania is free all the time. You can check out contemporary art at any time by taking a free tour of the city's many vibrant **murals** (🌐 *www.muralarts.org*).

HISTORY TOURS

Take yourself on a walk by downloading and printing the self-guided **Constitutional Walking Tour** of more than 30 sites around historic Philadelphia from 🌐 *www.theconstitutional.com*. **Elfreth's Alley,** the nation's oldest continuously inhabited street, is free to stroll through; two houses, now a museum, are open for a small fee. Go solo with a call-in cell-phone tour of **Valley Forge National Historical Park** (☎ *484/396–1018*). In the summer, look for the elaborately costumed storytellers with **Once Upon a Nation,** who set up at 13 benches throughout Philadelphia's historic area. Hop from bench to bench for a free, interactive tour, during which actors in character relay stories of Philadelphia in Colonial times.

Philadelphia with Kids

Philadelphia has fantastic activities and sights for tots. Best of all, these stops appeal to adults as well.

HISTORIC AREA

The **National Constitution Center**'s interactive exhibits are way better than learning from a textbook. Nearby **Franklin Square,** however, is the perfect place to take a break from all the history. There's a carousel, miniature-golf course (with Philadelphia landmarks), and an excellent burger stand that also serves up Cake Shakes (milk shakes made with Butterscotch Krimpet Tastykakes). Located in a restored 1902 firehouse near **Elfreth's Alley,** the **Fireman's Hall Museum** is home to some of the nation's earliest firefighting equipment. Kids can try on fire coats and boots, and it's free. For something spookier, check out one of the **Ghost Tours** offered around the Historic Area. If you're in need of a pick-me-up, head to **the Franklin Fountain,** a 1900s-style ice-cream and soda fountain, for handmade ice-cream treats.

FAIRMOUNT PARK

The **Please Touch Museum** is essentially a giant playground for kids. In its location in Fairmount Park's majestic Memorial Hall—one of the few remnants from the 1876 Centennial Exhibition—the museum is bigger (38,000 square feet of exhibits) and better than ever before. The nearby **Philadelphia Zoo** is another great spot, with a petting zoo, tree house, and "Big Cat Crossing," a series of overhead passageways that allows lions, tigers, pumas, and other large cats to roam. The sprawling indoor–outdoor **Smith Memorial Playground and Playhouse** nearby has a giant wooden slide and a mansionlike playhouse; check the website when the family summer concert series, Kidchella, occurs.

BENJAMIN FRANKLIN PARKWAY

At the **Franklin Institute,** kids can't resist walking through the giant heart and seeing their hair stand up in the static-electricity exhibit. The nearby **Academy of Natural Sciences** has great, kid-friendly exhibits about dinosaurs and architectural digs.

PENN'S LANDING

At **Penn's Landing** kids can climb in the bunks used in steerage or hop in a scull and row along the Schuylkill at the **Independence Seaport Museum.** Next take the **RiverLink Ferry** across the river to the Camden Waterfront to explore the **Adventure Aquarium.** The **Shark Realm,** an enormous tank filled with sharks, stingrays, and sawfish, is the central attraction here. The **Camden Children's Garden** is an interactive horticultural garden with exhibits that allow you to taste, smell, and touch different elements.

AROUND TOWN

There are plenty of great snacks to pick up for days on the go at the **Reading Terminal Market.** Kids will like watching the workers at **Miller's Twist** wind the dough into pretzel shapes. They can also feed pennies to Philbert, the bronze pig at the market's center (the money goes to local charities). For a sit-down meal option, the **City Tavern** is a great way into history, and it has a good kids' menu. If you're in the mood for a ball game, **Citizens Bank Park,** home to Major League Baseball's Phillies, is one of the most kid-friendly major-league ball parks, with features like the Phanatic Phun Zone play area.

OUTSIDE OF TOWN

About 40 minutes northwest of the city, **LEGOLAND Discovery Center Philadelphia** is a great place to take LEGO fans young and old.

What to Read and Watch

DISPATCHES FROM ELSEWHERE

Four strangers are brought together to solve mysterious puzzles in AMC's Dispatches from Elsewhere, an anthology series created by and starring Jason Segel. The show features a range of Philadelphia attractions including Rittenhouse Square, the Continental Restaurant and Martini Bar, Philadelphia's Magic Gardens, Parkway Central Library, the Curtis Center and Suburban Station.

PHILADELPHIA FIRE

Written by John Edgar Wideman, *Philadelphia Fire* explores the day in 1985 when the police firebombed a row home in West Philadelphia that was owned and occupied by an Afrocentric group known as MOVE. Tensions had long been high between MOVE and the Philadelphia police. The bombing took place at 6221 Osage Avenue and demolished 61 homes in the area.

SUCH A FUN AGE

Set in Philadelphia, this highly anticipated novel *Such a Fun Age* by newcomer Kiley Reid explores themes of race and privilege in an empathetic and funny-at-times story about a black babysitter and the white family she babysits for. The story opens in a high-end grocery store, where what should be an easy evening turns into so much more.

ROCKY (1976)

Philadelphia is perhaps best known for the classic film *Rocky,* which, even after decades, still has fans running up the Art Museum steps like the titular boxer every day. Starring Sylvester Stallone, the now-franchise features eight films that showcase Philadelphia's grit.

CREED (2015)

Included in the Rocky franchise is *Creed,* and the subsequent *Creed II,* both starring Michael B. Jordan and Sylvester Stallone. In the films, Adonis Creed moves to Philly to train with Rocky, and while he's here he falls in love with a Philly native who shows him spots like Johnny Brenda's and Max's Steaks. The iconic Rocky steps at the Art Museum also are seen on screen, and South Philadelphia's Victor Café plays a major role, too.

THE SIXTH SENSE (1999)

Director M. Night Shyamalan calls Philadelphia home, which is why he sets many of his films here. During one of his biggest films, *The Sixth Sense,* locations like St. Augustine Roman Catholic Church, St. Alban's Street in the Graduate Hospital neighborhood, and 20th and Delancey Streets are featured.

SILVER LININGS PLAYBOOK (2012)

This moving and endearing film explores mental illness, unexpected connections, and Philadelphia's intense love for its Philadelphia Eagles football team. Philadelphia Eagles's games and their home stadium, Lincoln Financial Field in South Philadelphia, are frequently seen on screen, along with views of Jeweler's Row, the Benjamin Franklin House, and a number of homes and restaurants right outside the city in Delaware County.

IT'S ALWAYS SUNNY IN PHILADELPHIA

The comedic television show about a group of quirky characters owning a bar in South Philadelphia shows off Philadelphia sights and South Philly attitudes throughout its 10-plus-year run. Much of the filming is done in Los Angeles, but a number of local spots are visible throughout the show, including Boathouse Row, the Benjamin Franklin Bridge, Penn's Landing, and Lincoln Financial Field during the opening credits, and the Italian Market and Rittenhouse Square during select episodes.

Chapter 2

TRAVEL SMART PHILADELPHIA

2

Updated by
Regan Stephens

POPULATION	EMERGENCIES	TIME
1,581,000	911	Eastern Time (same as New York)

POPULATION
1,581,000

LANGUAGE
English

$ CURRENCY
U.S. Dollar

AREA CODES
215, 267, and 445

EMERGENCIES
911

DRIVING
On the Right

ELECTRICITY
120-240 v/60 cycles; plugs have two or three rectangular prongs

TIME
Eastern Time (same as New York)

WEB RESOURCES
www.visitphilly.com

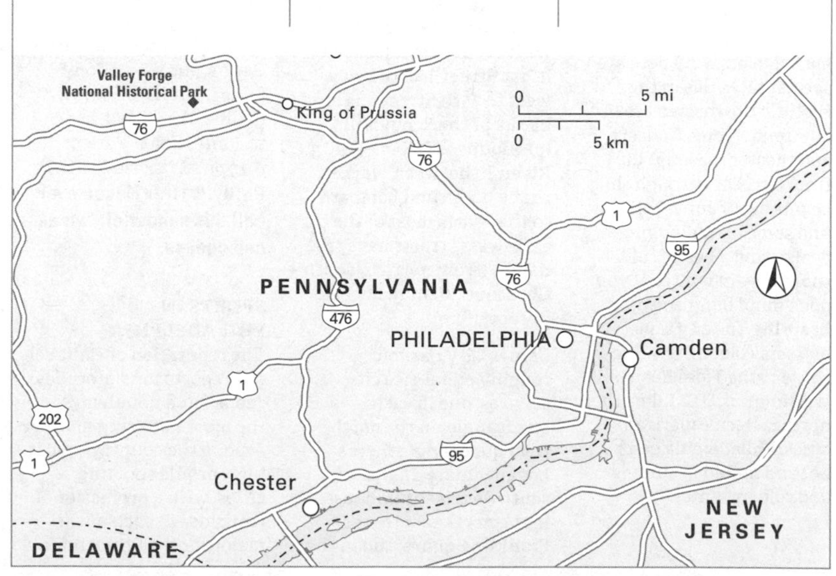

What You Need to Know Before You Go

When should I go to Philadelphia? How do I order a cheesesteak? Philly sports—are they really that important? Where can I buy booze and when? We've got answers and a few tips to help you make the most of your visit.

WHEN TO GO

Any time is right to enjoy the area's attractions, and a variety of popular annual events take place throughout the year. To avoid the largest crowds and be assured that all seasonal attractions are open, visit in May–June or September–October. If you don't mind waiting in longer lines to see popular attractions, visit around July 4, when the city comes alive with fireworks, parades, and festivals. The top draw is the Wawa Welcome America! festival, which often includes a performance by a blockbuster musician or two. There are special activities in the Historic Downtown area all summer long. Concert and theater seasons run from October through the beginning of June. You may find some better lodging deals—and a beautiful snowfall—in winter, if you don't mind bundling up. In spring, the city's cherry blossoms bloom, rivaling those of the Tidal Basin in Washington, D.C. Like other northeastern American cities, Philadelphia can be hot and humid in summer and cold in winter.

WHERE AM I?

If you ever feel lost, you can orient yourself by gauging where you stand in relation to the two main thoroughfares that intersect at the city's center: Broad (or 14th) Street, which runs north–south; and Market Street, which runs east–west. Where Broad and Market meet, neatly dividing the city center into four quadrants, you'll find massive City Hall, Philadelphia's center of gravity.

Within Center City, the numbered streets start on the eastern side, from the Delaware River, beginning with Front Street (consider it "1st Street") all the way west to 25th Street on the banks of the Schuylkill (pronounced "SKOO-kull") River. In between Market to the north and Lombard to the south, most of the east–west streets have tree names (from north to south: Chestnut, Walnut, Locust, Spruce, Pine).

Center City has four roughly equal-size city squares, one in each quadrangle. In the northwest quadrangle there's Logan Square; in the southwest is Rittenhouse; in the northeast there's Franklin Square; and in the southeast is Washington Square. Running along the banks of the Delaware River is Columbus Boulevard/Delaware Avenue.

ORDERING CHEESESTEAKS

Eating a cheesesteak is a must-do experience in Philly, but there is some lingo that you must know before you step up to the window—you don't want to get yelled at. And don't worry about temp. Most cheesesteaks are going to be well-done.

Step 1: Pick your cheese—Cheez Whiz, American, or provolone (never Swiss).

Step 2: Decide if you want onions or not.

Step 3: Order. If you want Cheez Whiz and onions, order "Whiz, wit." Don't like onions? Order "Whiz, witout."

So where should you get your cheesesteak? Everyone has a favorite, and loyalty is fierce. The most well-known are Pat's, Geno's, Jim's, and Tony Luke's, but if you want to dine like a local, head to John's Roast Pork or Angelo's Pizzeria South Philly. ■ TIP→ **Never, ever call this sandwich "steak and cheese."**

SPORTS IN PHILADELPHIA

The reputation of Philadelphia sports fans precedes them—and not always in the most flattering manner. Among the country's most high-profile sporting cities, with a professional franchise in each of the major sports, Philly has a long and storied athletic heritage that translates to a deep passion for the local teams. That passion sometimes manifests itself in blunt and at times inelegant ways, but the large-scale vilification of Philly supporters is mostly overblown and unfair. Should you find yourself in a game-time environment, expect good-natured heckling if you're with the opposing team. And if you're there supporting the Eagles, Phillies, Flyers, or Sixers, prepare to be welcomed with open arms.

The Philadelphia Phillies (baseball) play at Citizens Bank Park from April to October. Philadelphia 76ers (basketball) play at the Wells Fargo Center from November to April. College basketball fans may want to check out the Collegiate Big Five basketball rivalry that includes LaSalle, St. Joseph's, Temple, the University of Pennsylvania, and Villanova; the season runs from December to March. The Philadelphia Eagles, the 2018 Super Bowl champs (this is important to know), play at Lincoln Financial Field (aka the Linc) from September through January. The Philadelphia Flyers (hockey) hit the ice at the Wells Fargo Center from October to April.

On weekends April through October, parts of the Martin Luther King Jr. Drive (West River Drive) are closed to car traffic, making this a prime spot for running and cycling. Breathtaking trails for running, biking, and hiking thread through Fairmount Park. Walking along Forbidden Drive, a gravel trail along the Wissahickon Creek, you'll understand why artists from Thomas Eakins to Edgar Allan Poe felt inspired to immortalize the park in their work. Shafts of sunlight filter through the trees, while birdcalls complement the dense chorus of crickets bellowing from the mossy woods.

SAFETY

Philadelphia once had a bad rap for its high crime rate, but when Mayor Michael Nutter took office in 2008, overall violent crime dropped significantly. Following the trend in cities around the country, it has continued to do so under Mayor Jim Kenney. As in any major city, visitors should always exercise caution and be aware of their surroundings.

SHOP 'TIL YOU DROP

Pennsylvania has a statewide law that shoes and clothes are tax-free. This may be good news when you find out that two of the country's busiest outlets—Philadelphia Mills and Philadelphia Premium Outlets—plus King of Prussia, the biggest mall on the East Coast, are easily accessible by SEPTA bus from the city center. Most luxury designers and big brand names operate stores on Walnut or Chestnut Streets, near Rittenhouse Square, while independents fill in the surrounding small streets and pop up in neighborhoods like East Passyunk, Fishtown, and Old City.

LIQUOR LAWS

Philadelphia has notoriously complicated rules surrounding the purchase and consumption of alcohol (which loosened slightly in 2017). You can buy wine and liquor at Fine Wine & Good Spirits, state-run stores (locals call them "state stores") that are spread all around the city. These stores, which don't open till 11 am on Sundays (an arcane regulation that endures today) don't sell beer. You can also buy wine and beer at some supermarkets and at independently owned bottle shops; if you want something rare, unusual, or from a small producer, a bottle shop is your best bet. There's no law prohibiting you from buying alcohol on Sundays, but there are limits: up to 3,000 milliliters of wine (three liters, or four 750 milliliter bottles) and up to 192 ounces of beer. (Technically, you can leave and return to purchase more. The law limits the purchase on a single transaction.)

Bars and restaurants with liquor licenses can serve alcohol until 2 am. Ones with special social club licenses can go till 3 am, but you typically need to be a member (or the guest of a member) to get into these spots. Due to the prohibitive cost of obtaining a liquor license in Philly, many restaurants opt to let diners bring their own bottle (BYOB). Always check with a restaurant in advance so you don't show up empty-handed.

Getting Here and Around

 Air

Flying time from Boston is 1 hour, 20 minutes; from Chicago, roughly 2 hours; from Miami, 2 hours, 40 minutes; from Los Angeles, 5 hours, 40 minutes.

AIRPORTS

The major gateway to Philadelphia is Philadelphia International Airport (PHL), a seven-terminal airport located roughly 7 miles southwest from downtown. Elaborate renovations over the past decade-plus, adding multiple dining and shopping venues in addition to entire new terminals, have brought PHL into modern times and added some decent retail and dining options.

An alternative is Newark Liberty International Airport (EWR), about 85 miles northeast of Philadelphia in New Jersey. From EWR, a United Airlines hub, you can take an AirTrain shuttle to the Newark Airport station, then take a NJ Transit train to Trenton, and from Trenton ride a Southeastern Pennsylvania Transportation Authority (SEPTA) train into Philly. Expect a cost of roughly $40 per person and a minimum of an additional two hours to your travel time.

GROUND TRANSPORTATION

For $8, you can take SEPTA's Airport rail line directly into Center City directly from any of the airport terminals. It leaves the airport every 30 minutes from 5:09 am to 12:13 am. The trip to Center City takes about 20 minutes. Trains serve the Eastwick, University City, 30th Street, Suburban (Center City), Jefferson, and Temple University stations.

By car from the airport, the city is accessible via I–95 south or I–76 east. Allow at least a half hour, more during rush hour, for the 8-mile trip. Taxis at PHL are plentiful; follow signs in the airport and wait in line to catch one. Destinations that fall within the zone demarcated by Fairmount Avenue to the north, South Street to the south, the Delaware River to the east, and 38th Street to the west are eligible for a $28.50 flat rate, not including tip. If you're heading to a location south of South Street, you can ask the driver to run the meter, as you'll likely end up paying less than the flat rate.

Limousine and shuttles are also available from PHL. Shuttle buses cost $10 and up per person and will make most requested stops downtown as well as the suburbs. You can make shuttle arrangements at the centralized ground transportation counter in the baggage claim areas.

FLIGHTS

Most major U.S. airlines offer service to and from Philadelphia (PHL), which is a hub for American Airlines.

 Bicycle

While it still lacks the bipedal cachet of cities like San Francisco, Portland, and Denver, Philadelphia has made great bounds in becoming a progressive, bicycle-friendly town. Major streets, like Pine and Spruce Streets through Center City, feature spacious bike-only lanes adjacent to traffic lanes, and other highly trafficked drags, like Broad Street and Spring Garden Street, are equipped with bike lanes as well. Cyclists looking for a more isolated riding experience can visit paths along the Schuylkill River, in Fairmount Park, and in Wissahickon Valley Park. Many of Philly's older, narrower, single-lane streets are frequented by cyclists, though they might prove trickier to navigate for inexperienced riders or visitors.

It's completely legal for a rider to use a lane in the same manner as a motor vehicle, though some cyclists opt to move to one side of the street to let auto traffic pass. Like many cities, there is intermittent friction between cyclists and motorists when it comes to issues of road sharing, traffic laws, and safety. It's wise to obey all signs and directives as if one were in a car when riding a bike in Philly.

The most difficult part of biking in the city may be finding a safe place to stash your bike while you run into a restaurant for lunch or a historic site for a visit. The installation of street racks designed for bicycle lock-ups hasn't increased to meet the amount of active riders just yet, though more permanent racks and corrals seem to be popping up regularly. Invest in a quality, heavy-duty lock, whether you're locking up your bike at a rack or on a fence or street sign.

Visitors who haven't brought along their own bicycles can rent them in the short term via Indego, Philadelphia's bike-sharing program. Dozens of bike-stocked Indego kiosks are scattered throughout the city, offering instant rentals via a high-tech kiosk system. Conveniently, you're able to pick up a bike in one area and drop it off at the kiosk closest to your destination.

Boat and Ferry

The RiverLink Ferry, a seasonal (May–September) passenger ferry, offers service between Philadelphia and Camden, site of the Adventure Aquarium, the BB&T Pavilion, the battleship *New Jersey,* and Campbell's Field. Ferries depart every hour from Penn's Landing daily between 10 and 6 Monday through Thursday, and 10 and 7 Friday through Sunday, and from Camden's waterfront on the half hour, daily from 9:30 to 5:30 Monday through Thursday, and 9:30 to 6:30 Friday through Sunday, with extended hours and continuous service for Penn's Landing and BB&T Pavilion concerts, and Camden Riversharks baseball games. The cost is $9 round-trip ($7 for children and seniors, under age two is free), the ride takes 12 minutes, and the ferry is wheelchair accessible.

■ **TIP→ Tickets can be bought via mobile app, online, or at the ticket booth.**

Bus

A bus is generally the cheapest option to reach Philadelphia, particularly when you are coming from New York City. New Jersey Transit stops at the Greyhound terminal and offers service between Philadelphia and Atlantic City and other New Jersey destinations. There is a Bolt Bus and Megabus stop adjacent to 30th Street Station, offering service to and from midtown Manhattan in New York City. Tickets are best purchased online prior to your trip.

Car

Getting around Philadelphia by car can sometimes be difficult—and at rush hour, it can be a nightmare. The main east–west freeway through the city, the Schuylkill Expressway (I–76), is notorious for its traffic and delays. The main north–south highway through Philadelphia is the Delaware Expressway (I–95). To reach Center City heading southbound on I–95, take the Vine Street exit.

From the west the Pennsylvania Turnpike begins at the Ohio border and intersects the Schuylkill Expressway (I–76) at Valley Forge. The Schuylkill Expressway has several exits in Center City. The Northeast Extension of the turnpike, renamed

Getting Here and Around

I–476 and often called "the Blue Route" by locals, runs from Scranton to Plymouth Meeting, north of Philadelphia. From the east the New Jersey Turnpike and I–295 access U.S. 30, which enters the city via the Benjamin Franklin Bridge, or New Jersey Route 42 and the Walt Whitman Bridge into South Philadelphia.

With the exception of a few thoroughfares (e.g. the Benjamin Franklin Parkway, Broad Street, Vine Street, Spring Garden Street, parts of Market Street), streets in Center City are narrow and one way. Philadelphia's compact 5-square-mile downtown is laid out in a grid. The traditional heart of the city is Broad and Market Streets, where City Hall stands. Market Street divides the city north and south; 130 South 15th Street, for example, is in the second block south of Market Street. The diagonal Benjamin Franklin Parkway breaks the grid pattern by leading from City Hall out of Center City into Fairmount Park.

PARKING

In most cases, a spot at a Philadelphia parking meter will cost $2 an hour. Parking garages are plentiful, especially around Independence Hall, City Hall, and the Pennsylvania Convention Center, and rates vary. Philadelphia Parking Authority (PPA) employees are famously vigilant about ticketing illegally parked cars and vehicles with expired meters. Fortunately, Center City is compact, and you can easily get around downtown on foot or by bus after you park. If you plan to stay in a hotel in Center City, check ahead of time to see if it has its own parking facility or if the hotel will direct you to a nearby parking garage for a reduced rate, as this can significantly affect your parking expenses.

ROAD CONDITIONS

Traffic flows relatively freely through the main thoroughfares of the city. Just pay attention: you will often see Philly natives employing both the "rolling stop" at stop signs (found plentifully in South Philly) and the "red light jump" when drivers sitting at a red light will drive through it just as (or just before) it turns green. Road and house construction is a way of life for residents, particular in South Philly neighborhoods, so be prepared to detour if you plan on driving in and around this area. Use extra caution when maneuvering the narrow one-way streets of Center City. Drivers on the Philadelphia stretch of the Schuylkill Expressway (I–76) routinely drive well over the speed limit, and frequent accidents on this highway attest to this. If you're a slower motorist, consider gentler, more scenic routes to your destination, such as Kelly Drive or Martin Luther King Jr. Drive (West River Drive).

RULES OF THE ROAD

Pennsylvania law requires all children under age four to be strapped into approved child-safety seats, and children from ages four to eight to ride in booster seats. All passengers must wear seat belts. In Pennsylvania, unless otherwise indicated, you may turn right at a red light after stopping if there's no oncoming traffic. When in doubt, wait for the green. Speed limits in Philadelphia are generally 35–40 mph on side streets, 55 mph on the surrounding highways.

CAR RENTALS

If you plan on spending the majority of your time within the immediate city confines, especially in Center City, you don't need to rent a car, but you may want to rent one if you plan to do a lot of day trips. For rental cars, rates in Philadelphia begin at around $50 to $60 a day.

Generally, you must be at least 21 years old to rent a car in Philadelphia and the surrounding areas, though there are a handful of areas that hold to a 25-and-over rule. (Rates may be higher if you're under 25.) Non-U.S. residents need a reservation voucher (for prepaid reservations that were made in the traveler's home country), a passport, a driver's license, and a travel policy that covers each driver, when picking up a car.

Ⓜ Public Transportation

Buses make up the bulk of the SEPTA system, with more than 120 routes extending throughout the city and into the suburbs. Although the buses are comfortable and reliable, they should be used only when you're not in a hurry, as traffic on the city's major thoroughfares can add some time to your trip. The distinctive purple minibuses you see around Center City are SEPTA's convenience line for visitors, the PHLASH. The 22 stops run from the Philadelphia Museum of Art through Center City to Penn's Landing, stopping near high-profile destinations such as the Barnes Foundation, Eastern State Penitentiary, the Philadelphia Zoo, and Reading Terminal Market. Since a ride on the PHLASH costs $2 for a one-way ticket (seniors, SEPTA pass holders, and children four and under ride free), consider the all-day, unlimited-ride pass available for $5 per passenger. These buses typically run daily in season from 10 am to 6 pm. There's service every 15 minutes.

The base cash fare for subways, trolleys, and buses is $2.50, paid with exact change or with a Key Card, which you can purchase at a kiosk and refill online. Transfers cost $1. Senior citizens with proof of age are permitted to ride free. Up to two children four or younger may ride free with each paying adult.

If you plan to travel extensively within Center City, consider a SEPTA pass. A one-day Convenience Pass costs $9 and is good for a total of eight rides on any SEPTA bus, trolley, or subway train, excluding regional rail. A one-day Independence Pass costs $13 and is good for 24 hours of unlimited use on all SEPTA vehicles within the city, including regional rail, the purple PHLASH bus, and the Airport Express train. Passes can be purchased both online and in the SEPTA sales offices, in the concourse below 15th and Market Streets; in the Jefferson Station (10th and Market Streets); and in 30th Street Station.

SEPTA, Philadelphia's subway system, runs regular trains throughout the day, but their geographic reach is somewhat limited, so trips may need to be supplemented with bus, taxi, or car service rides. The orange-colored Broad Street Line (BSL) runs from Fern Rock Station in the northern part of the city to Pattison Avenue, aka NRG Station, in South Philadelphia, where Citizens Bank Park, the Wells Fargo Center, Lincoln Financial Field, and XFINITY Live! are located. The blue-colored Market-Frankford Line (MFL) runs across the city, from the 69th Street Transportation Center in the western suburb of Upper Darby to Frankford in Northeast Philadelphia.

Sunday through Thursday, most trains on the BSL and MFL begin suspending service for the evening between midnight and 1 am, resuming around 5 am. During these times, "Night Owl" buses operate along the same routes. On Friday and Saturday nights, both lines run continuously throughout the night. While subway travel in Philadelphia does have its limitations, it's a safe, accessible, and affordable way to maneuver around

Getting Here and Around

the city without the cost and hassle of driving and parking.

Taxis are plentiful in Center City, especially along Broad, Market, Walnut, and Chestnut Streets and near major hotels and travel hubs. They're hailed street-side; smartphone users can also download 215GetACab, a free Android/iOS app that allows you to schedule pickups instantly. At night, during prime-time hours, try your luck on a busy street corner or ask a hotel doorman to hail a taxi for you.

Fares rise according to distance: $2.70, plus 23¢ for each one-tenth of a mile. The standard tip for cabdrivers is about 20% of the fare. All Philadelphia cabs accept credit cards, though most drivers prefer cash transactions.

Train

Philadelphia's beautifully restored 30th Street Station, at 30th and Market streets, is a major stop on Amtrak's Northeast Corridor line. The 90-minute Philadelphia–to–New York trip can cost anywhere from $50 to $200 each way, depending on the type of train, class, and when tickets are purchased. Both Amtrak's Northeast Regional trains and its high-speed Acela line cater to business travelers, and are equipped with conference tables and electrical outlets. You can travel by train between Philadelphia and New York City more cheaply by taking the SEPTA's Trenton rail line to Trenton, New Jersey, then transferring to a NJ Transit commuter line to Manhattan. The trip takes an extra 30 minutes, but the savings is considerable ($16 to $25.50 each way). Amtrak also serves Philadelphia from points west, including Harrisburg, Pittsburgh, and Chicago.

SEPTA's network of commuter trains serves both the city and the suburbs. The famous Main Line, a cluster of affluent suburbs, got its start—and its name—from the Pennsylvania Railroad route that ran westward from Center City. SEPTA commuter trains stop at 30th Street Station and connect to Suburban Station (16th Street and JFK Boulevard, near major hotels), and Jefferson Station (10th and Market Streets), which is close to historic Old City. Fares, which vary according to route and time of travel, range from $3.75 to $10 each way. These trains are your best bet for reaching neighborhoods to the northwest, like Germantown and Chestnut Hill, as well as numerous suburbs.

The PATCO (Port Authority Transit Corporation) High Speed Line trains run underground, from 16th and Locust Streets to Lindenwold, New Jersey. Trains stop at 12th and Locust, 9th and Locust, 8th and Market, and City Hall, then continue across the Delaware River to Camden. It's one way to get to the Adventure Aquarium or the BB&T Pavilion; round-trip fares range from $2.80 to $6.

Trolley

Philadelphia once had an extensive trolley network, and a few good trolley lines are still in service and run by SEPTA. Route 10 begins west and north of Center City and ends on Market Street; Routes 11, 13, 34, and 36 each come from the west and south of Center City and also end on Market.

Essentials

Dining

Philadelphia's dining landscape has exploded in the last decade, making it one of the country's buzziest, with a growing roster of talented chefs, a thriving vegan scene, and, according to the James Beard Association, the country's best restaurant right now. Don't worry, though—Philly food purists can still find the country's best hoagies, cheesesteaks, and roast pork sandwiches at restaurants and delis throughout the city.

RESERVATIONS AND DRESS

Reservations are noted when they're essential or not accepted. Many top restaurants are typically booked a month ahead for Saturday night. Vetri is almost always booked two months ahead.

Most of Philadelphia's restaurants can be classified as business casual, with the exception of inexpensive spots or those in the University City area, where jeans and sneakers are de rigueur. Dress is mentioned in reviews only when men are required to wear a jacket or a jacket and tie.

WINE, BEER, AND SPIRITS

The most popular local beer, Yuengling, is made at one of the oldest breweries in the country. Other area breweries include Victory, Flying Fish, and Yards.

One happy development to come from Pennsylvania's somewhat arcane alcohol laws is the proliferation of BYOB restaurants—where you can bring your own bottle(s) of wine, beer, or liquor and enjoy them with your meal free of corkage fees. Many different cuisines are available, including Italian, Mexican, Thai, French, and Mediterranean. They are found throughout the city but are perhaps most highly concentrated in the Bella Vista and Queen Village neighborhoods in South Philly.

State-run liquor stores, called state stores, sell wine and other spirits. Beer is sold on a take-out basis by some bars and restaurants, or you can get beer at some supermarkets and bottle shops.

What it Costs in U.S. Dollars

	$	$$	$$$	$$$$
RESTAURANTS	under $15	$15–$19	$20–$24	over $24

Health and Safety

A new novel coronavirus brought all travel to a virtual standstill in the first half of 2020. Although the illness is mild in most people, some experience severe and even life-threatening complications, especially older adults. The same is true for people with weaker immune systems or those with certain medical conditions. Two weeks before a trip, be on the lookout for some of the following symptoms: cough, fever, chills, trouble breathing, muscle pain, sore throat, new loss of smell or taste. If you experience any of these symptoms, do not travel.

While traveling, wash your hands often. Limit your time in public places, and, when you are out and about, wear a cloth face mask that covers your nose and mouth.

Bring extra supplies, such as disinfecting wipes, hand sanitizer (12-ounce bottles were allowed in carry-on luggage at this writing), and a first-aid kit with a thermometer.

Consider protecting yourself by purchasing a travel insurance policy for costs related to COVID-19 related cancellations. Be sure to always read the fine print.

Essentials

Lodging

Philadelphia has lodgings for every style of travel. The city is in the midst of a hotel building boom, adding nearly 500 rooms in 2019, with about 1,700 more expected in 2020. Some midprice chains have moved into town or have spruced up their accommodations, and if you have greater expectations, you need look no further than the city's handful of swank hotels, each with its own gracious character.

Budget, moderate, and luxury properties are spread throughout the downtown area. The Historic Area, on the east side of downtown, centers on Independence Hall and extends to the Delaware River, and is a good base for sightseeing. Old City and Society Hill lodgings are also convenient for serious sightseeing; Society Hill is the quietest of the three areas. For business-oriented trips, Center City encompasses the heart of the downtown business district, centered around Broad and Market Streets, and Rittenhouse Square hotels are also nearby.

If you prefer to keep your distance from the tourist throngs, check out the Benjamin Franklin Parkway–Museum Area along the parkway from 16th Street to the Philadelphia Museum of Art. There are also a couple of hotels in University City—just across the Schuylkill River in West Philadelphia and close to the University of Pennsylvania and Drexel University—a 5- to 10-minute drive or taxi ride from Center City.

RESERVATIONS

Even with the large number of hotel rooms, sometimes it's difficult to find a place to stay, so advance reservations are advised. Philadelphia has no real off-season, but many hotels offer discount packages when the demand from business travelers and groups subsides. Besides substantially reduced rates, these packages often include an assortment of freebies, such as breakfast, parking, cocktails, and the use of exercise facilities.

PARKING

Most downtown hotels charge an average of $25 a night for parking, but some include it in the rate and it can be much higher at some hotels. You can find street parking if you're willing to put in the effort, but it can be difficult—even for natives. The best time to try is in the early morning or in the early evening, before the nightlife starts up. However, many streets have two-hour time limits until 10 pm, and the two-hour rule goes into effect at 8 am, even on Sunday in many places.

HOTEL PRICES

When pricing accommodations, always ask what's included and what costs extra.

What it Costs in U.S. Dollars

	$	$$	$$$	$$$$
HOTELS	Under $150	$150–$225	$226–$300	Over $300

Nightlife

Bars and clubs can sometimes close, change hands, or turn over with very short notice, so stay abreast of the latest by following the entertainment pages and respective websites of the *Philadelphia Inquirer* and *Philadelphia Daily News* (🌐 *philly.com*); the *Philadelphia Weekly* (🌐 *phillyweekly.com*); the *Philadelphia Gay News* (🌐 *epgn.com*); and *Philadelphia* magazine (🌐 *phillymag.com*).

Where Should I Stay?

	VIBE	PROS	CONS
Old City and Historic Downtown	Old City is home to some of the oldest buildings, streets, and attractions.	Its walkability makes it easy to get around and the dining options make it easy to stay fueled.	During the more touristy months, the areas can get busy.
Society Hill and Penn's Landing	While Society Hill is largely residential, adjacent Penn's Landing promises parks, waterfront views, and high-energy festivals.	Some of the city's most celebrated pop-up parks are here, along with town homes, cozy restaurants, and waterfront attractions.	Busy Columbus Boulevard, which runs through the area, can feel busy and overwhelming at all hours of the day.
Center City East and Chinatown	Expect everything from designer-brand shopping to dining at the city's most authentic Chinese restaurants.	Centrally located, these neighborhoods can be explored by foot. There's plenty of restaurants, shopping, and more.	Panhandlers frequent Center City East due to its central location, and traffic can be very heavy.
Center City West and Rittenhouse Square	A mix of retail and residential, expect the historic and affluent with an array of restaurants, bars, and shops.	Centrally located with some of the city's best food, drinks, shopping, hotels, and museums within a stone's throw of each other.	Hotel accommodations and overnight parking can be expensive, and traffic can be a problem, especially during rush hour.
Parkway Museum District and Fairmount Park	Home to some of the country's best museums and the city's largest municipal park.	Beautiful, clean, safe, and walkable, there are excellent hotels, museums, restaurants, parks, and shops all within a small radius.	Due to the number of attractions in the area, vehicular and foot traffic can be heavy—it's also a festival hub.
South Philadelphia and East Passyunk	What was once an old-school Italian neighborhood is now a diverse area with cuisines and residents from all over the world.	Something for everyone—from *Top Chef*–run restaurants to local pizza spots and toy stores and bookshops.	Parking is a challenge; it's so bad that people park in the middle of bustling Broad Street.
University City and West Philadelphia	It's an even mix of diverse West Philly and cutting-edge development.	Cultural diversity means international eateries and a multitude of languages and traditions.	It can still feel far away from some of the things that Philadelphia is known for.
Northern Liberties and Fishtown	Philly's hippest neighborhoods offer local shopping, global dining, and plenty of Instagrammable spots for hanging out.	The neighborhoods are full of energy and an array of things to do, including some of the city's best restaurants, bars, and festivals.	Bars can be rowdy and too crowded. Fishtown, while generally safe, is adjacent to Kensington, a part of the city where safety is a concern.

Essentials

In Philadelphia, last call for bars and clubs is 2 am, though there are a handful of places with special licenses that allow for legal after-hours service. Cover charges can range from free to about $12. While Philly tends toward the casual in many of its nightlife venues, there are dress codes enforced in some clubs. Best to check online to make certain if you're venturing into new territory.

People from outside the city might be surprised to see just how popular dancing is here. The persuasive DJ culture has permeated the city, especially in Old City, Northern Liberties/Fishtown, and on South Street.

Philadelphia has a rich jazz and blues heritage that includes such greats as the late, legendary jazz saxophonist John Coltrane and Grover Washington Jr. That legacy continues today in clubs around town.

Though a number of Philly rock/pop venues are owned by Live Nation, a good variety of touring bands is still represented on a nightly basis. And with the advent of the Fishtown live-music scene at venues such as Johnny Brenda's and Kung Fu Necktie, as well as the popular Union Transfer on Spring Garden, and Boot & Saddle and the Theatre of Living Arts (TLA) in South Philly, there is a greater variety of live music available than ever before.

Packing

Philadelphia is a fairly casual city, although men will need a jacket and tie in some of the better restaurants. Jeans and sneakers or other casual clothing is fine for sightseeing. You'll need a heavy coat and boots for winter, which can be cold and snowy. Summers are hot and humid, but woman may wish to bring a shawl or light jacket for air-conditioned restaurants. Many areas are best explored on foot, so bring good walking shoes.

 Performing Arts

Of all the performing arts, it's music for which Philadelphia is most renowned and the Philadelphia Orchestra of which its residents are most proud. Though the Orchestra has undergone some financial hardships in recent years, the hope is it can rebound and regain its place among the world's elite. The city also serves as a major stop for touring productions of shows from *Hello, Dolly!* to *Hamilton,* and the local theater scene, which supports more than two dozen regional and local companies, is thriving.

Since the opening of the Kimmel Center in 2001, Philadelphia has enjoyed an embarrassment of riches when it comes to performance space. The Academy of Music, the Philadelphia Orchestra's previous home, remains open in all its finery; the Annenberg and Painted Bride house everything from theater to performance art; and both the Mann Center and the BB&T Pavilion remain premier outdoor amphitheaters.

Classical music in Philadelphia begins with the world-renowned Philadelphia Orchestra, which, under music director Yannick Nézet-Séguin, has kept its remarkable pedigree. But there is also the Chamber Orchestra, which is also housed in the glorious Kimmel Center; the venerable Philly Pops; and the very talented students of the Curtis Institute, to round out the bill.

INFORMATION AND TICKETS

For current performances and listings, the best guides to Philly's performing arts are the "Guide to the Lively Arts" in the daily *Philadelphia Inquirer,* the "Weekend" section of the Friday *Inquirer,* and the "Friday" section of the *Philadelphia Daily News.*

Shopping

Shopaholics love the City of Brotherly Love for its style—funky artwork and highbrow housewares, fine jewels, and haute couture.

Indeed, Philadelphia has spawned some influential fashion retailers. The Urban Outfitters chain was born in a storefront in West Philadelphia. Its sophisticated sister, Anthropologie, also has its roots in Philadelphia. Lagos, the popular high-end jewelry line, was founded here, and all items are still produced locally. High-fashion boutiques Joan Shepp and Elle Lauri, in the Rittenhouse Square area, are well regarded by locals for designer clothing and accessories.

Some of the most spirited shopping in town is also pleasing to the palate. The indoor Reading Terminal Market and the outdoor Italian Market are bustling with urban dwellers buying groceries and visitors searching for the perfect Philadelphia cheesesteak. Equally welcoming is the city's quaint, cobblestone Antiques Row, the three-block stretch of Pine Street crammed with shops selling everything from estate jewelry to stained glass and vintage furniture. Also worth a trip is the Third Street Corridor in Old City, home to scads of independent, funky boutiques.

Taxes

The main sales tax in Philadelphia and the surrounding areas is 8%. This tax also applies to restaurant meals. Various other taxes—including a 10% liquor tax—may apply. There's no sales tax on clothing. Hotel taxes are 8.5% in Philadelphia, 5% in Bucks County, and 3.9% in Lancaster County.

Visitor Information

ONLINE RESOURCES

Arts and Entertainment. Billing itself as a guide to experiencing Philly like a local, **Uwishunu** (🌐 *www.uwishunu.com)* is an in-the-know blog extension of the city's more comprehensive visitor site. Written by a diverse staff with different interests, it lives up to its local point of view. **Visit Philly** (🌐 *www.visitphilly.com*) is a comprehensive guide to events throughout the year; it also includes new entries in Philly dining, attractions, and shopping.

For events listings and more local blogging, visit *Philadelphia* magazine's website (🌐 *www.phillymag.com*), where staffers hold forth on everything from street style to restaurants to shopping. **Philly.com**, the online home of the *Philadelphia Inquirer* and *Philadelphia Daily News,* covers many of these same topics, as well.

Food. Philly has more than its fair share of food blogs, which just shows you how important the dining scene is to Philadelphians. **Foobooz** (🌐 *foobooz.com*), which is part of *Philadelphia* magazine, mixes news of restaurant openings and closings with food-industry gossip and restaurant reviews. It also acts as a clearinghouse for other online reviews. **Eater** (🌐 *philly.eater.com*) has a very active Philly branch. Those who pride themselves on being in the know about the restaurant scene check out "Table Talk" by Michael Klein in the *Philadelphia Inquirer,* as well as Klein's blog, **The Insider** (🌐 *philly.com/theinsider*).

Contacts

Air

AIRPORTS Philadelphia International Airport. (*PHL*). *8000 Essington Ave., South Philadelphia* *215/937–6937, 800/ PHL–GATE automated flight information* *www.phl.org*. **Newark Liberty International Airport.** (*EWR*). *3 Brewster Rd.* *973/961–6000* *www.panynj.gov/airports/newark-liberty.html*.

SHUTTLES Allways Transportation. *Northeast Philadelphia Airport, 11301 Norcom Rd., Suite 1* *215/669–0522*. **Carey Limousine Philadelphia.** *610/667–1576* *www.carey.com*. **Priority Shuttle.** *215/632–2885* *www.priorityshuttle.com*.

Bicycle

Bicycle Coalition of Greater Philadelphia. *215/242–9253* *bicyclecoalition.org*. **Indego.** *844/446–3346* *www.rideindego.com*.

Boat

RiverLink Ferry. *Columbus Blvd. and Walnut St.* *215/625–0221* *www.delawareriverwaterfront.com/places/riverlink-ferry*.

Bus

Bolt Bus. *boltbus.com*. **Megabus.** *www.megabus.com*. **Philly PHLASH.** *484/881–3574* *www.phlvisitorcenter.com/tour/philly-phlash*.

Car

CAR RENTALS Avis. *800/633–3469* *www.avis.com*. **Budget.** *800/218–7992* *www.budget.com*. **Hertz.** *800/654–3131* *www.hertz.com*. **National Car Rental.** *888/826–6890* *www.nationalcar.com*.

Train

Amtrak *800/872–7245* *www.amtrak.com*.

New Jersey Transit *973/275–5555* *www.njtransit.com*.

Port Authority Transit Corporation (*PATCO*). *215/922–4600* *www.ridepatco.org*.

Southeastern Pennsylvania Transportation Authority (*SEPTA*). *215/580–7800* *www.septa.org*.

Visitor Information

CONTACTS Independence Visitor Center. *1 N. Independence Mall W, 6th and Market Sts., Old City* *800/537–7676* *www.phlvisitorcenter.com*. **Pennsylvania Office of Travel and Tourism.** *800/847–4872* *www.visitpa.com*. **Philadelphia Convention & Visitors Bureau.** *1601 Market St., Suite 200, Center City West* *215/636–3300* *www.discoverphl.com*. **Visit Philly.** *215/599–0776* *www.visitphilly.com*.

What Did They Just Say?

The Philly accent is an interesting one. Water is wooder. The Eagles are the Iggles. And jeet? That's how Philadelphians ask if you've eaten. But, there's also a certain vocabulary that's used as well. We suggest familiarizing yourself with the below list before you visit the City of Brotherly Love.

- **The Birds:** What Philadelphia Eagles fans call their football team.
- **Blue Route:** Another name for 476, the highway that cuts through Philadelphia suburbs and connects with the Schuylkill (see below).
- **CHOP:** Nickname for The Children's Hospital of Philadelphia.
- **Go Birds:** Literally means "Go Eagles," but it has morphed into an everyday greeting that's used in place of "thank you" and "have a good day."
- **gravy:** A South Philly term for red sauce.
- **Gritty:** The googly-eyed Flyers mascot.
- **hoagie:** A hero or sub sandwich.
- **Iggles:** Also what Philadelphia Eagles fans call their football team.
- **jawn:** A fill-in-the-blank word that can represent a person, place, or thing.
- **jimmies:** Sprinkles (for ice cream) to almost everyone else.
- **The Linc:** Nickname for Lincoln Financial Field, where the Iggles play.
- **Mummers:** Costumed musicians and partygoers who parade down Broad Street on New Year's Day.
- **Passyunk:** Pronounced *pash-shunk.* Popular South Philadelphia neighborhood; also an avenue.
- **Schuylkill:** Pronounced skool-kil. Another name for I-76; also referred to as "the Expressway." Also the name of the river the parallels the Expressway along the city's west side.
- **Shore:** This refers to the Jersey Shore (i.e. "I'm going down the shore"), a popular summer vacation spot for Philadelphians. It's also good to note that one goes "down the shore" not "to the shore."
- **water ice:** Pronounced *wood-er ahys.* Italian flavored ice treat.
- **Wawa:** A convenience store native to the Philadelphia region where locals go for hoagies; it's a sacred spot for many Philadelphians.
- **whiz:** a respected cheese option for cheesesteaks.
- **wit/witout:** with or without onions on cheesesteaks; if you say wit, you're getting fried onions on your cheesesteak.
- **youse:** "You guys."
- **Yo:** Greeting; used to get someone's attention.

A Historic Walk through the Old City

Touring through Old City, the neighborhood that encompasses the majority of Philly's Historic Downtown, doesn't have to begin and end with the Liberty Bell. Rely on this walk to make sure you hit all the highlights—and some under-the-radar locations as well.

A JUMPING-OFF POINT

Start off with a stop at the **Independence Visitor Center,** where you can get your bearings, talk to park rangers and concierges, and take in two short films chronicling Philadelphia's Revolutionary War history. The Center also has a café, public restrooms, and free Wi-Fi.

INDEPENDENCE NATIONAL HISTORIC PARK AND VICINITY

From here, it's off to the **Liberty Bell Center,** which is close by. Admission to lay eyes upon this gargantuan beacon of American freedom is free, but it's also very popular, so expect lines. You should also anticipate consistent crowds at **Independence Hall,** though there's quite a bit more to this portion of the Independence National Historical Park than the one-and-done Bell. Timed tours of the birthplace of both the Constitution and the Declaration of Independence are available free of charge; the most popular times are available on a first-come, first-served basis, though you can also reserve tickets over the phone or online for a small fee. Don't miss the other features of the park complex, including **Carpenter's Hall** (site of the First Continental Congress); and **Franklin Court,** Benjamin Franklin's former residence, featuring a mix of original architecture and restored features, including a fully operational post office.

Walk just a few blocks east down Market Street and you'll find the **Christ Church,** the beautifully maintained circa-1695 house of worship that also happens to be Franklin's final resting place. Three blocks

A Historic Walk through the Old City

WHERE TO START
Independence Visitor Center, 6th and Market Streets

GETTING HERE
It's a few minutes' walk from 30th Street Station to the visitor center, or you can park directly underneath it. Underground parking (✉ *41 N. 6th St.*) costs $14 if you arrive before 9 and leave by 6, Monday–Friday. Otherwise, it's $23 for up to 24 hours.

LENGTH
Less than 2 miles (but seeing all the sights can take a full day).

WHERE TO STOP
If you continue beyond Elfreth's Alley, consider stopping at the Betsy Ross House (✉ *239 Arch St.*), which is near the Constitution Center.

BEST TIME TO GO
When the weather is conducive to strolling outdoors.

WORST TIME TO GO
Sunday morning, when the National Constitution Center is closed, or on particularly cold or wet days, when walking isn't fun.

WRITER'S CHOICE
On weekends, Olde Bar is a good lunch stop, with happy hour starting at 4 pm. Royal Boucherie offers $2 martinis with the purchase of a lunch entrée during the week.

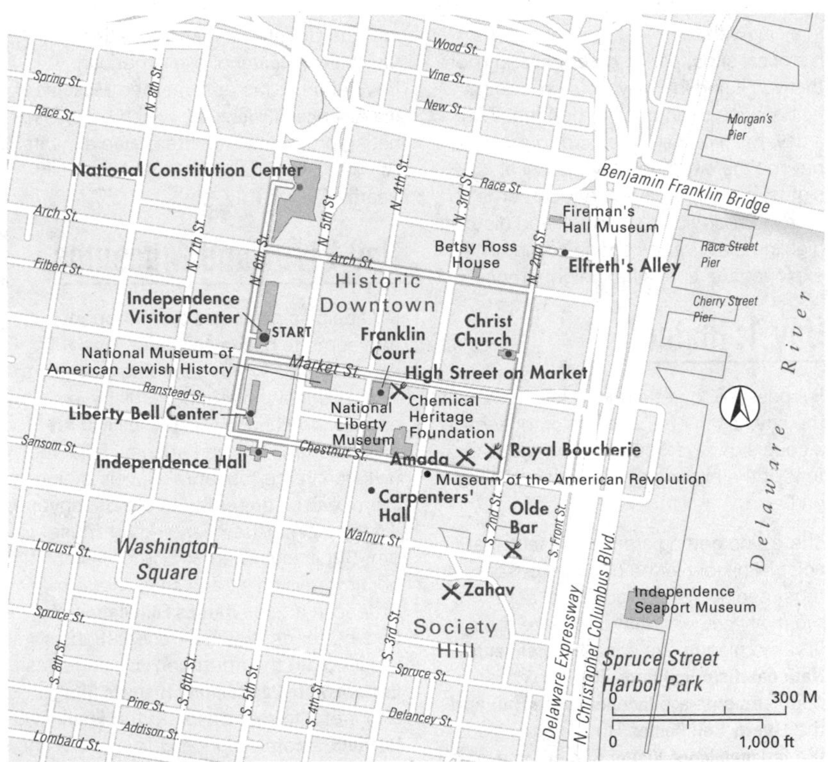

from here: the **National Constitution Center,** a gorgeous modern structure dedicated to celebration and analysis of America's most important political document. One block northeast of the church sits **Elfreth's Alley,** considered one of the oldest residential blocks in America. Two adjoined houses in the alley, which featured mostly hybrid business-residences in its heyday, serve as a museum and gift shop. Around the holidays, current residents host "Deck The Alley," an open-house fund-raiser with food, drink, and costumed revelry.

BEYOND THE BIGGIES

There are plenty of other draws worthy of your attention besides the "big five." The **National Museum of American Jewish History,** the **National Liberty Museum,** the **Chemical Heritage Foundation, Betsy Ross House,** the **Independence Seaport Museum,** the **Museum of the American Revolution,** and the **Fireman's Hall Museum** are but a few of the historic/academic draws in the neighborhood. Attractions like **Race Street Pier, Morgan's Pier, Cherry Street Pier,** and **Spruce Street Harbor Park** allow visitors to enjoy a view of the Delaware River.

REFRESHMENT STOPS

Old City also has a number of well-regarded, award-winning bars, restaurants, and cafés enjoyed by locals; look for High Street on Market, Zahav, Royal Boucherie, or Olde Bar.

How to Spend 3 Days in Philadelphia

In a city with the wealth of museums, historical sites, parks, gardens, and more that you'll find in Philly, you risk seeing half of everything or all of nothing. With a day, you'll be hard-pressed to move beyond the city's primary historical sights, but three days is enough time to take in Philadelphia's cultural and historic highlights as well as spend some time exploring the appealing neighborhoods.

Day 1: History

It's possible to get a good taste of what the city has to offer even if you only have a couple of days. You'll want to get the tour of the historic sights accomplished on Day 1.

There's no getting around the fact that colonial history is the primary reason most people visit Philadelphia, and most visitors will want to devote their first morning to exploring **Independence National Historical Park.** The two most popular sights are **Independence Hall** and the **Liberty Bell Center.** But don't neglect the **Independence Visitor Center,** where you must make a reservation (March through December) to tour Independence Hall; be sure to set aside 28 minutes from your schedule to see the film *Independence,* directed by John Huston, or the 20-minute *Choosing Sides.* There are usually lines to see the Liberty Bell, so do that while you wait for your tour time. If you have extra time, visit the Benjamin Franklin Museum on Franklin Court. Have lunch at nearby **Reading Terminal Market.** In the afternoon, you have a choice. You can keep up your historical pursuits, staying in Old Town to see more historic sights, including the **Carpenter's Hall, Christ Church,** the **Betsy Ross House,** and **Elfreth's Alley,** or you can delve deeper into the Constitution at the **National Constitution Center** or the American Revolution at the aptly named **Museum of the American Revolution,** which have fascinating programs and interactive exhibits. At night, dinner and nightlife beckon in nearby Center City.

Day 2: Art and Museums

Philadelphia has more than enough museums to occupy a visitor for a full week, but it's worth spending one day to visit a couple that are particularly interesting. The **Philadelphia Museum of Art** on Benjamin Franklin Parkway, followed by lunch in the museum's lovely dining room, will be enjoyable to almost anyone; it's the city's widest-ranging art museum. But if your interest is impressionist, postimpressionist, and early modern American art, **the Barnes Foundation** may be a better destination (reservations required). In the afternoon you could visit **Eastern State Penitentiary Historic Site** for a tour of a former prison or the **Franklin Institute.** Another option is to explore one of Philadelphia's distinct neighborhoods. Stroll around **Rittenhouse Square** and stop in at the **Rosenbach Museum and Library,** which has a diverse collection ranging from the original manuscript of James Joyce's *Ulysses* to the works of beloved children's author Maurice Sendak. There's also Society Hill, Queen Village, and South Philadelphia for the **Mummer Museum** on 9th Street and the outdoor **Italian Market.** Set aside time to dine in one of the city's best restaurants or take in a concert.

Day 3: Neighborhood Exploration

With more time, you can go deeper into your personal interests, whether they include art, shopping, history, the outdoors, or keeping your kids happy and occupied.

The best way to do that is to delve into more Philly neighborhoods. Check out Chinatown or Northern Liberties, or take a drive through Germantown and Chestnut Hill (stopping at **Cliveden**). If the weather's nice, you can drive or bike to the northwestern tip of **Fairmount Park** and check out the **Wissahickon**—a local favorite for all sorts of activities, from strolling to cycling. Afterward, head back into the city to check out the **Penn Museum of Archaeology and Anthropology** in University City and stroll down Locust Walk, the heart of University of Pennsylvania's leafy urban campus. In the evening, drive or take the SEPTA Market-Frankford line to Fishtown, where you can have dinner in one of the neighborhood's restaurants, and catch some live music afterwards.

Philadelphia in 1 Day

Sign up at the **Independence National Historical Park Visitor Center** for a walking tour hosted by a National Park Service guide, or try a go-at-your-own-pace tour offered by **the Constitutional Audio Walking Tour** (🌐 *www.theconstitutional.com*). At the very least you'll want to see the Liberty Bell, Independence Hall, the Carpenter's Hall, and Franklin Court. If you get started early, you can finish all that in about three or four hours. For lunch, visit **Reading Terminal Market,** where you can sample the cuisine Philadelphia is known for—like cheesesteaks, soft pretzels, and Bassetts ice cream. If you're interested in art (and make a reservation in advance), you can visit **the Barnes Foundation** on Benjamin Franklin Parkway. Then walk nine blocks east on Arch Street to Old City; **Christ Church,** the **Betsy Ross House,** and **Elfreth's Alley** are all in close proximity. In the late afternoon, head back toward Independence Hall for a horse-drawn carriage ride. Have dinner in Old City; then catch the **Lights of Liberty** 3-D show.

Best Tours

With a fine assortment of Colonial architecture, many museums, and some of the country's most significant historical artifacts and edifices, Philadelphia is perfect for a tour. In a relatively small area, the city offers history buffs, artisans, and architecture aficionados a wealth of fascinating material. The most-frequented tourist destination remains Old City, home to Independence Mall, which encompasses Independence Hall, the Liberty Bell, and the National Constitution Center, among other highlights. But there are many other historic and architectural tours to enjoy throughout the city. The mode of transportation largely dictates the type of tour, be it boat, bus, on foot, or horse and buggy, but you can explore everything from the cuisine of the city to the vast number of gorgeous giant art murals on the city's buildings.

Bicycle Tours

Bike tours are a great way to see a wide expanse of Philadelphia in a short period of time. Philly Bike Tour Co. offers both private and group tours, and bike rentals come with helmets and water; tours start at $59. You can also organize an independent tour of sorts by renting an Indego bicycle from one of the many kiosks situated throughout the city.

CONTACTS Indego. ☎ *844/446–3346* 🌐 *www.rideindego.com.* **Philly Bike Tour Co..** ✉ *2015 Fairmount Ave.* ✣ *Near Eastern State Penitentiary and the Art Museum* ☎ *267/521–2150* 🌐 *www.phillybiketours.com.*

Boat Tours

The *Spirit of Philadelphia* runs lunch and dinner cruises along the Delaware River. This three-deck ship leaves Penn's Landing for lunch, dinner, and a variety of specialty cruises. Dinner cruises include entertainment and music. Between April and October, Patriot Harbor Lines offers cruises on both the Delaware and Schuylkill Rivers, including wine-centric events and a ride to Bartram's Garden, a National Historic Landmark in Philly's southwest.

CONTACTS Patriot Harbor Lines. ☎ *800/979–3370* 🌐 *www.phillybyboat.com.* ***Spirit of Philadelphia.*** ☎ *866/455–3866* 🌐 *www.spiritcruises.com/philadelphia.*

Bus and Trolley Tours

Philadelphia Trolley Works offers narrated tours in buses designed to resemble Victorian-style open-air trolleys. Trolleys depart frequently from the corner of 5th and Market; the $35 fare is an all-day pass, allowing unlimited stops. There are nearly 30 sights on a route covering the Historic Area, the Benjamin Franklin Parkway, the Avenue of the Arts, Fairmount Park, the Philadelphia Zoo, Eastern State Penitentiary, and Penn's Landing. For a different kind of Philly experience, you can also try the Philadelphia Mural Arts Tour, a trolley ride that visits some of the more than 2,000 public murals the city has to offer; or the Philly By Night Tour, which gives patrons a chance to see the city under the stars in the comfort of a double-decker open-top bus.

CONTACTS Mural Arts Tour. ☎ *215/925–3633* 🌐 *www.muralarts.org/tour.* **Philadelphia Trolley Works.** ☎ *215/389–8687* 🌐 *www.phillytour.com.* **Philly By Night Tour.** ☎ *215/389–8687* 🌐 *www.phillytour.com.*

Carriage Rides

Numerous horse-drawn carriages wind their way through the narrow streets of the Historic Area. Tours last anywhere from 20 minutes to an hour and cost from $50 to $120 for up to four people. Carriages line up on 5th and Chestnut Streets near Independence Hall between 10:30 am and 3:30 pm and 6:30 pm and 10:30 pm Monday through Friday, and 10:30 am to 10:30 pm Saturday and Sunday. Carriages operate year-round, weather permitting.

CONTACTS '76 Carriage Company. ☎ *215/923–8516* 🌐 *www.phillytour.com.*

Segway Tours

Philly by Segway operates tours on motorized Segway scooters that travel throughout the city, allowing patrons to zip around the museum corridor, through historic Old City, and more. The tours, which run from two to three hours depending on destination, include hands-on Segway training, and start at $55.

CONTACTS Philly by Segway. ☎ *215/523–5827* 🌐 *phillybysegway.com.*

Walking Tours

Founding Footsteps offers highly rated tours of Independence Park led by informative and energetic guides. The Philly Phables tour has you literally retracing the footsteps of our Founding Fathers around Philadelphia; the BYOB tour aboard a trolley allows you to sip cold beer along the way. For food buffs, the Taste of Philadelphia tour of Reading Terminal Market offers a fascinating look behind some of Philly's most well-loved edibles, including soft pretzels and cheesesteaks. That tour is offered at 10 am every Wednesday and Saturday morning ($16.95 adults, $9.95 children). The more gourmet-minded might appreciate the City Food Tours Decadent Gourmet, which leads you through Center City to meet with chefs and owners of multiple establishments, tasting cheeses, Middle Eastern fare, desserts like chocolate and gelato, and more ($39 adults). Founding Father fanatics should take right to a Constitutional Walking Tour or a tour of noted Philly landmarks, with the multifaceted Lights of Liberty experience juggling history and entertainment. Finally, mild scares can be found during the Spirits of '76 Ghost Tour ($19 adult, $12.50 children. $55 for a family four pack), which begins at 4th and Chestnut Streets and guides its patrons through some of the ancient architecture of Old City, including famous film locations from spooky Philly-based films like *The Sixth Sense*.

CONTACTS City Food Tours Decadent Gourmet. ☎ *215/546–1234* 🌐 *www.cityfoodtours.com.* **Constitutional Walking Tour.** ☎ *215/525–1776* 🌐 *www.the-constitutional.com.* **Founding Footsteps.** ☎ *609/795–1776* 🌐 *foundingfootsteps.com.* **Landmark Tours.** ☎ *215/925–2251* 🌐 *www.philalandmarks.org.* **Spirits of '76 Ghost Tour.** ☎ *215/525–1776* 🌐 *www.spiritsof76.com.* **Taste of Philadelphia: Walking Tour.** ☎ *215/545–8007* 🌐 *www.readingterminalmarket.org.*

On the Calendar

January

Mummers Parade. One of Philadelphia's most unique traditions, the annual New Year's Day celebration is a bacchanal of music, dance, and ridiculous costumes with roots in 17th-century European folk celebrations. The parade begins at City Hall and proceeds south down Broad Street. 🌐 *www.phillymummers.com*

February

Blue Cross RiverRink Winterfest. Strap on your ice skates and glide around the seasonal pop-up that features a sprawling rink, a fire pit, warming cabins, and plenty of seasonal treats. 🌐 *delawareriverwaterfront.com/places/blue-cross-riverrink-winterfest*

Mummers Mardi Gras. Daylong festival with family-friendly activities and live music from Philadelphia Mummers String Bands. 🌐 *www.mummersmardigras.com*

Philly Theatre Week. Experience more than 100 events—including live performances, concerts, and panels—over 10 entertaining days. 🌐 *theatrephiladelphia.org*

March

Philadelphia Flower Show. One of the city's most high-profile happenings, Philly's flower show is the world's oldest continuously running indoor floral exhibition. Attracting more than a quarter-million viewers, the show features rare and ornate displays, a judged competition, hands-on instruction, and live entertainment. 🌐 *theflowershow.com*

April

Cherry Blossom Festival. The Japan Society of Greater Philadelphia organizes the city's take on the elaborate welcome-to-spring celebrations held in Japan and beyond, with events throughout the city and its suburbs. The occasion culminates with "Sakura Sunday," a vibrant celebration at the Horticulture Center of Fairmount Park. 🌐 *subarucherryblossom.org*

Penn Relays. Established in 1895 by the University of Pennsylvania, the Penn Relays are among America's oldest athletic traditions, now an international affair that attracts teams from around the globe to race over a three-day period. Held at Penn's historic Franklin Field, it regularly draws six-figure crowds. 🌐 *www.thepennrelays.com*

May

Jefferson Dad Vail Regatta. More than 100 colleges and universities from the United States and Canada participate in North America's largest collegiate regatta. 🌐 *www.dadvail.org*

Philadelphia Chinese Lantern Festival. Held through mid-July, the festival features lantern displays, folk artists, and authentic Chinese performances. 🌐 *historicphiladelphia.org*

Rittenhouse Row Spring Festival. This annual festival, which takes place along the main vein of Walnut Street, highlights all the neighborhood's offerings and is a bit more democratic in its invite policy than some of the more exclusive goings-on in the area, including food, drink, live music, and entertainment. It's a great way to see this often exclusive neighborhood. 🌐 *rittenhouserow.org*

Roots Picnic. Even though they're now the big-time house band for *The Tonight Show Starring Jimmy Fallon,* Philly's own The Roots still show a heavy amount of love for their hometown. Their annual one-day music festival has attracted A-List talent to Festival Pier at Penn's Landing since 2008. Past acts have included everyone from Erykah Badu and Snoop Dogg to Nas and Vampire Weekend. The Roots, of course, make their way onstage, too. *rootspicnic.com*

June

Philly Beer Week. Conceived as a way to bring together regional craft breweries and their out-of-town cohorts, Philly Beer Week has blossomed into one of the nation's largest and most ambitious brew-centric events. The schedule comprises hundreds of events (tastings, dinners, rare releases, meet the brewer, etc.) hosted at an equally dizzying array of area bars, restaurants, and venues. A steadily growing tourism draw, Beer Week stretches across a 10-day span from late May to early June. *phillybeerweek.org*

July

Wawa Welcome America! Wawa, the region's best-loved convenience store chain, sponsors this ambitious celebration on Independence Day with a multitude of patriotic happenings, from a massive block party on Benjamin Franklin Parkway to free museum access and historical tours. It all culminates with a concert and fireworks extravaganza held on the parkway that is attended by thousands. *www.welcomeamerica.com*

August

Philadelphia Folk Festival. Located just outside Philadelphia in Schwenksville, Pennsylvania, this family-friendly festival has been entertaining folk fans for nearly 60 years. Expect food, drink, hands-on educational activities, and entertainment, all with a backdrop of beautiful, bucolic countryside. *pfs.org*

2nd Street Festival. Art, music, crafts, and food festival celebrating the Northern Liberties neighborhood. *www.2ndstfestival.org*

September

FEASTIVAL. The artistic community links up with the culinary at FEASTIVAL, FringeArts' annual fund-raising soiree, featuring top restaurants commingling with performers and patrons. *www.phillyfeastival.com*

FringeArts. Taking place every autumn, FringeArts is a celebration of cutting-edge and avant garde theater and performance art. Inspired by the comparable approach taken by Fringe Festival organizers in cities like Edinburgh, Philly's Fringe has grown into a formidable cultural and artistic force, attracting talent from around the world to stage shows in Philly over a 17-day stretch. *fringearts.com*

Made in America. Held over the long Labor Day weekend, the unofficial end of summer, Made in America is a multiday musical festival founded by Jay-Z. The event, which takes over the Benjamin Franklin Parkway, typically features world-renowned acts; past installments have seen Beyoncé, Pearl Jam, Drake, Calvin Harris, and Run-DMC grace the stage. *a.madeinamericafest.com*

On the Calendar

October

Head of the Schuylkill Regatta. One of the world's largest rowing competitions takes place annually in Fairmount Park, attracting thousands of athletes and spectators. 🌐 *hosr.org*

Philadelphia International Film Festival. Organized by the Philadelphia Film Society, the city's annual film fest screens titles both high-profile and under-the-radar every fall. First established in 1991, the fest brings together a diverse slate of entries, with categories such as "World Narratives" (for global cinema), "Documentary," "Graveyard Shift" (horror and sci-fi), and "Filmadelphia" (films shot locally, or with a local connection). Screenings are held at theaters throughout the city. 🌐 *filmadelphia.org*

November

Franklin Square Holiday Festival. Held through December, this free festival features the Electrical Spectacle light show with more than 75,000 lights. There's food and shopping, too. 🌐 *historicphiladelphia.org*

Made in Philadelphia Holiday Market. Situated in Dilworth Park, across the street from the Christmas Village at LOVE Park, over 40 vendors showcase crafts, confections, and other gifts, all locally made. 🌐 *madeinphila.com/holiday-market/*

Philadelphia Marathon Weekend. Started in 1994, this is one of the country's top marathons. 🌐 *philadelphiamarathon.com*

The Rothman Institute Ice Rink. This picturesque ice rink, sponsored by the local medical orthopedic center, is centrally located in Dilworth Park, on the northwest side of City Hall. A seasonal attraction running from November to February, it offers affordable admission as well as skate rentals ($9). 🌐 *www.ccdparks.org/dilworth-park/rothmanicerink*

December

Christmas Village at LOVE Park. Iconic LOVE Park is transformed into a festive outdoor market inspired by historic German Christmas markets. Vendors sell ornaments, gifts, and seasonal treats like gingerbread and mulled wine. 🌐 *philachristmas.com*

Macy's Christmas Light Show. Throughout the month of December, Macy's Center City hosts a dazzling show in which more than 100,000 LED lights take the shape of merry holiday motifs, accompanied by a holiday concert featuring the Wanamaker historic grand organ. 🌐 *visitmacysusa.com/philadelphia*

Chapter 3

OLD CITY AND HISTORIC DOWNTOWN

Updated by
Drew Lazor

Sights	Restaurants	Hotels	Shopping	Nightlife
★★★★★	★★★★☆	★★★★☆	★★★★★	★★★★☆

VISITING INDEPENDENCE NATIONAL HISTORICAL PARK

Independence Hall is one of the most popular sights in Philadelphia.

Independence National Historical Park (INHP) welcomes more than 4 million visitors every year. Several of the country's most important historic sites are here, including the Liberty Bell, Congress Hall, the National Constitution Center, and Independence Hall (a UNESCO World Heritage site).

Your first stop should be the Independence Visitor Center, where you can buy tickets for tours and pick up maps and brochures. From here you can easily explore the park on your own; in each building a park ranger can answer all your questions. In summer more than a dozen storytellers wander through the park, perching on benches to tell tales of the times. Special paid guided tours are also available through the Independence Visitor Center. **■ TIP→ Visitors are required to join a ranger-led tour to see Independence Hall, Congress Hall, Dolley Todd House, and the Bishop White House, as well as the Germantown White House in Germantown. Tours of Independence Hall last 30 to 45 minutes.**

WHAT'S HERE

There are more than 20 sites in Independence National Historical Park (INHP), including Carpenters' Hall, Christ Church, Congress Hall, First Bank of the United States, Franklin Court, the National Constitution Center, and the President's House Site. Some of the lesser known sites include Declaration House, Dolley Todd House, Bishop White House, and the Merchants' Exchange Building. **■ TIP→ The Germantown White House, in Germantown, is also part of the park.**

HOURS AND FEES

The Independence Visitor Center is open daily 8:30–6, and Independence Hall and the Liberty Bell Pavilion are open daily year-round 9–5. In summer the closing times are often later. Other park buildings are also open daily, although their hours may vary from season to season. Call ☎ *800/537–7676*, the 24-hour hotline, for hours plus a schedule of park programs; or visit 🌐 *www.nps.gov/inde*.

Timed entry tickets are free but required for Independence Hall between March and December, and can be picked up for that day at the Independence Visitor Center starting at 8:30 am. Reserved tickets for up to a year in advance are available by calling ☎ *877/444–6777* or online at 🌐 *recreation.gov*; still free, but there's a $1 per ticket processing fee.

Most other attractions run by the park are free, but there are some exceptions, including the Benjamin Franklin Museum ($5) and the National Constitution Center ($14.50). To save, consider the NCC's discounted ticket packages bundled with sites outside the INHP's purview, such as the Museum of the American Revolution and the African American Museum.

This statue of Commodore John Barry is located behind Independence Hall.

The Presidents House: Freedom and Slavery in the Making of a New Nation is located next to the Liberty Bell.

WHEN TO GO

Visit America's birthplace on America's birthday for the Wawa Welcome America! party (June 27 to July 4). There are more than 50 free events, including parades (the Mummers and an illuminated boat procession), outdoor concerts, historical reenactments, and fireworks. The rest of the summer is filled with plays, musicals, and parades.

If you want to avoid the crowds, plan your visit in the summer or winter, as much of the spring and fall sees heavy visitation from school field trips. Day of, prioritize the Liberty Bell Center and Independence Hall as your earliest stops for the most manageable crowds.

HOW LONG TO STAY

Budget a full day here. An early start lets you reserve timed tickets for a tour of the Todd and Bishop White houses and adjust your schedule to catch some of the special events on the visitor center's daily schedule. Allow about 40 minutes for the Independence Hall tour and another hour each at Franklin Court and the Todd and Bishop White houses. Allow 30 minutes each at Declaration House and the visitor center, where it's a good idea to see the film *Independence* before you set out. Dine in the area before wrapping up for the day.

NEIGHBORHOOD SNAPSHOT

TOP EXPERIENCES

■ **African American Museum:** One of the nation's first museums created to commemorate black history, there's a deep focus here on the lives of African Americans in the nation's first century.

■ **Art, Boutiques, Shopping:** Old City is packed with history, but it also happens to be populated by an appealing concentration of art galleries, indie boutiques, and local book and record shops.

■ **Elfreth's Alley:** Stroll down this charming, cobblestone lane—the country's oldest continuously occupied street—and imagine yourself in Colonial times.

■ **Independence Hall:** The United States literally got its start in this modest redbrick building, where the Declaration of Independence was signed and the U.S. Constitution was adopted.

■ **Liberty Bell:** Yes, the bell really does have a giant crack, but more importantly, it still resonates as a symbol of the right of all Americans to be free.

■ **Museum of the American Revolution:** This relative newcomer to the Old City circuit offers a refreshing new perspective on the American Revolution.

GETTING HERE

It's an easy walk from Center City—check out pedestrian-friendly City Hall along the way—but SEPTA's Blue Line is one way to get here fast. From Center City, ride the train east from 15th Street/City Hall to the 5th Street or 2nd Street stops. Rides are $2.50 each (have exact change if paying in cash). A number of SEPTA's bus routes, including the 9, 17, 21, and 42, will get you down here painlessly, too.

PLANNING YOUR TIME

Old City is busy every day in high season; school months see plenty of student groups on weekdays in addition to the usual tourists. Visit iconic sites like Independence Hall and the Liberty Bell as early as possible to beat the rush, then break for lunch before more leisurely museum visits.

QUICK BITES

■ **Cafe Ole.** This charming Euro-like café does a wide range of sandwiches, salads, and breakfast dishes, but it's best known for its *shakshuka*, the soulful tomato-and-egg stew made here in the Tunisian style. ✉ *147 N. 3rd St., Old City* 🌐 *www.facebook.com/phillycafeole*

■ **Campo's.** Feeding Philly since the 1940s, Campo's is a respected name in the city's sandwich and cheesesteak game. ✉ *214 Market St., Old City* 🌐 *www.camposdeli.com*

■ **Sonny's Famous Steaks.** It doesn't enjoy the same notoriety of other shops, but connoisseurs know the friendly Sonny's slings a mean version of the iconic sandwich. ✉ *228 Market St., Old City* 🌐 *www.sonnyscheesesteaks.com*

GOOD TO KNOW

■ If you've put on your walking shoes and are good at negotiating the cobblestones, you can wander through this area in about two hours. But the city's atmospheric historic district warrants a slower pace, and built-in time for the many sights of interest. While there are ample parking lots and garages as well as metered street spots, it's really a neighborhood best absorbed on foot.

In Colonial days, wealthy folks in Society Hill derisively whispered of those who lived "north of Market," referencing the neighborhood between Front and 5th Streets and Chestnut and Vine Streets. This was traditionally a commercial district for industry and wholesale distributors, filled with wharves, warehouses, and taverns, plus the modest homes of craftsmen and artisans. Old City, so dubbed in 1972 to distinguish it from Independence National Historical Park, deserves its name: it's one of the nation's most historic neighborhoods, and millions visit from around the world each year to immerse themselves in the birthplace of modern democracy.

Despite its touristic heartbeat, Old City is still very much an artistic and residential neighborhood, with personality unto itself. It shares stylistic similarities with Manhattan's SoHo in its architectural mix. Many cast-iron building facades and ghost signs remain, while rugged old warehouses with telltale names like the Sugar Refinery and the Hoopskirt Factory now house modern loft space. There are small theaters—Painted Bride, Arden Theatre Company—and numerous galleries, boutiques, and restaurants. On the First Friday of each month, the Old City Arts Association coordinates a sprawling, ever-changing happening that sees businesses host show openings, receptions, and special events. The First Friday sidewalk scene is equally lively, coaxing out a creative class of street artists, vendors, and performers.

Sights

Any visit to Old City, whether you have one day or several, should begin in the area that comprises Independence National Historical Park. Philadelphia was the birthplace of the United States, the home of the country's first government, and nowhere is the spirit of those early days—the audacious beginnings of a brand-new nation—more palpable than along these cobbled streets.

In the late 1940s, before civic-minded citizens banded together to save the area, the neighborhood was crowded with factories and run-down warehouses. The city, state, and federal governments finally took interest. Some buildings were restored, while others were reconstructed on their original sites; several attractions were built for the 1976 Bicentennial celebration. In recent years, development has again spread across the area, with notable additions like an expanded visitor center, a more attractive home for the Liberty Bell, and museums examining the Constitution, the Revolution, African Americans, and Jewish Americans. It remains a destination for art and nightlife lovers, too. Within the National Park Service's 52-acre footprint and well beyond it, mindful development and renewal have ensured Old City will preserve its heritage and charm.

African American Museum in Philadelphia
MUSEUM | Opened in the Bicentennial year of 1976, this is the first museum of its kind funded and built by a city. The centerpiece is "Audacious Freedom: African Americans in Philadelphia 1776–1876," an interactive and immersive exhibit that uses technology to tell the stories of pioneers in the freedom movement. The list includes Frances Ellens Watkins Harper, a suffragist and conductor on the Underground Railroad; Thomas Morris Chester, the first black lawyer to argue before the U.S. Supreme Court; and Elizabeth Taylor Greenfield, a renowned singer who performed for Queen Victoria. Visiting and rotating exhibitions dive deep into the artistic, cultural, and political contributions of African American women and men. The museum's gift shop stocks one of the city's widest selections of books on black culture, history, fiction, poetry, and drama, along with textiles, sculpture, jewelry, prints, and tiles. ✉ *701 Arch St., Old City* ☎ *215/574–0380* 🌐 *www.aampmuseum.org* 🎫 *$14* 🕒 *Closed Mon. and Tues.*

Arch Street Meeting House
RELIGIOUS SITE | This site has been home to a Quaker gathering place since 1682. The current simple-lined building, constructed in 1804 for the Philadelphia Yearly Meeting of the Society of Friends, is still used for that purpose, as well as for weekly services. Among the most influential members in the 19th century was Lucretia Mott (1793–1880), a leader in the women's suffrage, antiwar, and antislavery movements. A small museum in the building presents a series of dioramas and slide show depicting the life and accomplishments of William Penn (1644–1718), who gave this land to the Society of Friends. Tours take place during the day April through October, and by appointment only November through March. ✉ *320 Arch St., at 4th St., Old City* ☎ *215/627–2667* 🌐 *www.archstreetmeetinghouse.org* 🎫 *$2 suggested donation.*

Benjamin Franklin Bridge
BRIDGE/TUNNEL | When the bridge opened in 1926, its 1,750-foot main span made it the longest suspension bridge in the world. Paul Cret, architect of the Rodin Museum, was the designer. The bridge has been having some rust problems of late, but a massive, multiyear project has restored its glorious blue paint job. The bridge is most impressive when it's lighted at night. Start the 1¾-mile walk (one way) from either the Philadelphia side, two blocks north of the U.S. Mint, or the Camden, New Jersey, side. ✉ *5th and Vine Sts., Old City* ☎ *215/218–3750* 🌐 *www.drpa.org* 🎫 *Free* ☞ *Weather and construction conditions may restrict access to the walkway. For updates call 856/968–2255 or 215/218–3750 Ext.*

2255 (weekdays 9–5). All other times call DRPA Police Radio at 856/968–3301 or 215/218–3750 Ext. 3301.

The Benjamin Franklin Museum (*Franklin Court*)
MUSEUM | FAMILY | This museum built on the site that was Benjamin Franklin's first permanent home in Philadelphia was thoroughly renovated in 2013, reopening as the Benjamin Franklin Museum. The exhibits combine the latest touch-screen displays and computer-generated animation with a chess set, eyeglasses, and other items actually used by the Renaissance man. Franklin's multifaceted roles as scientist, inventor, philosopher, writer, politician, and businessman are represented in various rooms via interactive displays. Franklin, publisher of *Poor Richard's Almanac,* helped draft the Declaration of Independence and negotiate peace with Great Britain. He also helped found Pennsylvania Hospital, the University of Pennsylvania, the Philadelphia Contributionship, and the American Philosophical Society. In the courtyard adjacent to the museum, architect Robert Venturi erected a steel skeleton of Franklin's former home. You can peek through "windows" into cutaways to see wall foundations, outdoor privies, and other original elements uncovered during excavation. At the Market Street side are several houses, now exhibition halls, that Franklin rented in addition to his main home. Here, too, you can find a restoration of a Colonial-era print shop and an operational post office. Don't forget to get a letter hand-stamped with a "b. free franklin" cancellation. ✉ *314–322 Market St., or enter from Chestnut St. walkway, Old City* ☎ *267/514–1522* 🌐 *www.nps.gov* 🎟 *$5.*

Betsy Ross House
MUSEUM | FAMILY | It's easy to find this little brick house with the gabled roof: just look for the 13-star flag displayed from its second-floor window. Whether Betsy Ross, also known as Elizabeth Griscom Ross Ashbourn Claypoole (1752–1836), actually lived here and whether she really made the first Stars and Stripes is debatable. Nonetheless, the house, built around 1740, is a splendid example of a Colonial Philadelphia home. The eight-room house overflows with artifacts such as a family Bible and Ross's chest of drawers and reading glasses. You may have to wait in line, as this is one of the city's most popular attractions. The house, with its winding narrow stairs, is not accessible to people with disabilities. Alongside the house is a courtyard with a fountain, as well as the graves of Ross and her third husband, John Claypoole. Visitors can meet Betsy in her upholstery shop (the only working Colonial upholstery shop in the country) and enjoy free, interactive historical programming. ✉ *239 Arch St., Old City* ☎ *215/629–5801* 🌐 *www.historicphiladelphia.org/betsy-ross-house/what-to-see* 🎟 *$8.*

Bishop White House
HOUSE | Built in 1787, this restored upper-class house embodies Colonial and Federal elegance. It was the home of Bishop William White (1748–1836), rector of Christ Church, first Episcopal bishop of Pennsylvania, and spiritual leader of Philadelphia for 60 years. White, a founder of the Episcopal Church after the break with England, was chaplain to the Continental Congress and entertained many of the country's first families, including Washington and Franklin. The second-floor study contains much of the bishop's own library. The house tour is not recommended for small children. Tours are available by appointment only; timed tickets are available at the Independence Visitor Center. ✉ *309 Walnut St., Old City* ☎ *215/965–2305* 🌐 *www.nps.gov/inde/learn/historyculture/places-bishopwhitehouse.htm* 🎟 *Free* ☞ *Tickets are required for tours and available on a first-come, first-served basis at the Independence Visitor Center daily; tours are limited to 10 adults at a time.*

Old City and Historic District
A
B
C
D
E
F
1
2
3
4
5
6
7
8
9
Old City
Historic Downtown
Washington Park
Society Hill
Penn's Landing
N. 8th St.
N. 7th St.
N. 6th St.
N. 5th St.
N. 4th St.
N. 3rd St.
N. 2nd St.
N. Christopher Columbus Blvd.
Arch St.
Market St.
Chestnut St.
Bank St.
Walnut St.
S. 2nd St.
S. Front St.
S. 3rd St.
S. 6th St.
S. 5th St.
S. 4th St.
Delancey St.
Rodman St.
Gaskill St.
South St.
Kater St.
95

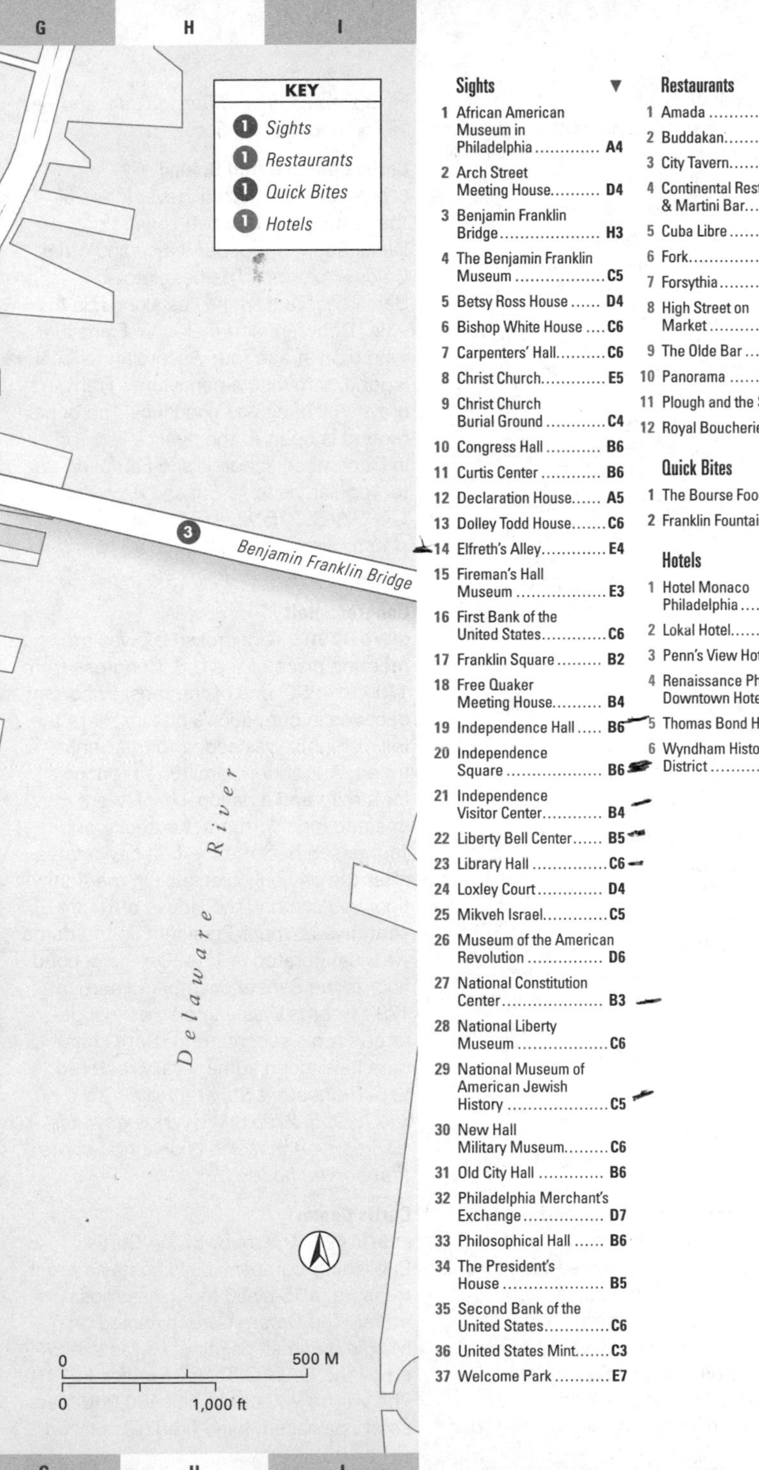

Sights

1 African American Museum in Philadelphia A4
2 Arch Street Meeting House.......... D4
3 Benjamin Franklin Bridge.................... H3
4 The Benjamin Franklin Museum C5
5 Betsy Ross House D4
6 Bishop White House C6
7 Carpenters' Hall.......... C6
8 Christ Church............ E5
9 Christ Church Burial Ground C4
10 Congress Hall B6
11 Curtis Center B6
12 Declaration House...... A5
13 Dolley Todd House....... C6
14 Elfreth's Alley............. E4
15 Fireman's Hall Museum E3
16 First Bank of the United States............. C6
17 Franklin Square B2
18 Free Quaker Meeting House.......... B4
19 Independence Hall B6
20 Independence Square B6
21 Independence Visitor Center............ B4
22 Liberty Bell Center...... B5
23 Library Hall C6
24 Loxley Court D4
25 Mikveh Israel............. C5
26 Museum of the American Revolution D6
27 National Constitution Center.................... B3
28 National Liberty Museum C6
29 National Museum of American Jewish History C5
30 New Hall Military Museum......... C6
31 Old City Hall B6
32 Philadelphia Merchant's Exchange D7
33 Philosophical Hall B6
34 The President's House B5
35 Second Bank of the United States............. C6
36 United States Mint....... C3
37 Welcome Park E7

Restaurants

1 Amada D6
2 Buddakan................. C6
3 City Tavern............... D7
4 Continental Restaurant & Martini Bar............. E5
5 Cuba Libre D5
6 Fork....................... D5
7 Forsythia D6
8 High Street on Market.................... C5
9 The Olde Bar E7
10 Panorama E5
11 Plough and the Stars.... E6
12 Royal Boucherie D6

Quick Bites

1 The Bourse Food Hall ... C5
2 Franklin Fountain E5

Hotels

1 Hotel Monaco Philadelphia C6
2 Lokal Hotel............... D4
3 Penn's View Hotel E5
4 Renaissance Philadelphia Downtown Hotel......... C6
5 Thomas Bond House.... E6
6 Wyndham Historic District C4

Carpenters' Hall

MUSEUM | This handsome, patterned red-and-black brick building dating from 1770 was the headquarters of the Carpenters' Company, a guild founded to support carpenters, who were both builders and architects in this era, and to aid their families. In September 1774 the First Continental Congress convened here and addressed a declaration of rights and grievances to King George III. Today re-creations of Colonial settings include original Windsor chairs and candle sconces and displays of 18th-century carpentry tools. The Carpenters' Company still owns and operates the building. ✉ *320 Chestnut St., Old City* ☎ *215/925–0167* 🌐 *www.carpentershall.org* 🎫 *Free; donations accepted* ⏲ *Closed Mon. Mar.–Dec.; closed Mon. and Tues. in Jan. and Feb.*

Christ Church

RELIGIOUS SITE | The Anglicans of the Church of England built a wooden church on this site in 1697. When they outgrew it, they erected a new church, the most sumptuous in the colonies, probably designed by Dr. John Kearsley and modeled on the work of famed English architect Sir Christopher Wren. The symmetrical, classical facade with arched windows, completed in 1754, is a fine example of Georgian architecture; the church is one of the city's treasures. The congregation included 15 signers of the Declaration of Independence. The bells and the soaring 196-foot steeple, the tallest in the colonies, were financed by lotteries run by Benjamin Franklin. Brass plaques mark the pews of George and Martha Washington, John and Abigail Adams, Betsy Ross, and others. Two blocks west of the church is Christ Church Burial Ground. Guided tours are available throughout the day. ✉ *20 N. American St., 2nd St. north of Market St., Old City* ☎ *215/922–1695* 🌐 *www.christchurchphila.org* 🎫 *$5 for Christ Church admission and guided tour, $8 for Burial Ground admission and guided tour* ⏲ *Closed Mon. and Tues. in Jan. and Feb.* Ⓜ *2nd and Market Sts.*

Christ Church Burial Ground

CEMETERY | Weathered gravestones fill the resting place of five signers of the Declaration of Independence and other Colonial patriots. The best known is Benjamin Franklin; he lies alongside his wife, Deborah, and their son, Francis, who died at age four. According to local legend, throwing a penny onto Franklin's grave will bring you good luck. The burial ground is open to the public—except in December, January, and February—for regular visits. ✉ *5th and Arch Sts., Old City* ☎ *215/922–1695* 🌐 *www.christchurchphila.org* 🎫 *$3, $8 with guided tour* ⏲ *Closed Dec.–Feb.*

Congress Hall

HISTORIC SITE | Congress Hall was the meeting place of the U.S. Congress from 1790 to 1800, one of the most important decades in our nation's history. Here the Bill of Rights was added to the Constitution; Alexander Hamilton's proposals for a mint and a national bank were enacted; and Vermont, Kentucky, and Tennessee became the first new states after the original colonies. On the first floor you can find the House of Representatives, where President John Adams was inaugurated in 1797. On the second floor is the Senate chamber, where in 1793 George Washington was inaugurated for his second term. Both chambers have been authentically restored. ✉ *520 Chestnut St., at 6th St., Old City* ☎ *215/965–2305* 🌐 *www.nps.gov/inde* 🎫 *Free* ☞ *Admission is on a first-come, first-served basis.*

Curtis Center

PUBLIC ART | The lobby of the Curtis Publishing Company building has a great treasure: a 15-by-50-foot glass mosaic mural, *The Dream Garden,* based on a Maxfield Parrish painting. It was executed by the Louis C. Tiffany Studios in 1916. The work's 260 colors and 100,000 pieces of opalescent hand-fired glass laced with gold leaf make it perhaps the finest Tiffany mural in the world. The mural was also designated a "historic object" by the Philadelphia Historical Commission after its owner, the estate of a local art patron, put it up for sale for $9 million in 1998; the designation, the first in the city's history, stopped the sale and the mural remains in public view, under the auspices of the Pennsylvania Academy of the Fine Arts. ✉ *601–45 Walnut St., at 6th St., Old City* ☎ *215/627–7280* 🎫 *Free* ☞ *The mural is open to the public whenever the building is open.*

Declaration House

MUSEUM | In a second-floor room that he had rented from bricklayer Jacob Graff, Thomas Jefferson (1743–1826) drafted the Declaration of Independence in June 1776. The home was reconstructed for the Bicentennial celebration; the bedroom and parlor in which Jefferson lived that summer were re-created with period furnishings. The first floor has a Jefferson exhibition. The display on the Declaration of Independence shows some of the changes Jefferson made while writing it. You can see Jefferson's original version—which would have abolished slavery had the passage not been stricken by the committee that included Benjamin Franklin and John Adams. ✉ *701 Market St., at 7th St., Old City* ☎ *215/965–2305* 🌐 *www.nps.gov/inde* 🎫 *Free* 🕒 *Call for hrs.*

Dolley Todd House

HOUSE | Built in 1775 by John Dilworth, Todd House has been restored to its 1790s appearance, when its best-known resident, Dolley Payne Todd (1768–1849), lived here. She lost her husband, the Quaker lawyer John Todd, to yellow fever in 1793. The widow later married James Madison, our fourth president. Her time as a hostess in the White House was quite a contrast to her years in this simple home. There's an 18th-century garden next to Todd House. **■ TIP→ Open by tour only; free tickets available at the Independence Visitor Center in advance.** ✉ *400 Walnut St., at 4th St., Old City* ☎ *215/965–2305* 🌐 *www.nps.gov/inde/learn/historyculture/places-dolley-toddhouse.htm* 🎫 *Free* ☞ *Tickets are required for tours and available on a first-come, first-served basis at the Independence Visitor Center; limit 10 adults per tour.*

★ Elfreth's Alley

HISTORIC SITE | This alley is the oldest continuously occupied residential street in America, dating back to 1702. Much of Colonial Philadelphia resembled this area, with its cobblestone streets and narrow two- or three-story brick houses. These were modest row homes rented by craftsmen, such as cabinetmakers, silversmiths, pewterers, and those who made their living in the shipping industry. The earliest houses have pent eaves; taller houses, built after the Revolution, show the influence of the Federal style. The Elfreth's Alley Museum includes two homes that have been restored by the Elfreth's Alley Association: No. 124, home of a Windsor chair maker, and No. 126, a Colonial dressmaker's home, with authentic furnishings and a Colonial kitchen. In early June residents celebrate Fete Day, when some of the 30 homes are open to the public for tours hosted by guides in Colonial garb. In December, residents again welcome visitors for "Deck the Alley," a holiday-themed celebration. Both of these special events require advance tickets. ✉ *Front and 2nd Sts. between Arch and Race Sts., 124–126 Elfreth's Alley, Old City* ☎ *215/627–8680* 🌐 *www.elfrethsalley.org* 🎫 *$3 for self-guided Museum House tour, $8 for guided tour.*

Fireman's Hall Museum

MUSEUM | **FAMILY** | Housed in an authentic 1876 firehouse, this museum traces the history of firefighting, from the volunteer company founded in Philadelphia by Benjamin Franklin in 1736 to the professional departments of the 20th century. The collection includes early hand- and horse-drawn fire engines, such as an 1796 hand pumper, an 1857 steamer, and a 1907 three-horse Metropolitan steamer; fire marks (18th-century building signs marking them as insured for fire); uniforms; other memorabilia; and a 9/11 memorial. There is also a gift shop on-site and online. ✉ *147 N. 2nd St., Old City* ☎ *215/923–1438* 🌐 *www.firemanshall.org* 🎫 *Free; donations requested* 🕒 *Closed Sun. and Mon.*

First Bank of the United States
GOVERNMENT BUILDING | A fine example of Federal architecture, the oldest bank building in the country was headquarters of the government's bank from 1797 to 1811. Designed by Samuel Blodget Jr., it was an imposing structure in its day, exemplifying strength, dignity, and security. Head first to the right to find a wrought-iron gateway topped by an eagle. Pass through it into the courtyard, and you magically step into Colonial America. Before you do so, check out the bank's pediment. Executed in 1797 by Clodius F. Legrand and Sons, its cornucopia, oak branch, and American eagle are carved from mahogany—a late-18th-century masterpiece that has withstood weather better than the bank's marble pillars. ✉ *120 S. 3rd St., Old City.*

Franklin Square
CITY PARK | One of five squares William Penn placed in his original design, this park is now a family-friendly destination. In addition to the water-dancing fountain, there's a modern playground and carousel; a food stand with burgers, fries, and shakes; and an 18-hole miniature-golf course, boasting scale models of Independence Hall, the Philadelphia Museum of Art, Ben Franklin Bridge, and other local landmarks. ✉ *200 N. 6th St., at Race St., Old City* ☎ *215/629–4026* 🌐 *www.historicphiladelphia.org* 🎫 *Park free; attraction prices vary.*

Free Quaker Meeting House
RELIGIOUS SITE | This was the house of worship for the Free "Fighting" Quakers, a group that broke away from the Society of Friends to support the cause against the British during the Revolutionary War. The building was designed in 1783 by Samuel Wetherill, one of the original leaders of the group, after they were disowned by their pacifist flock. Among the 100 members were Betsy Ross and Timothy Matlack, colonel in Washington's Army and assistant secretary of the Continental Congress. After the Free Quaker group dissolved, the building was used as a school, library, and warehouse. The meetinghouse, built in the Quaker plain style with a brick front and gable roof, has been carefully restored. **■ TIP→ No tickets are required, but call the Independence National Historical Park to check on availability.** ✉ *500 Arch St., at 5th St., Old City* ☎ *215/965–2305* 🌐 *www.nps.gov/inde/learn/historyculture/places-freequaker.htm* 🎫 *Free* 🕒 *Call for schedule.*

★ Independence Hall
HISTORIC SITE | The birthplace of the United States, this redbrick building with its clock tower and steeple is one of the nation's greatest icons. It was constructed in 1732–56 as the Pennsylvania State House. What happened here between 1775 and 1787 changed the course of American history—and the name of the building to Independence Hall. The delegates to the Second Continental Congress met in the Assembly Room in May 1776, united in anger over British troops firing on citizens in Concord, Massachusetts. In this same room, George Washington was appointed commander in chief of the Continental Army, Thomas Jefferson's eloquent Declaration of Independence was signed, and later the Constitution of the United States was adopted. Here the first foreign minister to visit the United States was welcomed; the news of Cornwallis's defeat was announced, signaling the end of

Home to the annual Philadelphia Chinese Lantern Festival, family-friendly Franklin Square also has a carousel and an 18-hole Philly-inspired mini-golf course.

the Revolutionary War; and, later, John Adams and Abraham Lincoln lay in state. The memories this building holds linger in the collection of polished muskets, the silver inkstand used by delegates to sign the Declaration of Independence, and the "Rising Sun" chair in which George Washington sat. (After the Constitution was adopted, Benjamin Franklin said about the carving on the chair: "I have the happiness to know that it is a rising and not a setting sun.")

In the **East Wing**—attached to Independence Hall by a short colonnade—you can embark on free tours that start every 15 to 20 minutes and last 35 minutes. Admission is first-come, first-served; pick up free, timed tickets from the visitor center to avoid waiting in line. The **West Wing** of Independence Hall contains an exhibit of our nation's founding documents: the final draft of the Constitution, a working copy of the Articles of Confederation, and the first printing of the Declaration of Independence.

In front of Independence Hall, next to the statue of George Washington, note the plaques marking the spots where Abraham Lincoln stood on February 22, 1861, and where John F. Kennedy delivered an address on July 4, 1962. With Independence Hall in front of you and the Liberty Bell behind you, this is a place to stand for a moment and soak up a sense of history. From March through December and on major holidays, free, timed tickets from the Independence Visitor Center are required for entry. Tickets also can be reserved online (🌐 *www.recreation.gov*) . ✉ *520 Chestnut St., between 5th and 6th Sts., Old City* ☎ *215/965–2305, 877/444–6777 advance tickets* 🌐 *www.nps.gov/inde* 🎫 *Free.*

Independence Square

PLAZA | On July 8, 1776, the Declaration of Independence was first read in public here. Although the square is not as imposing today, it still has great dignity. You can imagine the impact the reading had on the colonists. ✉ *Bounded by Walnut and Chestnut Sts. and 5th and*

Philadelphia's Place in American History 

William Penn founded the city in 1682, and chose to name it Philadelphia—Greek for "brotherly love"—after an ancient Syrian city, site of one of the earliest and most venerated Christian churches. Penn's Quakers settled on a tract of land he described as his "greene countrie towne." After the Quakers, the next waves of immigrants to arrive were Anglicans and Presbyterians (who had a running conflict with the "stiff Quakers" and their distaste for music and dancing). The new residents forged traditions that remain strong in parts of Philadelphia today: united families, comfortable houses, handsome furniture, and good education. From these early years came the attitude Mark Twain summed up as: "In Boston, they ask: 'What does he know?' In New York, 'How much does he make?' In Philadelphia, 'Who were his parents?'"

The city became the queen of the English-speaking New World from the late 1600s to the early 1800s. In the latter half of the 1700s Philadelphia was the largest city in the colonies, a great and glorious place. So when the delegates from the colonies wanted to meet in a centrally located, thriving city, they chose Philadelphia. They convened the First Continental Congress in 1774 at Carpenters' Hall. It is here that the Declaration of Independence was written and adopted, the Constitution was framed, the capital of the United States was established, the Liberty Bell was rung, the nation's flag was sewn by Betsy Ross (though scholars debate this), and George Washington served most of his presidency.

6th Sts., Old City 🌐 *www.nps.gov/inde* 🎫 *Free* ☞ *Visitors may have to pass through a security checkpoint at 5th and Chestnut Sts.*

Independence Visitor Center

HISTORIC SITE | This is the city's official visitor center as well as the gateway to Independence National Historical Park. Here, you'll find a fully staffed concierge-and-trip-planning desk, which provides information on the Park, the Philadelphia Museum of Art, the Philadelphia Zoo, and other attractions, as well as a reservation and ticketing service. Before you set off on a walking tour, acquaint yourself with Colonial American history by watching the Founding Fathers come to life in the 30-minute movie Independence, one of the films shown in the center's two theaters. There's also a café operated by the Hershey's brand, and an excellent bookstore, where you can stock up on books, videos, brochures, prints, wall hangings, and souvenirs of historic figures and events. An atrium connects the visitor center to a renovated underground parking area. ✉ *1 N. Independence Mall W, 6th and Market Sts., Old City* ☎ *215/965–7676, 800/537–7676* 🌐 *www.independencevisitorcenter.com* ☞ *Hrs may be extended during holidays and peak seasons.*

★ Liberty Bell Center

HISTORIC SITE | The bell fulfilled the words of its inscription when it rang to "proclaim liberty throughout all the land unto all the inhabitants thereof," beckoning Philadelphians to the State House yard to hear the first reading of the Declaration of Independence. Ordered in 1751 and originally cast in England, it cracked during testing and was recast in Philadelphia by Pass and Stow two years later. To keep it from falling into British hands during the Revolution—they would have melted it down for ammunition—it was spirited away by horse and wagon to Allentown, 60 miles to the north. The Liberty Bell is the subject of much legend; one story says it cracked when tolled at the funeral of Chief Justice John Marshall in 1835. Actually, the bell cracked slowly over a period of years. It was repaired but cracked again in 1846 and was then forever silenced. It was called the State House Bell until the 1830s, when a group of abolitionists adopted it as a symbol of freedom and renamed it the Liberty Bell.

After more than 200 years inside Independence Hall, the bell was moved to a glass-enclosed pavilion for the 1976 Bicentennial, which for many seemed an incongruous setting for such a historic object. In mid-2003 it once again moved to another glass-enclosed pavilion with redbrick accents. This time, great care was taken to improve access and viewing of its former home at Independence Hall, which is seen against the backdrop of the sky—rather than 20th-century buildings. The Liberty Bell complex houses a bell chamber, an interpretive exhibit area with historic displays and memorabilia, and a covered area for waiting in line.

During construction for the bell's current home, the foundation and other archaeological remains of The President's House, the home of the nation's chief executives before the capital shifted to Washington, D.C., were discovered, as well as evidence of slaves owned by President George Washington who lived there during his time in office. A new permanent installation includes a series of video panels focusing on the stories of the nine enslaved African Americans, as well as glass panels through which you can view the remains of the structure's foundation. ✉ *6th and Chestnut Sts., 526 Market St., Old City* ☎ *215/965–2305* 🌐 *www.nps.gov/inde/liberty-bell-center.htm* 🎫 *Free.*

Library Hall

LIBRARY | This 20th-century building is a reconstruction of Franklin's Library Company of Philadelphia, the first public library in the colonies. The American Philosophical Society, one of the country's leading institutions for the study of science, has its library here. The vaults contain such treasures as a copy of the Declaration of Independence handwritten by Thomas Jefferson, William Penn's 1701 Charter of Privileges, and journals from the Lewis and Clark expedition of 1803–06. The library's collection also includes first editions of Newton's *Principia Mathematica*, Franklin's *Experiments and Observations*, and Darwin's *On the Origin of Species.* The APS also offers a small, rotating exhibit of its rare books and manuscripts in the lobby of its first floor. ✉ *105 S. 5th St., Old City* ☎ *215/440–3400* 🌐 *www.amphilsoc.org* 🎫 *Free* Ⓜ *5th and Market Sts.*

Loxley Court

NEIGHBORHOOD | One of the restored 18th-century houses in this lovely court was once home to Benjamin Loxley, a carpenter who worked on Independence Hall. The court's claim to fame, according to its residents, is as the spot where Benjamin Franklin flew his kite in his experiment with lightning; the key tied to it was the key to Loxley's front door. ✉ *321–323 Arch St., Old City* 🕓 *Closed to public* ☞ *The residences are gated and privately owned. There is no admittance for the public.*

Mikveh Israel

RELIGIOUS SITE | Nathan Levy, a Colonial merchant whose ship, the *Myrtilla,* brought the Liberty Bell to America, helped found this Jewish congregation in 1740, making it the oldest in Philadelphia and the second oldest in the United States. The original synagogue was at 3rd and Cherry Streets; the congregation's current space, where it has been since 1976, is in the Sephardic style (following Spanish and Portuguese Jewish ritual).

William Penn and His Legacy

William Penn was a rebel with a cause. Born in London in 1644 into a nobleman's family, he attended Oxford University, studied law, and tried a military career (in emulation of his father, an admiral in the British Navy). It was at Oxford that Penn first heard Quaker preachers professing that each life is part of the Divine spirit, and that all people should be treated equally. At age 23, Penn joined the Religious Society of Friends (Quakers), who at the time were considered religious zealots.

Penn was imprisoned in the Tower of London for his heretical pamphlets, but he was spared worse persecution because of his father's support of King Charles II. He petitioned the king to grant him land in the New World for a Quaker colony; he was given a 45,000-square-mile tract along the Delaware River in payment of a debt Charles owed to his late father. Indeed, the king named the land Pennsylvania in honor of the admiral.

On Penn's first visit to his colony, from 1662 to 1664, he began his "Holy Experiment," establishing his haven for Quakers. His laws guaranteed religious freedom and an elected government. He bought land from the Native Americans and established a peace treaty that lasted for 70 years.

Penn was called back to England in 1684 and remained there until 1699, caring for his ill wife, Gulielma Maria Springett, who would die without seeing his beloved Pennsylvania. Penn was suspected of plotting with the former Catholic king, James II, to overthrow the Protestant monarchy of William and Mary, who revoked his charter in 1692 for 18 months.

Penn made his second trip to America with his second wife, Hannah Callowhill Penn, in 1699. The couple moved into Pennsbury Manor along the upper Delaware River, where, while preaching about a life of simplicity, he lived in luxury. Penn issued a new frame of government, the Charter of Privileges, which became a model for the U.S. Constitution. He had to return to England yet again in 1701; there he was consumed by the political and legal problems of his colony, a term in prison for debt, and then illness. Penn died before he could return to Pennsylvania. After his death, his wife honored him by assuming the governorship for nine years.

Although Penn spent only 4 of his 74 years in Pennsylvania, his legacy is profound. As a city planner, he mapped out a "greene countrie towne" with broad, straight streets. He positioned each house in the middle of its plot, so that every child would have play space; he named its streets—Walnut, Spruce, Chestnut—for trees, not for men. His original city plan has survived. As a reformer, Penn replaced dungeons with workhouses; established the right of a jury to decide a verdict without harassment by a judge; provided schools where boys—and girls—could get a practical education; and limited the death penalty to two offenses—murder and treason—rather than the 200 mandated by English criminal law.

The synagogue's Spruce Street Cemetery (about eight blocks away, beyond Old City) dates from 1740 and is the oldest surviving Jewish site in Philadelphia. It was the burial ground for the Spanish-Portuguese Jewish community. Guided tours of the synagogue and the cemetery are available by appointment. ✉ *44 N. 4th St., Old City* ☎ *215/922–5446* 🌐 *www.mikvehisrael.org* 🎫 *Free; donations accepted* ☞ *The daily minyan (7:30 weekdays, 8:30 Sun. and holidays) and Shabbat services (Fri. 7:15 pm, Sat. 9 am) are open to all.*

★ Museum of the American Revolution

MUSEUM | Within walking distance of the Liberty Bell, Independence Hall, the Constitution Center, and the First Bank of the United States, the Museum of the American Revolution resides in the heart of historic Philadelphia. Divided into four parts—Road to Independence (1760–75), The Darkest Hour (1776–78), A Revolutionary War (1778–83), A New Nation (1783–present)—the museum's impressive collection has been in the making for more than a century. Several thousand artifacts, many of which have never been shown before, include General George Washington's actual tent that he used as his war headquarters; a pair of English holster pistols carried throughout the war by a German American brigadier general; an early-19th-century summer coat worn by a Revolutionary War soldier; and a pair of infant shoes crafted from the stolen coat of a British soldier. ✉ *101 S. 3rd St., Old City* ☎ *215/253–6731* 🌐 *www.amrevmuseum.org* 🎫 *$25.*

★ National Constitution Center

MUSEUM | This 160,000-square-foot attraction brings the U.S. Constitution to life with exhibits tracing the development and adoption of the nation's guiding document. The interactive "The Story of We the People" takes you from the American Revolution through the Constitution's ratification to major events in the nation's constitutional history, including present-day events like the inauguration of President Barack Obama, Hurricane Katrina, and the recent economic crisis. Later, you can play the role of a Supreme Court justice deciding an important case, walk among the framers in Signers' Hall, and add your signature to the list of Founding Fathers. The facility has 100-plus exhibits, and plays host to many events with major historians, authors, and political figures. ✉ *525 Arch St., Independence Mall, Old City* ☎ *215/409–6700* 🌐 *www.constitutioncenter.org* 🎫 *$14.50 (with extra charges for some special exhibits)* Ⓜ *SEPTA; the Market-Frankfurt subway line stops 1 block from the Center at 5th and Market Sts.*

National Liberty Museum

MUSEUM | Using interactive exhibits, video, and works of art, the museum aims to combat bigotry in the United States by putting a spotlight on the nation's rich traditions of freedom and diversity. Galleries celebrate outstanding Americans and contemporary heroes from around the world. The Live Like a Hero exhibit celebrates everyday heroes, including teachers, first responders, and extraordinary children working to better their communities. The museum's collection of glass art is symbolic of the fragility of peace; its highlight is Dale Chihuly's 21-foot-tall red glass sculpture *Flame of Liberty*. Sandy Skoglund's colorful *Jelly Bean People* are a reminder that many of our differences are only skin-deep. ✉ *321 Chestnut St., Old City* ☎ *215/925–2800* 🌐 *www.libertymuseum.org* 🎫 *$12.*

National Museum of American Jewish History

MUSEUM | Established in 1976, this museum in 2011 moved to a new, $150 million, contemporary building near Independence Hall. The 100,000-square-foot facility, via multimedia displays, historic objects, and ephemera, traces the history of American Jews from 1654 to the present. Highlights include "Only in America," a showcase of the accomplishments

Located on Independence Mall, the interactive National Constitution Center is a great place to learn about the U.S. Constitution.

of famed Jewish Americans, including Jonas Salk, Barbra Streisand, and Irving Berlin; a three-level timeline covering immigration, the formation of Israel, the civil rights movement, and *Seinfeld*; a Contemporary Issues Forum, where you can share your views on Post-it-style notes that are electronically scanned and displayed; and "It's Your Story," where you can record clips about your family history. The museum's exterior offers two contrasting sculptures symbolizing how American Jewish history is intertwined with the nation's story: a 19th-century marble monument dubbed *Religious Liberty*, and an LED torch atop the corner of the facility's glass facade. ✉ *5th and Market Sts., 101 S. Independence Mall E, Old City* ☎ *215/923–3811* 🌐 *www.nmajh.org* 🎟 *$15* ⏲ *Closed Mon.*

New Hall Military Museum

MUSEUM | When it was originally built in 1791, this building housed the U.S. Department of War. Today's reconstruction outlines early American military history, and the formation of the Army, Navy, and Marine Corps. On display are Revolutionary uniforms, medals, and authentic weapons, including powder horns, swords, and a blunderbuss. Dioramas depict highlights from the Revolutionary War through the late 18th century, and there are several scale models of warships and frigates, as well. This museum is typically open for special events and occasions only. ✉ *320 Chestnut St., east of 4th St., Old City* ☎ *215/965–2305* 🌐 *www.nps.gov/inde/learn/historyculture/places-newhallmilitarymuseum.htm* 🎟 *Free.*

Old City Hall

MUSEUM | Independence Hall is flanked by Congress Hall to the west and Old City Hall to the east: three distinctive Federal-style buildings erected to house the city's growing government. But when Philadelphia became the nation's capital in 1790, the just-completed city hall was lent to the federal government. It housed the U.S. Supreme Court from 1791 to 1800; John Jay was the Chief Justice. Later, the boxlike building with a peaked roof and cupola was used as the city hall. Today an exhibit presents information about the early days of the federal judiciary. ✉ *5th and Chestnut Sts., Old City* ☎ *215/965–2305* 🌐 *www.nps.gov/inde/old-city-hall.html* 🎟 *Free.*

Philadelphia Merchant's Exchange
BUILDING | Designed by the well-known Philadelphia architect William Strickland and built in 1832, this impressive Greek Revival building served as the city's commercial center for 50 years. It was both the stock exchange and a place where merchants met to trade goods. In the tower a watchman scanned the Delaware River and notified merchants of arriving ships. The exchange stands behind Dock Street, a cobblestone thoroughfare. The building houses a small exhibit on its history and now serves as the headquarters for Independence National Park. ✉ *143 S. 3rd St., Old City* ☎ *215/965–2305* 🌐 *www.nps.gov/inde/learn/historyculture/places-merchantsexchange.htm* 🎟 *Free* ⏲ *Closed weekends.*

Philosophical Hall
BUILDING | This is the headquarters of the American Philosophical Society, founded by Benjamin Franklin in 1743 to promote "useful knowledge." The members of the oldest learned society in America have included Washington, Jefferson, Lafayette, Emerson, Darwin, Edison, Churchill, and Einstein. Erected between 1785 and 1789 in what has been called a "restrained Federal style" (designed to complement, not outshine, adjacent Independence Hall), Philosophical Hall is brick with marble trim, has a handsome arched entrance, and houses the Society's museum, open to the public Thursday to Sunday. The society's library is across the street in Library Hall. ✉ *104 S. 5th St., Old City* ☎ *215/440–3400* 🌐 *www.apsmuseum.org* 🎟 *$2 suggested donation* ⏲ *Closed Mon.–Wed. and Jan.–mid-Apr.*

The President's House
ARCHAEOLOGICAL SITE | This site commemorates the location of the home to U.S. presidents George Washington and John Adams from 1790 to 1800, as well as nine enslaved Africans who worked as household staff. The outdoor monument, which is open 24 hours a day, shows video clips that bring the house's history alive. Inside, take note of the bow window, which is thought to have inspired the shape of the Oval Office at the White House, as well as the remains of a passage torn down in 1832 that connected the main house to the slave quarters. ✉ *600 Market St., Old City* ☎ *215/965–2305* 🌐 *www.phila.gov/presidentshouse* 🎟 *Free* ☞ *The outdoor site is accessible at all times, but the interactive exhibits run concurrent with the Liberty Bell Pavilion hrs.*

Second Bank of the United States
MUSEUM | When Second Bank president Nicholas Biddle held a design competition for a new building, he required all architects to use the Greek style; William Strickland, one of the foremost architects of the 19th century, won. Built in 1824, the bank, with its Doric columns, was based on the design of the Parthenon and helped establish the popularity of Greek Revival architecture in the United States. The interior hall, though, was Roman, with a dramatic barrel-vault ceiling. Housed here are portraits of prominent Colonial Americans by noted artists such as Charles Willson Peale, William Rush, and Gilbert Stuart. Don't miss Peale's portraits of Jefferson and Lewis and Clark: the former is the only one that shows the third president with red hair, and the latter is the only known portrait of the famous explorers. The permanent exhibition, "The People of Independence," has a life-size wooden statue of George Washington by William Rush; a mural of Philadelphia in the 1830s by John A. Woodside Jr.; and the only known likeness of William Floyd, a lesser-known signer of the Declaration

of Independence. *420 Chestnut St., Historic Area* *215/965–2305* *www.nps.gov/inde/learn/historyculture/places-secondbank.htm* *Free* *Call ahead for availability.*

United States Mint

MUSEUM | The first U.S. mint was built in Philadelphia at 16th and Spring Garden Streets in 1792, when the Bank of North America adopted dollars and cents instead of shillings and pence as standard currency; the current mint was built in 1971. During a self-guided tour you can see blank disks being melted, cast, and pressed into coins, which are then inspected, counted, and bagged. Historic artifacts such as the Key to the First Mint and the gold medal awarded to General Anthony Wayne for his capture of Stony Point during the Revolutionary War are displayed. Seven Tiffany glass tile mosaics depict coin making in ancient Rome. A shop in the lobby sells special coins and medals—in mint condition. *151 N. Independence Mall E, 5th and Arch Sts., Old City* *215/408–0112* *www.usmint.gov* *Free* *No tours Sept.–May weekends, June–Aug. Sun.* *The mint is subject to U.S. Homeland Security rules. If the Homeland Security threat is raised to "orange," no public tours will be allowed.*

Welcome Park

PLAZA | A scale model of the William Penn statue that tops City Hall sits on a 60-foot-long map of Penn's Philadelphia, carved in the pavement of Welcome Park. (The *Welcome* was the ship that transported Penn to America.) The wall surrounding the park displays a timeline of Penn's life, with information about his philosophy and writings. The park was the site of the slate-roof house where Penn lived briefly and where he granted the Charter of Privileges in 1701, which served as Pennsylvania's constitutional framework until 1776; the Liberty Bell was commissioned to commemorate the charter's 50th anniversary. *129 Sansom Walk, 2nd St. and Sansom Walk, Old City* *www.ushistory.org/tour/welcome-park.htm* *Free.*

Restaurants

Amada

$$$ | **SPANISH** | At Amada, the first of chef-restaurateur Jose Garces's restaurants, the Ecuadorian-American chef reinterprets regional cuisine with choice ingredients and a modern touch that feature in more than 50 tapas, from the crab-stuffed peppers with toasted almonds to the flatbread topped with artichoke, black truffle, and manchego. Ingredients—including even more glorious cheeses—are sourced from northern Spain, the main inspiration for the menu. **Known for:** Andalusian cuisine; Spanish meats and cheeses; lively scene. *Average main: $20* *217–19 Chestnut St., Old City* *215/398–6968* *www.amadarestaurant.com* *No lunch.*

Buddakan

$$$$ | **ASIAN** | This Stephen Starr restaurant is presided over by a 10-foot-tall gilded Buddha who seems to approve of the fusion food that pairs Pan-Asian ingredients with various cooking styles. The truffled edamame dumplings and tuna tartare spring rolls are tasty, but much of the appeal is in the theatrical decor and people-watching, also prevalent at Buddakan's outposts in New York and Atlantic City. **Known for:** creative Pan-Asian cooking; eye-catching decor; lively scene. *Average main: $29* *325 Chestnut St., Old City* *215/574–9440* *www.buddakan.com* *No lunch weekends.*

City Tavern

$$$$ | **AMERICAN** | You can time-travel to the 18th century at this authentic re-creation of historic City Tavern, where the atmosphere suggests that Adams, Washington, and Jefferson dined here (they didn't; the restaurant was built under the supervision of the National Park Service

Adams, Washington, and Jefferson never ate at City Tavern, but this authentically recreated tavern is a great way to relive Philadelphia in the late-1700s.

in 1994, to the specifications of the original 1773 tavern). The food is rich—West Indies pepper-pot soup, cornmeal-crusted oysters, and braised rabbit are prepared from enhanced period recipes and served on handsome Colonial-patterned china or pewter. **Known for:** Early American cooking; Colonial garb; historic surroundings. $ *Average main: $31* ✉ *138 S. 2nd St., Old City* ☎ *215/413–1443* 🌐 *www.citytavern.com.*

Continental Restaurant & Martini Bar

$$ | **ECLECTIC** | Light fixtures fashioned like olives pierced with toothpicks are a tip-off to the theme at this cool watering hole that's installed in a classic diner shell in the center of Old City's action. The first of Stephen Starr's trendy restaurants, the Continental serves lively (but not outré) food in generous portions to people who know how to enjoy it. **Known for:** specialty martinis; crowd-pleasing snacks; lively bar scene. $ *Average main: $18* ✉ *138 Market St., Old City* ☎ *215/923–6069* 🌐 *www.continentalmartinibar.com.*

Cuba Libre

$$$$ | **LATIN AMERICAN** | People who have been to Havana swear this place is a dead ringer; in any event, it's lovely, with balconies and fancy streetlights, and even a leaded-glass window on the interior. An entire drinks menu is devoted to rum from everywhere in the Caribbean and Central and South America, including Cuba Libre's own brand, and of course, the mojitos are excellent. **Known for:** Cuban cuisine; mojitos; salsa dancing. $ *Average main: $25* ✉ *10 S. 2nd St., Old City* ☎ *215/627–0666* 🌐 *www.cubalibrerestaurant.com.*

★ Fork

$$$$ | **AMERICAN** | Happy sounds are always emanating from eaters at this comfortable, elegant eatery, one of Old City's most respected and longest-running dinner destinations. The kitchen is known for its innovative pastas and breads, in-house fermentation, and the celebration of local meats and produce. **Known for:** creative new American food; excellent service; elegant dining

room. $ *Average main: $36* ✉ *306 Market St., Old City* ☎ *215/625–9425* 🌐 *www.forkrestaurant.com* ⏲ *No lunch weekdays.*

★ Forsythia

$$$$ | FRENCH | Well traveled and well trained, chef Christopher Kearse presents his unique take on French cuisine at the modern Forsythia. Start with shareable canapés, like smoked trout rillettes or sweet-and-sour crispy pig tails, before digging into small plates, pastas, and shareable mains (try the tuna collar amandine) that split the difference between edgy and accessible. **Known for:** modern French cuisine; beautiful room; bar scene. $ *Average main: $29* ✉ *233 Chestnut St., Old City* ☎ *215/644–9395* 🌐 *www.forsythiaphilly.com* ⏲ *No lunch.*

★ High Street on Market

$$$$ | AMERICAN | This sunny younger sibling of perennial favorite Fork is half clubhouse for Old City neighbors, half food-tourist magnet. Grain-brained High Street will take you from cortados (an espresso drink) and *kouign-amann* (a French pastry) in the morning to beet-cured salmon sandwiches in the afternoon to creative alt-flour pastas—spelt pappardelle, anyone?—at night. **Known for:** all-day service; creative breads; innovative pastas. $ *Average main: $29* ✉ *308 Market St., Old City* ☎ *215/625–0988* 🌐 *www.highstreetonmarket.com.*

The Olde Bar

$$$ | SEAFOOD | This Jose Garces spot is located in the historic bones of Old Original Bookbinders, a fish house that catered to politicians, bigwigs, and celebrities in its day. The menu isn't elaborate, but manages well with updates on seafood classics like snapper soup and lobster rolls, and the East and West Coast oysters are pristine, but the deep catalog of cocktails both classic and nouveau is the real reason to come—seasonal Old Fashioneds, elaborate swizzles, and sours as foamy as the ocean surf satisfy tipplers of all tastes. **Known for:** raw bar; cocktails; historic atmosphere. $ *Average main: $20* ✉ *125 Walnut St., Old City* ☎ *215/253–3777* 🌐 *www.theoldebar.com* ⏲ *No lunch.*

Panorama

$$$$ | ITALIAN | The name refers to a lovely mural rather than a window view from this lively spot inside the Penn's View Hotel. The restaurant has the largest wine cruvinet (storage system) in the country. **Known for:** Italian cuisine; relaxed atmosphere; wide wine selection. $ *Average main: $32* ✉ *Penn's View Hotel, 14 N. Front St., Old City* ☎ *215/922–7800* 🌐 *www.pennsviewhotel.com* ⏲ *No lunch Sun.*

Plough and the Stars

$$$ | IRISH | The cheery first floor of a renovated bank feels like a genuine Irish pub. A long bar with a dozen spigots is invariably spouting several imported and a few local brews. **Known for:** Irish hospitality; Guinness; Irish music. $ *Average main: $20* ✉ *123 Chestnut St., enter on 2nd St., Old City* ☎ *215/733–0300* 🌐 *www.ploughstars.com.*

Royal Boucherie

$$$$ | FRENCH | A collaboration between award-winning chef Nicholas Elmi and the owners of local favorites Royal Tavern, Cantina Los Caballitos, and Khyber Pass Pub, Royal Boucherie is a polished operation set in a moody and intimate bi-level 2nd Street space. A classic brasserie in approach, it specializes in luscious raw-bar selections, house-made charcuterie, and rib-sticking plates like steak au poivre, pork schnitzel, and handwrought pastas. **Known for:** raw bar; cocktails; intimate space. $ *Average main: $27* ✉ *52 S. 2nd St., Old City* ☎ *267/606–6313* 🌐 *www.royalboucherie.com.*

Coffee and Quick Bites

The Bourse Food Hall

$ | **INTERNATIONAL** | Built in 1895 as a stock, maritime, and commodities exchange, the Bourse building is an icon of Philadelphia commerce. The skylighted Great Hall, with its Corinthian columns, marble, wrought-iron stairways, and Victorian gingerbread details, has been meticulously maintained, but the space has also been updated to house an internationally inspired food hall with local roots. **Known for:** historic architecture; wide culinary options; space for big groups. *Average main: $10 111 S. Independence Mall E, 5th St. across from Liberty Bell Pavilion, Old City 215/625–0300 www.theboursephilly.com.*

★ Franklin Fountain

$ | **CAFÉ** | **FAMILY** | You can't throw a wet walnut in Philly without hitting an artisanal-ice-cream maker these days, but brothers Ryan and Eric Berley and their charming Colonial-inspired scoop shop have newcomers beat by years. On summer nights, long lines ripple out the door into the warm Old City night, but the wait (half an hour isn't uncommon in summer) is worth it for the house-made seasonal flavors like fresh peach, brooding black raspberry, and honeycomb made with booty from the Fountain's rooftop hives. Just down the block, the Berleys also operate Shane Confectionery, a candy shop informed by the same bygone era. **Known for:** old-timey uniforms and decor; handmade ice cream; long lines. *Average main: $5 116 Market St., Old City 215/627–1899 www.franklinfountain.com.*

Hotels

★ Hotel Monaco Philadelphia

$$$ | **HOTEL** | Opened in 2012, Hotel Monaco offers style, sass, and LEED certification in the heart of Philly's historic center, along with the beloved perks of the Kimpton brand, including free bike rentals, yoga mats in every room, complimentary evening wine hours nightly from 5 to 6 pm, and pet-friendly accommodations. **Pros:** central location; lots of great perks and freebies; service with a smile; popular on-site dining and drinking; lovely past-meets-present design. **Cons:** note that it's pet-friendly, if you have allergies; crowded part of town; pricey valet parking. *Rooms from: $259 433 Chestnut St., Historic Area 215/925–2111 www.monaco-philadelphia.com 268 rooms No meals.*

Lokal Hotel

$$$$ | **HOTEL** | A unique boutique hotel that stands out from Old City's numerous big-brand options, Lokal is owned by a husband-and-wife team that preaches the merits of "invisible service"—no front desks or on-site staff, with check-ins, deliveries, and the like handled by the guest via tech innovations and mobile apps. **Pros:** private boutique feel; fully equipped kitchens; in-suite washer and dryer. **Cons:** no elevator; not wheelchair accessible; pricier than traditional hotel. *Rooms from: $390 139 N. 3rd St., Old City 267/702–4345 www.staylokal.com 6 rooms No meals.*

Penn's View Hotel

$$ | **HOTEL** | This cosmopolitan little hotel in a refurbished 19th-century commercial building on the fringe of Old City offers its own brand of urban charm. **Pros:** good service; generous continental breakfast including waffles; romantic atmosphere. **Cons:** gym is tiny; rooms facing I–95 can be noisy; slightly dated decor. *Rooms from: $169 14 N. Front St., Old City 215/922–7600 www.pennsviewhotel.com 53 rooms Free breakfast.*

Renaissance Philadelphia Downtown Hotel

$$$ | **HOTEL** | **FAMILY** | An ornate fireplace dominates the breathtaking marble lobby of this towering hotel in the historic district, which recently joined the Marriott family of hotels. **Pros:** excellent location for historic touring and Old City

revelry; boutique feel; good service; nice views; known to offer good sale rates. **Cons:** crowded part of town; surrounding area can be noisy; pricey valet parking. *Rooms from: $249* *401 Chestnut St., Old City* *215/925–0000* *renaissance-hotels.marriott.com/renaissance-philadelphia-downtown-hotel* *152 rooms* *No meals.*

Thomas Bond House

$$ | **B&B/INN** | This bed-and-breakfast in the heart of Old City is great for travelers who want an authentic taste of historic Philadelphia—built in 1769 by a prominent local physician (an enormous family tree detailing his descendents hangs from a wall in a common living room), the four-story Georgian house has undergone a faithful, meticulous revival. **Pros:** historic home; good service; complimentary wine and snacks. **Cons:** some guests complain of noise when nearby bars let out at 2 am; there are also some complaints about closet space and hot water; no elevator. *Rooms from: $170* *129 S. 2nd St., Old City* *215/923–8523, 800/845–2663* *www.thomasbondhousebandb.com* *12 rooms* *Free breakfast.*

Wyndham Historic District

$$$ | **HOTEL** | This eight-story hotel sits within what is billed as the country's "most historic square mile," within a block and a half of the Liberty Bell and Independence Hall. **Pros:** can be a relative bargain located close to major tourist attractions; 24-hour gym; paid airport shuttle. **Cons:** lots of tourists and large groups; rates very high in busy seasons; noisy part of town. *Rooms from: $279* *400 Arch St., Old City* *215/923–8660, 800/843–2355* *www.phillydowntownhotel.com* *371 rooms* *No meals.*

Nightlife

MUSIC CLUBS

Khyber Pass Pub

BARS/PUBS | Operated as a saloon since 1876, the bi-level Khyber earned renown as a loud and fast punk rock club in the 1970s through the 1990s. In more recent years, it has been reinvented as a restaurant serving authentic New Orleans cuisine (try the po'boys and gumbo), alongside a serious craft beer selection (22 taps). The upstairs space still plays host to a wide slate of live performances and special events. *56 S. 2nd St., Old City* *215/238–5888* *www.khyberpasspub.com.*

★ Sassafras

BARS/PUBS | A classic and classy Old City watering hole, Sassafras is a stately stop for a well-made cocktail, a hideaway for grownups among the neighborhood's most boisterous and youthful hangouts. In addition to drinks and dinner, they host live jazz musicians Sunday to Thursday. *48 S. 2nd St., Old City* *215/925–2317* *www.sassafrasbar.com.*

Shopping

Lofts, art galleries, furniture stores, and unique home-decor shops line the streets of the Old City in the Historic Downtown; there are also wonderful clothing stores with work by local up-and-coming designers. After dark, crowds flock to the neighborhood's bars and clubs. Some great restaurants can also be found here. One of the best times to explore Old City's gallery scene is during First Friday. As the name implies, on the first Friday of each month, Old City galleries are open to the public late into the evening. Many offer refreshments, and the street scene becomes quite festive, too.

ART GALLERIES

The Center for Art in Wood

CRAFTS | This hub for the international wood-art community cultivates and promotes education and creative expression of the form. The space features a store stocked with gorgeous work, some by the accomplished artists whose work has been displayed in the adjacent gallery, including those who come every year as part of the organization's annual Windgate ITE International Residency program. There is also a free museum on the premises. ✉ *141 N. 3rd St., Old City* ☎ *215/923–8000* 🌐 *www.centerforartinwood.org* ☞ *Closed Sun.-Mon.*

Clay Studio

ART GALLERIES | A nonprofit organization runs the gallery and conducts classes as well as an outreach program to inner-city schools. There are clay works and pottery by well-known artists; the gallery has juried shows and group exhibits. ✉ *137–139 N. 2nd St., Old City* ☎ *215/925 3453* 🌐 *www.theclaystudio.org.*

Larry Becker Contemporary Art

ART GALLERIES | Gallerist Becker and his wife, Heidi Nivling, display the kind of austere, abstract art that prompts people who don't know any better to say, "Hey, my kid could do that." Look more closely at the conceptual paintings featured in this small gallery and you'll notice the great skill required to make minimalist art with maximal effect. ✉ *43 N. 2nd St., Old City* ☎ *215/925–5389* 🌐 *www.artnet.com/galleries/larry-becker-contemporary-art* ☞ *Closed Sun.-Thurs. or by appt.*

Muse Gallery

ART GALLERIES | Established in 1978 by the Muse Foundation for the Visual Arts, Muse Gallery is an artists' cooperative committed to increasing the visibility of local artwork and presenting experimental work in a variety of mediums. ✉ *52 N. 2nd St., Old City* ☎ *215/627–5310* ☞ *Closed Mon-Tues.*

Wexler Gallery

ART GALLERIES | This gallery is known for specializing in historic and contemporary glass, but it always has an interesting mix of 20th- and 21st-century handcrafted furnishings and art. ✉ *201 N. 3rd St., Old City* ☎ *215/923–7030* 🌐 *www.wexlergallery.com* ☞ *Closed Sun.-Mon.*

CLOTHING AND ACCESSORIES

Lost & Found

CLOTHING | This laid-back shop has something for everyone (women and men both) with its well-curated mix of young, contemporary designers from Asia, Europe, and the United States. It also has a range of delightful accessories including vintage belt buckles, printed canvas totes, and unique jewelry. Prices here are lower than at many of the neighboring boutiques. ✉ *133 N. 3rd St., Old City* ☎ *215/928–1311* 🌐 *www.facebook.com/lostandfoundboutique.*

Sugarcube

CLOTHING | Some know Sugarcube as a vintage boutique; others go for its stock of hard-to-find designers like A.P.C., Dunderdon, Lavender Brown, and Penumbra. The stylish, friendly owner is usually on hand to advise how to match your Williamsburg Garment Company jeans with your Rag and Bone shawl-collar cardi. ✉ *124 N. 3rd St., Old City* ☎ *215/238–0825* 🌐 *www.sugarcube.us.*

Vagabond

CLOTHING | The two designing women/co-owners of Vagabond pioneered a formula—selling vintage wares alongside new, edgy labels and featuring under-the-radar brands like their own (Stellapop and City of Brotherly Love). It's been imitated plenty ever since, but this boutique still does it best. ✉ *37 N. 3rd St., Old City* ☎ *267/671–0737* 🌐 *www.vagabondboutique.com.*

GIFTS AND SOUVENIRS

Art in the Age

SPECIALTY STORES | A one-stop shop for craft cocktail enthusiasts, Art in the Age stocks a curated selection of spirits, including locally distilled whiskies and its own line of unique products (black trumpet/blueberry cordial; chicory root vodka). In addition to cocktail books, tools, gift items, and accessories, there's a full bar in the rear that accommodates tastings and pre-purchase sampling; it's regularly used for special events and parties. ✉ *116 N. 3rd St., Old City* ☎ *215/922–2600* 🌐 *www.artintheage.com* ⏲ *Closed Mon.-Tues.*

Scarlett Alley

GIFTS/SOUVENIRS | Founded by Mary Kay Scarlett and her daughter Liz, and now owned by Liz alone, this delightful shop at the corner of 3rd and Race near the Betsy Ross House features an ever-changing assortment of unique jewelry, housewares, and stationery, as well as toys, soaps, and teas. Items are displayed on furniture designed and handcrafted by Richard Scarlett, Liz's father; it's also for sale or custom order. ✉ *241 Race St., Old City* ☎ *215/592–7898* 🌐 *www.scarlettalley.com* Ⓜ *2nd and Market.*

Xenos Candy 'N' Gifts

GIFTS/SOUVENIRS | Asher chocolates and Philly souvenirs from key chains to T-shirts are stocked here, near the sights of the historic district. ✉ *231 Chestnut St., Old City* ☎ *215/922–1445* 🌐 *www.xenosgifts.com.*

JEWELRY

Millésimé

JEWELRY/ACCESSORIES | This high-design concept store sells a mix of furniture and home decor curated by a Paris-centric store owner, including plush couches, modern-art-inspired mirrors, colorful wall hangings and charmingly offbeat kitchenware. ✉ *33 N. 2nd St., Old City* ☎ *267/455–0374* 🌐 *www.millesime.us* ⏲ *Sun. and Mon. appt. only.*

Chapter 4

SOCIETY HILL AND PENN'S LANDING

Updated by
Drew Lazor

Sights	Restaurants	Hotels	Shopping	Nightlife
★★★★★	★★☆☆☆	★★★★☆	★★★☆☆	★★☆☆☆

NEIGHBORHOOD SNAPSHOT

TOP EXPERIENCES

■ **Battleship *New Jersey*:** Walk the decks of this World War II–era ship, one of the U.S. Navy's most decorated military vessels.

■ **Headhouse Shambles:** Peruse the wares from local farmers and artisans at this historic open-air marketplace.

■ **House museums:** See how the Colonial era's high society lived at two of the city's most gracious residences, the Hill-Physick and Powel houses.

■ **Mother Bethel A.M.E. Church:** This historic house of worship was also an Underground Railroad stop.

■ **Race Street Pier:** This reimagined pier along Philly's waterfront offers free Wi-Fi and water views.

■ **Washington Square:** One of William Penn's original squares, it's a great place to picnic or people watch.

GETTING HERE

Society Hill is easy to reach on foot for those staying in Center City. Stroll eastward along Locust, Spruce, or Pine Streets for an enjoyable pedestrian experience (i.e. sightseeing, snacking, and shopping). SEPTA's 12 bus goes from Rittenhouse Square to Society Hill in about 15 minutes.

Penn's Landing is also within walking distance of Old City and Society Hill, or can be accessed by SEPTA. To reach it, cross the Walnut Street Bridge at Front Street, which deposits you at the Independence Seaport Museum. The RiverLink Ferry connects Penn's Landing to Camden, New Jersey.

PLANNING YOUR TIME

It's about one hour to walk through Society Hill, more if you tour the Powel and Physick houses. However, you can easily spend a whole day in Penn's Landing. If kids are in tow, allow an hour and a half for the Independence Seaport Museum and its historic boats and another two or three hours for the ferry ride and visit to the Adventure Aquarium in Camden, followed by a tour of the battleship *New Jersey*.

QUICK BITES

■ **Bodhi Coffee.** Eco-friendly in ethos and in practice, this sunny Headhouse café produces nondairy milk with local oats, and offers ice cream and coffee drinks, as well. ✉ *410 S. 2nd St., Society Hill* 🌐 *www.bodhi2go.com*

■ **Cavanaugh's.** A traditional sports bar, Cav's is worth a drop-in thanks to its incredible, idiosyncratic bones–this multilevel, multiroom tavern has been slaking Philadelphia's collective thirst since the 1780s (try the wings). ✉ *421 S. 2nd St., Society Hill* 🌐 *www.cavsheadhouse.com*

■ **The Victoria Freehouse.** This U.K.-inspired pub on Front Street serves proper pub fare (shepherd's pie, bangers and mash) and authentic cask ales; it's a popular hangout for fans of English soccer. ✉ *10 S. Front St., Penn's Landing* 🌐 *www.victoriafreehouse.com*

GOOD TO KNOW

■ If walking is your aim, visit on a warm day, because it can be quite windy along the waterfront. On summer weekends revitalized Penn's Landing bustles with festivals and pop-up parks, and Headhouse Square turns into a farmers' market with locally grown products and baked goods.

The Historic District teaches us what the earliest Philadelphians did; Society Hill shows us how they lived. This residential neighborhood offers a postcard-perfect view of post-Colonial America, with cobblestone streets, historic private residences, and centuries-old churches. And thanks to its central location, exploring the area is as easy as it is transportative.

Comprising the far edge of Society Hill and overlapping with Old City, Penn's Landing refers to the sliver of land separating the easternmost neighborhoods of Center City with the Delaware River, which in turn separates Philadelphia and Camden, New Jersey. Long in developmental flux as the civic powers that be determine how to capitalize on its potential as a waterfront entertainment district, Penn's Landing has a bright future—but there are many points of interest ready to explore right now.

Society Hill

During the 18th century Society Hill was Philadelphia's showplace. A carefully preserved district, it remains the city's most photogenic neighborhood, filled with hidden courtyards, delightful decorative touches such as chimney pots and brass door knockers, wrought-iron foot scrapers, and other remnants from the days of horse-drawn carriages and muddy, unpaved streets. Here time has not quite stopped but meanders down the cobblestone streets, whiling away the hours.

A trove of Colonial- and Federal-style brick row houses, churches, and narrow streets, Society Hill stretches from the Delaware River to 8th Street, south of Independence National Historical Park. Those homes built before 1750 in the Colonial style generally have 2½ stories and a dormer window jutting out of a steep roof. The less heavy, more graceful houses built after the Revolution were often in the Federal style, popularized in England during the 1790s.

Here lived the "World's People," wealthier Anglicans who arrived after William Penn and loved music and dancing—pursuits the Quakers shunned when they set up their enclave in Old City, north of Market Street, in a less desirable commercial area. The "Society" in the neighborhood's moniker refers, however, to the now-defunct Free Society of Traders, a group of business investors who settled here on William Penn's advice.

Today many Colonial homes in this area have been lovingly restored by modern pioneers who moved into the area nearly 50 years ago and rescued Society Hill from becoming a slum. Inspired urban renewal efforts have transformed vast empty factory spaces into airy lofts; new town houses were carefully designed to blend in with the old. As a result, Society Hill is not just a showcase for historic churches and mansions but a living, breathing neighborhood.

Sights

Athenaeum

LIBRARY | Housed in a national landmark Italianate Revival brownstone built in the mid-19th century, the Athenaeum is a research library specializing in architectural history and design with a collection that features millions of items. The library, founded in 1814, contains significant materials on the French in America and on early American travel, exploration, and transportation. Besides books, the Athenaeum has notable paintings and period furniture; changing exhibits are presented in the gallery. Research is by appointment only. ✉ *219 S. 6th St., Society Hill* ☎ *215/925–2688* 🌐 *www.philaathenaeum.org* ⏲ *Closed weekends* Ⓜ *4 blocks from the 5th and Market stop.*

Bouvier's Row

NEIGHBORHOOD | Three of the Victorian brownstones on a stretch of 3rd Street near Locust Street, often called Bouvier's Row, were once owned by the late Jacqueline Kennedy Onassis's ancestors. Michel Bouvier, her great-great-grandfather—the first of the family to come from France—and many of his descendants lie in the family vault at Old St. Mary's Church, a few blocks away on 4th Street. ✉ *258–262 S. 3rd St., Society Hill.*

★ Headhouse Square

PLAZA | This open-air Colonial marketplace, extending from Pine Street to Lombard Street, is a reminder of the days when people went to central outdoor markets to buy food directly from farmers. It was first established as New Market in 1745, and George Washington was among those who came here to buy butter, eggs, meat, fish, herbs, and vegetables. The Head House, a boxy building with a cupola and weather vane, was built in 1803 as the office and home of the market master, who tested the quality of the goods. Today it's the site of a year-round farmers' market, featuring dozens of vendors selling local, seasonal produce, plus everything from honey and flowers to pickles and pastries. On some summer weekends, the square is also home to an arts-and-crafts fair featuring the work of Delaware Valley artists. ✉ *200 Pine St., Society Hill* ☎ *215/413–3713* 🌐 *www.southstreet.com.*

Hill-Physick House

HOUSE | Built in 1786, this is one of the oldest freestanding houses in Society Hill, with elegantly restored interiors and some of the finest Federal and Empire furniture in Philadelphia. Touches of Napoléon's France are everywhere—the golden bee motif woven into upholstery; the magenta-hue Aubusson rug; and stools in the style of Pompeii, the Roman city rediscovered at the time of the house's construction. Upstairs in the parlor, there's an inkstand that retains Benjamin Franklin's actual fingerprints. Originally built by a wealthy wine importer, the house's most famous owner was Philip Syng Physick, the "Father of American Surgery" and a leading physician in the days before anesthesia. His celebrated patients included President Andrew Jackson and Chief Justice John Marshall. The garden planted outside the house is filled with plants common during the 19th century; complete with an Etruscan sarcophagus, a natural grotto, and antique cannon, it's one of the city's loveliest. ✉ *321 S. 4th St., Society Hill* ☎ *215/925–7866* 🌐 *www.philalandmarks.org/physick-house* 🎫 *$8* ⏲ *Tours offered Thurs.–Sat. Apr.–Nov. and weekends Mar. and Dec.*

With hidden courtyards, cobblestone streets, and brass door knockers, the carefully preserved Society Hill district is the city's most photogenic neighborhood.

Mother Bethel A.M.E. Church

RELIGIOUS SITE | In 1787, Rev. Richard Allen, a former slave, galvanized fellow black congregants who left St. George's Methodist Church in a protest against segregated worship. Allen purchased this site in 1791, and it's believed to be the country's oldest parcel of land continuously owned by African Americans. When the African Methodist Episcopal Church, America's first black congregation, was formed in 1816, Allen was its first bishop. The current church is an example of the 19th-century Romanesque Revival style, with broad arches, opalescent stained glass, and stunning woodwork. An earlier building on these grounds was a stop on the Underground Railroad. Allen's tomb and a small museum are on the lower level. ✉ *419 S. 6th St., Society Hill* ☎ *215/925–0616* 🎫 *Donation requested.*

Old Pine Street Presbyterian Church

RELIGIOUS SITE | Designed by Robert Smith in 1768, Old Pine is the only remaining Colonial Presbyterian church and churchyard in Philadelphia. Badly damaged during the Revolution, it served as a hospital and then a stable. In the mid-19th century, its exterior had a Greek Revival face-lift that introduced Corinthian columns. In the 1980s, the interior walls and ceiling were stenciled with thistle and wave motifs, a reminder of Old Pine's true name—Third, Scots, and Mariners Presbyterian Church, which documented the congregation's mergers. The beautifully restored church is painted in soft shades of periwinkle and yellow. In the churchyard are the graves of 100 Hessian soldiers from the Revolution; and that of Eugene Ormandy, former conductor of the Philadelphia Orchestra. ✉ *412 Pine St., Society Hill* ☎ *215/925–8051* 🌐 *www.oldpine.org* 🎫 *Free; donations accepted* ☞ *Guided tours by appointment.*

Old St. Joseph's Church

RELIGIOUS SITE | In 1733 a tiny chapel was established by Jesuits for Philadelphia's 11 Catholic families. It was one of the first places in the English-speaking colonies where Catholic mass could be legally celebrated, a right granted under

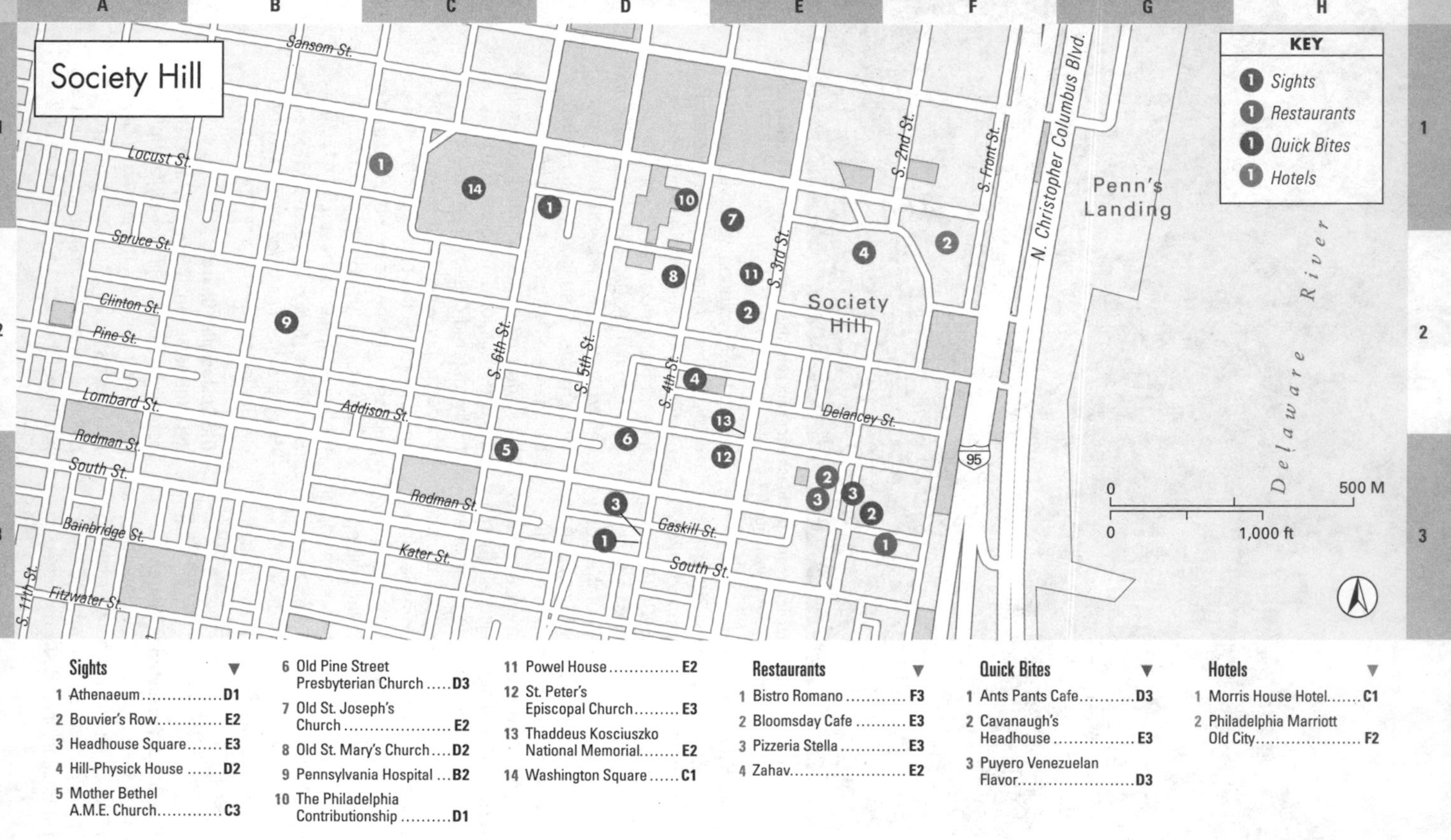

Sights

1 Athenaeum D1
2 Bouvier's Row E2
3 Headhouse Square E3
4 Hill-Physick House D2
5 Mother Bethel A.M.E. Church C3
6 Old Pine Street Presbyterian Church D3
7 Old St. Joseph's Church E2
8 Old St. Mary's Church D2
9 Pennsylvania Hospital B2
10 The Philadelphia Contributionship D1
11 Powel House E2
12 St. Peter's Episcopal Church E3
13 Thaddeus Kosciuszko National Memorial E2
14 Washington Square C1

Restaurants

1 Bistro Romano F3
2 Bloomsday Cafe E3
3 Pizzeria Stella E3
4 Zahav E2

Quick Bites

1 Ants Pants Cafe D3
2 Cavanaugh's Headhouse E3
3 Puyero Venezuelan Flavor D3

Hotels

1 Morris House Hotel C1
2 Philadelphia Marriott Old City F2

William Penn's 1701 Charter of Privileges, which guaranteed religious freedom. But freedom didn't come easy; on one occasion Quakers had to patrol St. Joseph's to prevent a Protestant mob from disrupting services. The present church, built in 1839, is the third on this site. The late-19th-century stained-glass windows are notable. ✉ *321 Willings Alley, Society Hill* ☎ *215/923–1733* 🌐 *www.oldstjoseph.org* 🎫 *Free* ☞ *A free, self-guided audio tour is available for download on the church's website.*

Old St. Mary's Church

CEMETERY | The city's second-oldest Catholic church, circa 1763, became its first cathedral when the archdiocese was formed in 1810. Though the interior was renovated in the 1960s, the stained-glass windows and brass chandeliers that once hung in the Founders Room of Independence Hall are historic highlights. Commodore John Barry, a Revolutionary War naval hero, and other famous Philadelphians are buried in the small churchyard. ✉ *252 S. 4th St., Society Hill* ☎ *215/923–7930* 🌐 *www.oldstmary.com* 🎫 *Free.*

Pennsylvania Hospital

HOSPITAL—SIGHT | Inside the fine 18th-century original buildings of the oldest hospital in the United States are the nation's first medical library and first surgical amphitheater (an 1804 innovation, with a skylight). The hospital also has a portrait gallery, early medical instruments, art objects, and a rare-book library with items dating from 1762. The artwork includes the 1817 Benjamin West painting *Christ Healing the Sick in the Temple.* Today Pennsylvania Hospital is a full-service modern medical center four blocks southwest of the Athenaeum. Guided tours are available by appointment only. ✉ *800 Spruce St., at 8th St., Society Hill* ☎ *215/829–3370* 🌐 *www.pennmedicine.org/for-patients-and-visitors/penn-medicine-locations/pennsylvania-hospital.*

The Philadelphia Contributionship

MUSEUM | The Contributionship, the nation's oldest fire insurance company, was founded by Benjamin Franklin in 1752; the present Greek Revival building with fluted marble Corinthian columns dates from 1836 and has some magnificently elegant salons (particularly the boardroom, where a seating plan on the wall lists Benjamin Franklin as the first incumbent of seat Number One). The architect, Thomas U. Walter, was also responsible for the dome and House and Senate wings of the U.S. Capitol in Washington, D.C. This is still an active business, but a small museum is open to the public by appointment. ✉ *210 S. 4th St., Society Hill* ☎ *215/627–1752 Ext. 1286 to arrange a tour* 🌐 *www.1752.com* 🎫 *Free.*

Powel House

HOUSE | Built in 1765 and later purchased by Samuel Powel, the last mayor of Philadelphia under the Crown and the first in the new republic, this brick Georgian house remains one of the city's most elegant historic homes. It's furnished with important pieces of 18th-century furniture. A mahogany staircase from Santo Domingo embellishes the front hall, and there is a signed Gilbert Stuart portrait in the parlor. In the second-floor ballroom, renowned hostess Mrs. Powel served floating islands and whipped syllabubs to distinguished guests (Adams, Franklin, Lafayette) on Nanking china that was a gift from George and Martha Washington. Today the ballroom can be rented for parties and special events. ✉ *244 S. 3rd St., Society Hill* ☎ *215/627–0364* 🌐 *www.philalandmarks.org/powel-house* 🎫 *$8.*

St. Peter's Episcopal Church

RELIGIOUS SITE | St. Peter's has been in continuous use since its first service on September 4, 1761. The brick Palladian-style building was designed by Scottish architect Robert Smith, also responsible for Carpenters' Hall and the steeple on Christ Church. William

Strickland's simple steeple, a Philadelphia landmark, was added in 1842. Notable features include the grand Palladian window on the chancel wall, high-back box pews that were raised off the floor to eliminate drafts, and the unusual arrangement of altar and pulpit at either end of the main aisle. The design has been called "restrained," but what is palpable on a visit is the silence and grace of the stark white interior. In the churchyard lie Commodore John Hazelwood, a Revolutionary War hero; painter Charles Willson Peale; and seven Native American chiefs who died of smallpox on a visit to Philadelphia in 1793. A guide may be on hand Saturday from 11 to 1 and on Sunday from 1 to 3. *313 Pine St., Society Hill* *215/925–5968* *www.stpetersphila.org* *Free; donations accepted* *Audio tour of the church accessible by calling 215–554–6161* *SEPTA buses 12, 40, and 57 all stop alongside St. Peter's campus.*

Thaddeus Kosciuszko National Memorial

HOUSE | A Polish general who later became a national hero in his homeland, Kosciuszko came to the United States in 1776 to fight in the Revolution, one of the first foreign volunteers in the war. The plain three-story brick house, built around 1776, features a series of exhibits that feature artifacts from six Polish museums, depicting Kosciuszko's life in his homeland as well as some of his original possessions. An eight-minute film (in English and Polish) portrays the general's activities during the Revolution. *301 Pine St., Society Hill* *215/965–2305 phone number for Independence Visitor Center, call to check availability* *www.nps.gov/thko* *Free* *Closed Nov.–Mar., and weekdays Apr.–Oct.*

Washington Square

PLAZA | This leafy area resembling a London park has been through numerous incarnations since it was set aside by William Penn. From 1705 until after the Revolution, the square was lined on three sides by houses and on the fourth by the Walnut Street Prison. The square served as a burial ground for victims of the 1793 yellow fever epidemic and for 2,600 British and American soldiers who perished during the Revolutionary War. The square holds a Tomb of the Unknown Soldier, erected to commemorate those lost in that conflict. By the 1840s the square had gained prestige as the center of the city's most fashionable neighborhood. It later became the city's publishing center. *Bounded by 6th and 7th Sts. and Walnut and Locust Sts., Society Hill* *www.nps.gov/inde/washington-square.htm* *Free.*

Restaurants

Bistro Romano

$$$$ | **ITALIAN** | **FAMILY** | Copious portions of regional Italian cuisine are served in the brick-walled dining room of this early-18th-century granary. Don't miss the acclaimed Caesar salad prepared tableside by the genial owner, who thoroughly enjoys animated conversations with his guests. **Known for:** hearty Italian cuisine; romantic dining room; weekly lobster special. *Average main: $31* *120 Lombard St., Society Hill* *215/925–8880* *www.bistroromano.com* *No lunch.*

Bloomsday Cafe

$$$$ | **AMERICAN** | Bloomsday begins daily service bright and early, with coffee, creative egg dishes, and fresh-baked pastry. After a brief break, the sunny, plant-laden space opens for late afternoon and evening service, where a curated selection of natural wines and local beers and spirits complements heartier seasonal plates using local ingredients. **Known for:** natural wine; specialty coffee; seasonal cuisine. *Average main: $25* *414 S. 2nd St., Society Hill* *267/319–8018* *www.bloomsdaycafe.com* *No dinner Sun.*

Pizzeria Stella

$$ | **PIZZA** | **FAMILY** | Restaurateur Stephen Starr logged countless hours researching how to make the very best pizza, agonizing over the dough, oven type, ideal temperature, and every other conceivable variable. The resulting artisanal, 12-inch rounds, with ingredients like black truffle, fresh prosciutto, and earthy chanterelles, keep this cozy 80-seater overflowing with neighborhood duos and families. (No-reservations policy necessitates getting here early or late if you don't want to wait.) All tables are good tables—each has a view of the red-and-white-tiled Neapolitan pizza oven and Headhouse Square through plenty of tall café windows. **Known for:** Neapolitan pizza; outdoor seating; charming location. *Average main: $16 ✉ 420 S. 2nd St., Society Hill ☎ 215/320–8000 www.pizzeriastella.net.*

★ Zahav

$ | **MEDITERRANEAN** | Chef Michael Solomonov's Zahav is steeped in the milk and honey and hummus and lamb of his native Israel, as well as the cultures that have left a mark on that Promised Land. Taking advantage of its dramatic perch above one of the city's oldest streets, the restaurant relies on picture windows and soaring ceilings to create spectacle, but the open kitchen is the true stage. **Known for:** Israeli cuisine; creative cocktails; hopping dining room. *Average main: $14 ✉ 237 St. James Pl., Society Hill ☎ 215/625–8800 www.zahavrestaurant.com No lunch.*

Coffee and Quick Bites

Ants Pants Cafe

$ | **AUSTRALIAN** | A Society Hill offshoot of the South Street original, Ants Pants is a breakfast, brunch, and lunch spot with an Australian approach. Specialties include omelets, stuffed French toast, and dill scrambled eggs; look for down under drinks like the flat white and the Spider (vanilla ice cream, strawberry soda, whipped cream). **Known for:** brunch and coffee; BYOB and cash only; Australian specialties. *Average main: $13 ✉ 526 S. 4th St., Society Hill ☎ 215/309–2877 www.antspantscafe.com No dinner No credit cards.*

Cavanaugh's Headhouse

$$ | **AMERICAN** | A traditional sports bar, Cav's is worth a drop-in thanks to its incredible, idiosyncratic bones—this multi-level, multi-room tavern has been slaking Philadelphia's collective thirst since the 1780s. The menu has all the pub food you could want, but try the wings; they are dry-rubbed and fried to order and come hot, mild, or 3rd degree. **Known for:** wings; plenty of TVs to watch whatever game you're looking for; location on the historic Headhouse Square. *Average main: $15 ✉ 421 S. 2nd St., Society Hill ☎ 215/928–9307 www.cavsheadhouse.com No lunch Mon.-Thurs.*

Puyero Venezuelan Flavor

$ | **SOUTH AMERICAN** | Owned by a team of young Venezuelans, the vibrant Puyero offers a fun fast-casual take on their country's cuisine. The main focus is crispy cornmeal arepas filled with a variety of meats, cheeses, and veggies; they also offer *patacones* (fried plantain sandwiches), *cachacas* (thinner cornmeal pancakes), and rotating specials. **Known for:** traditional arepas; Venezuelan food; fun environment. *Average main: $9 ✉ 524 S. 4th St., Society Hill ☎ 267/928–4584 www.puyeroflavor.com Closed Mon.*

Hotels

Morris House Hotel

$$ | **B&B/INN** | This is a lovely bed-and-breakfast option in leafy Society Hill. **Pros:** great, low-key location; historic; has its own restaurant and bar. **Cons:** no gym; no parking; not a good fit for families. *Rooms from: $219 ✉ 225 S. 8th St., Society Hill ☎ 215/922–2446 www.morrishousehotel.com 17 rooms Free breakfast.*

Philadelphia Marriott Old City

$$$ | **HOTEL** | Convenient to downtown sights, this Colonial-style building is two blocks from Penn's Landing, three blocks from Headhouse Square, and four blocks from Independence Hall. **Pros:** pleasant, airy lobby; newly updated fitness center; within walking distance of Old City nightlife. **Cons:** pricey valet parking; fee for high-speed Wi-Fi; removed from main attractions. *Rooms from: $229 ✉ 1 Dock St., Society Hill ☎ 215/238–6000, 800/325–3535 🌐 www.marriott.com 364 rooms 🍽 No meals.*

Penn's Landing

Named in honor of Philadelphia founder William Penn's first steps ashore in 1682—the actual spot is in nearby Chester—Penn's Landing runs along the western bank of the Delaware River, providing views of moored pleasure boats and chugging cargo ships alike. Attractions along the stretch of Penn's Landing abutting Old City include the world's largest four-masted tall ship, the *Moshulu,* which doubles as a restaurant. The waterfront is also the scene of July 4 fireworks, as well as jazz and big-band concerts, cultural festivals, and children's events. Recent years have seen the development of the walkable Race Street Pier, where you can take in views of the Benjamin Franklin Bridge looming overhead. There's also the mixed-use Cherry Street Pier, and seasonal gathering places like Spruce Street Harbor Park, Morgan's Pier, and the Blue Cross RiverRink Winterfest, all popular places for snacking, sipping, and family-friendly recreation. An ambitious, multimillion-dollar redevelopment of this area, which will introduce a cap park connecting Old City with its riverfront, is expected to be completed by 2024.

GETTING HERE AND AROUND

The RiverLink Ferry makes a 15-minute trip across the Delaware River, traveling between the Philadelphia side and waterfront attractions in Camden, New Jersey, including the Adventure Aquarium, the Camden Children's Museum, BB&T Pavilion, and the battleship *New Jersey.* It operates seasonally, and round-trip tickets cost $9. Though the closest access point is at 8th and Market Streets, about a 15-minute walk from Penn's Landing, the PATCO Speedline is another efficient and affordable means of transportation between both sides of the Delaware River. Round-trip fares are $9.

RiverLink Ferry

This passenger ferry makes a 15-minute trip across the Delaware River; it travels back and forth between Penn's Landing and Camden's waterfront attractions, including the Adventure Aquarium, the Camden Children's Museum, BB&T Pavilion, and the battleship *New Jersey.* A ride on the ferry provides picturesque views of Philadelphia's skyline and the Ben Franklin Bridge. It runs daily from June through August and weekends only in May and September. Besides its daytime seasonal schedule, in the summer months and on select weekends through the fall, the ferry runs express, extended services for BB&T Pavilion concerts and events. Round-trip tickets cost $9. *✉ Penn's Landing, Columbus Blvd. and Walnut St., Penn's Landing ✣ Near Independence Seaport Museum ☎ 856/964–5465 🌐 www.delawareriverwaterfront.com/places/riverlink-ferry.*

Sights

Penn's Landing attractions include historic vessels like the *Moshulu,* the world's largest four-masted tall ship. There's also access to Camden's waterfront attractions, including the Adventure Aquarium, the Camden Children's Museum, and the battleship *New Jersey* via the RiverLink Ferry.

Penn's Landing's Irish Memorial honors those who lost their lives during the Great Famine and well as those who were forced to emigrate.

Adventure Aquarium

ZOO | **FAMILY** | This high-tech, hands-on science education center is the home of "Shark Realm," a 550,000-gallon tank stretching two stories high and thick with sharks, stingrays, and sawfish. The daring can traverse "Shark Bridge," a V-shaped rope suspension bridge just above the exhibit. In the "Hippo Haven," hippopotamuses cohabitate with birds, lizards, and tortoises also native to Africa. There are also up-close "animal experiences," penguin feedings, live animal talks, and immersive 3-D theater presentations. To get here, drive or take the ferry from Penn's Landing. Tickets are cheaper if you purchase online ahead of time. ✉ *1 Riverside Dr., Camden Waterfront, Camden* ☎ *844/474–3474* 🌐 *www.adventureaquarium.com* 🎟 *$32.*

Battleship *New Jersey*

NAUTICAL SITE | **FAMILY** | The World War II–era USS *New Jersey,* one of the most decorated battleships in the history of the U.S. Navy, is now a floating museum. It's docked in Camden, New Jersey, just south of the BB&T Pavilion amphitheater. A 90-minute guided tour takes you around the upper and lower decks of the ship, or you can explore on your own. Families and groups can arrange to tour, dine, and sleep on the vessel overnight. ✉ *62 Battleship Pl., Camden Waterfront, Camden* ☎ *866/877–6262* 🌐 *www.battleshipnewjersey.org* 🎟 *$29.95.*

Camden Children's Garden

GARDEN | **FAMILY** | Located adjacent to the Adventure Aquarium on the Camden waterfront, this delightful 4-acre garden is an interactive horticultural playground with theme exhibits. You can smell, hear, touch, and even taste some of the elements in the Dinosaur, Cityscapes, Picnic, and Storybook exhibits, as well as in the gardens and the Butterfly House. Other attractions include Amaze, Carousel, Train Ride, Tree House, and more. To get here, drive or take the ferry from Penn's Landing. ✉ *3 Riverside Dr., Camden Waterfront, Camden* ☎ *856/365–8733* 🌐 *www.camdenchildrensgarden.org* 🎟 *$9.*

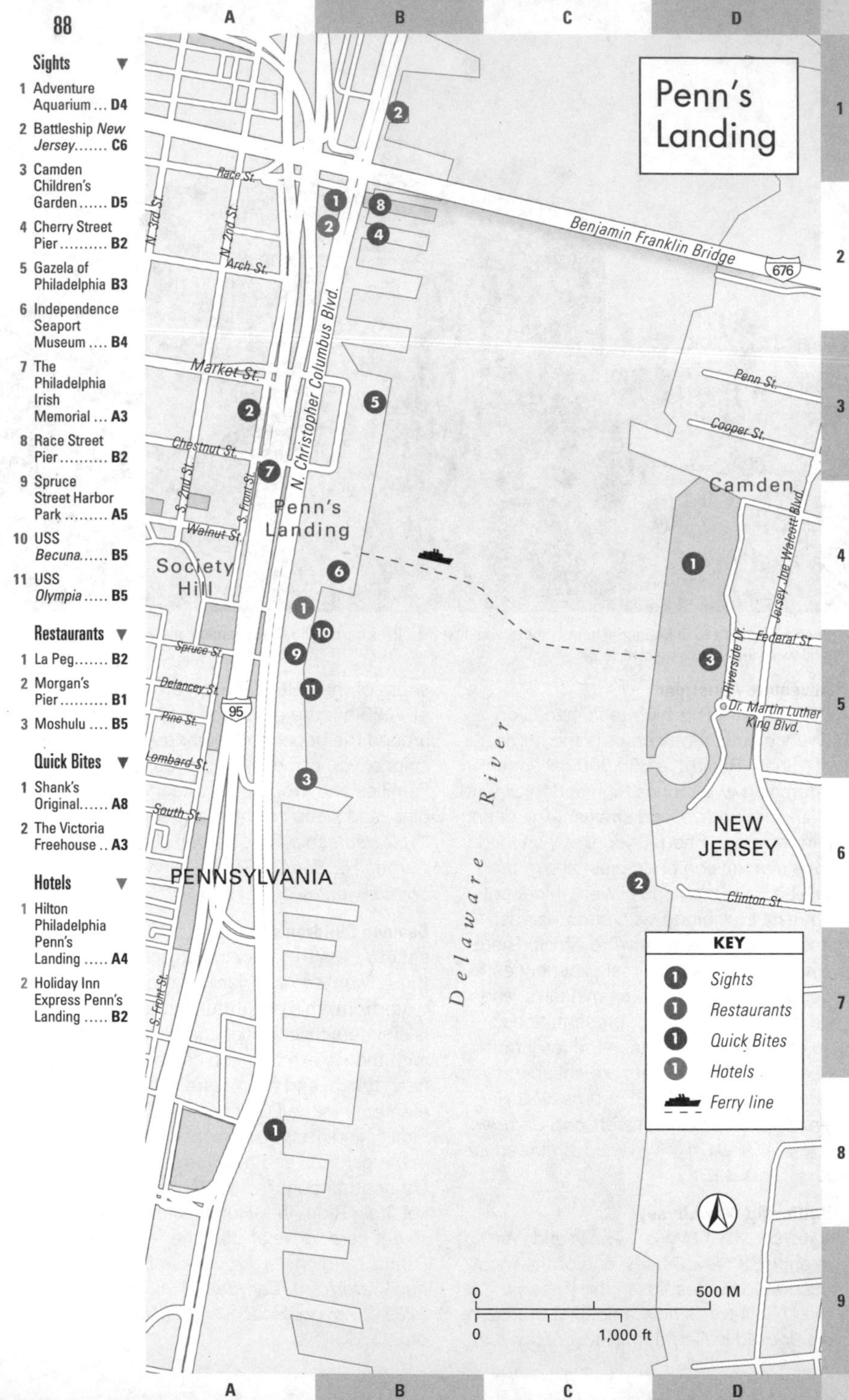
Sights
1 Adventure Aquarium ... D4
2 Battleship New Jersey....... C6
3 Camden Children's Garden...... D5
4 Cherry Street Pier.......... B2
5 Gazela of Philadelphia B3
6 Independence Seaport Museum B4
7 The Philadelphia Irish Memorial ... A3
8 Race Street Pier.......... B2
9 Spruce Street Harbor Park......... A5
10 USS Becuna...... B5
11 USS Olympia..... B5
Restaurants
1 La Peg....... B2
2 Morgan's Pier.......... B1
3 Moshulu B5
Quick Bites
1 Shank's Original...... A8
2 The Victoria Freehouse .. A3
Hotels
1 Hilton Philadelphia Penn's Landing A4
2 Holiday Inn Express Penn's Landing B2
Penn's Landing
A
B
C
D
1
2
3
4
5
6
7
8
9
Race St.
N. 3rd St.
N. 2nd St.
Arch St.
Benjamin Franklin Bridge
676
N. Christopher Columbus Blvd.
Market St.
Chestnut St.
S. 2nd St.
S. Front St.
Walnut St.
Penn's Landing
Society Hill
Spruce St.
Delancey St.
Pine St.
95
Lombard St.
South St.
PENNSYLVANIA
S. Front St.
Delaware River
Penn St.
Cooper St.
Camden
Jersey Joe Walcott Blvd.
Federal St.
Riverside Dr.
Dr. Martin Luther King Blvd.
NEW JERSEY
Clinton St.
KEY
Sights
Restaurants
Quick Bites
Hotels
Ferry line
0
500 M
0
1,000 ft

Cherry Street Pier

MARINA | Spread out across 55,000 square feet, the multiuse Cherry Street Pier is among the newer gems of Philadelphia's slow but gradual Delaware River revitalization efforts. There are artists' studios, artisan craft fairs, and performances throughout the versatile space, but the diversity of snacks available is a more immediate draw. Popular concessions include a variety of sweets, local brews and comfort foods, and even authentic Indonesian cuisine from the popular South Philly restaurant Hardena. ✉ *121 N. Columbus Blvd., Penn's Landing* ☎ *215/923–0818* 🌐 *www.cherrystreetpier.com.*

***Gazela* of Philadelphia**

NAUTICAL SITE | Built in 1883 and formerly named *Gazela Primeiro*, this 177-foot square rigger is the last of a Portuguese fleet of cod-fishing ships, retired from regular service in 1969. As the Port of Philadelphia's ambassador of goodwill, the *Gazela* sails from June to October to participate in harbor festivals and celebrations up and down the Atlantic coast. She's also a ship school and a museum, and has been featured in movies like *Interview with the Vampire*. An all-volunteer crew works on maintenance while the vessel is in port. ✉ *101 S. Christopher Columbus Blvd., Penn's Landing* ☎ *215/238–0280* 🌐 *www.philashipguild.org/ships/gazela.*

Independence Seaport Museum

MUSEUM | FAMILY | Philadelphia's maritime museum houses many nautical artifacts, figureheads, and ship models, as well as interactive exhibits that convey just what the Delaware and Schuylkill rivers have meant to the city's fortunes over the years. You can climb in the gray, cold, wooden bunks used in steerage; unload cargo from giant container ships with a miniature crane; or even try your hand at designing your own boat. Enter the museum by passing under the three-story replica of the Benjamin Franklin Bridge, and be sure to check out the Ship Model Shack, where members of the Philadelphia Ship Model Society put together scale-model ships in front of visitors' eyes. Tickets to tour the USS *Becunia* and USS *Olympia* in addition to the museum cost slightly more. ✉ *211 S. Columbus Blvd., at Walnut St., Penn's Landing* ☎ *215/413–8655* 🌐 *www.phillyseaport.org* 🎟 *$10 museum only, $18 for museum and historic vessels.*

The Philadelphia Irish Memorial

MEMORIAL | Erected in 2003 to honor the victims of the Irish Famine (1845–1849), the memorial features 35 life-size bronze figures that depict the famine in Ireland, as well as people moving to and arriving in America; more than 1 million people died in the famine and more than 1 million people left the country. The memorial was designed by Glenna Goodacre. ✉ *100 Chestnut St., Penn's Landing* 🌐 *www.irishmemorial.org.*

Race Street Pier

PROMENADE | The first in a planned series of parks along the Delaware River, this green space offers dramatic views of the overhead Benjamin Franklin Bridge and allows for up-close views of the river itself. Designed by the same firm behind New York's popular High Line, the terraced promenade features lush plantings, including some three dozen trees and many perennials, as well as amphitheater-style seating near the river's edge, plenty of benches and green lawns for relaxing, and regular donation-based yoga classes during the summer months. ✉ *N. Columbus Blvd. and Race St., Penn's Landing* ☎ *215/922–2386* 🌐 *www.delawareriverwaterfront.com/places/race-street-pier* 🎟 *Free.*

Spruce Street Harbor Park

NATIONAL/STATE PARK | FAMILY | This seasonal oasis—referred to by some as an urban beach—is a combination of three landscaped barges, a hammock lounge, and floating gardens along that hug the Delaware River. More than 50 hammocks are strung throughout the park, and there's an award-winning beer garden that pours more than 15 local brews. You can get food from the Franklin Fountain and Chickie's & Pete's as well as pizza, classic boardwalk foods, and more. There's even a boardwalk that's lined with swings, hammocks, bocce courts, Ping-Pong, shuffleboard, and shipping containers that have been converted into an arcade with skeeball, air hockey, and other classic games. ✉ *Marina at Penn's Landing, 301 S Christopher Columbus Blvd., Penn's Landing* ☎ *215/922–2386* 🌐 *www.sprucestreetharborpark.com* ⏲ *Closed Oct.–Apr.*

USS *Becuna*
NAUTICAL SITE | FAMILY | You can tour this 307-foot-long "guppy class" submarine, which was launched in 1944 and conducted search-and-destroy missions in the South Pacific. A free audio tour, available with the price of admission, tells amazing stories of what life was like for a crew of 80 men, at sea for months at a time, in these claustrophobic quarters. Then you can step through the narrow walkways, climb the ladders, and glimpse the torpedoes in their firing chambers. Tickets are available at the Independence Seaport Museum. ✉ *211 S. Columbus Blvd., at Walnut St., Penn's Landing* ☎ *215/413–8655* 🌐 *www.phillyseaport.org/becuna* 🎟 *$18 for museum and historic vessels, $10 for historic vessels only.*

USS *Olympia*
NAUTICAL SITE | FAMILY | Commodore George Dewey's flagship at the Battle of Manila in the Spanish-American War is the oldest still-afloat steel warship in the world. Dewey entered Manila Harbor after midnight on May 1, 1898. At 5:40 am he told his captain, "You may fire when you are ready, Gridley," and by 12:30 they had destroyed the entire Spanish fleet. You can tour the entire restored ship, including the officers' staterooms, galley, gun batteries, and pilothouse. Tickets can be purchased at the Independence Seaport Museum. ✉ *211 S. Columbus Blvd., at Walnut St., Penn's Landing* ☎ *215/413–8655* 🌐 *www.phillyseaport.org/olympia* 🎟 *$18 for museum and historic vessels, $10 for historic vessels only.*

Restaurants

La Peg
$$$$ | AMERICAN | Peter Woolsey, whose tenured Bella Vista bistro, La Minette, is beloved by Francophiles, bet big on an out-of-the-way Penn's Landing sequel named for his wife, Peggy. Housed in a former water pumping station, the digs are catnip for engineering and architecture nerds; rivet-studded I-beams crisscross the ceiling like a catwalk, and soaring arched windows overlook the brontosaurus hoof—like supports of the Ben Franklin Bridge. **Known for:** waterfront views; impressive architecture; theatrical touches. 💲 *Average main: $26* ✉ *140 N. Christopher Columbus Blvd., Penn's Landing* ☎ *215/375–7744* 🌐 *www.lapegbrasserie.com* ⏲ *No lunch Mon.-Sat.*

Morgan's Pier
$ | AMERICAN | This waterfront open-air beer garden has made a splash every year since its 2012 debut, offering exciting new eats with each new season—the "chef-in-residence" program, which sees a new chef shaping the culinary approach at the start of each spring season, keeps things fresh. Expect a high-low approach, mixing beer-friendly snacks with more creative fare; a wide range of craft beer, cocktails, and specialty beverages, along with DJs and other live music, make this an appealing stop in the warmer months. **Known for:** craft cocktails; casual alfresco dining; craft beer. 💲 *Average main: $10* ✉ *221 N. Columbus Blvd., Penn's Landing* ☎ *215/279–7134* 🌐 *www.morganspier.com* ⏲ *Closed in winter months.*

Moshulu

$$$$ | **AMERICAN** | The altogether unexpected restaurant set aboard the *Moshulu,* the oldest and biggest still-floating rigged-sail vessel in the world, offers one of the city's more unique atmospheres. The 359-foot ship, built in 1904, once transported coal and other natural resources all over the world, but today it focuses on serving high-end (and often spendy) new American cuisine, with attention paid to seafood and local, seasonal produce. **Known for:** unique atmosphere; creative seafood; wine. *Average main: $37 401 S. Columbus Blvd., Penn's Landing 215/923–2500 www.moshulu.com No lunch weekdays.*

Coffee and Quick Bites

Shank's Original

$ | **ITALIAN** | A South Philly staple for decades, the relocated Shank's now slings its signature sandwiches on the waterfront. A cheesesteak is always a solid order, but longtime customers sing the praises of lesser-publicized signatures, such as the chicken cutlet "Italiano" (pick broccoli rabe or spinach) and vegetarian eggplant Parmesan. **Known for:** cheesesteaks; roast pork sandwiches; chicken cutlet sandwiches. *Average main: $8 Pier 40, 901 S. Columbus Blvd., Penn's Landing 215/218–4000 www.shanksoriginal.com Closed Mon.*

The Victoria Freehouse

$$ | **BRITISH** | This U.K.-inspired pub on Front Street serves proper pub fare (shepherd's pie, bangers and mash) and authentic cask ales. It's also a popular hangout for fans of English soccer. **Known for:** Sunday roast; craft beer and cask ale; weekend brunch. *Average main: $15 10 S. Front St., Penn's Landing 215/543–6089 www.victoriafreehouse.com No lunch Mon.-Thurs.*

Hotels

Hilton Philadelphia Penn's Landing

$$$ | **HOTEL** | **FAMILY** | The theme here is "room with a view," as this hotel on the banks of the Delaware offers dramatic river views from the 22-story tower; southern-facing rooms have views of both the river and the city. **Pros:** nice indoor pool with option to sit outside; great views; kid-friendly. **Cons:** separated from Old City by I–95; it can feel isolated; expensive valet parking. *Rooms from: $283 201 S. Columbus Blvd., Penn's Landing 215/521–6500 www.hilton-pennslanding.com 350 rooms No meals.*

Holiday Inn Express Penn's Landing

$$ | **HOTEL** | Situated on a busy corner, the 10-story location can be noisy, but the affordable rates are the main attraction; if you have a room on an upper floor facing the Delaware River you can enjoy excellent views of the Benjamin Franklin Bridge. **Pros:** cheaper alternative to staying in Old City; nice views of the river and Benjamin Franklin Bridge; free shuttle to Center City. **Cons:** isolated from Center City; immediate area can be desolate; can be noisy due to traffic. *Rooms from: $190 100 N. Columbus Blvd., Penn's Landing 215/627–7900, 215/627–7900 www.hiepennslanding.com 184 rooms Free breakfast.*

Performing Arts

BB&T Pavilion

CONCERTS | Across the Delaware River in Camden, New Jersey, this urban amphitheater programs everything from classical to hip-hop and rock in an adaptable space. Between the outdoor lawn and seated pavilion, it can host crowds as large as 25,000, with the indoor portion able to accommodate 7,000. *1 Harbor Blvd., Camden 856/365–1300 ticket information and directions www.livenation.com/venues/14115/bb-t-pavilion.*

PECO Multicultural Series

FESTIVALS | PECO, Philadelphia's primary electric provider, sponsors a series of free-to-attend summer festivals along Penn's Landing. Each installment focuses on a different cultural tradition, welcoming food, music, dance, and vendors from around the world. Programming changes yearly, but recent slates have included ACANAfest, by the African Cultural Alliance of North America; Brazilian and Mexican independence celebrations; the Philadelphia Irish Festival; and the Islamic Heritage Festival. ✉ *Great Plaza at Penn's Landing, 101 Columbus Blvd., at Chestnut St., Penn's Landing* ☎ *215/922–2386* 🌐 *www.delawareriverwaterfront.com.*

The Philadelphia Fringe Festival

THEATER | This performing arts festival takes over the city for about four weeks each September. More than 1000 perfromances include cutting-edge dance and theater from international and local groups, some produced by Fringe and some produced independently. ✉ *FringeArts, 140 N. Columbus Blvd. , at Race St., Penn's Landing* ☎ *215/413–1318* 🌐 *fringearts.com.*

Chapter 5

CENTER CITY EAST AND CHINATOWN

Updated by
Drew Lazor

Sights ★★★★☆ | Restaurants ★★★★★ | Hotels ★★★★☆ | Shopping ★★★☆☆ | Nightlife ★★★☆☆

READING TERMINAL MARKET 101

Reading Terminal Market is a great place to grab a counter

The roots of the Reading Terminal Market date to 1890, when the Reading Railroad Company, wishing to build a grand terminal at 1100 Market Street, struck a deal with existing merchants on the block to construct a new home for them to vend. The market you see today opened for business in 1893, and though much has changed, it still provides a throw-back experience to an older, simpler Philadelphia.

WHAT TO EXPECT

There are more than 80 stalls in the market. Amish and Mennonite merchants from Lancaster County sell baked goods and produce straight from their farms, alongside butchers, bakers, fishmongers, candymakers, cheese specialists, and many other artisan makers. Breakfast and lunch options abound, with everything from cheesesteaks, Cajun cuisine, and a Jewish deli to vegetarian dishes, sushi, and soul food.

NON-FOOD VENDORS

It's not all about food at the Reading Market. Retail vendors sell exotic spices, flowers, crafts, jewelry, clothing, gifts, and local spirits.

WHAT NOT TO MISS

Don't miss Miller's Twist for piping-hot, freshly rolled soft pretzels; Bassetts, America's oldest ice-cream makers; Metropolitan Bakery, for hearty breads and light pastries; and Down Home Diner for affordable Southern-style fare. And while arguing over food is a time-honored pastime in Philly, pretty much everyone agrees on pancakes and scrapple at the Dutch Eating Place, roast pork sandwiches at DiNic's, whoopie pies at Flying Monkey, and chocolate chip cookies at Famous 4th Street. Hershel's East Side Deli has your reliable corned beef and pastrami fix; Fox & Son will fix you a high-end corndog, while Beiler's big ol' doughnuts and fritters draw long lines daily. And if you need a drink to calm the nerves enough to navigate the madness, stop by the friendly Molly Malloy's; they'll pour you a brew in a to-go cup you can sip as you stroll around and shop.

WHEN TO GO

Hours: The market is open daily 8 am to 6 pm, but some vendors close earlier, and popular items often sell out before the end of the day, so if there's something specific you're after, go early. ■ **TIP→ Most of the Amish and Mennonite shops are not open on Sundays.**

Take a Tour: Seventy-five-minute tours, offered every Wednesday and Saturday, highlight the market's history and offerings. Tickets are $16.95 for adults and $9.99 for children, and reservations are required; call ☎ *800/838–3006* or visit ⊕ *tasteofphillyfoodtour.com* to book in advance.

If you love food, plan to spend a few hours exploring the markets stocked shelves.

Hot dogs and hot beef sausages wrapped in pastry. Yum.

OTHER MARKETS WORTH VISITING

Though Reading Terminal Market has a tourist-friendly reputation, note that it is also a popular destination with everyday Philadelphians looking to do their weekly grocery shopping, given the high number of affordable produce, meat, and seafood purveyors. For a slightly different glimpse into how locals shop, check out the **Rittenhouse Farmers' Market** (✉ *18th and Walnut, Rittenhouse Square*; ⊕ *friendsofrittenhouse.org*), held every Saturday morning year-round, along with Tuesdays on a seasonal basis; the **Headhouse Farmers Market** (✉ *2nd and Lombard, Society Hill,* ⊕ *thefoodtrust.org*), which operates on Sunday mornings year-round; and the **South 9th Street Italian Market** (✉ *9th St., between Fitzwater St. and Wharton St., South Philadelphia* ⊕ *www.italianmarketphilly.org*), another year-round option (see Chapter 8 South Philadelphia and East Passyunk for more details).

CONTACT INFO

✉ *51 N. 12th St. at Arch St.*
☎ *215/922–2317* ⊕ *www.readingterminalmarket.org*

NEIGHBORHOOD SNAPSHOT

TOP EXPERIENCES

■ **Reading Terminal Market:** Sample a wide range of cuisines at dozens of stalls at this bustling market.

■ **City Hall:** Take the elevator to the observation deck for commanding views of the city.

■ **The Comcast Center:** The city's tallest building offers a seasonal sidewalk café and an entertaining video installation in its lobby.

■ **Macy's:** The Wanamaker Building is a city landmark. It's home to Macy's, the world's largest pipe organ, and a spectacular holiday light show.

■ **Pennsylvania Academy of the Fine Arts:** The High Victorian building housing this collection of American art is worth a visit in itself.

■ **Chinatown:** Stop by this colorful district to sample authentic Asian cuisine or shop for ingredients to make your own meal at home.

GETTING HERE

The heart of Center City is an easy 10- to 15-minute stroll from the Historic Area, or about a 20- to 25-minute walk from Penn's Landing. To orient yourself, Broad Street (the name for what would be 14th Street) serves as a delineation for Center City East and Center City West, while City Hall, located at Broad and Market Streets, is the diving line for north–south addresses on the numbered streets. You also can use SEPTA bus lines on Market or Walnut Streets, or the underground Blue Line on Market Street, to reach points west of the Historic Area, or take the seasonal PHLASH. The City Hall SEPTA station is a major hub that includes connections for the north–south Orange Line, as well as the east—west Blue and Green Lines.

Chinatown is easily reached by foot from anywhere in greater Center City, or by riding the Blue Line east to the 11th or 8th Street stations. Street parking is available, but it's often challenging; opt for a pay lot, or leave the vehicle behind at your hotel or garage.

QUICK BITES

■ **Merkaz.** Zahav chef Michael Solomonov's quick-serve whips up Israeli-style lunch, fresh hot pitas filled with tasty meat and veg. ✉ *1218 Sansom St., Center City East* 🌐 *merkazphilly.com*

■ **Kanella Grill.** Popular for lunch and dinner, this casual Cypriot corner spot offers killer Mediterranean cuisine. ✉ *1001 Spruce St., Center City East* 🌐 *kanellarestaurant.com*

■ **Greenstreet Coffee Co.** What this minute shop lacks in size it makes up for in expertly pulled espresso. ✉ *1101 Spruce St., Center City East* 🌐 *greenstreetcoffee.com*

PLANNING YOUR TIME

■ To get a feel for the city at work, save exploring City Center East for a weekday, when the streets are bustling, but even on weekends you'll encounter plenty of people strolling and shopping. Besides, the City Hall Observation Tower is open weekdays only, and the Masonic Temple is closed on Sunday and Monday. You could walk through the neighborhood in 45 minutes, but reserve about half a day, with an hour each at the Masonic Temple, City Hall Tower, and the Pennsylvania Academy of the Fine Arts.

City Hall is the heart of Philadelphia, geographically and culturally. The densely packed surrounding blocks, especially those east of Broad Street, are home to the buildings, businesses, and people that make Philly tick. From historic landmarks and the humming nightlife scene of 13th Street to vibrant Chinatown, this area exudes urban energy.

For a grand introduction to the heart of downtown, climb the steps to the plaza in front of the Municipal Services Building at 15th Street and John F. Kennedy Boulevard. You'll be standing alongside a 10-foot-tall bronze statue of the late Frank L. Rizzo. A controversial figure in Philadelphia history, Rizzo was the city's police commissioner and two-term mayor. Beloved and reviled, depending on who you ask, Rizzo regardless shaped the political scene, just as the structures that surround you—City Hall, the Philadelphia Saving Fund Society Building, the Art Museum, the skyscrapers at Liberty Place, Oldenburg's *Clothespin*, and more—shape its architectural landscape.

The story behind this skyline begins with City Hall, which reaches to 40 stories and was the tallest structure in the metropolis until 1987. No law prohibited taller buildings, but the tradition sprang from a gentleman's agreement not to build higher. In May 1984, when a developer introduced plans to build two office towers that would break the 491-foot barrier, it became evident how entrenched this tradition was: the proposal provoked a public outcry. Traditionalists contended that the height limitation made Philadelphia a city of human scale, gave character to its streets and public places, and showed respect for tradition. Those opposed thought a dramatic new skyline would shatter the city's conservative image and encourage economic growth. After much debate, the go-ahead was granted. In short order midtown became the hub of the city's commercial center, Market Street west of City Hall became a district of high-rise office buildings, and the area became a symbol of the city's ongoing transformation from a dying industrial town to a center for service industries. Here, too, are a number of museums, the Reading Terminal Market and the convention center, and Chinatown.

Center City East

Though geographically accurate, Center City East is not the name Philadelphians use to refer to this zone, bounded by Broad Street to the west and Old City to the east. Instead, you might hear them name-drop sub-neighborhoods, like Midtown Village, a dining-and-shopping juggernaut that has grown up along formerly derelict 13th Street. Or the Gayborhood, the historic HQ for LGBTQ Philly, where the street signs are etched in rainbows. Or Washington Square West, a larger catchall for the area. There's a lot of overlap between the interloping districts of Center City East, but no matter what you call it, its core is leafy Washington Square, the eastern mirror to Rittenhouse Square across Broad. Thomas Jefferson University Hospital has claimed a lot of real estate here, so it's not uncommon to see flocks of eds and meds buzzing around the area in teal scrubs.

Sights

Avenue of the Arts

NEIGHBORHOOD | Broad Street, the city's main north–south thoroughfare, has been reinvented as a performing arts district. Although most of the cultural institutions are situated along South Broad Street from City Hall to Spruce Street, the avenue's cultural, education, and arts organizations reach as far south as Washington Avenue in South Philadelphia and as far north as Dauphin Street in North Philadelphia. The main venue is the Kimmel Center for the Performing Arts, at Broad and Spruce Streets, which includes a 2,500-seat concert hall designed for the Philadelphia Orchestra. The newest addition is the Suzanne Roberts Theatre, a 365-seat facility that is home to the Philadelphia Theatre Company. ✉ *408 S. Broad St., Center City East* ☎ *215/731–9668* 🌐 *www.avenueofthearts.org.*

★ City Hall

GOVERNMENT BUILDING | Topped by a 37-foot bronze statue of William Penn, City Hall provides an opportunity to study the trappings of government and get a panoramic view of the city. With close to 700 rooms, it's the largest city hall in the country and the tallest masonry-bearing building in the world: no steel structure supports it. Designed by architect John McArthur Jr., the building took 30 years to build (1871–1901). The result has been called a "Victorian wedding cake of Renaissance styles." Placed about the facade are hundreds of statues by Alexander Milne Calder, who also designed the statue of Penn, a 27-ton cast-iron work that is the largest single piece of sculpture on any building in the world. City Hall is also the center of municipal and state government. Many of the magnificent interiors—splendidly decorated with mahogany paneling, gold-leaf ceilings, and marble pillars—are patterned after the Second Empire salons of part of the Louvre in Paris. On a tour each weekday at 12:30 you can see the Conversation Hall, the Supreme Court of Pennsylvania, the City Council chambers, and the mayor's reception room. You can attend City Council meetings, held each Thursday morning at 10. To top off your visit, take the elevator from the seventh floor up the tower to the observation deck at the foot of William Penn's statue for a 30-mile view of the city and surroundings. The elevator holds only six people per trip and runs every 15 minutes; the least crowded time is early morning. The 90-minute building tour, including a trip up the tower, steps off weekdays at 12:30. The tour office is in Room 121. ✉ *Broad and Market Sts., Center City East* ☎ *215/686–2840, 215/686–2840 tour information* 🌐 *www.phlvisitorcenter.com/cityhall* 🎫 *$18 for interior and tower tour, $10 for tower tour only.*

Dilworth Park

NATIONAL/STATE PARK | This welcoming outdoor space has a café and a spacious Great Lawn for relaxing. There's a fountain for cooling off in the summer, and the space transforms into the Rothman Orthopaedics Ice Rink in the winter. It's also home to free events throughout the year including the Made in Philadelphia Holiday Market. ✉ *1 S. 15th St., west* *side of City Hall, Center City East ⊕ centercityphila.org/parks/dilworth-park.*

Fashion District Philadelphia

COMMERCIAL CENTER | An elaborate revamp of the long-standing Gallery shopping complex, the Fashion District consists of more than 800,000 square feet of shopping, dining, and entertainment destinations. Big-name retailers include Century 21, Eddie Bauer, H&M, Levi's, and Nike. There's a state-of-the-art AMC movie theater, the large-scale City Winery, as well as smaller, more affordable dining options, and Round1, a multi-entertainment facility that has bowling, billiards, karaoke, and more than 250 arcade games. Wonderspaces is an art installation space and there are rotating Instagram-friendly interactive exhibits like Candytopia. ✉ *901 Market St., Center City East* ☎ *215/925–7162* ⊕ *www.fashiondistrictphiladelphia.com.*

Masonic Temple

BUILDING | One of the city's architectural jewels, this temple remains a hidden treasure even to many Philadelphians. Historically, Freemasons were skilled stoneworkers who relied on secret signs and passwords. Their worldwide fraternal order—the Free and Accepted Masons—included men in the building trades, plus many honorary members; the secret society prospered in Philadelphia during Colonial times. Brother James Windrim designed this elaborate temple as a home for the Grand Lodge of Free and Accepted Masons of Pennsylvania. The ceremonial gavel used here at the laying of the cornerstone in 1868, while 10,000 brothers looked on, was the same one that Brother George Washington used to set the cornerstone of the U.S. Capitol. The temple's ornate interior consists of seven lavishly decorated lodge halls built to exemplify specific styles of architecture: Corinthian, Ionic, Italian Renaissance, Norman, Gothic, Oriental, and Egyptian. The Egyptian hall, with its accurate hieroglyphics, is the most famous. The temple also houses an interesting museum of Masonic items, including Benjamin Franklin's printing of the first book on Freemasonry published in America and George Washington's Masonic Apron. ✉ *1 N. Broad St., Center City East* ☎ *215/988–1917* ⊕ *www.pamasonictemple.org* 🎫 *$7 for library and museum only; tours $15* ⊗ *Closed Sun. and Mon.*

Pennsylvania Convention Center

CONVENTION CENTER | It's big: a massive expansion completed in 2011 covers 20 acres of central Philadelphia. And it's beautiful: the 2.3 million square feet of space are punctuated by the largest permanent collection of contemporary art in a building of its kind. Many city and state artists are represented in the niches, nooks, and galleries built to house their multimedia works. To see the architectural highlight of the building—the Reading Terminal's magnificently restored four-story-high Victorian train shed, which has been transformed into the Convention Center's Grand Hall—enter the building through the century-old Italian Renaissance Headhouse structure on Market Street between 11th and 12th Streets and ride up the escalator. ✉ *1101 Arch St., Center City East* ☎ *215/418–4700* ⊕ *www.paconvention.com* 🎫 *Free.*

★ Reading Terminal Market

MARKET | The sprawling market—a food heaven for Philadelphians and visitors alike—has more than 80 food stalls and other shops, selling items from hooked rugs and handmade jewelry to South American and African crafts. Here, amid the local color, you can sample Bassett's ice cream, Philadelphia's best; down a cheesesteak, a hoagie, a bowl of snapper soup, or a soft pretzel; or nibble Greek, Mexican, Thai, and Indian specialties. The Amish from Lancaster County cart in their goodies, including Lebanon bologna, shoofly pie, and scrapple. Many stalls have their own counters with seating; there's also a central eating area. An

Center City East
A
B
C
D
E
F
1
2
3
4
5
6
7
8
9
Vine Street Expressway
N. 18th St.
N. 17th St.
N. 16th St.
N. 15th St.
North Broad Street
N. 13th St.
N. 12th St.
N. 11th St.
Race St.
Chinato
JFK Plaza
Arch St.
Filbert St.
Center City
Market St.
Chestnut St.
Sansom St.
Walnut St.
Latimer St.
Locust St.
Spruce St.
Clinton St.
Pine St.
Addison St.
Lombard St.
Rodman
South St.
Kater St.
South Broad Street
KEY
Sights
Restaurants
Quick Bites
Hotels

Sights

1 Avenue of The Arts C5
2 City Hall C4
3 Dilworth Park............... C4
4 Fashion District Philadelphia..... G4
5 Masonic Temple D3
6 Pennsylvania Convention Center E2
7 Reading Terminal Market E3
8 Wanamaker Building.............. D4

Restaurants

1 Barbuzzo............... D5
2 Capital Grille............... C5
3 Lolita D5
4 Mercato............... D7
5 Mixto D8
6 Morimoto H5
7 Talula's Garden............... H7
8 Vedge D6
9 Vetri D7

Quick Bites

1 Destination Dogs E6
2 Greenstreet Coffee Co............... E7
3 Kanella Grill F7
4 La Colombe............... C4
5 Merkaz............... D6
6 Middle Child............... E7

Hotels

1 Alexander Inn............... E7
2 Canopy by Hilton Philadelphia Center City............... E5
3 Days Inn Philadelphia Convention Center............... E2
4 DoubleTree by Hilton Philadelphia Center City............... C6
5 Four Points by Sheraton Philadelphia City Center E2
6 Hampton Inn Philadelphia Center City-Convention Center.... E2
7 Hilton Garden Inn Philadelphia Center City............... F3
8 Holiday Inn Express Midtown.... D6
9 The Independent............... D7
10 Loews Philadelphia Hotel.......... E5
11 The Notary Hotel............... D4
12 Philadelphia Mariott Downtown............... E4
13 Residence Inn Philadelphia Center City D4
14 Roost East Market............... E4

open kitchen offers regular demonstrations by some of the region's top chefs. You can also take a guided Market Tour on Wednesdays and Saturdays at 10 am. The entire building is a National Historic Landmark, and the Reading Railroad train shed is a National Engineering Landmark. ✉ *51 N. 12th St., at Arch St., Center City East* ☎ *215/922–2317* 🌐 *www.readingterminalmarket.org* Ⓜ *SEPTA's Blue Line subway.*

★ Wanamaker Building

STORE/MALL | The former John Wanamaker department store is almost as prominent a Philadelphia landmark as the Liberty Bell. Wanamaker began with a clothing store in 1861, and became one of America's most innovative and prominent retailers. The massive building was designed by Chicago architect Daniel H. Burnham; its focal point is a 2,500-pound statue of an eagle, a remnant of the 1904 Louisiana Purchase Exposition in St. Louis. Today, the building is home to Macy's and the store's 30,000-pipe organ—the largest ever built—which is used for free concerts every day but Sunday. There's a spectacular holiday light show in the atrium between Thanksgiving and New Years, as well as Macy's Dickens Christmas Village. ✉ *1300 Market St., at 13th St., Center City East* ☎ *215/241–9000* 🌐 *thewanamakerbuilding.com.*

Restaurants

In Center City East (meaning the blocks east of Broad Street), most restaurants are near Washington Square and a few blocks west, along the bustling 13th Street corridor.

Barbuzzo

$$ | MEDITERRANEAN | This buzzing Mediterranean tapas joint has inspired an almost religious devotion among nearly every demographic of Philadelphian. Diners happily stuff themselves into the cramped tables at this long, narrow eatery for a fix of the cheese boards, the egg-and-truffle pizza, and the house-made charcuterie. **Known for:** creative pizzas; caramel budino; lively crowd. $ *Average main: $19* ✉ *110 S. 13th St., Center City East* ☎ *215/546–9300* 🌐 *www.barbuzzo.com* ⏲ *No lunch Sun.*

The Original Centre Square

Philadelphia's founder, William Penn, designed the city around five main squares including Centre Square, which became the site of the city's magnificent City Hall. Today, Dilworth Park, at the foot of City Hall, re-creates the original Centre Square's goal of being a public gathering point for the community.

Capital Grille

$$$$ | STEAKHOUSE | It's only fair to question whether Capital Grille is a restaurant or an art gallery. When you first enter the Philadelphia dining room of this high-end national chain, you'll find walls covered with exquisitely framed paintings and pedestals bearing bronze statues. **Known for:** high-end steaks and chops; business crowd; power lunch. $ *Average main: $52* ✉ *1338 Chestnut St., Center City East* ☎ *215/545–9588* 🌐 *www.thecapitalgrille.com* ⏲ *No lunch weekends.*

Lolita

$$ | MEXICAN | The first restaurant opened by prolific restaurateurs Marcie Turney and Valerie Safan, Lolita has evolved over the years from a scrappy Mexi-esque BYOB to the slick, sophisticated (and liquor-licensed) Midtown Village cantina it is today. The street food–influenced menu includes specialty guacamoles; seafood small plates, like Veracruz octopus tostadas; and all manner of creative tacos on house-made tortillas, with a build-your-own "taquizas" option for the table.

Guided tours of City Hall, the country's largest municipal building, include a trip to the observation deck which provides amazing panoramic city views.

Known for: specialty margaritas; creative taco toppings; inviting bar scene. *Average main: $15 ✉ 106 S. 13th St., Center City East ☎ 215/546–7100 🌐 www.lolitaphilly.com ⊗ No lunch Sun.*

Mercato

$$$ | ITALIAN | This BYOB in a former corner market is noisy, cramped, and cash only. They have, however, started taking reservations and keep packing them in. **Known for:** pasta dishes; classic Italian; close quarters. *Average main: $24 ✉ 1216 Spruce St., Center City East ☎ 215/985–2962 🌐 www.mercatobyob.com ▭ No credit cards ⊗ No lunch.*

Mixto

$$ | LATIN AMERICAN | Latin American and Caribbean cuisine mix in an airy, two-story space on historic Antique Row, a few blocks below Broad Street. The place feels like a well-loved neighborhood joint, with its friendly vibe, heaping portions of slightly greasy food, and Latin music that sets the mood for some of the city's best mojitos. **Known for:** mojitos; Pan-Latin cuisine; music/dance scene. *Average main: $18 ✉ 1141 Pine St., Center City East ☎ 215/592–0363 🌐 www.mixtorestaurante.com ⊗ No brunch Mon.–Thurs.*

Morimoto

$$$$ | JAPANESE | Stunning (and expensive) dishes created by celebrity chef Masaharu Morimoto (of the Food Network's *Iron Chef*) are served in an elegant, slightly futuristic setting. White plastic tables and benches glow beneath multicolored lights; the ceiling is undulating bamboo. **Known for:** sushi; Japanese fine dining; sleek atmosphere. *Average main: $35 ✉ 723 Chestnut St., Center City East ☎ 215/413–9070 🌐 www.morimotorestaurant.com ⊗ No lunch weekends.*

★ Talula's Garden

$$$$ | AMERICAN | Aimee Olexy's Talula's Table in Kennett Square was an unlikely phenomenon; the little country market had a months-long backlog of reservations for its lone farmhouse table. Olexy's urban extension of that runaway success is a sprawling, high-ceilinged space decorated with Alice Waters quotations printed on the walls, a charming outdoor

Philadelphia Flower Show

It takes one week; 7,000 Belgian blocks; 3,500 volunteers; thousands of plumbers, carpenters, and electricians; more than a million plants; and 50 tractor-trailer loads of mulch to transform the Pennsylvania Convention Center into the annual Philadelphia Flower Show (⊕ *www.theflowershow.com*), the world's largest indoor horticultural event. But the exhibitors—nursery owners, landscapers, and florists from the region and from Africa, Japan, and Europe—spend the better part of a year planning their displays. Each year the show has a theme, and the show's designers think big—very big. The astonishing, fragrant results of their efforts arrive in the city as a touch of spring in early March.

It's a fitting tribute to William Penn that Philadelphia hosts this extravaganza, for this was Penn's "greene countrie town," which he laid out on a grid punctuated with tree-lined streets, pocket parks, small squares, and large public parks. It's also appropriate that this city gave root to the Pennsylvania Horticultural Society, the nation's first such organization. In 1829, two years after its founding, the society hosted its first show at the Masonic Hall in an 82-by-69-foot exhibition space; 25 society members showed off their green thumbs.

Today the show fills 10 acres of exhibition space at the convention center and spills throughout the area as local restaurants, hotels, and attractions offer special deals. (The show's website may have discounts and coupons.) Along with the more than 50 major exhibits, amateur gardeners contribute more than 2,000 entries in 330 competitive categories—from pressed plants and miniature settings to spectacular jewelry designs that use flowers. There are free cooking and gardening demonstrations, lectures, and an area where you can try out the latest gardening gadgets. Hundreds of vendors sell plants, birdhouses, topiaries, watering systems, botanical prints, and more.

Many people plan trips to Philadelphia during the run of the flower show, so be sure to make reservations early. Wear good walking shoes, check your coat, and bring spending money for the many horticultural temptations. To avoid crowds, which can be daunting, arrive after 4 on weekdays and stay until the 9 pm closing, or show up when the doors open on weekend mornings at 8.

If you've made reservations, you can rest your weary feet during Garden Tea at the Flower Show, a proper English tea served at 12:30 and 3:45.

courtyard with a garden that glows under twinkly lights, and an elegant seasonal menu. **Known for:** farm-to-table cuisine; charming courtyard; cheese boards. *$ Average main: $34 ✉ 210 W. Washington Sq., Center City East ☎ 215/592–7787 ⊕ www.talulasgarden.com ⊘ No lunch Mon.-Sat.*

Vedge

$$ | MODERN AMERICAN | Less a restaurant than a roving dinner party spread among several rooms in a tony Center City brownstone, Vedge marked a shift for chefs Rich Landau and Kate Jacoby. At their longtime vegan spot, Horizons, the focus was on making non-meat look and taste like meat, but at Vedge, it's a true celebration of vegetables, many of them

Located in the Wanamaker Building which is now the home of Macy's, the 30,000-pipe organ—the largest ever built—is used for free concerts every day but Sunday.

sourced from nearby farms. **Known for:** elevated vegan cuisine; local/seasonable produce; creative desserts. *Average main: $18* *1221 Locust St., Center City East* *215/320–7500* *www.vedgerestaurant.com* *No lunch.*

Vetri

$$$$ | ITALIAN | Philadelphia's foremost practitioner of Italian cooking, Marc Vetri, can still be found at his eponymous ristorante just off Broad Street. In this lovely, sepia-toned town house (the original home of the late Le Bec-Fin) you can expect exquisite but superexpensive custom-built tasting menus (no à la carte) that may involve freshly milled alt-grain pastas, quivering buffalo-milk mozzarella flown in from Campania, and long-standing classics like the golden onion crepe and roasted suckling goat. **Known for:** elaborate tasting menus; elegant pastas; top-tier service. *Average main: $165* *1312 Spruce St., Center City East* *215/732–3478* *www.vetriristorante.com* *No lunch Sat.-Thurs.*

Coffee and Quick Bites

Destination Dogs

$ | INTERNATIONAL | The concept here, as the name might suggest, is hot dogs inspired by countries and cuisines from around the world. Named for airport codes, these can range from conventional (MSP, aka Minneapolis, is a breakfast sausage with fried potatoes, bacon, syrup, and fried egg) to eye-popping (the BKK, repping Bangkok, features a sausage made from python). **Known for:** high-end hot dogs; cocktails; hopping bar scene. *Average main: $6* *1111 Walnut St., Center City East* *267/773–7750* *www.destinationdogs.com.*

Greenstreet Coffee Co.

$ | CAFÉ | What this minute shop lacks in size it makes up for in expertly pulled espresso. The tiny neighborhood café is the public-facing portion of the locally owned Greenstreet, which imports its beans from around the world and roasts and packages them in a South Philadelphia facility. **Known for:** international coffee selection; espresso drinks; cozy seating. *Average main: $5* *1101 Spruce St., Center City East* *610/504–3934* *greenstreetcoffee.com* *No dinner.*

Kanella Grill

$ | **MEDITERRANEAN** | Popular for lunch and dinner, this casual Cypriot corner spot offers killer Mediterranean cuisine. Center City workers on their lunch breaks and bottle-toting evening groups alike (BYOB) enjoy the ever-changing "dips of the day," with warm pita; a remarkable rendition of Greek salad; and kebabs of pork loin, lamb kofta, or seiftalia, Cypriot lamb-and-pork sausages made in-house. **Known for:** Cypriot cooking; charming dining room; Mediterranean flavors. *Average main: $12* *1001 Spruce St., Center City East* *267/928–2058* *kanellarestaurant.com* *Closed Mon.*

La Colombe

$ | **CAFÉ** | Though they nowadays have 30 cafés (and counting) across six states, La Colombe is still very much a Philadelphia company. Looking out onto Dilworth Plaza, this European-style shop scores points in the centralized location and built-in views categories, making it the perfect stopover during exploring for a quick espresso shot and a light snack. **Known for:** expert espresso; laid-back pace; baked goods. *Average main: $5* *Dilworth Plaza, 1414 S. Penn Sq., Center City East* *215/977–7770* *www.lacolombe.com* *No dinner.*

Merkaz

$ | **ISRAELI** | Zahav chef Michael Solomonov's colorfully appointed quick-serve concept serves up Israeli-style breakfast and lunch, featuring fresh hot pitas filled with tasty meat and veg. Must-orders include the zesty shakshuka, served daily before 11 am; and the fried eggplant and Jerusalem Grill sandwiches. **Known for:** coffee; Israeli cuisine; fresh-baked pita. *Average main: $11* *1218 Sansom St., Center City East* *267/768–8111* *merkazphilly.com.*

Middle Child

$ | **CAFÉ** | In Midtown Village, Middle Child represents the new guard in the land of hoagies and cheesesteaks. Their So Long Sal—with spicy lemon artichoke spread, Duke's mayo, meat, cheese, and arugula on a Sarcone's roll—draws lines out the door, as does their vegan, hoisin-eggplant Phoagie, but don't miss out on the breakfast options either. **Known for:** phone in your order if you're in a rush; weekends get crowded; sandwiches like the So Long Sal and the Phoagie. *Average main: $12* *248 S 11th St., Center City East* *267/930–8344* *www.middlechildphilly.com* *Closed Mon. No dinner.*

Hotels

Alexander Inn

$$ | **HOTEL** | The well-maintained rooms at this small hotel have an art deco feel, while location puts you close to the Pennsylvania Convention Center, Avenue of the Arts, and most downtown attractions. **Pros:** excellent location between Rittenhouse Square and historic district; great service; cheap parking. **Cons:** tiny gym; no laundry facilities or services; bar downstairs can get noisy. *Rooms from: $169* *301 S. 12th St., Center City East* *215/923–3535* *www.alexanderinn.com* *48 rooms* *Free breakfast.*

Canopy by Hilton Philadelphia Center City

$$$ | **HOTEL** | Taking over the historic Stephen Girard Building, Canopy's hotel melds the city's R&B culture with local history—think luxury department store-style that was present in the neighborhood at the start of the early 20th century. **Pros:** complimentary bikes to explore the city; filtered water stations on every floor; close to the city's must-see sights. **Cons:** onsite parking is expensive. *Rooms from: $259* *1180 Ludlow St., Center City East* *215/258–9400* *canopy3.hilton.com* *236 rooms* *No meals.*

Days Inn Philadelphia Convention Center
$$ | **HOTEL** | On the edge of Chinatown, this small hotel has a location as good as many other downtown hotels but charges much less. **Pros:** affordable option for Center City; equipped for work travelers; free breakfast. **Cons:** feels congested; neighborhood can seem desolate at night; dominated by convention goers. *Rooms from: $203* *1227 Race St., Center City East* *215/564–2888, 800/578–7878* *www.daysinn.com* *60 rooms* *Free breakfast.*

Doubletree By Hilton Philadelphia Center City
$$$ | **HOTEL** | The hotel's sawtooth design ensures that each room has a peaked bay window with an eye-popping 180-degree view. **Pros:** great location for the theatergoer; good views; sunny and unique lobby. **Cons:** lots of groups can make for a hectic lobby; expensive parking; Broad Street is noisy. *Rooms from: $239* *237 S. Broad St., Center City East* *215/893–1600, 800/222–8733* *www.philadelphia.doubletree.com* *481 rooms* *No meals.*

Four Points by Sheraton Philadelphia City Center
$$$$ | **HOTEL** | With its understated boutiquelike charms, this Four Points offers a practical yet homey alternative to some of its larger neighbors in the Pennsylvania Convention Center area. **Pros:** 24-hour gym; free Wi-Fi; modern yet intimate. **Cons:** no tub for those who like baths; better dining outside hotel; block can be desolate at night. *Rooms from: $340* *1201 Race St., Center City East* *215/496–2700* *www.fourpointsphiladelphiacitycenter.com* *92 rooms* *No meals.*

Hampton Inn Philadelphia Center City-Convention Center
$$ | **HOTEL** | This hotel bills itself as the "best value hotel in Center City" and backs it up with a gym, business center, and, weather permitting, complimentary breakfast on a patio facing 13th Street. **Pros:** excellent value for convention center events; friendly service; recently renovated. **Cons:** immediate area can be desolate at night; pricey parking; small guest laundry. *Rooms from: $159* *1301 Race St., Center City East* *215/665–9100, 800/426–7866* *www.hamptoninn.com* *250 rooms* *Free breakfast.*

Hilton Garden Inn Philadelphia Center City
$$$ | **HOTEL** | This hotel is an affordable alternative to other hotels near the Pennsylvania Convention Center. **Pros:** nice rooms; good value; indoor pool. **Cons:** neighborhood can be desolate at night; pricey parking; area can be noisy. *Rooms from: $296* *1100 Arch St., Center City East* *215/923–0100, 800/774–1500* *www.hiltongardenphilly.com* *279 rooms* *No meals.*

Holiday Inn Express Midtown
$$ | **RENTAL** | What this hotel lacks in frills it more than makes up for with its central location, on-site, 24-hour fitness center, and complimentary breakfast bar. **Pros:** free Wi-Fi; big rooms; outdoor seasonal pool. **Cons:** small lobby can get cramped with groups; funky smells in common areas; lots of congested traffic during daylight hours. *Rooms from: $189* *1305 Walnut St., Center City East* *215/735–9300, 800/564–3869* *www.himidtown.com* *168 rooms* *Free breakfast.*

The Independent
$$$ | **HOTEL** | The Independent is among a handful of newer boutique alternatives to Philadelphia's big convention hotels. **Pros:** tasteful, warm decor makes you feel like you're staying with friends; rooms larger than some luxury properties; good on-site restaurants. **Cons:** noisy neighborhood; no on-site parking; no room service. *Rooms from: $228* *1234 Locust St., Center City East* *215/772–1440* *www.theindependenthotel.com* *24 rooms* *Free breakfast.*

Loews Philadelphia Hotel

$$ | **HOTEL** | **FAMILY** | Topped by the red neon letters PSFS (for the former tenant, Pennsylvania Savings Fund Society), this 1930s building was the country's first skyscraper in the ultramodern international style. **Pros:** architectural gem; cool style throughout; amazing views; special amenities for kids. **Cons:** some guests have complained about the smell of smoke in rooms; you might need a cab to get to nightlife destinations; pricey parking. *Rooms from: $189* *1200 Market St., Center City East* *215/627–1200, 800/235–6397* *www.loewshotels.com* *593 rooms* *No meals.*

The Notary Hotel

$$$ | **HOTEL** | This hotel is in the historic City Hall Annex, and the brass, copper, and bronze details, as well as the lobby's ceiling and chandelier, are original from 1926. **Pros:** centrally located; architecturally beautiful; good service. **Cons:** central location can make for difficulty in picking up and dropping off car; no complimentary breakfast; old elevators are slow. *Rooms from: $299* *21 N. Juniper St., Center City East* *215/496–3200, 215/496–3200* *www.marriott.com* *499 rooms* *No meals.*

Philadelphia Marriott Downtown

$$$ | **HOTEL** | This bustling convention hotel fills an entire city block, and for an intrinsically impersonal type of place, the Marriott tries hard to meet special needs; it also offers some of the lowest rates in its price category. **Pros:** centrally located; clean rooms; good for traveling families or businesspeople. **Cons:** crowds, crowds, and more crowds; parking is a whopping $56 or more a night; the sheer size can be impersonal. *Rooms from: $249* *1201 Market St., Center City East* *215/625–2900* *www.philadelphiamarriott.com* *1332 rooms* *No meals.*

Residence Inn Philadelphia Center City

$$ | **HOTEL** | **FAMILY** | Originally the Market Street National Bank, this building from the 1920s has a beautifully restored art deco facade. **Pros:** centrally located; novel amenities; nice option for families. **Cons:** pricey parking; central location makes it hard to drop off and pick up your car; no on-site dinner option. *Rooms from: $209* *1 E. Penn Sq., corner of Market and Juniper Sts., Center City East* *215/557–0005, 800/331–3131* *www.residenceinn.com* *324 rooms* *Free breakfast.*

Roost East Market

$$$ | **HOTEL** | The furnished accommodations at this "apartment hotel," part of the locally based Roost brand, are well equipped for weekly and even monthly stays, offering full-size kitchens (groceries can be delivered), in-room washer and dryer, and light-filled living and work spaces enlivened with house plants. **Pros:** full kitchens ideal for longer stays; sophisticated design and decor; 24-hour front desk and maintenance teams. **Cons:** no daily housekeeping; no on-site dining; area of town can be noisy. *Rooms from: $269* *1199 Ludlow St., Center City East* *267/737–9000* *www.myroost.com* *60 rooms* *No meals.*

Nightlife

BARS AND LOUNGES

The Bike Stop

BARS/PUBS | A multifloored space, down a side alley, the Bike Stop caters specifically to those seeking leather-clad adventures. *206 S. Quince St., Center City East* *215/627–1662* *www.thebikestop.com.*

Dirty Frank's

BARS/PUBS | Its outside walls decorated with famous Franks throughout history (Frankenstein's monster, FDR, Sinatra, Zappa, etc.), Dirty Frank's is a Philadelphia classic. A glorious mixture of students, artists, journalists, and resident characters crowds around the horseshoe-shaped bar and engages in friendly, beer-soaked mayhem. ✉ *347 S. 13th St., Center City East* ☎ *215/732–5010* 🌐 *www.facebook.com/dirtyfranksbar.*

Fergie's Pub

BARS/PUBS | Fergus "Fergie" Carey is the jovial proprietor of this casual, cozy, and beloved bar, which has been around longer than most establishments of its ilk in Philly. The taproom, which serves solid craft beer and comfort food, hosts regular entertainment, including music, poetry, Quizzo, and even live theater. There are no televisions on the premises, as Carey believes in the lost art of conversation. ✉ *1214 Sansom St., Center City East* ☎ *215/928–8118* 🌐 *www.fergies.com.*

Franky Bradley's

BARS/PUBS | A former supper club that attracted movers and shakers of yesteryear, the updated Franky's is now under the watch of Mark Bee, architect of N. 3rd and Silk City. A kitschy dining room decorated with Bee's Technicolor flea market finds gives way to an upstairs performance space used by DJs and live acts. They serve food until 1 am every night except Friday and Saturday, when the kitchen closes at midnight. ✉ *1320 Chancellor St., Center City East* ☎ *215/735–0735* 🌐 *www.frankybradleys.com.*

McGillin's Olde Ale House

BARS/PUBS | For longevity alone, McGillin's stands proud. Open since 1860, it's the oldest continually operating pub in the city, as well as one of the oldest in the country. But though there are nostalgic touches, it's a modern watering hole, featuring a bevy of TVs for sports and hugely popular karaoke nights. The beer list, featuring 30 choices on draft, tends toward the local, including a series of signature house ales brewed by Adamstown, Pennsylvania's Stoudts. ✉ *1310 Drury St., Center City East* ☎ *215/735–5562* 🌐 *www.mcgillins.com.*

Tavern on Camac

BARS/PUBS | Three venues in one, Tavern features a popular piano bar, a top-floor dance club called Ascend, and a late-night restaurant, which serves rib-sticking comfort food until midnight on weekdays and 1 am Friday and Saturday. Specialties include grilled cheese, a beefy Tavern burger, and beer can barbecue chicken; they make creative cocktails, too. ✉ *243 S. Camac St., Center City East* ☎ *215/545–1102* 🌐 *www.tavernphilly.com.*

Woody's

BARS/PUBS | Philadelphia's most popular gay nightlife destination is spread over two levels, offering several bars—with monitors playing music videos and campy moments from TV shows and movies—and a large dance floor upstairs. Themed nights include Latin music on Thursdays and house, EDM, and hip-hop on Fridays. ✉ *202 S. 13th St., Center City East* ☎ *215/545–1893* 🌐 *www.woodysbar.com.*

Zavino

BARS/PUBS | A small but bustling pizzeria and bar on par with European-style alfresco cafés, Zavino slings creative Neapolitan-style pies and a taut selection of wine and beer. In warmer months, the large open windows and sidewalk seating make for a humming outdoor scene. ✉ *112 S. 13th St., Center City East* ☎ *215/732–2400* 🌐 *cc.zavino.com.*

DANCE CLUBS

Voyeur

DANCE CLUBS | This gay-friendly after-hours joint offers late-night thrills, courtesy of diverse DJ booking and a potent light-and-sound system. Two massive dance floors are filled with gyrating bodies, and a third-level catwalk gives those wanting a rest (or further libations) an excellent vantage point. ✉ *1221 St. James St., Center City East* ☎ *215/735–5772* 🌐 *www.voyeurnightclub.com* ☞ *Closed Mon.*

MUSIC CLUBS

MilkBoy

MUSIC CLUBS | One of two public outposts of MilkBoy recording studios in North Philly, this space features a down-to-earth café and bar on the street level, with a narrow, intimate performance space up top. It attracts mostly indie rock acts, both locals and touring outfits. ✉ *1100 Chestnut St., Center City East* ☎ *215/925–6455* 🌐 *www.milkboyphilly.com.*

Philadelphia Clef Club of Jazz & Performing Arts

MUSIC | Dedicated solely to jazz, including its history and instruction, the Clef Club boasts a 240-seat theater for live concerts, celebrating both the present and past of Philly jazz. ✉ *738 S. Broad St., Center City East* ☎ *215/893–9912* 🌐 *www.clefclubofjazz.org.*

Time

MUSIC CLUBS | A rocking big-city club from the same owners of the nearby Vintage Wine Bar, Time features three concepts in one—a whiskey-heavy cocktail bar; a dining room with a bar and live music seven nights a week; and an upstairs lounge and music venue. Downstairs acts tend toward the jazz persuasion, while DJs tend to dominate up top. ✉ *1315 Sansom St., Center City East* ☎ *215/985–4800* 🌐 *www.timerestaurant.net.*

Performing Arts

FILM FESTIVALS

Philadelphia Film Festival

FESTIVALS | This two-week extravaganza in late October organized by the Philadelphia Film Society is filled with screenings, seminars, and events attended by critics, scholars, filmmakers, and cinema buffs. It's held at various venues around the city. ✉ *Philadelphia* 🌐 *www.filmadelphia.org.*

qFLIX Philadelphia

FESTIVALS | This annual festival of contemporary LGBTQ+ cinema takes place in a variety of venues around the city. qFLIX Philadelphia hosts other film-related events throughout the year. ✉ *Philadelphia* 🌐 *www.qflixphilly.com.*

THEATER

Forrest Theatre

THEATER | The Forrest is the place to catch Broadway blockbusters in Philadelphia. Eight to 10 high-profile shows are presented each season—think hits like *The Book of Mormon, Bullets Over Broadway, Pippin,* and *The Sound of Music.* ✉ *1114 Walnut St., Center City East* ☎ *215/923–1515* 🌐 *www.forrest-theatre.com.*

Walnut Street Theatre

THEATER | Founded in 1809, this is the oldest English-language theater in continuous use in the United States. The schedule includes musicals, comedies, and dramas in a lovely 1,084-seat auditorium where almost every seat is a good one. Smaller stages showcase workshop productions of new plays, and are rented by other theater companies. ✉ *825 Walnut St., Center City East* ☎ *215/574–3550* 🌐 *www.walnutstreettheatre.org.*

Wilma Theater

THEATER | Under founding artistic directors Blanka and Jiri Zizka, Czech natives who joined the Wilma Project feminist collective as its artists-in-residence in the late 1970s, this experimental theater has grown in size and renown, gaining favorable critical notices for innovative presentations of American and European drama. (Blanka remains at the helm; Jiri passed away in 2012.) Its season runs from September to June. ✉ *265 S. Broad St., at Spruce St., Center City East* ☎ *215/546–7824* 🌐 *www.wilmatheater.org.*

Shopping

There are many upscale chains in Center City West, especially along Walnut Street between Broad and 18th Streets, including Cole Haan, Banana Republic, Madewell, and Barneys Co-Op.

ANTIQUES

Antique Row

SHOPPING NEIGHBORHOODS | Pine Street from 9th Street to 12th Street has long been Philadelphia's Antique Row. The three-block area has a good number of antiques stores and curio shops, many specializing in expensive period furniture and Colonial heirlooms. ✉ *Center City East.*

Arader Galleries

ANTIQUES/COLLECTIBLES | This is the flagship store of a highly respected national chain that stocks the world's largest selection of 16th- to 19th-century prints and maps, specializing in botanicals, birds, and the American West. ✉ *1308 Walnut St., Center City East* ☎ *215/735–8811* 🌐 *www.aradergalleries.com* ☞ *Closed Sun.*

Blendo, Past and Present

ANTIQUES/COLLECTIBLES | More like an irreverent flea market than an antiques shop, Blendo is stocked with loads of finds so plentiful they overflow onto the sidewalk. There are new, retro-flavored items and plenty of vintage goodies including clothing, lamps and small furniture, jewelry, prints, and linens. It has the magical, memorable effect of grandma's attic, assuming grandma had cultured and eclectic tastes. ✉ *1002 Pine St., Center City East* ☎ *215/351–9260* 🌐 *www.shopblendo.com* Ⓜ *Bus 40.*

M. Finkel & Daughter

ANTIQUES/COLLECTIBLES | The country's leading dealer of antique needlework samplers, M. Finkel & Daughter also specializes in carefully selected furniture and folk art, making this an important outpost for lovers of Americana. Call ahead of visiting, as public hours of operation can vary. ✉ *936 Pine St., Center City East* ☎ *215/627–7797* 🌐 *www.samplings.com.*

ART GALLERIES

Fabric Workshop and Museum

ART GALLERIES | A nonprofit arts organization runs this center and store dedicated to creating new work in fabric and other materials, working with emerging and nationally and internationally recognized artists. ✉ *1214 Arch St., Center City East* ☎ *215/561–8888* 🌐 *www.fabricworkshopandmuseum.org* 🎫 *$3 adults; children under 12 free.*

Show of Hands

ART GALLERIES | You'll find one-of-a-kind artisan crafts—exquisite jewelry, colorful vases, textiles, Murano glass, and unique lamps—in a wide range of price points here. The friendly owner is on hand to answer questions and encourages you to handle the fragile objects. ✉ *1006 Pine St., Center City East* ☎ *215/592–4010.*

BOOKSTORES

Philly AIDS Thrift @ Giovanni's Room

BOOKS/STATIONERY | Although longtime owner Ed Hermance retired and closed this historic bookstore in 2014, Philly AIDS Thrift, now owner of both the business and building, revived it for a new generation interested in LGBTQ fiction and nonfiction. Focusing on books dealing with gay, lesbian, and feminist topics, Giovanni's Room stocks an extensive inventory and sponsors many author appearances. This inventory is paired with a selection of clothing, home goods, and art. ✉ *345 S. 12th St., Center City East* ☎ *215/923–2960* 🌐 *www.queerbooks.com* Ⓜ *Walnut–Locust on the Broad St. Line.*

COSMETICS

Duross & Langel

PERFUME/COSMETICS | This shop makes eco-friendly soaps, organic scrubs, shampoos, and other skin- and hair-care products locally and infuses them with scents like cherry almond bark and coconut lime. They have also expanded their product line into hand-poured candles, natural perfumes, and a variety of giftable selections. ✉ *117 S. 13th St., Center City East* ☎ *215/592–7627* 🌐 *www.durossand-langel.com* 🕙 *Closed Mon.*

DEPARTMENT STORES

Macy's

DEPARTMENT STORES | Macy's displays the chain's classic merchandise in the spacious former John Wanamaker department store, a Philadelphia landmark. Its focal point is the nine-story grand court with its nearly 30,000-pipe organ—the largest ever built—and a 2,500-pound statue of an eagle, both remnants of the 1904 Louisiana Purchase Exposition in St. Louis. During Christmastime, the space is filled with families and office workers gazing (and listening) in awe at the store's legendary holiday sound-and-light show and organ performances. ✉ *Surrounded by 13th, Juniper, Market, and Chestnut Sts., 1300 Market St., Center City East* ☎ *215/241–9000* 🌐 *l.macys.com/philadelphia-pa.*

GIFTS AND SOUVENIRS

Verde

GIFTS/SOUVENIRS | If you're hunting for a gift that makes you look thoughtful, this is the place to go—here you'll find jewelry, scarves, and handbags with a handcrafted look. This is also the home of Marcie Blaine Artisanal Chocolates, which offers delicious custom chocolates, caramels, and barks with unique flavor combinations. ✉ *108 S. 13th St., Center City East* ☎ *215/546–8700* 🌐 *www.verdephiladelphia.com.*

HOME DECOR

Open House

HOUSEHOLD ITEMS/FURNITURE | This modern, hip, urban home boutique strikes the balance between edgy hipster and hip hostess. The furniture, baby clothes, jewelry, candles, and soaps all manage to be clever and quirky. It's as fun to browse as it is to buy, as there's no pressure from the friendly sales staff. ✉ *107 S. 13th St., Center City East* ☎ *215/922–1415* 🌐 *www.openhouseliving.com.*

Ten Thousand Villages

HOUSEHOLD ITEMS/FURNITURE | Woven rugs, pottery, carvings, and other handcrafted gifts made by skilled artisans in 38 countries such as Kenya, Thailand, and India make this fair-trade store a favorite for innovative gifts with a social conscience. ✉ *The Philadelphia Building, 1315 Walnut St., Center City East* ☎ *445/444–0632* 🌐 *www.tenthousandvillages.com/philadelphia.*

JEWELRY

Halloween

JEWELRY/ACCESSORIES | If the sheer quantity of baubles crammed into this tiny shop doesn't take your breath away, the gorgeous, one-of-a-kind designs will. The shelves, drawers, displays, and even the second-floor balcony overflow with rings, necklaces, earrings, bracelets, pins, and much more. The jewelry ranges from classic pearls to mystical amber. Owner Henri David (who designs some pieces) is well known for his lavish and outrageous Halloween fetes. He can do custom work, such as creating mates for single earrings. Proudly old-fashioned, the shop does not have a website, and does not accept credit cards. ✉ *1329 Pine St., Center City East* ☎ *215/732–7711* ☞ *Closed Sun.-Mon.*

Chinatown

Centered on 10th and Race Streets two blocks north of Market Street, Chinatown serves as the residential and commercial hub of the city's Chinese community. Chinatown has grocery stores, souvenir and gift shops, martial arts studios, a fortune cookie store, bilingual street signs, and more than 50 restaurants. Over the past 20 years Chinatown's population has become more diverse, reflecting the increase in immigration from Vietnam, Cambodia, Thailand, and Myanmar. One

Originally settled in the mid-19th century, Philadelphia's Chinatown is home to Chinese, Korean, Thai, Malaysian, Burmese, and Vietnamese restaurants and stores.

striking Chinatown sight is the Chinese Friendship Gate, straddling 10th Street at Arch Street. This intricate and colorful 40-foot-tall arch—the largest authentic Chinese gate outside China—was created by Chinese artisans, who brought their own tools and construction materials. The citizens of Tianjin, Philadelphia's sister city in China, donated the building materials, including the ornamental tile.

Sights

Chinatown Friendship Arch

PUBLIC ART | Conceptualized by the late Sabrina Soong, a Chinese-American architect/artist and Philadelphia resident, the 40-foot-tall, 88-ton "China Gate" has welcomed visitors to historic Chinatown since its introduction in 1984. Designed in a manner reminiscent of China's Qing dynasty, it features materials and cultural flourishes fabricated by artisans from Philadelphia's sister city of Tianjin, China. The Chinese characters emblazoned on the "Friendship Arch" translate simply to "Philadelphia Chinatown," a paean to the neighborhood's historic importance and resilience. ✉ *1000 Arch St., Chinatown* 🌐 *www.associationforpublicart.org/artwork/the-china-gate/.*

Restaurants

Chinatown Square

$ | **ASIAN FUSION** | A contemporary food hall dishing up a little something for everyone, Chinatown Square covers plenty of international ground with its vendor lineup; choose from Cambodian meat skewers, Japanese street food, modern Chinese bao buns, and even Middle Eastern platters from the Halal Guys chain. Upstairs, check out karaoke and frenetic bar-lounge scene. **Known for:** multiple cuisine options; cocktails; upper-level lounge. $ *Average main: $10* ✉ *1016 Race St., Chinatown* ☎ *215/925–1111* 🌐 *www.chinatownsq.com.*

Lee How Fook Tea House

$$ | **CHINESE** | Literally translated as "good food for the mouth," this unprepossessing BYOB spot is now being run by a

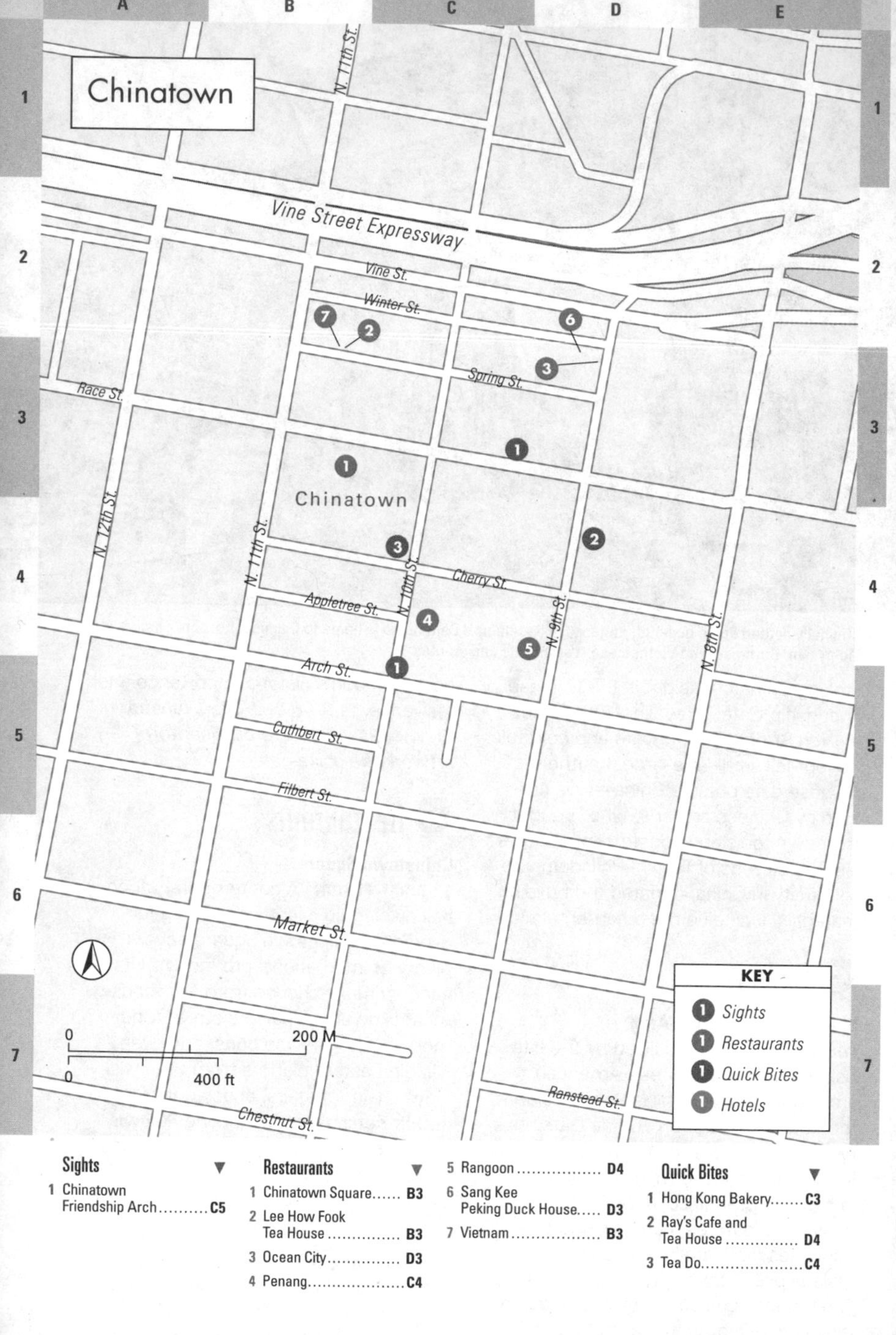

Sights

1 Chinatown Friendship Arch C5

Restaurants

1 Chinatown Square B3
2 Lee How Fook Tea House B3
3 Ocean City D3
4 Penang C4
5 Rangoon D4
6 Sang Kee Peking Duck House..... D3
7 Vietnam B3

Quick Bites

1 Hong Kong Bakery C3
2 Ray's Cafe and Tea House D4
3 Tea Do C4

second generation of restaurateurs. They do an excellent job with the most straightforward fare, like General Tso's chicken, hot-and-sour soup, and steamed pork dumplings, but they are best known for their salt-baked seafood and their hot pots. **Known for:** salt-baked seafood; hot pots; dumplings. *Average main: $15* *219 N. 11th St., Chinatown* *215/925–7266* *www.newleehowfook.com.*

Ocean City

$ | **CHINESE** | It's largely locals eating at this smallish banquet space on the edge of Chinatown, and things can get a bit hectic with big-screen TVs hanging from every corner, spangly chandeliers overhead, and dim sum carts racing through the aisles. Snag a seat next to the kitchen to flag down the carts as they emerge—the dim sum is excellent and well priced. **Known for:** dim sum; seafood; large groups. *Average main: $14* *234 N. 9th St., Chinatown* *215/829–0688.*

★ Penang

$ | **MALAYSIAN** | The juxtaposition of bamboo and exposed pipes is indicative of the surprising mix of flavors in this perennially busy Malaysian restaurant. A taste of India creeps into a scintillating appetizer of *roti canai,* handkerchief-thin crepes served with a small dipping dish of spicy chicken curry, and the wide variety of soups are tasty and filling; *satay,* Singapore rice noodles, and *chow kueh teow* (Malaysian stir-fried flat rice noodles) are among the other popular dishes. **Known for:** Malaysian cuisine; roti canai; Southeast Asian noodles. *Average main: $13* *117 N. 10th St., Chinatown* *215/413–2531* *penang-philly.com* *No credit cards.*

Rangoon

$ | **BURMESE** | The distinctive and delightful cooking of Myanmar features native flavors and seasonings that will appeal to fans of Chinese, Indian, and greater Southeast Asian cuisine. The spring ginger salad and thousand-layer bread served with a potato-curry dipping sauce are both excellent; "Firecracker" lentil fritters are a mega-popular appetizer, for vegetarians and omnivores alike. **Known for:** Burmese cuisine; vegetarian-friendly; authentic spice levels. *Average main: $14* *112 N. 9th St., Chinatown* *215/829–8939* *www.rangoonphilly.com.*

Sang Kee Peking Duck House

$$ | **CHINESE** | Open since 1980, this Chinatown barbecue stalwart hasn't missed a beat dishing up delicious plates based around its famously flavorful duck. Egg or rice noodles come in different styles and are simmered with duck, pork, or beef brisket; if you wish, you can customize your soup with both noodles, plus fat, tender wontons. **Known for:** Peking duck; noodle soups; dumplings. *Average main: $16* *238 N. 9th St., Chinatown* *215/925–7532* *www.sangkeechinatown.com.*

★ Vietnam

$ | **VIETNAMESE** | Owner Benny Lai took this humble noodle shop founded by his immigrant parents and built it into a chic restaurant with an upstairs lounge serving small plates and wacky cocktails like the Bachelor's Downfall and the Flaming Volcano (two straws included). In the dining room the best bets are the crispy spring rolls, salted squid, barbecue platter, and soups with rice noodles. **Known for:** strong cocktails; spring rolls; noodle soups. *Average main: $10* *221 N. 11th St., Chinatown* *215/592–1163* *www.eatatvietnam.com.*

Coffee and Quick Bites

Hong Kong Bakery

$ | **BAKERY** | For a savory or sweet Chinese snack, stop at the Hong Kong Bakery. Sample the steam buns, moon cakes, or a sweet egg-custard tart. **Known for:** Chinese pastry; egg tarts; bubble tea. *Average main: $5* *917 Race St., Chinatown* *215/925–1288* *No credit cards.*

Ray's Cafe and Tea House

$ | CHINESE | Pouring specialty coffee decades before it was cool, Ray's is renowned for its special syphon brewing system, a complex (and photogenic) technique that relies on the vacuum pressure to produce transcendent java. But this charming family-run café cooks up simple eats, too, like steamed or panfried dumplings, noodle soups, and rotating specials. **Known for:** high-end coffees; syphon brewing; homemade Chinese snacks. *Average main: $12* *141 N. 9th St., Chinatown* *215/922–3299* *www.rayscafe.com* *Closed Sun.*

Tea Do

$ | CAFÉ | A bustling bubble tea parlor with a young, cool clientele, Tea Do offers a wide-spanning selection of boba-laden beverages, including milk bubble tea, black- and green tea-based drinks, and blended fruit smoothies. There are also light Pan-Asian snacks, like *onigiri,* edamame, and *shumai.* **Known for:** bubble tea; smoothies; light snacks. *Average main: $5* *132 N. 10th St., Chinatown* *215/925–8889* *www.tea-do.com.*

Nightlife

BARS AND LOUNGES

Hop Sing Laundromat

BARS/PUBS | Run by the mononym'd owner Lê, a one-of-a-kind personality, Hop Sing is a spirituous haven for bargoers who prefer their cocktails clandestine. Hopeful patrons wait in front of a nondescript door in Chinatown, adhering to a strict no-phones policy to gain admission. Once inside, the high-end spirits and creative cocktails flow in a moody, mismatched, haunted-library-esque room unlike any other in the city. **■ TIP→ Open Thursday to Saturday only.** *1029 Race St., Chinatown* *www.hopsinglaundromat.com.*

Chapter 6

CENTER CITY WEST AND RITTENHOUSE SQUARE

Updated by
Jillian Wilson

Sights ★★★★★ | Restaurants ★★★★★ | Hotels ★★★★★ | Shopping ★★★★★ | Nightlife ★★★★★

NEIGHBORHOOD SNAPSHOT

TOP EXPERIENCES

■ **Academy of Music and the Kimmel Center:** Opera, ballet, music, theater—it can all be found within the walls of these great cultural centers.

■ **Delancey Place:** Stroll the 2000 block to check out some of the city's most elegant town houses.

■ **Rittenhouse Square:** This lush park offers a lovely retreat in the heart of the city.

■ **Comcast Technology Center:** The city's new tallest building has restaurants, a coffee shop, bars, a soaring hotel, and sweeping city views.

GETTING HERE

The heart of Center City is an easy 10- to 15-minute stroll from the Historic Area, or about a 20- to 25-minute walk from Penn's Landing. To orient yourself, Broad Street serves as a delineation for Center City East and Center City West, while City Hall, located at Broad and Market Streets, is the dividing line for north–south addresses on the numbered streets. You also can use SEPTA bus lines on Market or Walnut Streets, or the underground Market-Frankford line, to reach points west of the Historic Area, or take the seasonal PHLASH. The City Hall SEPTA station is a major hub that includes connections for the north–south Broad Street line, as well as the east–west Market-Frankford line and trolley lines.

PLANNING YOUR TIME

You could walk through City Center West in 45 minutes, but reserve about half a day, with an hour each at the Masonic Temple, City Hall Tower, and the Pennsylvania Academy of the Fine Arts. If you get an early start, you can finish with lunch at the Reading Terminal Market.

Rittenhouse Square is one of the loveliest neighborhoods for strolling. Two hours allows enough time to wander through the area and visit the Rosenbach Museum and Library. Add at least another hour for a stroll along South Broad Street and a pop into the Ritz-Carlton.

QUICK BITES

■ **The Concourse at Comcast Center.** Below the bustling Comcast Center hides the best grab-a-bite scenario this side of Reading Terminal Market. There's sandwiches and salads from Di Bruno Bros., nigiri by Tokyo Sushi, and cannoli by Termini Brothers. ✉ *1701 John F. Kennedy Blvd., Center City West* 🌐 *comcastcentercampus.com/concourse/* Ⓜ *City Hall, Suburban Station*

■ **Di Bruno Bros.** This uptown outpost of the original Italian Market location is a one-stop gourmet shop with eat-in and take-out options. ✉ *1730 Chestnut St., Rittenhouse Square* 🌐 *dibruno.com*

■ **Federal Donuts** Come for breakfast, lunch, or coffee to try inventive donut flavors like marble coffee cake and strawberry lavender, in addition to fried chicken, breakfast sandwiches, and fried-chicken sandwiches. ✉ *1632 Sansom St., Rittenhouse Square* 🌐 *www.federaldonuts.com* Ⓜ *Broad Street Line, Walnut-Locust Street*

GOOD TO KNOW

■ City Hall Observation Tower is open weekdays only, and the Masonic Temple is closed on Sunday and Monday.

Philadelphia's evolution into a must-visit city began in Rittenhouse Square and Center City West with the fine-dining establishments, cocktail bars, boutiques, high-end hotels, and palpable energy that still fill the neighborhoods today. The city's business district lives here, along with some of the best restaurants, shops, and public spaces in the area.

Always busy and always exciting, Rittenhouse Square and Center City West offer an experience for all, with bars slinging drinks until 2 am, museums showcasing Philadelphia history, trendy restaurants that transport guests across the world, happy hours that draw the after-work crowd, and shopping that rivals any other big city. The neighborhood is known for large festivals throughout the year that draw crowds of thousands for everything from arts celebrations in the centrally located Rittenhouse Square park to a multiblock food and drink festival on Rittenhouse's bustling Walnut Street.

Center City West

Stretching from the eastern banks of the Schuylkill River to Broad Street, Center City West is Philly's entertainment and business hub. Oriented around leafy Rittenhouse Square (the name of the park as well as the posh surrounding neighborhood), this side of Center City is where you can expect to do the bulk of shopping and dining. You'll find big brands and luxury labels along Walnut Street and Chestnut Street, with independent boutiques on the little side streets that fan out to the south, and restaurants that follow suit. This is also where most hotels set up shop in Philly.

Four blocks east of the square is the Avenue of the Arts, also known as Broad Street. "Let us entertain you" could be the theme of the ambitious cultural development project that has transformed North and South Broad Street from a commercial thoroughfare to a performing arts district. Dramatic performance spaces have been built, old landmarks have been refurbished, and South Broad Street has been spruced up with landscaping, cast-iron lighting fixtures, special architectural lighting of key buildings, and decorative sidewalk paving.

■ **TIP→ For this book, we have used the boundaries of 16th Street east to South Broad Street and Chestnut Street north to Arch Street to determine what properties are in City Center West.**

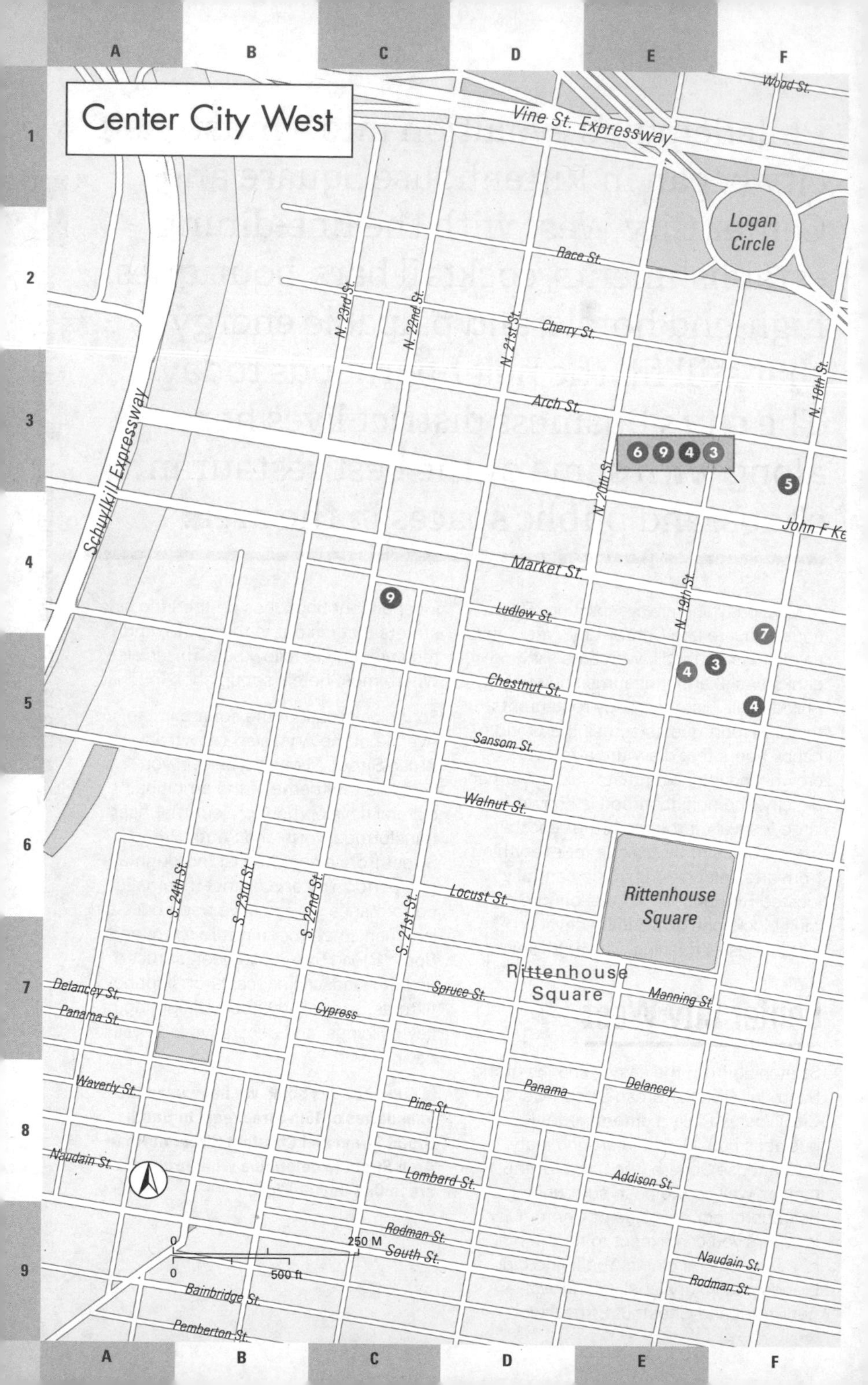

Center City West
A
B
C
D
E
F
1
2
3
4
5
6
7
8
9
Vine St. Expressway
Wood St.
Logan Circle
Race St.
Cherry St.
Arch St.
N. 23rd St.
N. 22nd St.
N. 21st St.
N. 20th St.
N. 19th St.
N. 18th St.
John F Ke
Schuylkill Expressway
Market St.
Ludlow St.
Chestnut St.
Sansom St.
Walnut St.
Locust St.
Rittenhouse Square
S. 24th St.
S. 23rd St.
S. 22nd St.
S. 21st St.
Delancey St.
Panama St.
Cypress
Spruce St.
Manning St.
Waverly St.
Panama
Delancey
Pine St.
Naudain St.
Lombard St.
Addison St.
Rodman St.
South St.
Naudain St.
Rodman St.
Bainbridge St.
Pemberton St.
0
250 M
0
500 ft
6
9
4
3
5
9
7
4
3
4

Sights

1 Academy of Music H7
2 The Bellevue Hotel H7
3 *Clothespin* H5
4 The Comcast Center.............. G3
5 Comcast Technology Center F3
6 Historical Society of Pennsylvania I7
7 Kimmel Center for the Performing Arts H8
8 Liberty Place One and Two....... G5
9 Mütter Museum C4

Restaurants

1 Aqimero I5
2 Butcher & Singer H7
3 Condesa F5
4 Continental Mid-town F5
5 Harp & Crown.............. H6
6 Jean-Georges Philadelphia F3
7 XIX (Nineteen) H7
8 The Palm Philadelphia H7
9 Vernick Fish F3

Quick Bites

1 The Concourse at Comcast Center G3
2 La Colombe Coffee Roasters H5
3 The Shops at Liberty Place Food Court.............. G5
4 Vernick Coffee Bar F3

Hotels

1 The Bellevue Philadelphia H7
2 Club Quarters Hotel in Philadelphia G5
3 Four Seasons Hotel Philadelphia at the Comcast Technology Center F3
4 Pod Philly Hotel F5
5 Ritz-Carlton Philadelphia I5
6 ROOST Apartment Hotel H6
7 Sonesta Philadelphia Downtown.............. F4
8 Westin Philadelphia G5

Sights

★Academy of Music

ARTS VENUE | FAMILY | The only surviving European-style opera house in America is the current home of the Opera Philadelphia and the Pennsylvania Ballet; for the past century, it was home to the Philadelphia Orchestra. Designed by Napoleon Le Brun and Gustav Runge, the 1857 building has a modest exterior; the builders ran out of money and couldn't put marble facing on the brick, as they had intended. The lavish interior, modeled after Milan's La Scala, has elaborate carvings, murals on the ceiling, and a huge Victorian crystal chandelier. ✉ *Broad and Locust Sts., Center City West* ☎ *215/893–1999 box office* 🌐 *www.academyofmusic.org* 🎫 *Free.*

The Bellevue Hotel

HOTEL—SIGHT | Though its name has been changed many times, this building will always be "the Bellevue" to Philadelphians. The hotel has had an important role in city life, much like the heroine of a long-running soap opera. The epitome of the opulent hotels characteristic of the early 1900s, the Bellevue Stratford was the city's leading hotel for decades. It closed in 1976 after the first outbreak of Legionnaires' disease, which spread through the building's air-conditioning system during an American Legion convention. The hotel has reopened several times since then, and now includes upscale shops and restaurants and a food court in its basement, but its character seems to have remained the same. ✉ *200 S. Broad St., at Walnut St., Center City West* ☎ *215/893–1234* 🌐 *www.bellevuephiladelphia.com.*

Clothespin

PUBLIC ART | Claes Oldenburg's 45-foot-high, 10-ton steel sculpture stands in front of the Center Square Building, above one of the entrances to SEPTA's City Hall subway station. Lauded by some and scorned by others, this pop-art piece contrasts with the traditional statuary so common in Philadelphia. ✉ *1500 Market St., at 15th St., Center City West.*

★The Comcast Center

BUILDING | Now Philadelphia's second-tallest building, the 975-foot Comcast Center is also one of its most eco-friendly: the 58-story design by Robert A.M. Stern Architects uses 40% less water than a traditional office building and also deploys its glass-curtain-wall facade to reduce energy costs significantly. Not to be missed is *The Comcast Experience*, a 2,000-square-foot high-definition video "wall" in the building's lobby, which also features "Humanity in Motion," an installation of 12 life-size figures by Jonathan Borofsky that appear to be striding along girders 110 feet above. The building is also the site of an upscale food court, a steak house, and a seasonal, outdoor café. ✉ *1701 John F. Kennedy Blvd., Center City West.*

Comcast Technology Center

COMMERCIAL CENTER | With a height of 1,121 feet—that's 60 floors—Philadelphia's new tallest building is home to restaurants like Vernick Fish and Jean-Georges Philadelphia, a coffee shop, bars, the soaring Four Seasons Hotel Philadelphia, and sweeping views of the entire city. ✉ *1800 Arch St., Center City West* 🌐 *corporate.comcast.com.*

Historical Society of Pennsylvania

LIBRARY | Following a merger with the Balch Institute for Ethnic Studies in 2002 and the Genealogical Society of Pennsylvania in 2006, this superlative special-collections library now contains more than 500,000 books, 300,000 graphic works, and 21 million manuscript items; the emphasis is on Colonial, early national, and Pennsylvania history, as well as immigration history and ethnicity. Founded in 1824, the society also owns one of the largest family history libraries in the nation. This is the place to go to trace your family roots. Notable items from the collection include the Penn family archives, President James Buchanan's

The Academy of Music—the country's oldest known opera house continuously in use—is home to Opera Philadelphia and the Pennsylvania Ballet.

papers, a printer's proof of the Declaration of Independence, and the first draft of the Constitution. ✉ *1300 Locust St., Center City West* ☎ *215/732–6200* 🌐 *www.hsp.org* 🎟 *$8.*

★ Kimmel Center for the Performing Arts
ARTS VENUE | FAMILY | Intended to make a contemporary design statement, the Kimmel Center for the Performing Arts has some architectural oomph with its dramatic vaulted glass roof. The 450,000-square-foot venue by architect Rafael Viñoly includes the 2,500-seat Verizon Hall, the more intimate 650-seat Perelman Theater, Jose Garces's restaurant Volvér, a café, central plaza, and a rooftop terrace. Making their home at the Kimmel are the Philadelphia Orchestra, Philadanco, Philadelphia Chamber Music Society, Chamber Orchestra of Philadelphia, and the Philly Pops. Free performances are given before some performances and on many weekends in the center's Commonwealth Plaza. ✉ *300 S. Broad St., Center City West* ☎ *215/790–5800, 215/893–1999 call center/tickets, 215/790–5886 tour info* 🌐 *www.kimmelcenter.org* 🎟 *Free.*

Liberty Place One and Two
BUILDING | FAMILY | **One Liberty Place** is the 945-foot office building designed by Helmut Jahn that propelled Philadelphia into the "ultrahigh" skyscraper era. Built in 1987, it became the city's tallest structure; however, that distinction now belongs to the 975-foot Comcast Center. Vaguely reminiscent of a modern version of New York's Chrysler Building, One Liberty Place is visible from almost everywhere in the city. On the 57th floor is the **One Liberty Observation Deck**, which offers panoramic views of the Philadelphia skyline. Downstairs are dozens of stores and a food court. In 1990 the adjacent tower, **Two Liberty Place,** opened. Zeidler Roberts designed this second building with Murphy & Jahn, which now holds the Westin Philadelphia, luxury condominiums, and a restaurant on the 37th floor. ✉ *One Liberty Pl., 1650 Market St., Center City West* ☎ *215/561–3325* 🌐 *onelibertyplace.com* 🎟 *One Liberty Observation Deck $15.*

Mütter Museum

MUSEUM | Skulls, antique microscopes, and a cancerous tumor removed from President Grover Cleveland's mouth in 1893 form just part of the unusual medical collection in the Mütter Museum, at the College of Physicians of Philadelphia. The museum has hundreds of anatomical and pathological specimens, medical instruments, and organs removed from patients, including a piece of John Wilkes Booth's neck tissue. The collection contains 139 skulls; items that belonged to Marie Curie, Louis Pasteur, and Joseph Lister; and a 7-foot, 6-inch skeleton, the tallest on public exhibition in the United States. ✉ *19 S. 22nd St., Center City West* ☎ *215/560–8564* 🌐 *muttermuseum.org* 🎟 *$20.*

Aqimero

$$$$ | **LATIN AMERICAN** | Far below the Ritz-Carlton's 140-foot-tall rotunda sits this Latin-inspired grill by chef Richard Sandoval who creates meals that match the grandeur and excitement of the historic building. Many visit Aqimero for its wood-fired meats and fish, as well as its endless Champagne weekend brunch. **Known for:** wood-fired meats and fish; endless Champagne weekend brunch; swanky setting. $ *Average main: $28* ✉ *10 Avenue of the Arts, Center City West* ☎ *215/523–8200* 🌐 *www.aqimero.com.*

Butcher & Singer

$$$$ | **STEAKHOUSE** | One of restaurateur Stephen Starr's many ventures is housed in an old wood-paneled and marbled brokerage (from which it borrows its name). Here the dishes are traditional rather than fancy (wedge salad, filet Oscar), portions are hefty, and the sides classic (green beans amandine, creamed spinach). **Known for:** juicy steaks; weekday lunch options; baked Alaska. $ *Average main: $38* ✉ *1500 Walnut St., Center City West* ☎ *215/732–4444* 🌐 *www.butcherandsinger.com* ⏲ *No lunch weekends.*

★ Condesa

$$$ | **MODERN MEXICAN** | In a neighborhood full of beautifully designed restaurants with exciting food to boot, it's hard to pick favorites, but new-to-the-neighborhood Condesa certainly holds its own. Inspired by the flavors and style of Mexico City, the restaurant expands over an outdoor space, indoor dining room, lounge, and a bar, seating 140 people. **Known for:** margaritas; house-made corn tortillas; well-designed interior. $ *Average main: $20* ✉ *1830 Ludlow St., Center City West* ☎ *267/930–5600* 🌐 *www.condesaphilly.com* ⏲ *No lunch weekends.*

Continental Mid-town

$$ | **ECLECTIC** | **FAMILY** | You're not sure what decade you're in once you enter the vast, retro playground that shares a name with the Old City martini lounge, also from blockbuster restaurateur Stephen Starr. The cognoscenti have moved on, but others still line up for a spot on the popular rooftop lounge or sit inside, in a swinging wicker basket chair, a sunken banquette, or a baby-blue vinyl booth. **Known for:** large portions; solid martinis; rooftop bar. $ *Average main: $15* ✉ *1801 Chestnut St., Center City West* ☎ *215/567–1800* 🌐 *www.continentalmid-town.com.*

Harp & Crown

$$$ | **AMERICAN** | Dimly lit with exceptionally designed interiors, this Sansom Street haunt is a frequent stop for those looking for a cool space to enjoy new American–style bites. In this case, that means doughy pizzas, inspired veggie dishes, hearty meat-based meals, artisanal toasts, and a selection of raw dishes, in addition to a hefty drink list. **Known for:** happy hour with $5 drinks and $3–$5 snacks; pizzas; downstairs bowling. $ *Average main: $20* ✉ *1525 Sansom St., Center City West* ☎ *215/330–2800* 🌐 *harpcrown.com* ⏲ *No lunch weekdays.*

★ Jean-Georges Philadelphia
$$$$ | **FRENCH FUSION** | Perched atop the Comcast Technology Center, 59 stories above street level, lives chef Jean-Georges Vongerichten's opulent, breathtaking, and elevated French-American restaurant. Offering prime views of the entire city—every table has a view, and an open floor plan allows everyone to enjoy the skyline—Jean-Georges Philadelphia marks Vongerichten's first foray into Philly's dining scene with a seasonally changing menu that features a number of exclusive-to-Philadelphia dishes, in addition to the egg toast and caviar and caramelized foie gras that draw thousands to his other locations. **Known for:** city views; egg toast with caviar; seasonal tasting menu. *Average main: $80* *1 N. 19th St., Center City West* *215/419–5000* *www.fourseasons.com.*

XIX (Nineteen)
$$$$ | **AMERICAN** | Occupying the 19th floor of the historic Hyatt at the Bellevue, XIX is a sophisticated American brasserie with Continental favorites like its juicy steaks, artisanal charcuterie, and crab cakes. Though the menu is not particularly unique, XIX remains a scene for its raw bar, weekend brunch, and jaw-dropping views. **Known for:** city views; elegant dining options; decadent weekend brunch. *Average main: $30* *200 S. Broad St., Center City West* *215/790–1919* *nineteenrestaurant.com.*

The Palm Philadelphia
$$$$ | **STEAKHOUSE** | Local movers and shakers broker deals here in the buzzing space off the lobby of the Hyatt at the Bellevue and beneath their own caricatures hanging on the wall. The steak-house ambience comes complete with bare floors, harried waiters, and huge steaks, chops, and salads whizzing by. **Known for:** convenient Broad Street location; three-course theater dinner; tender steaks. *Average main: $42* *200 S. Broad St., Center City West* *215/546–7256* *www.thepalm.com* *No lunch weekends.*

★ Vernick Fish
$$$$ | **SEAFOOD** | The formidable chef Greg Vernick used his Jersey Shore vacations as inspiration for Vernick Fish, an oyster bar reminiscent of the restaurants that dot the Jersey Shore—albeit, with an elevated vibe. Located on the first floor of the soaring Comcast Technology Center, the seafood-focused restaurant serves lunch and dinner daily with a special focus on raw fish and fish-forward tartares. **Known for:** tartares; scallops; bar seating. *Average main: $30* *1876 Arch St., Center City West* *215/419-5055* *www.vernickfish.com.*

Coffee and Quick Bites

The Concourse at Comcast Center
$ | **ECLECTIC** | **FAMILY** | A go-to spot for many who work in Center City, the Concourse on the bottom floor of the Comcast Center is a dining hall made up of Philadelphia favorites, in addition to nationwide food brands. From sushi to Italian pastries, there are plenty of options for a quick meal or snack beneath the towering Comcast Center. **Known for:** affordable meals; grab-and-go lunch; diverse food options. *Average main: $9* *1701 John F. Kennedy Blvd., Center City West* *215/496–1810* *Closed Sun.*

★ La Colombe Coffee Roasters
$ | **CAFÉ** | Adjacent to City Hall, the 9-to-5-ers flock to La Colombe Coffee Roasters for their morning, afternoon, and evening cup of coffee among the hustle and bustle of Center City. The shop is small, but the staff is efficient, which keeps the line moving no matter how busy it may look from the outside. **Known for:** draft cold brew; impressive selection of pastries; oat milk latte. *Average main: $4* *1414 S. Penn Sq., Center City West* *215/977–7770* *www.lacolombe.com.*

The Shops at Liberty Place Food Court

$ | **ECLECTIC** | The Shops at Liberty Place house a large food court on the second level, above the retail stores. You can find anything from salad to burritos to those familiar Philly cheesesteaks. **Known for:** grab-and-go food options; selection of global fare; lots of seating. *Average main: $8 1625 Chestnut St., between Liberty One and Liberty Two, Center City West 215/851–9055 www.shopsatliberty.com No breakfast Sun. Suburban Station.*

★ Vernick Coffee Bar

$ | **CAFÉ** | Chef Greg Vernick has two spots within the Comcast Technology Center, including Vernick Coffee Bar, a high-end café with some of the best baked goods in the city. Located up the escalator in the second-floor lobby of the skyscraper, the coffee shop offers a space for to-go beverages, baked goods, and salads, in addition to a 40-seat café for a sit-down breakfast or lunch. **Known for:** baked goods; toasts; open-air seating. *Average main: $9 1800 Arch St., Center City West 215/419–5052 vernickcoffeebar.com Closed weekends. No dinner.*

Hotels

The Bellevue Philadelphia

$$$$ | **HOTEL** | **FAMILY** | A Philadelphia institution for almost a century, The Bellevue offers elegant lodging at the very heart of the city. **Pros:** centrally located; shopping downstairs; old-school elegance; amazing gym. **Cons:** rooms and hallways could use an upgrade; noise from Broad Street; lackluster room service. *Rooms from: $300 200 S. Broad St., Center City West 215/893–1234, 800/233–1234 www.bellevuephiladelphia.com 185 rooms No meals.*

Club Quarters Hotel in Philadelphia

$$ | **HOTEL** | Hoping to capture the look and feel of an old Scotch-and-cigar parlor, Philadelphia's Club Quarters, sometimes branded as "CQ Hotel," has a little more style than the typical business-minded lodge. **Pros:** excellent location; accommodations for both typical pleasure travelers and extended business travelers; "Sleep Better Kit" available to guests. **Cons:** studio kitchens only have a microwave; no on-site parking. *Rooms from: $165 1628 Chestnut St., Center City West 215/282–5000 www.clubquartershotels.com/philadelphia 275 rooms No meals.*

★ Four Seasons Hotel Philadelphia at the Comcast Technology Center

$$$$ | **HOTEL** | Sweeping views of Philadelphia, a world-class spa, luxurious accommodations, and multiple spaces for eating and drinking make up the Four Seasons Hotel atop the Comcast Technology Center. **Pros:** views of Philadelphia; comfortable beds; high-quality restaurants. **Cons:** expensive room rates; pricey parking; long waits at hotel bars and restaurants without reservation. *Rooms from: $570 1 N. 19th St., Center City West 215/419–5000 www.fourseasons.com 219 rooms No meals.*

★ Pod Philly Hotel

$ | **HOTEL** | Philadelphia's first location of microhotel-brand Pod, a seriously cool hotel with more spacious rooms than one would expect, features 252 rooms that range from 150 to 300 square feet, allowing for two people in the smaller rooms and three to four people in the larger. **Pros:** modern design; excellent dining options within hotel; central location. **Cons:** small rooms; long waits at hotel restaurant; no room service. *Rooms from: $130 31 S. 19th St., Center City West 267/494–0440 www.thepodhotel.com 252 rooms No meals.*

★ Ritz-Carlton Philadelphia

$$$$ | **HOTEL** | **FAMILY** | You'll feel like you're checking into the Pantheon when you enter this neoclassical hotel set in a century-old bank building—more than 60,000 square feet of Georgian white marble

Within walking distance of City Hall and the Pennsylvania Convention Center, the Ritz-Carlton resides in the former home of The Girard Trust Company.

makes up the dramatic lobby; a 2015 renovation modernized both the lobby (textures reminiscent of currency, in a nod to the building's banking past) and guest rooms (work and play spaces, set in a contemporary neutral palette with metallic touches). **Pros:** stunning architecture (the lobby bar is unparalleled); attentive and friendly service; modern in-room amenities. **Cons:** rooms are smaller than some luxury competitors; street noise can be a problem; pricey parking; elevators can be slow; gym is spare. *$ Rooms from: $400 ✉ 10 S. Broad St., Center City West ☎ 215/523–8000, 800/241–3333 ⊕ www.ritzcarlton.com ⇆ 299 rooms 🍴 No meals.*

ROOST Apartment Hotel

$$ | HOTEL | Nestling thoughtful hyper-modern amenities in the bones of the venerable Packard Building, ROOST is an extended-stay establishment designed with the modern traveler in mind. **Pros:** stylish, thoughtfully curated design; excellent location for Center City; apartment-style rooms. **Cons:** not always the best fit for shorter stays; parking can be far from the hotel; can be loud on weekend nights. *$ Rooms from: $155 ✉ 111 S. 15th St., Center City West ☎ 267/737–9000 ⊕ www.myroost.com ⇆ 27 suites 🍴 No meals.*

Sonesta Philadelphia Downtown

$$ | HOTEL | FAMILY | Center City's Sonesta pairs an urbane design aesthetic—heavy on the blacks and reds and minimalist furniture—that touches both common areas and private guest rooms, with an interesting collection of amenities. **Pros:** great central location; can be a bargain compared to other Center City options; outdoor seasonal pool. **Cons:** some guests complain about careless service; noise level can be a problem; expensive parking. *$ Rooms from: $179 ✉ 1800 Market St., Center City West ☎ 215/561–7500, 800/227–6963 ⊕ www.sonesta.com ⇆ 447 rooms 🍴 No meals.*

★ Westin Philadelphia

$$$$ | HOTEL | FAMILY | If luxurious accommodations and plenty of shopping are your top priorities, you're not going to beat the Westin. **Pros:** close to best shopping areas; excellent beds; comfortable furniture; quiet. **Cons:** pricey parking; common spaces could use updating; busy valet parking area. *Rooms from: $300 ✉ 99 S. 17th St., at Liberty Pl., Center City West ☎ 215/563–1600, 800/937–8461 🌐 www.westin.com/philadelphia 294 rooms No meals.*

Nightlife

BARS AND LOUNGES

Continental Mid-town

BARS/PUBS | A more elaborate offshoot of Stephen Starr's Old City martini lounge, the Continental Mid-town spreads the cocktail and global small-plates concept across three whimsically appointed floors, including an indoor-outdoor rooftop space. The items on the comprehensive food menu run the gamut from cheesesteak egg rolls to lobster macaroni and cheese. *✉ 1801 Chestnut St., Center City West ☎ 215/567–1800 🌐 www.continentalmidtown.com.*

XIX (Nineteen)

BARS/PUBS | Perched on the 19th floor of the Hyatt at the Bellevue, this high-end lounge bestows beautiful vistas of the city, solid cocktails, a seafood-centric menu, a roaring fireplace, and elegant decorative accents. It's certainly pricey, but the views make up for it. *✉ 200 S. Broad St., Center City West ☎ 215/790–1919 🌐 nineteenrestaurant.com.*

MUSIC CLUBS

Chris' Jazz Café

MUSIC CLUBS | An intimate hangout off the Avenue of the Arts (aka Broad Street), Chris' showcases top talent Monday through Saturday. The jazz club stays accessible by doing the simple things right—friendly service, fair prices, great performers. The lunch and dinner menus feature some light New Orleans–style touches. *✉ 1421 Sansom St., Center City West ☎ 215/568–3131 🌐 www.chrisjazzcafe.com ☞ Closed Sun.*

Performing Arts

CLASSICAL MUSIC

Chamber Orchestra of Philadelphia

MUSIC | Directed by Dirk Brossé, this prestigious group performs chamber music from September to May at the Perelman Theater at the Kimmel Center for the Performing Arts. *✉ 300 S. Broad St., Center City West ☎ 215/893–1999 box office, 215/545–5451 administrative office 🌐 www.chamberorchestra.org.*

Philadelphia Chamber Music Society

CONCERTS | From October to May, the society presents 60 concerts featuring nationally and internationally known musicians. The schedule is packed with a piano, vocal, and chamber music series, a special-events and jazz series, and string recitals. Performances are held in the Perelman Theater at the Kimmel Center for the Performing Arts, at the Philadelphia Museum of Art, and at other locations in the city. *✉ Center City West ☎ 215/569–8587 information, 215/569–8080 box office 🌐 www.pcmsconcerts.org.*

Philadelphia Orchestra

CONCERTS | Considered one of the world's best symphony orchestras, the Philadelphia Orchestra is overseen by the effervescent Yannick Nézet-Séguin. The orchestra's present home is the cello-shaped Verizon Hall at the Kimmel Center for the Performing Arts. The 2,500-seat hall is the centerpiece of the performing-arts center at Broad and Spruce Streets—a dynamic complex housed under a glass-vaulted roof. Orchestra concerts during the September–May season are still among the city's premier social events. In summer the orchestra performs at the Mann Center for the Performing Arts. *✉ 300 S. Broad St., Center City West ☎ 215/893–1999 box office, 215/893–1900 info 🌐 www.philorch.org.*

The Philly Pops
CONCERTS | FAMILY | Music director Todd Ellison leads an orchestra of local musicians in programs that swing from Broadway to big band, or from ragtime to rock and roll, with ease. They perform mainly at the Kimmel Center in the fall, winter, and spring. ✉ *300 S. Broad St., Center City West* ☎ *215/893–1900* 🌐 *www.phillypops.com.*

DANCE

★ Pennsylvania Ballet
DANCE | FAMILY | Artistic director Angel Corella leads the company through a season of classic favorites and new works; they dance on the stage of the Academy of Music and at the Merriam Theater at the University of the Arts. Their annual production of George Balanchine's *The Nutcracker* is a holiday favorite. ✉ *Broad and Locust Sts., Center City West* ☎ *215/551–7000* 🌐 *www.paballet.org.*

Philadelphia Dance Company
DANCE | This modern troupe, also known as PHILADANCO, is recognized for its innovative performances that weld contemporary and classical forms and the traditions of other cultures, with a particular emphasis on African American dance heritage. ✉ *Broad and Spruce Sts., Center City West* ☎ *215/387–8200* 🌐 *www.philadanco.org.*

OPERA

★ Opera Philadelphia
OPERA | Recently, the city's premier opera company rebranded as Opera Philadelphia with an emphasis on creating programming that welcomes broader audiences. Its season begins with Festival O annually in September, a week-plus-long extravaganza featuring free and more affordably priced shows. Following the festival, the group stages four or five productions a year between October and May at the Academy of Music; some operas have international stars. All performances are in the original language, with English supertitles above the stage. ✉ *240 S. Broad St., Center City West* ☎ *215/732-8400* 🌐 *www.operaphila.org.*

THEATER

Merriam Theater
THEATER | Built in 1918 as the Shubert, the ornate 1,688-seat theater has had many stage greats, including Al Jolson, Helen Hayes, Katharine Hepburn, Sammy Davis Jr., Angela Lansbury, and Sir Laurence Olivier. Named after a local benefactor, the lavishly decorated Merriam hosts a full schedule of national tours of Broadway shows, modern dance companies, and solo performers, from the magicians Penn & Teller to tap dancer Savion Glover. ✉ *250 S. Broad St., Center City West* ☎ *215/893–1999* 🌐 *www.kimmelcenter.org.*

Philadelphia Film Center
FILM | Formerly the Prince Music Theater, the theater has evolved into a regular venue for movie screenings and the society's fall film festival, though it also hosts concerts, cabaret, opera, comedy, and more. ✉ *1412 Chestnut St., Center City West* ☎ *267/239–2941* 🌐 *filmadelphia.org.*

Philadelphia Theatre Company
THEATER | Philadelphia and world premieres of works by contemporary American playwrights are performed here. In 2007 the Philadelphia Theatre Company moved to their new permanent home, the 365-seat Suzanne Roberts Theatre on the Avenue of the Arts. ✉ *480 S. Broad St., between Lombard and Pine Sts., Center City West* ☎ *215/985–0420* 🌐 *www.philadelphiatheatrecompany.org.*

Shopping

There are many upscale chains in Center City West, especially along Walnut Street between Broad and 18th Streets, including Cole Haan, Banana Republic, Madewell, and Barneys Co-Op.

CLOTHING

Children's Boutique

CLOTHING | FAMILY | The store carries a look between conservative and classic in infant to preteen clothes and shoes. You can buy complete wardrobes, specialty gifts, and handmade items by a range of designers from all over the country and throughout Europe. An extensive toy department carries the latest in kiddie crazes. ✉ *The Shops at Liberty Place, 1625 Chestnut St., Center City West* ☎ *215/732–2661* 🌐 *www.shopsatliberty.com.*

GIFTS AND SOUVENIRS

Holt's Cigar Company

GIFTS/SOUVENIRS | Stogie aficionados make a point of stopping by this cigar emporium, whose Philadelphia roots date back more than 100 years. The shop features a comfortable smoking lounge and one of the nation's largest walk-in humidors. Find private-label Ashton cigars, a wide array of smoking accessories and humidors, and writing instruments from Mont Blanc, Waterman, and Cross. Upstairs is the Ashton Cigar Bar, which pairs cigars with rare whiskeys and also specialty cocktails. ✉ *1522 Walnut St., Center City West* ☎ *215/732–8500* 🌐 *www.ashtoncigarbar.com.*

Loop Yarn

TEXTILES/SEWING | Loop is a knitting store stocked with supplies including natural fiber, luxury, and hand-dyed yarn in a rainbow of hues artfully arranged in stark-white ceiling-high cubbies, softened by the addition of comfy couches where crafty types can (and do) bond. ✉ *1914 South St., Center City West* ☎ *215/893–9939* 🌐 *www.loopyarn.com.*

HOME DECOR

Kitchen Kapers

HOUSEHOLD ITEMS/FURNITURE | From one store in South Jersey, this family business has grown to be one of the largest independent kitchenware stores in the United States. Kitchen Kapers is a good source for fine cookware, French copper, cutlery, coffees, and teas. ✉ *213 S. 17th St., Center City West* ☎ *215/546–8059* 🌐 *www.kitchenkapers.com/ba2.html.*

Usona

HOUSEHOLD ITEMS/FURNITURE | Furniture and accessories are what the owner calls "global modern," reflecting a fusion of different styles, periods, and materials. Accent pieces, like picture frames and mirrors, are interesting and affordable. ✉ *1633 Locust St., Center City West* ☎ *215/496–0440* 🌐 *www.usonahome.com* ☞ *Weekends by appt. only.*

MALLS

Shops at the Bellevue

SHOPPING CENTERS/MALLS | The elegant Shops at the Bellevue have started to succumb to the fierce retail competition in the area, but staples like Tiffany & Co. and a Williams-Sonoma cookware store remain within the historic building. A downstairs food court is bustling at lunchtime; several upscale restaurants in the historic building, which also houses an elegant hotel, are popular in the evening. ✉ *Broad and Walnut Sts., Center City West* 🌐 *www.bellevuephiladelphia.com.*

Shops at Liberty Place

SHOPPING CENTERS/MALLS | At 16th and Chestnut Streets is the Shops at Liberty Place. The complex features a food court and popular stores, including Loft, Aveda, Victoria's Secret, Express, J. Crew, and Bloomingdales Outlet. More than 20 stores and restaurants are arranged in two circular levels within a strikingly handsome 90-foot glass-roof atrium. ✉ *1625 Chestnut St., Center City West* ☎ *215/851–9055* 🌐 *www.shopsatliberty.com.*

SHOES

Sherman Brothers Shoes

SHOES/LUGGAGE/LEATHER GOODS | This discount retailer of shoes has name-brand merchandise and excellent service. The store stocks extra-wide and extra-narrow widths, as well as sizes up to 16 in men's shoes. Look for classic comfort shoes by Cole Haan, Clarks, and Johnston & Murphy. ✉ *1520 Sansom St., Center City West* ☎ *267/421-5379* 🌐 *www.sherman-brothers.com.*

Rittenhouse Square

Rittenhouse Square has long been one of the city's swankiest addresses. The square's entrances, plaza, pool, and fountains were designed in 1913 by Paul Cret, one of the people responsible for the Benjamin Franklin Parkway. The square was named in honor of one of the city's 18th-century stars: David Rittenhouse, president of the American Philosophical Society. The first house facing the square was erected in 1840, soon to be followed by other grand mansions. Almost all the private homes are now gone, replaced by hotels, apartments, cultural institutions, and elegant restaurants and stylish cafés. The area south and west of the square is still largely residential and lovely, with cupolas and balconies, hitching posts and stained-glass windows. Peek in the streets behind these homes or through their wrought-iron gates and into well-tended gardens.

■ TIP→ For this book, we have used the boundaries of 16th Street west to 23rd Street and Chestnut Street south to Lombard Street to determine what properties are in Rittenhouse Square. It is important to keep in mind that Rittenhouse Square is part of the larger City Center West neighborhood as well.

Sights

Curtis Institute of Music

ARTS VENUE | Graduates of this tuition-free school for outstanding students include Leonard Bernstein, Samuel Barber, Ned Rorem, and Anna Moffo. The school occupies four former private homes and Lenfest Hall for student housing and practice rooms; the main building is in the mansion that belonged to banker George W. Childs Drexel. Built in 1893 by the distinguished Boston firm of Peabody and Stearns, it's notable for Romanesque and Renaissance architectural details. Free student and faculty concerts are given from October through May, usually on Monday, Wednesday, and Friday evenings. ✉ *1726 Locust St., Rittenhouse Square* ☎ *215/893–5261 recital hotline, 215/893–7902 ticket office* 🌐 *www.curtis.edu* Ⓜ *Walnut/Locust stop; Broad Street Line.*

Delancey Place

NEIGHBORHOOD | Cypress Street, north of Delancey Place, and Panama Street (especially the 1900 block, one block south of Delancey) are two of the many intimate streets lined with trees and town houses characteristic of the area. At No. 2010 is the Rosenbach Museum and Library. ✉ *Rittenhouse Square.*

★ Rittenhouse Row

COMMERCIAL CENTER | **FAMILY** | Shop-'til-you-droppers make a beeline for Rittenhouse Row, the area between Broad and 21st Streets and Spruce and Market Streets. Lately chains like Madewell, H&M, and Lululemon have been taking over Walnut Street between Rittenhouse Square and Broad Street, but this is still the greatest concentration of swanky stores, tony boutiques, and jewelers you'll find in the city. ✉ *Center City West* 🌐 *www.rittenhouserow.org.*

★ Rittenhouse Square

NEIGHBORHOOD | Once grazing ground for cows and sheep, Philadelphia's most elegant square is reminiscent of a Parisian park. One of William Penn's original five city squares, the park was named in 1825 to honor David Rittenhouse, 18th-century astronomer, clock maker, and the first director of the United States Mint. Many of Philadelphia's celebrities have lived here. Extra paths were made for Dr. William White, a leader in beautifying the square, so he could walk directly from his home to the exclusive Rittenhouse Club across the square and lunch with

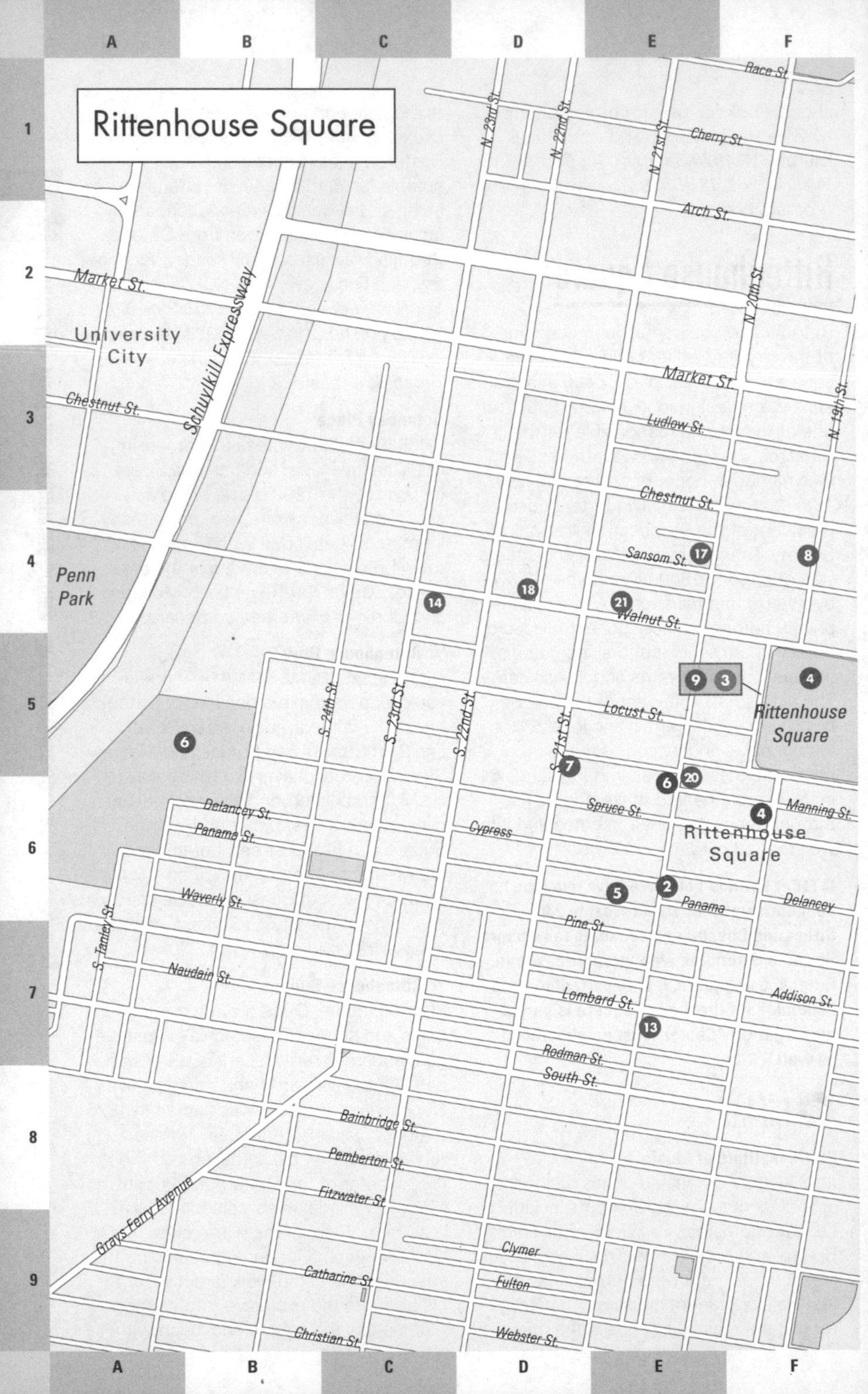
Rittenhouse Square
A
B
C
D
E
F
1
2
3
4
5
6
7
8
9
Race St.
Cherry St.
Arch St.
N. 23rd St.
N. 22nd St.
N. 21st St.
N. 20th St.
N. 19th St.
Market St.
University City
Schuylkill Expressway
Chestnut St.
Market St.
Ludlow St.
Chestnut St.
Sansom St.
Walnut St.
Penn Park
Locust St.
Rittenhouse Square
S. 24th St.
S. 23rd St.
S. 22nd St.
S. 21st St.
Spruce St.
Manning St.
Delancey St.
Panama St.
Cypress
Rittenhouse Square
Waverly St.
Panama
Delancey
Pine St.
S. Tanley St.
Naudain St.
Lombard St.
Addison St.
Rodman St.
South St.
Bainbridge St.
Pemberton St.
Fitzwater St.
Grays Ferry Avenue
Clymer
Catharine St.
Fulton
Christian St.
Webster St.
1
2
3
4
5
6
7
8
9
13
14
17
18
20
21

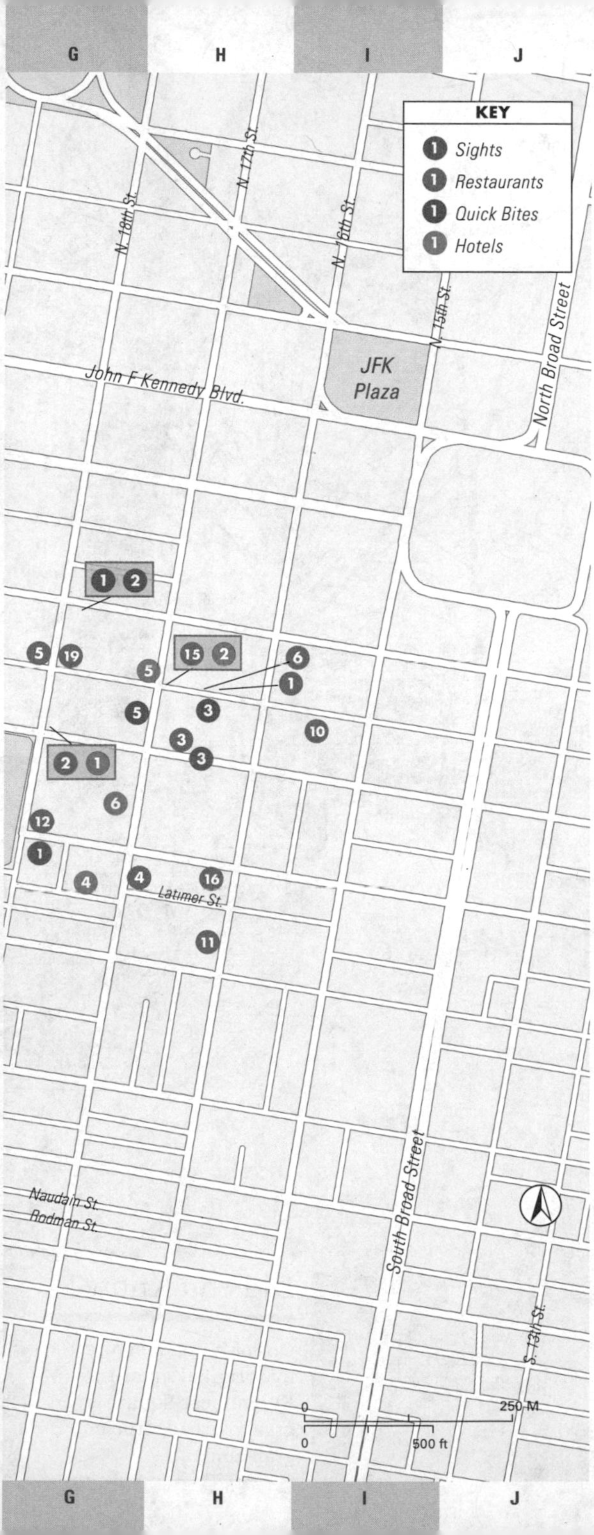

KEY
Sights
Restaurants
Quick Bites
Hotels

Sights

1 Curtis Institute of Music G6
2 Delancey Place E6
3 Rittenhouse Row H5
4 Rittenhouse Square F5
5 Rosenbach Museum and Library E6
6 Schuylkill River Park B5

Restaurants

1 Abe Fisher H5
2 a.kitchen G5
3 Alma de Cuba H5
4 Black Sheep G6
5 The Dandelion G4
6 Dizengoff H5
7 Friday Saturday Sunday E6
8 K'Far F4
9 Lacroix at The Rittenhouse F5
10 Mission Taqueria I5
11 Monk's Cafe H6
12 PARC G5
13 Pub & Kitchen E7
14 Res Ipsa Cafe C4
15 Square 1682 .... H4
16 Tequilas Restaurant H6
17 Tinto Wine Bar E4
18 Townsend D4
19 Tria Cafe Rittenhouse G4
20 Twenty Manning E6
21 Vernick Food & Drink E4

Quick Bites

1 Alimentari at Di Bruno Bros. G4
2 Di Bruno Bros. G4
3 Federal Donuts H4
4 Metropolitan Bakery F6
5 Sip-N-Glo Juicery H4
6 Spread Bagelry E6

Hotels

1 AKA Rittenhouse Square G5
2 Kimpton Hotel Palomar Philadelphia H4
3 The Rittenhouse F5
4 Rittenhouse 1715 .... G6
5 Sofitel Philadelphia at Rittenhouse Square G4
6 Warwick Hotel Rittenhouse Square G5

Did You Know?

One of William Penn's five original squares, Rittenhouse Square is a great place to stroll or grab lunch.

author Henry James. Until 1950 town houses bordered the square, but they have now been replaced on three sides by swank apartment buildings and hotels. Some great houses remain, including the former residence of Henry P. McIlhenny on the southwest corner. If you want to join the office workers who have lunch-hour picnics in the park, you can find many eateries along Walnut, Sansom, and Chestnut Streets east of the square. Or you can dine alfresco at one of several upscale open-air cafés across from the square on 18th Street between Locust and Walnut. The term "Rittenhouse Row" describes the greater Rittenhouse Square area, bordered by Pine, Market, 21st, and Broad Streets. ✉ *Walnut St. between 18th and 19th Sts., Rittenhouse Square.*

Rosenbach Museum and Library

LIBRARY | This 1863 three-floor town house and an adjoining building are filled with Persian rugs and 18th-century British, French, and American antiques (plus an entire living room that once belonged to poet Marianne Moore), but the real treasures are the artworks, books, and manuscripts here. Amassed by Philadelphia collectors Philip H. and A. S. W. Rosenbach, the collection includes paintings by Canaletto, Sully, and Lawrence; drawings by Daumier, Fragonard, and Blake; book illustrations ranging from medieval illuminations to the works of Maurice Sendak, author of *Where the Wild Things Are*; the only known copy of the first issue of Benjamin Franklin's *Poor Richard's Almanack*; and the library's most famous treasure, the original manuscript of James Joyce's *Ulysses.* The Rosenbach celebrates "Bloomsday" on June 16 with readings from *Ulysses* by notable Philadelphians. The library has more than 130,000 manuscripts and 30,000 rare books. ✉ *2008–10 Delancey Pl., Rittenhouse Square* ☎ *215/732–1600* 🌐 *www.rosenbach.org* 🎟 *$10.*

Schuylkill River Park

CITY PARK | **FAMILY** | On any given day, runners, cyclists, walkers, dog walkers, and loungers can be found at the expansive Schuylkill River Park. The park runs along the river from Lombard Street to Manning Street, spanning more than three city blocks on the edge of Center City before University City. Even during the coldest months, the park is packed with people and their dogs in the on-site dog parks, children on the playground, athletes shooting hoops at the basketball courts, and people enjoying the skyline vantage points. ✉ *300 S. 25th St., Rittenhouse Square* ☎ *215/309–5523* 🌐 *www.fsrp.org.*

Restaurants

Abe Fisher

$$ | **EASTERN EUROPEAN** | Having successfully turned the country into Israeli-food addicts, Michael Solomonov and Steve Cook have now turned their attention to the cuisines of the Ashkenazi Jews in Eastern Europe. Chef Yehuda Sichel is at the helm, creating incognito thrillers like matzo ball tamale, smoked salmon tartare, and veal schnitzel tacos. **Known for:** Montreal-style smoked short ribs; happy hour; retro-inspired digs. [$] *Average main: $18* ✉ *1623 Sansom St., Rittenhouse Square* ☎ *215/867–0088* 🌐 *www.abefisherphilly.com* ⏲ *No lunch.*

★ a.kitchen

$$$$ | **MODERN AMERICAN** | Smoke, coal, fire, and ash create a through line for the menu at a.kitchen, on the ground floor of the AKA Hotel. Attired in blond wood and Carrara marble, it looks like a spa in the Italian Alps, and its Rittenhouse address guarantees a scene, but the recent involvement of High Street Hospitality (Fork, High Street on Market) has transformed it into a "serious restaurant" with an ace sommelier and a steak tartare that cannot be missed. **Known for:** seasonal small plates; fresh oysters; sleek interior. [$] *Average main: $25* ✉ *135 S. 18th St.,*

Rittenhouse Square ☎ *215/825–7030* 🌐 *www.akitchenandbar.com.*

Alma de Cuba

$$$$ | **CUBAN** | A bit of scrolled ironwork greets diners, followed by a swank bar pulsating with Cuban music that lets everyone know this is a happening place; find a seat here because you may wait awhile, even with a reservation. The service is a bit chaotic, but the mojitos are refreshing and the menu contains a few genuine dishes, such as *lechon asado* (crispy roasted pork) and a wide selection of ceviche, all prepared by star chef Douglas Rodriguez. **Known for:** pre-Castro Havana decor; lechon asado (crispy roasted pork); refreshing mojitos. 💲 *Average main: $26* ✉ *1623 Walnut St., Rittenhouse Square* ☎ *215/988–1799* 🌐 *www.almadecubarestaurant.com* ⏲ *No lunch.*

Black Sheep

$$ | **IRISH** | Converted from a private club with blacked-out windows, this Dublin-style pub has been packing them in for rivers of Irish draft and kitchen specialties. Guinness-battered fish-and-chips could have been produced on the "auld sod," and the malt vinegar to sprinkle over it all does little to dampen the crisp crust. **Known for:** traditional pub fare; casual atmosphere; vast beer selection. 💲 *Average main: $17* ✉ *247 S. 17th St., Rittenhouse Square* ☎ *215/545–9473* 🌐 *www.theblacksheeppub.com.*

The Dandelion

$$ | **BRITISH** | This Stephen Starr–helmed pub is as close to an English pub as you'll get stateside—there's a snarling bear head mounted on one wall; an assortment of mismatched divans and armchairs; and toasties, fish-and-chips, and puddings on the menu. While the entrées are solid, the apps and desserts shine brightest at this sprawling, cozy venue. **Known for:** happy hour; weekend brunch; Sunday roast. 💲 *Average main: $18* ✉ *124 S. 18th St., Rittenhouse Square* ☎ *215/558–2500* 🌐 *www.thedandelionpub.com.*

Dizengoff

$ | **ISRAELI** | Think of Dizengoff as Zahav lite. This graffiti-tagged spin-off of the nationally acclaimed Israeli restaurant is modeled after the hummus stalls of Tel Aviv, specializing in the dreamy chickpea puree crowned with an array of creative, seasonal toppings. **Known for:** rotating hummus toppings; fluffy pita; frozen lemonanna. 💲 *Average main: $9* ✉ *1625 Sansom St., Rittenhouse Square* ☎ *215/867–8181* 🌐 *www.dizengoffphilly.com.*

★ Friday Saturday Sunday

$$$ | **AMERICAN** | What was once a Rittenhouse institution is now a Rittenhouse darling after the restaurant was sold to husband-and-wife team Chad and Hanna Williams and revitalized as a cozy yet elevated space with boundary-pushing but still familiar food and drinks. The new American fare ranges from a curated raw bar, featuring the likes of oysters and caviar, to delicate pastas coated in punchy sauces with proteins like lobster and pork cheek. **Known for:** delicate pastas; cozy corner setting; raw bar. 💲 *Average main: $24* ✉ *261 S. 21st St., Rittenhouse Square* ☎ *215/546–4232* 🌐 *www.fridaysaturdaysunday.com* ⏲ *Closed Mon. No lunch.*

★ K'Far

$$ | **ISRAELI** | The most exciting Rittenhouse restaurant opening recently is K'Far, one of the latest ventures by James Beard Award–winning chef Michael Solomonov's CookNSolo group. Helmed by Camille Cogswell, the former pastry chef of Solomonov's buzzy Zahav, K'Far is an ode to the all-day bakeries that populate Israel with traditional baked goods, coffee, and Jerusalem bagel sandwiches by morning, here expanded into lunch territory with grain bowls and salads. **Known for:** Jerusalem bagel sandwiches; full bar; fresh baked goods. 💲 *Average main: $15* ✉ *110 S. 19th St., Rittenhouse Square* ☎ *267/800–7200* 🌐 *www.kfarcafe.com.*

★ Lacroix at the Rittenhouse

$$$$ | **ECLECTIC** | Jonathan Cichon has proven himself to be a worthy successor to this luxe establishment and one who forges his own way with graceful dishes using seasonal, prestige ingredients. He is bigger on elegance and shorter on whimsy than his predecessors, with dishes like lobster crepes, and chicken liver and foie gras mousse with watermelon glaze. **Known for:** all-day dining options; Sunday brunch; expansive wine list. *Average main: $45 ✉ 210 W. Rittenhouse Sq., Rittenhouse Square ☎ 215/790–2533 🌐 www.lacroixrestaurant.com.*

★ Mission Taqueria

$ | **MEXICAN** | Within the highbrow Rittenhouse neighborhood, Mission Taqueria is the cool kid in town. Its neon signs, colorful digs, and collaborative games draw the crowds, while the fresh tacos, delectable dips, and margaritas in a multitude of flavors keep them full and happy. **Known for:** happy hour including $3 beer, $2 tacos, and $6 margaritas; cheap drinks and snacks; colorful digs. *Average main: $14 ✉ 1516 Sansom St. , 2nd fl., above Oyster House, Rittenhouse Square ☎ 215/383–1200 🌐 www.missiontaqueria.com.*

Monk's Cafe

$$ | **BELGIAN** | If the rumors are true, and Philadelphians do drink more Belgian beer than Belgians do, then it's because of the owners of Monk's, the seminal café with a pipeline of sours, dubbels, and saisons straight from the motherland. Whether steamed in classic style with white wine and shallots or with cream, mussels are a high point at Monk's and the fries that accompany them draw raves from the regulars who crowd the place. **Known for:** Monk's Café Flemish Sour Ale; mussels; burgers. *Average main: $15 ✉ 264 S. 16th St., Rittenhouse Square ☎ 215/545–7005 🌐 www.monkscafe.com.*

★ PARC

$$$$ | **FRENCH** | Brass rails, silvered mirrors, claret-hued banquettes, and oak wainscoting reclaimed from now-shuttered Parisian restaurants, imbue patina—while small touches like newspapers on wooden poles, create extra realism—in the meticulous stage set placed on Philadelphia's most desirable corner by restaurateur Stephen Starr. Similarly, standard menu items (roasted chicken, trout amandine) hold their own, but the little things—desserts and salads, fresh-baked goods (including house-made macaroons), and excellent onion soup—stand out. **Known for:** onion soup; seafood tower; outdoor dining. *Average main: $25 ✉ 227 S. 18th St., Rittenhouse Square ☎ 215/545–2262 🌐 parc-restaurant.com.*

★ Pub & Kitchen

$$ | **MODERN AMERICAN** | **FAMILY** | Pub & Kitchen has been a favorite since it opened in 2009 with a daily selection of oysters and a menu that includes everything from a sweet-and-savory fried-chicken sandwich to a kick-ass cheeseburger. But even if the food menu wasn't a star, locals would flock to this energetic saloon to unwind with friends or catch the game. **Known for:** draft old-fashioned; weekend brunch; solid beer list. *Average main: $17 ✉ 1946 Lombard St., Rittenhouse Square ☎ 215/545–0350 🌐 www.thepubandkitchen.com ⏲ No lunch weekdays.*

★ Res Ipsa Cafe

$$$ | **AMERICAN** | The all-day café craze is alive and well in Philly, with some of the best spots in the city taking full advantage of the day-to-night trend. One such place is Res Ipsa Cafe, a café by day, serving breakfast sandwiches on house-made English muffins, pastries, protein-packed lunch sandwiches, salads, and more, and BYOB Italian dining experience by night. **Known for:** chef's tasting menu; BYOB format; grab-and-go breakfast sandwiches. *Average main: $20*

✉ 2218 Walnut St., Rittenhouse Square ☎ 267/519–0329 🌐 www.resipsaphilly.com ⏲ No dinner Tues.

Square 1682

$$$ | **MODERN AMERICAN** | With a deal-fueled happy hour and central location, Square 1682 at the Kimpton Hotel Palomar is a go-to spot for Center City dwellers all throughout the year. For dinner, you ascend a floating staircase to an upstairs dining room and settle into a plush banquette to sample deviled duck eggs, kale Caesar, and pea-and-carrot gnocchi scented with vanilla. **Known for:** affordable weeknight happy hour; meat-driven dinner menu; kid-friendly environment. *💲 Average main: $22 ✉ Kimpton Palomar Hotel, 121 S. 17th St., Rittenhouse Square ☎ 215/563–5008 🌐 www.square1682.com.*

Tequila's Restaurant

$$$ | **MEXICAN** | David and Annette Suro opened Tequila's way back in 1986, when the local culinary consciousness wasn't quite as familiar with mole poblano and chiles rellenos as it is now. Fortunately, the space was evocative enough (painted Day of the Dead figures, a long hardwood bar, Mexican glassware, colorful ceramics) to get the curious and unfamiliar in the door. **Known for:** authentic Mexican fare; margarita deals during happy hour; space for big groups. *💲 Average main: $23 ✉ 1602 Locust St., Rittenhouse Square ☎ 215/546–0181 🌐 www.tequilasphilly.com ⏲ No lunch weekends.*

Tinto Wine Bar

$$$$ | **SPANISH** | Chef Jose Garces went to Spain to research food and wine for Amada, his Old City tapas restaurant, and while he was there he fell in love with Basque Country. Tinto is his ode to the bars in San Sebastian that serve up *pinxtos* (small plates), *bocadillos* (sandwiches), charcuterie, and cheeses. **Known for:** paella; pintxo tasting menu; large selection of Spanish wines. *💲 Average main: $25 ✉ 114 S. 20th St., Rittenhouse Square ☎ 215/665–9150 🌐 www.tintorestaurant.com ⏲ No lunch.*

Townsend

$$$$ | **MODERN FRENCH** | Chef Townsend "Tod" Wentz moved his eponymous French eatery to Rittenhouse Square for more space, more foot traffic, and to welcome more visitors who come into town by public transit. The new space is larger and sleeker than the former East Passyunk digs, but the menu is still anchored in traditional French cuisine—think escargots, roasted duck, *pot de crème,* and sauces that cloak the tongue like silk pajamas. **Known for:** tasting menu; thoughtful wine list; late-night industry crowd. *💲 Average main: $28 ✉ 2121 Walnut St., Rittenhouse Square ☎ 267/639–3203 🌐 www.townsendrestaurant.com ⏲ Closed Mon. No lunch.*

Tria Cafe Rittenhouse

$ | **AMERICAN** | Tria's brown interior and minimalist signage give off a wallflower vibe, but the tables packed with chic urbanites grazing lightly contradict its inner beauty. The knowledgeable staff is serious about the restaurant's focus—the "fermentation trio" of wine, cheese, and beer—but not in a snobby way. **Known for:** lively crowd; huge wine list; cheese pairings. *💲 Average main: $12 ✉ 123 S. 18th St., Rittenhouse Square ☎ 215/972–8742 🌐 www.triaphilly.com.*

Twenty Manning

$$$ | **AMERICAN** | Large French windows open up onto the sidewalk where tables are always packed in the warmer months with chic young couples and groups sipping old-fashioneds and Bellinis and supping on plates like oysters on the half, spaghetti Bolognese, and steak tartare toast. **Known for:** prix-fixe options; outdoor seating; daily specials. *💲 Average main: $20 ✉ 261 S. 20th St., Rittenhouse Square ☎ 215/731–0900 🌐 www.twentymanning.com ⏲ No lunch.*

With numerous locations around the city, Federal Donuts is a great snack stop. Try the "fancy" menu—daily and seasonal specials—or the hot menu, i.e. made while you watch.

★ Vernick Food & Drink

$$$$ | **MODERN AMERICAN** | South Jersey native, and James Beard-award winning chef, Greg Vernick spent the bulk of his career opening restaurants around the world for Jean-Georges Vongerichten. When he and his wife, Julie, wanted to do their own place, they came back to the Delaware Valley and made waves with their bustling (but intimate) modern American restaurant whose ever-changing menu features delicious things on toast (avocado, foie gras, Maryland crab), Asian influences, and large-format proteins (whole chicken or rack of lamb) cooked in a wood-burning oven. **Known for:** thoughtful toasts like pumpkin, apple and brown butter or sea scallop and black truffle butter; roasted meats; raw bar. *Average main: $28 2031 Walnut St., Rittenhouse Square 267/639–6644 www.vernickphilly.com Closed Mon. No lunch.*

Coffee and Quick Bites

★ Alimentari at Di Bruno Bros.

$ | **ITALIAN** | Above Di Bruno Bros. Rittenhouse location lives Alimentari, a casual Italian restaurant with plenty of seating and enough space for large groups. **Known for:** mozzarella bar; charcuterie; Italian wine selection. *Average main: $14 1730 Chestnut St., 2nd fl., Rittenhouse Square 267/764–5143 dibruno.com/alimentari/.*

Di Bruno Bros.

$ | **CAFÉ** | This two-level gourmet shop has a dazzling array of prepared foods, mouthwatering pastries, and creamy gelato. Sampling the wares can make for a good snack, but if you require something more substantial, head to the recently redone café upstairs. **Known for:** grab-and-go lunch options; pastries; cheese selection. *Average main: $10 1730 Chestnut St., Rittenhouse Square 215/665–9220 www.dibruno.com.*

★ Federal Donuts

$ | CAFÉ | FAMILY | Cakey doughnuts are the star at this local-to-Philadelphia chain run by chefs Michael Solomonov and Steven Cook of the celebrated CookNSolo restaurants. The menu includes both a "fancy" doughnut menu, which includes daily and seasonal specials, along with a hot doughnut menu, which includes staples that are available throughout the year. **Known for:** inventive doughnut flavors; fried chicken and fried-chicken sandwich; breakfast sandwich. *Average main: $5 1632 Sansom St., Rittenhouse Square 215/665–1101 www.federaldonuts.com.*

Metropolitan Bakery

$ | CAFÉ | FAMILY | This Philadelphia institution was founded on the principle of artisanal baking, which explains why its loaves have such an intense flavor and crackly crust. Stop here for a round of cracked wheat or multigrain or for a small treat such as a chocolatey cookie or lemon bar. **Known for:** fresh breads; pizzas; sandwiches. *Average main: $5 262 S. 19th St., Rittenhouse Square 215/545–6655 bakery, 267/990–8055 café www.metropolitanbakery.com.*

Sip-N-Glo Juicery

$ | CAFÉ | When looking for a post-workout recovery shake, a cold-fighting juice, or a kale-packed smoothie, locals visit Sip-N-Glo Juicery, the city's resident smoothie and juice shop. Opt for one of their made-to-order smoothies for a more substantial snack, or sip a fresh, colorful juice for a lighter option. **Known for:** health-foused smoothies; cold-pressed juices; wheatgrass shots. *Average main: $9 257 S. 20th St., Rittenhouse Square 215/351–9300 www.sipnglo.com.*

★ Spread Bagelry

$ | CAFÉ | FAMILY | This Montreal-style bagel shop operates its self-proclaimed "Spreadquarters" with views of the Schuylkill River and bagels and beer to boot; the Walnut Street shop partnered with Workhorse Brewing Company, a brewery based in King of Prussia, Pennsylvania. The café offers a menu of fresh Spread bagels and bagel sandwiches, in addition to flatbreads, nachos, and other snacks made with Spread bagel dough. **Known for:** bagels; beer; river views. *Average main: $8 2401 Walnut St., Rittenhouse Square 267/692–2435 www.spreadbagelry.com.*

Hotels

AKA Rittenhouse Square

$$$$ | HOTEL | Though steps away from the popular park and surrounding shopping, this former apartment building operates in a below-the-radar fashion favored by visiting actors and athletes; the property offers homey studios and one- and two-bedroom suites that have lots of closet space and full kitchens with dishes, glassware, and large, stainless-steel refrigerators. **Pros:** large rooms; homey amenities and atmosphere; nice restaurant and bar. **Cons:** no parking; no room service; some of the lower rooms have views of a brick wall; gym lacks ample equipment. *Rooms from: $305 135 S. 18th St., Rittenhouse Square 215/825–7000, 888/252–0180 www.hotelaka.com 78 rooms No meals.*

★ Kimpton Hotel Palomar Philadelphia

$$ | HOTEL | FAMILY | The Palomar marks the apex of Philadelphia's recent surge of hip hotels; three brightly colored busts of Ben Franklin greet you in this Kimpton property's chic lobby alongside a comfy fireside living room. **Pros:** superhip yet comfortable; eco-friendly and LEED Gold certified; good location near Rittenhouse Square restaurants. **Cons:** allows pets, including barking dogs; standard rooms are cleverly designed but a bit small; main entrance is along a busy street. *Rooms from: $185 117 S. 17th St., Rittenhouse Square 215/563–5006, 888/725–1778 www.hotelpalomar-philadelphia.com 247 rooms No meals.*

The Rittenhouse

$$$$ | HOTEL | FAMILY | From providing personal items that travelers commonly forget to dressing the pillows of weekend guests with chocolate-covered strawberries, the staff is among the most accommodating in the city. **Pros:** great service without the stuffiness; 24-hour room service; complimentary Wi-Fi; among the largest rooms for luxury hotels; quiet. **Cons:** furniture can seem a bit dated; pricey; valet area can be busy. *Rooms from: $315* ✉ *210 W. Rittenhouse Sq., Rittenhouse Square* ☎ *215/546–9000, 800/635–1042* 🌐 *www.rittenhousehotel.com* *98 rooms* *No meals.*

★ Rittenhouse 1715

$$$$ | HOTEL | On a small street near Rittenhouse Square, this refined, European-style mansion offers the luxury of a large hotel in an intimate space. **Pros:** quiet option for downtown; romantic; unique, boutique-style rooms. **Cons:** no parking service; no laundry service; extra beds are an additional fee. *Rooms from: $300* ✉ *1715 Rittenhouse Sq., Rittenhouse Square* ☎ *215/546–6500, 877/791–6500* 🌐 *www.rittenhouse1715.com* *23 rooms* *Free breakfast.*

Sofitel Philadelphia at Rittenhouse Square

$$$$ | HOTEL | FAMILY | In the middle of the city's French Quarter, this luxury hotel has more of a hip feeling than some of its stuffier Federal-style neighbors. **Pros:** luxury with a hipper feel; excellent location; great service. **Cons:** its central location can make driving in and out of the hotel a pain; can be loud; some travelers complain that the front-desk staff is unfriendly. *Rooms from: $399* ✉ *120 S. 17th St., Rittenhouse Square* ☎ *215/569–8300, 800/763–4835* 🌐 *www.sofitel-philadelphia.com* *373 rooms* *No meals.*

Warwick Hotel Rittenhouse Square

$ | HOTEL | After a recent rebrand and remodel, the Warwick Hotel wlecomes guests into a sleek lobby featuring bulbous pendant lights, fireplaces, pop-art rugs and wall decor, and sofas upholstered with bold fabrics. **Pros:** historic hotel with modern amenities; great location; great service. **Cons:** smallish bathrooms; noise from busy street; expensive parking. *Rooms from: $129* ✉ *220 S. 17th St., Rittenhouse Square* ☎ *215/735–6000, 800/333–3333* 🌐 *www.radisson.com/philadelphiapa* *305 rooms* *No meals.*

Nightlife

BARS AND LOUNGES

a.bar

BARS/PUBS | Attached to the AKA hotel and its restaurant, a.kitchen, a.bar boasts one of the most enviable views in the city, looking right out onto Rittenhouse Square. The food and drink, with its emphases on fresh seafood and cutting-edge cocktails, will encourage return visits. ✉ *AKA Rittenhouse Square, 1737 Walnut St., Rittenhouse Square* ☎ *215/825–7035* 🌐 *www.akitchenandbar.com.*

The Bards

BARS/PUBS | A lively and authentic Irish pub, the Bards has an Irish crowd, Irish food, and a host of full-bodied beers. ✉ *2013 Walnut St., Rittenhouse Square* ☎ *215/569–9585* 🌐 *www.bardsirishbar.com.*

Black Sheep

BARS/PUBS | This handsome pub is just off Rittenhouse Square, in a refurbished town house with a fireplace on the main floor and a quiet dining space on the upper level. Beer lovers can choose from a solid selection of draft, bottled, and canned beers; the food, including U.K.-style entrées like shepherd's pie and bangers and mash, is straightforward and satisfying. ✉ *247 S. 17th St., Rittenhouse Square* ☎ *215/545–9473* 🌐 *www.theblacksheeppub.com.*

The Franklin Mortgage & Investment Co.
BARS/PUBS | One of the city's premier bars for cocktail lovers, the sexy, subterranean Franklin is named after a cover business established by infamous Philly gangster Max "Boo Boo" Hoff. Bartenders whip up potent and elaborate cocktails in a narrow parlor that often requires a wait; upstairs is a Mexican-inspired bar and eatery with Mexican street food and a focus on mezcal and tequila cocktails. ✉ *112 S. 18th St., Rittenhouse Square* ☎ *267/467–3277* 🌐 *www.thefranklinbar.com.*

Tria
BARS/PUBS | Wine, beer, and cheese is the celebrated trio at this branch of the well-loved collection of tasting-friendly bar-restaurants, which also features a lineup of clever small plates. The menu is packed with interesting info, as are the well-versed servers and bartenders. ✉ *123 S. 18th St., Rittenhouse Square* ☎ *215/972–8742* 🌐 *www.triaphilly.com.*

Twenty Manning Grill
BARS/PUBS | The sleek lounge area and bar at this spiffy restaurant-bar is a haven for Rittenhouse regulars, making for some solid people-watching. Though it's largely known in the area as a spot for socializing, it's also an excellent source of creative cocktails and reliable comfort food. ✉ *261 S. 20th St., Rittenhouse Square* ☎ *215/731–0900* 🌐 *www.twenty-manning.com.*

Vango Lounge & Skybar
BARS/PUBS | Upstairs from sister joint Byblos, this lively club and restaurant conjures up a Tokyo vibe, from its largely Japanese-themed menu to its emphasis on mod design. The real star, however, is the third-floor Skybar, offering panoramic views of the city. ✉ *116 S. 18th St., Rittenhouse Square* ☎ *215/568–1020* 🌐 *www.vangoloungeandskybar.com.*

COMEDY CLUBS

Comedy Sportz
COMEDY CLUBS | Anything goes during Comedy Sportz's nights of improvisational comedy, formatted as a high-energy competitive sport. The troupe hosts two shows every Saturday at the Adrienne Theater, while a minor-league troupe performs on Sunday. Audience participation is essential to the experience. ✉ *2030 Sansom St., Rittenhouse Square* ☎ *484/450–8089* 🌐 *www.comedysportz-philly.com.*

Helium Comedy Club
COMEDY CLUBS | Everyone from major comedians to comedy's up-and-comers stops at Rittenhouse Square's Helium Comedy Club, a cozy space where every seat in the house is a good one. In addition to shows featuring big names, the club also hosts open-mic nights, stand-up workshops, and more. ✉ *2031 Sansom St., Rittenhouse Square* ☎ *215/496–9001* 🌐 *philadelphia.heliumcomedy.com.*

DANCE CLUBS

Stir Lounge
DANCE CLUBS | A lesbian-owned bar and club with a dance-loving clientele, Stir prides itself on its inclusive nature and stiff drinks. It's got a primo location in Rittenhouse, though it's tucked out of the way on tiny Chancellor Street. ✉ *1705 Chancellor St., Rittenhouse Square* ☎ *215/732–2700* 🌐 *www.stirphilly.com.*

Performing Arts

CLASSICAL MUSIC

Curtis Institute of Music
MUSIC | The gifted students at this world-renowned music conservatory give free recitals several times a week from October through May. All of its students are on full scholarships; its alumni include such luminaries as Leonard Bernstein, Samuel Barber, and Anna Moffo. The school also has an opera and symphony orchestra series. ✉ *1726 Locust St., Rittenhouse Square* ☎ *215/893–5252*

hotline, 215/893–7902 ticket office ⊕ www.curtis.edu.

OPERA

AVA Opera Theatre

MUSIC | The resident artists at the Academy of Vocal Arts, a four-year, tuition-free vocal training program, present four or five fully staged opera productions during their September to May season. They are accompanied by the Chamber Orchestra of Philadelphia and perform at various venues in and around the city. ✉ *1920 Spruce St., Rittenhouse Square* ☎ *215/735–1685* ⊕ *www.avaopera.org.*

Shopping

There is more local flavor off the beaten path, down numbered streets and smaller streets around Rittenhouse Square. Parking is tough in this area, and you'll pay a pretty penny for a meter or a lot. You'll have more fun and see much more if you walk these lively streets and let yourself get a little lost.

ART GALLERIES

David David Gallery

ART GALLERIES | American and European paintings, drawings, and watercolors from the 16th to the 20th century are on display. ✉ *260 S. 18th St., Rittenhouse Square* ☎ *215/735-2922* ⊕ *www.daviddavidgallery.com* ☞ *Fri.-Sun. by appt. only.*

Gross McCleaf Gallery

ART GALLERIES | This gallery is a good place to see works by both prominent and emerging artists, with an emphasis on Philadelphia painters. The gallery is home to special, often Philadelphia-centric, exhibitions throughout the year. ✉ *127 S. 16th St., between Walnut and Chestnut Sts., Rittenhouse Square* ☎ *215/665–8138* ⊕ *www.grossmccleaf.com* ⏲ *Closed Sun.-Mon.*

The Print Center

ART GALLERIES | The frequent exhibitions at this two-story gallery down a charming side street attract fans of contemporary printmaking and photography. ✉ *1614 Latimer St., Rittenhouse Square* ☎ *215/735–6090* ⊕ *www.printcenter.org/100* ☞ *Closed Sun.-Mon.*

Schwarz Gallery

CRAFTS | American and European paintings of the 18th to 20th century are the focus, with an emphasis on Philadelphia artists. ✉ *1806 Chestnut St., Rittenhouse Square* ☎ *215/563–4887* ⊕ *www.schwarzgallery.com* ⏲ *Closed Sat.-Mon.*

Works on Paper

CRAFTS | The contemporary prints here by American masters like Chuck Close and Robert Rauschenberg and by artists represented by the gallery have won Works on Paper a reputation as one of the city's best. ✉ *1611 Walnut St., Suite B (mezzanine), Rittenhouse Square* ☎ *215/988–9999* ⊕ *www.worksonpaper.biz* ⏲ *Closed Sun.-Mon.*

BOOKSTORES

Fat Jack's Comicrypt

BOOKS/STATIONERY | For more than 30 years, Fat Jack's has been a mecca for local comic devotees with fresh-off-the-presses copies from major and independent publishers, including Japanese mangas plus 3-D posters, action figures, and the obligatory Dungeons & Dragons supplies. ✉ *2006 Sansom St., Rittenhouse Square* ☎ *215/963–0788* ⊕ *www.comicrypt.com.*

Joseph Fox

BOOKS/STATIONERY | Quaint and cozy, this small bookstore specializes in art, architecture, and design—all well organized in diminutive quarters. ✉ *1724 Sansom St., Rittenhouse Square* ✣ *Between 17th and 18th Sts.* ☎ *215/563–4184* ⊕ *www.foxbookshop.com* ⏲ *Closed Sun.*

CLOTHING

★ Anthropologie

CLOTHING | The flagship shop of the locally based national chain takes up three floors of an elegant Rittenhouse Square building (once someone's mansion, of course). The sales floors that encircle the grand stone staircase are brimming with lush colors, floral patterns, and vintage and unique styles that offer a departure from the ordinary. Pretty jewelry, stylish shoes and handbags, and other accessories add an enchanting femininity to fashion. Head downstairs for the brand's BHLDN bridal line featuring an array of dreamy wedding dresses, elegant jewelry, bridesmaid dresses and more. Downstairs also offers a selection of Anthropologie's lauded home line, including candles, glassware, pottery, pillows, and mirrors. Be sure to check out the third floor for racks of bargain-priced sale items, and don't forget to look up at the towering first-floor ceiling of the onetime front parlor. ✉ *1801 Walnut St., Rittenhouse Square* ☎ *215/568–2114* 🌐 *www.anthropologie.com/anthro/index.jsp.*

Born Yesterday

CLOTHING | FAMILY | This shop is filled with unique clothing and toys for haute tots. Specialties include handmade goods, imported fashions, Philadelphia-themed clothing, and styles not available elsewhere. ✉ *1901 Walnut St., Rittenhouse Square* ☎ *215/568–6556* 🌐 *www.bornyesterdaykids.com.*

Boyds

CLOTHING | Beneath the royal-blue canopy and white-marble entrance, you can find a large department store full of avant-garde Italian imports and dozens of other styles and designers, from Oscar de la Renta to Dior. The store has departments for extra tall, large, and short men; formal wear; and shoes; and there's free valet parking, and 60 tailors on the premises. ✉ *1818 Chestnut St., Rittenhouse Square* ☎ *215/564–9000* 🌐 *www.boydsphila.com* ⏲ *Closed Sun.* ☞ *Free valet parking.*

Jacques Ferber

CLOTHING | Since 1879, this famed furrier has been offering high-style furs in sable, mink, and more, as well as shearlings, outerwear, and accessories that make a fashion statement. ✉ *1708 Walnut St., Rittenhouse Square* ☎ *215/735–4173* 🌐 *www.jacquesferber.com.*

Joan Shepp

CLOTHING | Cutting-edge fashion is displayed in a setting reminiscent of a New York loft. Notable designers include Phillip Lim, Ivan Grundahl, Rich Owens, Etro, Marni, Moschino, and shoes by Maison Margiela. ✉ *1811 Chestnut St., Rittenhouse Square* ☎ *215/735–2666* 🌐 *www.joanshepp.com.*

Kiki Hughes

CLOTHING | This funky, luxe boutique on the corner of a residential street stocks unusual garments that stand out for their unexpected twists—a wide-leg pant in black velvet, a white oxford embroidered with flowers—as well as outright showstoppers like Asian tunics with mandarin collars and shimmering silk taffeta skirts. The owner designed the store interior herself, down to the hand-carved vines in the woodwork and the draped-fabric ceiling. ✉ *259 S. 21st St., Rittenhouse Square* ☎ *215/546–1534* 🌐 *www.kikihughes.com* ☞ *Closed Sun.-Mon.*

Skirt

CLOTHING | Personal stylists help you peruse the racks of labels like Vince, DVF, and J Brand at Skirt, whose clean-cut Rittenhouse location recently joined sister stores in Bryn Mawr and Stone Harbor. ✉ *212 S. 17th St., Rittenhouse Square* ☎ *215/309–8419* 🌐 *www.shop-skirt.com.*

Sophy Curson

CLOTHING | In this shop that dates back to 1929, women's fashions from top American and European designers, such as Blumarine and Krizia, are presented in a salon setting, with experienced sales staff selecting the latest styles that are totally you. ✉ *19th St. and Sansom St., Rittenhouse Square* ☎ *215/567–4662* 🌐 *www.sophycurson.com* ⏲ *Closed Sun.*

Urban Outfitters

CLOTHING | What started out as a storefront selling used jeans to students in West Philadelphia is now a trendsetting chain on campuses across the country. Three floors showcase an eclectic array of hip clothing, unusual books, and funky housewares that can go from the dorm room to the family room. ✉ *1627 Walnut St., Rittenhouse Square* ☎ *215/569–3131* 🌐 *www.urbanoutfitters.com/urban/stores/en/urban-outfitters-walnut-street.*

COSMETICS

Bluemercury

PERFUME/COSMETICS | Makeup and skin-care junkies can get their fix at this sleek shop featuring products from Caudalie, Supergoop, Bumble & Bumble, Fresh, Trish McEvoy, Nars, Laura Mercier, and many others. Sweetly scented candles and fragrances in intoxicating blends of fruits and spices fill the shop. In the back of the store, spa services are offered in a serene setting. ✉ *1707 Walnut St., Rittenhouse Square* ☎ *215/569–3100* 🌐 *www.bluemercury.com.*

Kiehl's Since 1851

PERFUME/COSMETICS | Step inside this store and you can feel like you're in an old-world apothecary—with a sleek, modern twist. The staff is friendly and helpful and knows everything about the extensive line of natural lotions, balms, and cosmetics. This chain is known for giving away generous samples. ✉ *The Shops at Liberty Place, 1625 Chestnut St., Rittenhouse Square* ☎ *215/636–9936* 🌐 *www.kiehls.com.*

Lush

PERFUME/COSMETICS | The soaps, lotions, and other unguents made by this Canadian-based chain are so boldly fragrant you can smell the place when you're still half a block away. This pioneer in the organic-cosmetics industry is loved for its ethical sourcing and anti-animal-testing policy as much as it is for its fizzy bath bombs and aromatic (in a good way) lotions and potions. ✉ *1525 Walnut St., Rittenhouse Square* ☎ *215/546–5874* 🌐 *www.lushusa.com.*

Sephora

PERFUME/COSMETICS | Locals rejoiced when the national cosmetic chain finally landed in Center City. It stocks lots of must-have makeup, skin-care, hair-care, and perfume brands, including Bare Minerals, Nars, Benefit, Laura Mercier, and Stila. ✉ *1714 Chestnut St., Rittenhouse Square* ☎ *215/563–6112.*

GIFTS AND SOUVENIRS

Omoi Zakka

GIFTS/SOUVENIRS | Owner Elizabeth Seiber studied in Japan as a teenager and came back with a taste for "zakka" shops—small stores carrying compelling, everyday things. She resolved to create one with Omoi, a cozy space on a residential block that carries cute, kitschy, and charming tchotchkes, jewelry, housewares, and stationery from Japan, France, and other places far and near. ✉ *1608 Pine St., Rittenhouse Square* ☎ *215/545–0963* 🌐 *www.omoionline.com.*

JEWELRY

Egan Day

JEWELRY/ACCESSORIES | A move to the tony Rittenhouse Hotel brought more foot traffic and an ultra-exclusive address to Egan Day's new location. In the new space, it continues to stock fine jewelry by contemporary designers, in addition to home decor, clothing, and giftable items. ✉ *210 W. Rittenhouse Sq., Rittenhouse Square* ☎ *215/433–1632* 🌐 *www.egan-day.com* 🕒 *Closed Sun.-Mon.*

LAGOS–The Store

JEWELRY/ACCESSORIES | Lagos jewelry, sold in upscale department stores, gets top billing here. All pieces are handcrafted and designed in Philadelphia by Steven Lagos. Aficionados are thrilled by the selection at the flagship location, including the Diamonds & Caviar, and Signature designs. ✉ *1735 Walnut St., Rittenhouse Square* ☎ *215/567–0770* 🌐 *www.lagos.com* Ⓜ *15th and Market.*

SHOES

Head Start Shoes

SHOES/LUGGAGE/LEATHER GOODS | Floor-to-ceiling windows showcasing a huge selection of Italian shoes and boots beckon to shoppers passing by this hip shop. Inside you can find footwear in the trendiest styles and of the highest quality. ✉ *126 S. 17th St., Rittenhouse Square* ☎ *215/567-3247* 🌐 *www.headstartshoes.com.*

SPORTING GOODS

Philadelphia Runner

SPORTING GOODS | Specializing in all things running, this independently owned running company offers a selection of sneakers and athletic wear, as well as a special shoe-fitting service to ensure all clients have the shoes that fit their needs. In addition to shopping, the retailer is home to a running club. ✉ *1601 Sansom St., Rittenhouse Square* ☎ *215/972-8333* 🌐 *philadelphiarunner.com/center-city.*

Activities

Hidden River Outfitters

KAYAKING | FAMILY | Departing from the easy-to-get-to Walnut Street Dock at the Schuylkill Banks, Hidden River Outfitters offers patrons a chance to get on the water and into a kayak via an instructor-led kayak tour of the Schuylkill River. The tours head up the river for vantage points of the Fairmount Dam, the Philadelphia Museum of Art, Fairmount Water Works, and the skyline. ✉ *2501 Walnut St., Rittenhouse Square* ☎ *215/309-5523* 🌐 *www.hiddenriveroutfitters.com.*

Chapter 7

PARKWAY MUSEUMS DISTRICT AND FAIRMOUNT PARK

Updated by
Linda Cabasin

Sights	Restaurants	Hotels	Shopping	Nightlife
★★★★★	★★★☆☆	★★☆☆☆	★☆☆☆☆	★★☆☆☆

PHILADELPHIA: AMERICA'S GARDEN CAPITAL

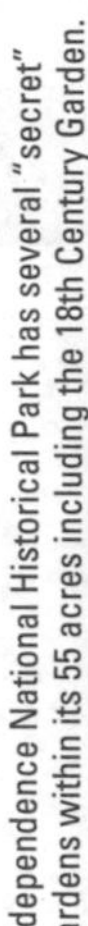

Independence National Historical Park has several "secret" gardens within its 55 acres including the 18th Century Garden.

With over 30 public gardens within 30 miles of the city, Philadelphia lays claim to being "America's Garden Capital." From arboretums to sprawling former estates, there's a garden for everyone.

This horticultural legacy began with Philadelphia's founding, and today garden treasures exist even within the city. William Penn's 1682 plan for a "greene countrie towne" included open green squares, many of which survive. The early Quaker settlers had an interest in nature, and this helped propel the young city as a horticultural center. Another Philadelphia tradition has been the conversion of private gardens to public ones.

WHEN TO GO

Gardens are often loveliest in spring and summer; note that Shofuso and Wyck close in winter. Morris Arboretum and Laurel Hill have vivid colors in fall, and Morris Arboretum runs a miniature holiday garden railway. April brings the city's popular Subaru Cherry Blossom Festival (🌐 *japanphilly.org*); Shofuso and Fairmount Park's Horticulture Center are prime sites. Wyck's roses bloom in June.

HOW TO SEE THE GARDENS

For an overview of area gardens, from wildflower preserves to grand former du Pont estates, see 🌐 *americasgarden-capital.org*; there's also a paper passport/guide. Some, like Bartram's Garden, Wyck, and Laurel Hill Cemetery, are free; tours and events may have a charge, though. There's no overall money-saving pass, but check for any reciprocal garden memberships.

THE CITY'S BEST GARDENS

Bartram's Garden: Quaker John Bartram, who founded the country's oldest surviving botanical garden in 1728, and his son William gathered and studied native plants at this 45-acre National Historic Landmark in southwest Philadelphia. John established a thriving transatlantic trade in plants; today the garden and his home continue to inspire the public. 🌐 *bartramsgarden.org*

Wyck: Relax and smell the roses at this house in Germantown, where nine generations of one family lived, beginning with Quaker owners in 1690. The 1820s rose garden, with its original layout, contains rare, fragrant varieties and fascinating historic plants. There's also a fruit and vegetable farm on-site, as there was for centuries. 🌐 *wyck.org*

Shofuso Japanese House and Garden: A horticultural gem in itself, Fairmount Park holds many surprises, not least of which is an outstanding traditional Japanese garden and a re-creation of a 17th-century guesthouse. A waterfall, koi pond, teahouse, and Japanese trees and shrubs enhance the serene setting. 🌐 *japanphilly.org*

Laurel Hill Cemetery: From its 1836 founding by Quaker John Jay Smith and his partners on a bluff above the Schuylkill, Laurel Hill has been a site for contemplation of nature as well as a final resting place. This Level II arboretum north of East Fairmount Park has river views and winding paths lined by almost 300 kinds of shrubs and trees. 🌐 *thelaurelhillcemetery.org*

Views of historic Laurel Hill Cemetery, which is north of East Fairmount Park.

The beautiful Shofuso Japanese House and Garden is located in Fairmount Park.

Morris Arboretum: In leafy Chestnut Hill, the 175-acre former estate showcases trees and plants from around the globe, cottage and rose gardens, and a Victorian fernery. Now Pennsylvania's official arboretum and part of the University of Pennsylvania, it began in 1887 as the summer home of Quaker brother and sister John and Lydia Morris. 🌐 *morris-arboretum.org*

PHILADELPHIA FLOWER SHOW

This nine-day winter wonder (late February–early March) fills acres of space in the Pennsylvania Convention Center with dramatic displays, gardening demonstrations, and floral competitions galore. The Pennsylvania Horticultural Society (🌐 *phsonline.org*) has sponsored the show (🌐 *theflowershow.com*), the world's longest-running and largest of its type, since 1829. The first show introduced the poinsettia, now a Christmas favorite, to the American public. PHS also supports community gardens and green initiatives.

NEIGHBORHOOD SNAPSHOT

TOP EXPERIENCES

- **Barnes Foundation:** This impressive collection of impressionist, postimpressionist, and early modern art is a unique Philadelphia treasure.
- **Eastern State Penitentiary Historic Site:** Gangster Al Capone lived in this enormous former prison.
- **Fairmount Park:** Boathouse Row and Shofuso Japanese House and Garden are some of this vast park's pleasures.
- **The Franklin Institute:** Learn about science and technology at this interactive museum.
- **Philadelphia Museum of Art:** Modeled after a Greek temple, the building holds one of the country's greatest art collections.
- **Philadelphia Zoo:** The nation's oldest zoo has lions and tigers and bears—oh, my!—as well as all kinds of wildlife.

GETTING HERE

The Parkway is easily walkable from Rittenhouse Square, but it's a 30-minute walk from the far eastern sections of the Historic Area. SEPTA or the seasonal PHLASH are good options. Drivers can find parking on metered spaces along the Parkway or on Pennsylvania Avenue; the Art Museum has a garage.

Boathouse Row on Kelly Drive and portions of Martin Luther King, Jr. Drive are easily reached on foot from the Art Museum. To reach the Philadelphia Zoo or the Please Touch Museum, drive or take SEPTA or PHLASH. The zoo and Please Touch are less than 15-minutes' drive from Center City West.

PLANNING YOUR TIME

The Parkway's trees and flowers are at their most colorful spring through fall. Plan to spend a day here. On Wednesday and Friday, the Philadelphia Museum of Art is open until 8:45 pm.

You can drive to attractions in Fairmount Park. The zoo loop of the hop-on, hop-off Big Bus takes you by some park sights, as does PHLASH.

QUICK BITES

- **Capriccio Café and Bar at Cret Park.** At the eastern end of the Parkway, the cafe is a convenient stop before or after exploring the area for coffee and tea, pastries and sandwiches, and even cocktails. ✉ *110 N. 16th St., Parkway Museums District* 🌐 *www.capricciocafe.com*
- **Cosmic Cafe.** This handy, casual spot has plenty of outdoor seating (and some indoors) and serves all-day breakfasts, plus sandwiches, soups, yogurts, and snacks prepared fresh on-site. ✉ *1 Boathouse Row, at Lloyd Hall, Fairmount Park* 🌐 *cafe.cosmicfoods.com*
- **OCF Coffee House.** Across from Eastern State Penitentiary, pop in for coffee and tea, breakfast, snack, and lunch choices (including vegetarian and vegan options). ✉ *2100 Fairmount Ave., Parkway Museums District* 🌐 *www.ocfrealty.com/coffee-house*

GOOD TO KNOW

- The iconic Love Park Welcome Center got a facelift in 2020 and is now home to Loveluck, a new 50-seat restaurant.

Alive with flowers, flags, and fountains, the Benjamin Franklin Parkway stretches northwest from John F. Kennedy Plaza to the Kelly (East) and MLK Jr. (West) River drives. This 250-foot-wide boulevard is crowned by the Philadelphia Museum of Art and other cultural institutions. To its north is the residential Fairmount neighborhood; to its northwest lies Fairmount Park.

The Parkway district adjoins the Fairmount neighborhood, named for the hill that is the site of the Philadelphia Museum of Art. This boulevard continues to expand its cultural footprint: at this writing, plans call for development in 2021 of a Herzog & de Meuron–designed space opposite the Barnes Foundation that will hold changing displays of works by sculptor and artist Alexander Calder, who is the third generation of Calders whose creations can be seen in Philadelphia.

Nearby, 2,000-acre Fairmount Park encompasses natural areas—woodlands, meadows, rolling hills, two scenic waterways, and a forested 5½-mile gorge. It also contains tennis courts, ball fields, playgrounds, trails, exercise courses, several celebrated cultural institutions, and some historic Early American country houses that are operated by various cultural institutions and open to visitors. Philadelphia has more works of outdoor art than any other city in North America, and more than 200—including statues by Frederic Remington, Jacques Lipchitz, and William Rush—are scattered throughout Fairmount Park. Some sections of the park that border depressed urban neighborhoods are neglected; it's better maintained along the Schuylkill.

Parkway Museums District

Modeled after the Champs-Élysées in Paris, the Benjamin Franklin Parkway (or simply, the Parkway, as locals call it) is the Philadelphia's grand boulevard. French architects Jacques Gréber and Paul Cret—the latter taught at the University of Pennsylvania—designed the Parkway in the 1920s. Stretching from City Hall to Logan Circle to the Art Museum on a diagonal and lined with international flags, the Parkway is where you'll find many of the city's major museums and institutions (as well as apartment buildings and some hotels), from the Franklin Institute to the Barnes Foundation to the Parkway Central Library. Near the last of these, at Vine and 17th Streets, the granite, neoclassical Philadelphia Pennsylvania Temple of the Church of Jesus Christ of Latter-Day Saints (closed to non-Mormons) rises dramatically, with a statue of the angel Moroni atop the highest spire. On a beautiful day, the Parkway is the most majestic stroll in town. Or you can grab a bike and ride the Parkway past the Art Museum into Fairmount Park. Just watch out for the *Rocky* runners.

Located north of the Parkway, Fairmount is a residential district popular with young families and the eds-and-meds crowd. It shares a name with nearby Fairmount Park but lies east of it. Mature trees, 19th-century row houses, and some new housing line the sleepy, strollable streets behind the main commercial strip, Fairmount Avenue. The neighborhood is also home to the hulking Eastern State Penitentiary, a decommissioned prison, now a historic site and a popular visitor attraction, that becomes a spectacular haunted house at Halloween.

VISITOR INFORMATION

Parkway Museums District website

The website of the Parkway Council, a group of institutions and businesses in the Parkway area, has historical and practical information, including public transportation and parking tips. It also offers coupons for $2–$5 off adult admission to five attractions. ✉ *Parkways Museum District* 🌐 *www.parkwaymuseumsdistrictphiladelphia.org.*

Academy of Natural Sciences of Drexel University

MUSEUM | **FAMILY** | The more than 35 dioramas of animals from around the world displayed in their natural habitats give this natural history museum an old-fashioned charm, but the most popular attraction is Dinosaur Hall, with reconstructed skeletons of a Tyrannosaurus rex and some 30 others of its ilk. Other popular areas are the "Big Dig," where you can hunt for real fossils, and "Outside-In," an interactive area where kids ages three–eight can climb into an eagle's nest, explore a sandy beach, and more. Another draw is "Butterflies!," where colorful, winged creatures take flight in a tropical garden setting. Founded in 1812, the academy is considered the oldest science-research institution in the western hemisphere and a world leader in the fields of natural-science research, education, and exhibition; the present building dates from 1876. Weekdays and late afternoons are generally less busy times to visit. ✉ *1900 Benjamin Franklin Pkwy., at 19th St., Parkways Museum District* ☎ *215/299–1000* 🌐 *ansp.org* 🎫 *$22; $20 if purchased online.*

★ Barnes Foundation

MUSEUM | One man's collection and now a Parkway treasure, the Barnes Foundation displays some of the most fabled paintings of impressionist, postimpressionist, and modern art—181 Renoirs, 69 Cézannes, 59 Matisses, 46 Picassos, 7 van Goghs, 6 Seurats, and plenty more—in a soaring, modern, limestone-and-glass museum. Highlights include Cézanne's *The Card Players*, Georges Seurat's *Models*, van Gogh's *The Postman (Joseph-Etienne Roulin)*, Monet's *Studio Boat*, Matisse's *La Danse I* triptych mural, Renoir's *The Artist's Family*, and Picasso's *Acrobat and Young Harlequin*. The collection was amassed after 1912 in Merion, Pennsylvania, by Dr. Albert C. Barnes (1872–1951), who made his fortune as co-inventor of an antiseptic; he conceived the foundation as an educational institution.

Barnes wanted to help people "see as an artist saw," and to do this, he created each gallery wall as an "ensemble" that reflected visual relationships: a Picasso could hang side by side with an African sculpture, and below an Old Master sketch and an iron door hinge. Barnes's will decreed that nothing in the displays could be changed, so when the collection moved—lock, stock, and Modigliani—to the Parkway in 2012, the

Set on four-and-a-half acres on the Ben Franklin Parkway, the Barnes Foundation features plenty of places to sit and reflect, including two outdoor water features.

building's rooms and arrangements were re-created within a spacious modern structure that contains special exhibition galleries and a large, high-ceilinged court where visitors can sit and reflect. ✉ *2025 Benjamin Franklin Pkwy., Parkways Museum District* ☎ *215/278–7000* 🌐 *www.barnesfoundation.org* 🎫 *$25* ⏲ *Closed Tues.*

Cathedral Basilica of Saints Peter and Paul
RELIGIOUS SITE | The basilica of the archdiocese of Philadelphia is the spiritual center for the Philadelphia area's 1.3 million Roman Catholics. Topped by a huge, distinctive copper dome, the large brownstone building was built between 1846 and 1864 in the Italian Renaissance style. Many of the interior decorations are by Constantino Brumidi, who painted the dome of the U.S. Capitol. Several Philadelphia bishops and archbishops are buried beneath the altar. Pick up a brochure for a self-guided tour by the entrance or gift shop, or see the website. ✉ *1723 Race St., at 18th St. and Benjamin Franklin Parkway, Parkways Museum District* ☎ *215/561–1313* 🌐 *cathedralphila.org* 🎫 *Free.*

Eastern State Penitentiary Historic Site
JAIL | Designed by John Haviland and built in 1829, Eastern State was at the time the most expensive building in America; this massive structure influenced international penal design and was the model for some 300 prisons from China to South America. Its system of solitary confinement (to encourage reflection and penitence) and firm discipline was ultimately recognized as flawed. Before it closed in 1971, the now-crumbling, atmospheric prison was home to Al Capone, Willie Sutton, and Pep the Dog, who allegedly killed the cat that belonged to a governor's wife. The excellent audio tour of the prison features narration by actor Steve Buscemi, and some thoughtful exhibits examine issues relating to criminal justice reform. You can also take a guided tour; check online in advance. The penitentiary, just a half mile north of the Rodin Museum, hosts changing art installations and Terror

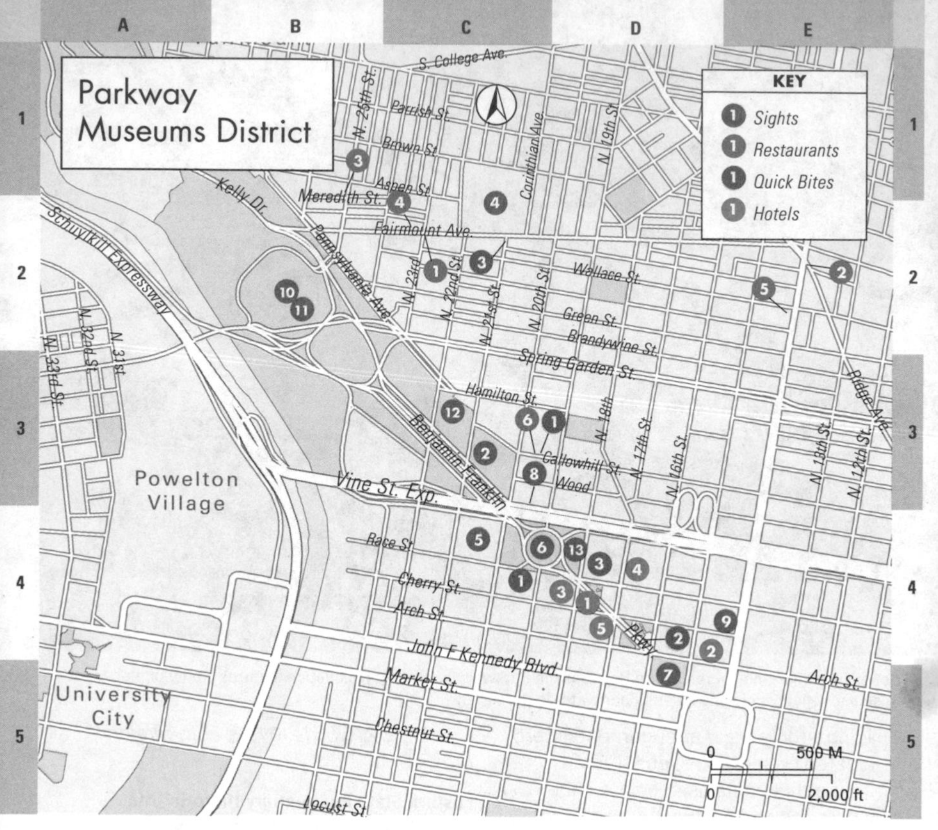

Sights

1. Academy of Natural Sciences of Drexel University **C4**
2. Barnes Foundation **C3**
3. Cathedral Basilica of Saints Peter and Paul **D4**
4. Eastern State Penitentiary Historic Site **C2**
5. The Franklin Institute **C4**
6. Logan Circle **D4**
7. LOVE Park **D5**
8. Parkway Central Library **C3**
9. Pennsylvania Academy of the Fine Arts **D4**
10. Philadelphia Museum of Art **B2**
11. The Rocky Statue and the "Rocky Steps" **B2**
12. Rodin Museum **C3**
13. Sister Cities Park **D4**

Restaurants

1. A Mano **C2**
2. Cicala **E2**
3. Figs **B2**
4. La Calaca Feliz **C2**
5. Osteria **E2**
6. Pizzeria Vetri **C3**

Quick Bites

1. Buena Onda **C3**
2. Capriccio Café and Bar at Cret Park **D4**
3. OCF Coffee House **C2**

Hotels

1. Embassy Suites by Hilton Philadelphia Center City **D4**
2. Le Méridien Philadelphia **D4**
3. The Logan Philadelphia, Curio Collection by Hilton **D4**
4. Philadelphia 201 Hotel **D4**
5. The Windsor Suites **D4**

Behind the Walls, a very popular group of haunted house experiences, around Halloween. At this writing, work was beginning on a new visitor center, but the site is still open. Also, most areas you visit are unheated, so bundle up well in winter. ✉ *2027 Fairmount Ave., at 22nd St., Fairmount* ☎ *215/236–3300* 🌐 *www.easternstate.org* 🎫 *$16 (check for online discount); seasonal Halloween-themed night attraction (separate admission; reserve in advance) "Terror Behind the Walls" $30–$50.*

★ The Franklin Institute

MUSEUM | FAMILY | Founded in 1824 to honor Benjamin Franklin, this large science museum is as clever as its namesake, thanks to many dazzling hands-on exhibits. To optimize your time, study the daily schedule of demonstrations and events online before visiting. Weekday afternoons are less busy. You can sit in the cockpit of a T-33 jet trainer and trace the route of a corpuscle through an enormous artificial heart (15,000 times life size). Popular exhibits include **Electricity**, which focuses on sustainable energy and displays Franklin's famous lightning rod; and **Changing Earth.** Don't miss the 30-ton white-marble statue of Franklin; you can see the likeness (and an accompanying 3½-minute multimedia presentation) without paying admission.

The **Franklin Air Show** celebrates powered flight with the Wright Model B Flyer and has virtual reality flight simulator experiences. Visitors to the interactive **Tech Studio** can engage with tech design processes. **The Sports Zone** conveys the physics, physiology, and material science behind your favorite sport by simulating surfing, testing your reaction time, and more. Shows in the **Fels Planetarium** focus on the stars, space exploration, comets, and other phenomena, and the Tuttleman iMAX Theater screens recent Hollywood films and special documentaries. Two **Escape Rooms** require an extra fee. ✉ *222 N. 20th St., at Benjamin Franklin Pkwy., Parkways Museum District* ☎ *215/448–1200* 🌐 *www.fi.edu* 🎫 *$23–$35 for adult admission and passes; some exhibitions require additional fees.*

Logan Circle

PLAZA | The focal point of Logan Circle, one of the city's gems, is the **Swann Fountain** of 1920, designed by Alexander Stirling Calder, son of Alexander Milne Calder, who created the William Penn statue atop City Hall. You can find many works by a third generation of the family, noted modern sculptor Alexander Calder (1898–1976), the mobile- and stabile-maker, in the nearby **Philadelphia Museum of Art.** The main figures in the fountain symbolize Philadelphia's three leading waterways: the Delaware and Schuylkill rivers and Wissahickon Creek. Around Logan Circle are some examples of Philadelphia's magnificent collection of outdoor art, including *General Galusha Pennypacker,* the Shakespeare Memorial (*Hamlet and the Fool,* by Alexander Stirling Calder), and *Jesus Breaking Bread.* One of William Penn's five squares, Logan Circle was originally a graveyard and execution grounds. In 1825 the square was named for James Logan, Penn's secretary; in the 20th century it became a circle. ✉ *Benjamin Franklin Pkwy., at 19th St., Parkways Museum District.*

LOVE Park

PLAZA | Also known as John F. Kennedy Plaza, LOVE Park at the start of the Parkway is the place to get your photo with *LOVE,* Robert Indiana's iconic red sculpture . You may need to stand in line awhile to do so, but people are quick and cheerful. The 6-foot sculpture, standing atop a 7-foot base, was placed in this area for the City of Brotherly Love's Bicentennial celebrations in 1976. (Another iteration of the sculpture is on the University of Pennsylvania campus.) Revamped in 2018, the plaza has a fountain, views of City Hall and the Parkway, and an *I "HEART" Philly* sculpture. It

One of the city's iconic sights, Robert Indiana's *LOVE* Sculpture can be found in John F. Kennedy Plaza (a.k.a Love Park), which is northwest of City Hall.

serves as the site of civic happenings like the Christmas Village Market, too. The southwest corner has a flying saucer–like building (a former visitor center from the mid-20th century) with large glass windows. At this writing it's due to become a restaurant called Loveluck, from popular local restaurateurs Safran Turney Hospitality, by late summer 2020. ✉ *Between 15th and 16th Sts., between Arch St. and John F. Kennedy Blvd., Parkways Museum District.*

Parkway Central Library

LIBRARY | Philadelphia calls its public-library system, founded in 1891, the Fabulous Freebie, and the central library embraces the present in ways that go beyond its more than 1 million volumes. A grand entrance hall, marble staircase, and enormous reading rooms make this Greek Revival building look the way libraries should, but it also holds a welcoming area for community gatherings, a space with practical business resources, and galleries with changing exhibitions. With more than 12,000 musical scores, the Edwin S. Fleisher collection (appointment recommended) is the largest of its kind in the world. The rare-book department is a beautiful suite of rooms housing first editions of Dickens, ancient Sumerian clay tablets, and medieval and other manuscripts, including the only known handwritten copy of Poe's "The Raven." (Also here is a taxidermied Grip, Dickens's pet raven.) The children's department houses the city's largest collection of children's books in a made-for-kids setting, and there's a special area for teens. **■TIP→ Check the website for events such as author readings, exhibits, and tours of parts of the library.** ✉ *1901 Vine St. , between 19th St. and Benjamin Franklin Pkwy., Parkways Museum District* ☎ *215/686–5322* 🌐 *freelibrary.org* 🎟 *Free.*

★ Pennsylvania Academy of the Fine Arts

MUSEUM | This High Victorian Gothic structure is a work of art in itself. Designed in 1876 by the noted, and sometimes eccentric, Philadelphia architects Frank Furness and George Hewitt, the multicolor stone-and-brick exterior is an extravagant blend of columns, friezes, and Richardsonian Romanesque and Moorish flourishes. The interior is just as lush, with rich hues of red, yellow, and blue and an impressive staircase. The nation's first art school and museum (founded in 1805) displays a fine collection that ranges from the Peale family, Gilbert Stuart, Benjamin West, and Winslow Homer to Andrew Wyeth and Red Grooms. *Fox Hunt* by Winslow Homer, and *The Artist in His Museum* by Charles Willson Peale, are just a few notable works. The academy faculty has included Thomas Sully, Charles Willson Peale, and Thomas Eakins. The latter painted what is now the museum's most prized work, *The Gross Clinic,* a dramatic depiction of Samuel D. Gross, a celebrated 19th-century surgeon, presiding over an operation under a skylighted roof; the masterwork is co-owned with the Philadelphia Museum of Art, and is displayed for six months at a time at each institution.

Supplementing the permanent collection are constantly changing exhibitions of sculptures, paintings, and mixed-media artwork in the adjacent Samuel M. V. Hamilton Building; the 11-story facility, which opened for the academy's 200th anniversary, is also the home to the Sculpture Study Center, which offers changing displays from the permanent collection, classrooms, group and private studios for more than 300 students, and Portfolio, the museum's gift shop. The 1400 block of Cherry Street, which runs between the two buildings, is a pedestrian plaza featuring *Paint Torch,* a 53-foot-tall sculpture of a paintbrush by Claes Oldenburg; Grumman Greenhouse, a Cold War–era plane sculpture by a Pennsylvania Academy of the Fine Arts graduate; a three-part serpentine bench, and outdoor seating. ✉ *118–128 N. Broad St., at Cherry St., Parkways Museum District* ☎ *215/972–7600* 🌐 *www.pafa.org* 🎫 *$15* 🕒 *Closed Mon.*

★ Philadelphia Museum of Art

MUSEUM | Set on a hill in a majestic 1928 building modeled after Greek temples, the city's premier cultural attraction is one of the country's leading art museums, with permanent collections focused on European, American, and Asian art. The museum's east entrance is the well-known site of the "Rocky steps," with people running up the 72 steps immortalized in the movie *Rocky* and lining up at street level for photos with A. Thomas Schomberg's *Rocky* statue. The museum is undergoing a massive multiyear reorganization and mostly underground expansion, based on a plan by Frank Gehry, but galleries remain open. The long-closed north entrance, at street level, has reopened; the now-closed west entrance will open during 2020. New, expanded first-floor galleries dedicated to the art of the Americas will open in late 2020. The John G. Johnson Collection covers Western art from the Renaissance to the 19th century; the Arensberg and A. E. Gallatin collections contain modern works by artists such as Brancusi, Braque, Matisse, and Picasso. Famous paintings include Van Eyck's *St. Francis Receiving the Stigmata,* van Gogh's *Sunflowers,* and Cézanne's *The Large Bathers.* The museum has the world's most extensive collection of works by Marcel Duchamp (*Nude Descending a Staircase*) and fine works by 19th-century Philadelphia artist Thomas Eakins. Some of the most spectacular objects are structures and rooms moved from around the world, such as a 17th-century Chinese palace hall and a Japanese teahouse. Children like the Kienbusch Collection of Arms and Armor. There's an outdoor sculpture garden, and the Perelman Building, across the street, presents exhibitions of photography, costume, and contemporary design. Museum visitors can eat in the Gehry-designed restaurant or café, and Friday evenings feature live music and food. ✉ *2600 Benjamin Franklin Pkwy., Parkways Museum District*

The Parkway Museums District is home to many of the city's museums and institutions including the Philadelphia Museum of Art (pictured), the Franklin Institute, and the Barnes.

215/763–8100 www.philamuseum.org $25 for 2-day access including the Rodin Museum and (when open) two historic houses; 1st Sun. of each month and every Wed. after 5 pm, pay what you wish Closed Mon.

The Rocky Statue and the "Rocky Steps"
PUBLIC ART | Created by artist A. Thomas Schomberg for the 1980 film *Rocky III*, the life-size statue was donated by the film's director and star, Sylvester Stallone, to the City of Philadelphia after filming. The statue has moved around, but since 2006, it's been located at the bottom of Philadelphia Museum of Art's stairs where it continues to be one of the city's most popular destinations as visitors lineup to get their selfie with the bronze version of the "Italian Stallion." *2600 Benjamin Franklin Pkwy., Parkways Museum District.*

★ Rodin Museum
MUSEUM | This small jewel of a museum holds the biggest collection outside France—almost 150 bronzes, plasters, and marbles—of the work of sculptor Auguste Rodin (1840–1917). Movie theater owner Jules Mastbaum acquired the works to found the museum, which opened in 1929. The building, designed by French architects Jacques Gréber and Paul Cret, honors Cret's original idea that inside and out offer a "unified setting" for the presentation of sculpture. Entering the museum, you pass through a landscaped courtyard to reach Rodin's *Gates of Hell*—a 21-foot-high sculpture with more than 100 human and animal figures. In the exhibition hall, the sculptor's masterworks are made even more striking by the use of light and shadow. The museum rotates works in thematic shows every two years but may include major works like *The Kiss, The Burghers of Calais, Balzac,*and *Eternal Springtime.* *2151 Benjamin Franklin Pkwy., between 21st and 22nd Sts., Parkways Museum District 215/763–8100 www.rodinmuseum.org $12 suggested donation; $25 2-day ticket with access to the Philadelphia Museum of Art and Perelman Building, and historic houses Mount Pleasant and Cedar Grove Closed Tues.*

Sister Cities Park
CITY PARK | FAMILY | Marking the city's connections with Florence, Italy; Tel Aviv, Israel; and eight other "sister cities," this small park has a prime location near Logan Circle, the Logan Philadelphia hotel, and the Cathedral Basilica of Saints Peter and Paul. The park is home to Robert Indiana's *AMOR* (Spanish and Latin for "love") sculpture, a companion to nearby LOVE Park's famous *LOVE*. An extensive play area for kids inspired by the local Wissahickon watershed features a rocky area to explore, discovery garden, and toy-sailboat pond; there's also a fountain kids can play in. The seasonal café (closed mid-December–early March), in an attractive building with floor-to-ceiling windows, has some kid-friendly fare. ✉ *210 N. 18th St., at Benjamin Franklin Pkwy., Parkways Museum District* ☎ *215/440–5500* 🌐 *centercityphila.org/parks/sister-cities-park* 🎫 *Free.*

Restaurants

A Mano
$$$$ | ITALIAN | The name of this cash-only, local-favorite BYOB from Townsend Wentz (of Townsend and Oloroso) means "by hand," and the sophisticated, well-crafted Italian dishes reflect careful attention to seasonal ingredients. Settle into the cozy, serene dining room with its green banquettes, white walls, and wooden tables and chairs; then put together your meal from the flavorful choices: an antipasti board, superb handmade pastas, mains including fish and meat choices, and satisfying sides. **Known for:** abbondanza, a four-course prix-fixe option; multiregion Italian fare; half portions of pastas. $ *Average main: $29* ✉ *2244 Fairmount Ave., Fairmount* ☎ *215/236–1114* 🌐 *www.amanophl.com* ⏲ *Closed Mon. No lunch* 💳 *No credit cards.*

★ Cicala
$$$$ | ITALIAN | Once the Divine Lorraine on North Broad Street's extensive remodel was complete, Cicala became the focal point of the neighborhood. A new restaurant from husband and wife Joe and Angela Cicala, the restaurant celebrates the food and drink of Southern Italy, along with the important history of the Divine Lorraine, which was home to some of the wealthiest Philadelphia residents in the 19th and 20th centuries, and later turned into the first fully racially integrated hotel in the country. **Known for:** fresh pastas; coal-grilled meats; Italian pastries. $ *Average main: $25* ✉ *699 N. Broad St., Fairmount* ☎ *267/886–9334* 🌐 *www.cicalarestaurant.com* ⏲ *No lunch.*

Figs
$$$ | MEDITERRANEAN | Away from the Parkway, this intimate, cash-only BYOB focuses on the flavors of Morocco and the Mediterranean, setting the mood with simple decor including Moroccan lamps, trays, and decorative items. The baked Brie in clay pot appetizer with honey and almonds is a standout; usually there's a good *tagine* (stew of meat or poultry simmered with vegetables, olives, garlic, and spices) on the menu, and fish options are plentiful. **Known for:** Mediterranean tapas plate; varied lunch menu; choices for non-meat eaters. $ *Average main: $24* ✉ *2501 Meredith St., Fairmount* ☎ *215/978–8440* 🌐 *www.figsrestaurant.com* 💳 *No credit cards* ⏲ *Closed Mon.*

La Calaca Feliz
$$ | MEXICAN | FAMILY | A colorful mural of freewheeling Day of the Dead skeletons gives this cheerful Fairmount cantina its name, but the polished ceviches, tacos, and enchiladas from Jose Garces veteran Tim Spinner are what will really make you happy. A deep tequila library informs the bar and cocktail list; try a flight of añejos or margaritas in flavors like lychee and chili. **Known for:** worthy happy hours;

Benjamin Franklin in Philadelphia

Unlike the bronze statue of William Penn perched atop City Hall, a marble likeness of Benjamin Franklin, the Benjamin Franklin National Memorial, is within **The Franklin Institute.** Perhaps that's as it should be: noble-born Penn above the people and common-born Franklin sitting more democratically among them.

Franklin (1706–90) was anything but a common man, though. In fact, biographer Walter Isaacson called him "the most accomplished American of his age." Franklin's insatiable curiosity, combined with his ability to solve problems in his own life, inspired his invention of bifocals, an odometer to measure postal routes, a "long arm" to reach books high on his shelves, and a flexible urinary catheter for his brother who was suffering with kidney stones. His great intellect inspired his launching of the American Philosophical Society, the oldest learned society in America. He was the only Founding Father who shaped and signed all of the nation's founding documents, including the Declaration of Independence, the Constitution, and treaties with France and England. He was a citizen of the world—a representative in the Pennsylvania General Assembly, a minister to France.

It's fortunate for Philadelphians that Franklin spent so many of his 84 years here. That might have been an act of fate or early recognition that "time is money," as he wrote in *Advice to a Young Tradesman* in 1748. Born in Boston in 1706, Franklin ran away from home and the oppression of his job as a printer's apprentice at his brother's shop. When he couldn't find work in New York, he didn't waste time; he moved on to Philadelphia. Within 10 years Franklin had opened his own printing office. His *Pennsylvania Gazette* was the most successful newspaper in the colonies; his humor propelled his *Poor Richard's Almanack* to best-seller status in the colonies. Learn more about Franklin's legacy at the engaging, lively **Benjamin Franklin Museum** in the **Franklin Court** complex, site of Ben's first permanent home in Philadelphia, and check out Franklin's Printing Office. At the nearby **B. Free Franklin Post Office & Museum**, you can get a letter hand-stamped with a "B. Free Franklin" cancellation.

Franklin had time and passion for civic duties. As postmaster, he set up the city's postal system. He founded the city's first volunteer fire company and the **Library Company of Philadelphia,** its first subscription library. After his famous kite experiment, he opened the first fire-insurance company, the **Philadelphia Contributionship for the Insurance of Houses from Loss by Fire.** He proposed the idea for the **University of Pennsylvania** and personally raised money to finance **Pennsylvania Hospital**, one of the nation's oldest hospitals.

Franklin was laid to rest alongside his wife, Deborah, and one of his sons, Francis, in the **Christ Church Burial Ground.**

vegetarian options; patio dining in season. $ *Average main: $17 ✉ 2321 Fairmount Ave., Fairmount ☎ 215/787–9930 🌐 www.lacalacafeliz.com ⏲ No lunch weekdays.*

Osteria

$$$$ | ITALIAN | After changing hands a number of times, Osteria is now under the careful direction of chef Jeff Michaud. The menu has everything from amazing brick-oven pizzas (try the Lombarda, with sausage and a soft-cooked egg) to delicate pastas tossed in creamy sauces to a 32-ounce rib-eye steak for two. **Known for:** house-made pastas; wood-fired pizza; 300-bottle Italian wine list. $ *Average main: $25 ✉ 640 N. Broad St., Fairmount ☎ 215/763–0920 🌐 www.osteriaphilly.com ⏲ No lunch.*

Pizzeria Vetri

$ | PIZZA | FAMILY | Started by noted Philly chef Marc Vetri, this small, very casual spot catercorner to the Barnes Foundation takes wood-fired pizza seriously, creating personal and larger-size pies both deliciously traditional (margherita, mushroom, and pepperoni) and more creative (seasonal wild boar pizza, fennel sausage, and others). Antipasti and salad bowls round out the menu, along with cocktails, wines, and a beer list with some good local juices: enjoy it all at the small bar or one of the communal wooden tables at this often-busy eatery. **Known for:** rotolo (pizza dough wrapped around mortadella and ricotta); fried pizza dough with nutella; soft-serve ice cream. $ *Average main: $14 ✉ 1939 Callowhill St., Fairmount ☎ 215/600–2629 🌐 pizzeriavetri.com.*

Coffee and Quick Bites

Buena Onda

$ | MEXICAN | Philadelphia chef-darling Jose Garces's beachy, casual spot in the City of Brotherly love serves Baja Peninsula–inspired fare that can be eaten in or taken away. Tacos, quesadillas, and margaritas rule the menu, but the buena bowls are good choices, too, as are the happy–hour specials. **Known for:** grilled fish tacos; frozen margaritas; great location near the museums, including the Barnes. $ *Average main: $10 ✉ 1901 Callowhill St., Fairmount ☎ 215/302–3530 🌐 www.buenaondatacos.com.*

Capriccio Café and Bar at Cret Park

$ | CAFÉ | At the far eastern end of the Parkway sits this small café, a glass-enclosed pavilion that offers good views of City Hall. On the menu are a range of good hot and cold coffee-based drinks, along with breakfast items, pastries, and familiar sandwiches and salads; you can also have a cocktail, beer, or wine at the little bar or at your table. **Known for:** alfresco dining or sipping in season; convenient spot at beginning or end of Parkway exploration; good pastries and cookies. $ *Average main: $7 ✉ 110 N. 16th St., in Cret Park, Parkways Museum District ☎ 215/735–9797 🌐 www.capricciocafe.com ⏲ No dinner.*

OCF Coffee House

$ | CAFÉ | At this large café opposite Eastern State Penitentiary, the tall windows, high ceilings with exposed ductwork, and dozens of wooden tables create an airy, casual space for trying delicious La Colombe coffee with breakfast, lunch, or a snack. The students and families who flock here appreciate the many fresh-tasting gluten-free and vegetarian options on the menu, as well as the build-your-own egg sandwiches, melts and other sandwiches, and salads. **Known for:** Fairmount Reuben; vegan pancakes and bagels; long list of tea choices as well as coffee drinks. $ *Average main: $9 ✉ 2100 Fairmount Ave., Fairmount ☎ 267/773–8081 🌐 www.ocfrealty.com/coffee-house ⏲ No dinner.*

Embassy Suites by Hilton Philadelphia Center City
$$ | **HOTEL** | **FAMILY** | The suites at this practical chain hotel on Logan Square, within walking distance of Boathouse Row, have separate living rooms with sofa beds, as well as kitchenettes and dining areas; many have stunning views of nearby Fairmount Park. **Pros:** spacious suites are good for families; plenty of restaurants nearby; good value compared to neighboring hotels. **Cons:** high-priced valet parking; often a wait for the elevators; basic decor. *Rooms from: $169 1776 Benjamin Franklin Pkwy., Parkways Museum District 215/561–1776, 800/362–2779 hilton.com/en/embassy 288 rooms Free breakfast.*

The Logan Philadelphia, Curio Collection by Hilton
$$$$ | **HOTEL** | The former home of the Four Seasons underwent renovations to become the Logan, part of Hilton's independent Curio Collection, in late 2105, and emerged with gracious, contemporary public areas and guest rooms that blend modern style with natural materials and Philly touches, from installations of local art to Rocky-themed bathrobes. **Pros:** convenient to Parkway museums, Fairmount Park, and convention center; secluded ambience in a busy area; notable rooftop bar. **Cons:** steak-house restaurant may not suit all tastes; spa has worthy but expensive treatments; rooftop bar gets crowded. *Rooms from: $480 1 Logan Sq., Parkways Museum District 215/963–1500, 844/634–3605 reservations www.theloganhotel.com 391 rooms No meals.*

Le Méridien
$$ | **HOTEL** | **FAMILY** | Opened in 2010, Le Méridien offers a welcome boutique alternative to the more standard hotels near the convention center. **Pros:** hip boutique alternative near convention center; good service; comfy beds; 24-hour gym; affordable relative to some luxury hotels. **Cons:** rooms could use some extra seating; immediate neighborhood can be a bit empty at night; can take a while to get your car back on busy check-out mornings. *Rooms from: $220 1421 Arch St., Parkways Museum District 215/422–8200, 800/543–4300 www.lemeridien.com 202 rooms No meals.*

Philadelphia 201 Hotel
$$ | **HOTEL** | Although it's a convenient convention hotel, this large Marriott hotel caters to both business and leisure travelers; at this writing ongoing renovations were due to be completed by mid-2020. **Pros:** good location between Parkway museums and convention center; contemporary rooms; great city or Parkway views from some rooms. **Cons:** large convention crowds; in-house dining not great; some service issues. *Rooms from: $170 201 N. 17th St., Parkways Museum District 215/448–2000, 888/236–2427 marriott.com 759 rooms No meals.*

The Windsor Suites
$$$$ | **HOTEL** | This 24-story all-suites hotel caters to corporate business travelers (some on extended stays) as well as vacationing families, and features both studio and one-bedroom spaces. **Pros:** good location near Parkway museums and Center City; some good views from rooms; responsive staff and service. **Cons:** rooftop pool closes seasonally; some rooms and areas need updating; may hear street noise. *Rooms from: $252 1700 Benjamin Franklin Pkwy., Parkways Museum District 215/981–5678, 877/784–8379 thewindsorsuites.com 199 suites No meals.*

MUSIC FESTIVALS

Wawa Welcome America! Festival
FESTIVALS | In the days leading up to Independence Day (July 4), Welcome America! highlights Philly's history with

patriotic happenings around downtown, from a massive block party on the Benjamin Franklin Parkway to concerts to free museum access to historical tours. It all culminates with a free July 4th Welcome America Concert and Fireworks extravaganza on the Parkway; past performers have included Jennifer Hudson, Meghan Trainor, and the U.S. Army Field Band. ✉ *20–24th Sts. and Benjamin Franklin Pkwy., Parkways Museum District* 🌐 *www.welcomeamerica.com.*

Shopping

The Philadelphia Museum of Art Store
GIFTS/SOUVENIRS | The store features items that are inspired by and reflect the museum's extraordinary collection including reproductions, note cards, jewelry, gifts for children, apparel, stationery, and items for the home. There's even a section devoted to items made in the Philadelphia area, as well the Northeast's largest selection of art books. There are additional locations at the Rodin Museum and the Perelman Building. ✉ *2600 Benjamin Franklin Pkwy., Parkways Museum District* ☎ *215/684–7960* 🌐 *store.philamuseum.org* ☞ *Closed Mon.*

Fairmount Park

Stretching from the edge of downtown to the city's northwest corner, Fairmount Park is the largest landscaped city park in the world. With more than 8,500 acres and 2 million trees (someone claims to have counted, and today the park is planting even more), the park winds along the banks of the Schuylkill River—which divides it into west and east sections—and through parts of the city. Historic houses and buildings, outdoor sculptures, the Please Touch Museum for kids, and a performing arts center enhance the park. On weekends the 4-mile stretch along Kelly Drive is crowded with joggers, bicycling moms and dads with children strapped into kiddie seats atop the back wheel, hand-holding senior citizens out for some fresh air, collegiate crew teams sculling on the river, and budding artists trying to capture the sylvan magic just as Thomas Eakins once did.

VISITOR INFORMATION

Fairmount Park Conservancy
The nonprofit Conservancy works with Philadelphia Parks & Recreation to support the city's parks, and its website has useful information about exploring Fairmount and other parks. In December, some of Fairmount Park's Historic Houses are decorated for Christmas and have special events; check 🌐 holidaysinthepark.com and 🌐 *parkcharms.com for information about this city tradition.* ✉ *Fairmount Park* ☎ *215/988–9334* 🌐 *myphillypark.org.*

Sights

Belmont Plateau
VIEWPOINT | Belmont Plateau has a view from 243 feet above river level, which will literally be the high point of a tour of Fairmount Park. In front of you are the park, the Schuylkill River winding down to the Philadelphia Museum of Art, and, 4 miles away, the Philadelphia skyline. ✉ *2000 Belmont Mansion Dr., W. Fairmount Park, Fairmount Park.*

★ **Boathouse Row**
BUILDING | These architecturally varied, quaint-looking 19th-century buildings—city icons built in Victorian Gothic, Gothic Revival, and Italianate styles—are home to the rowing clubs that make up the Schuylkill Navy, an association of boating clubs organized in 1858. These clubs host various races, including the Dad Vail Regatta and the Head of the Schuylkill. The view of the boathouses from the west side of the river is splendid—especially at night, when they're outlined with hundreds of small lights. Lloyd Hall, at 1 Boathouse Row, is a public recreation

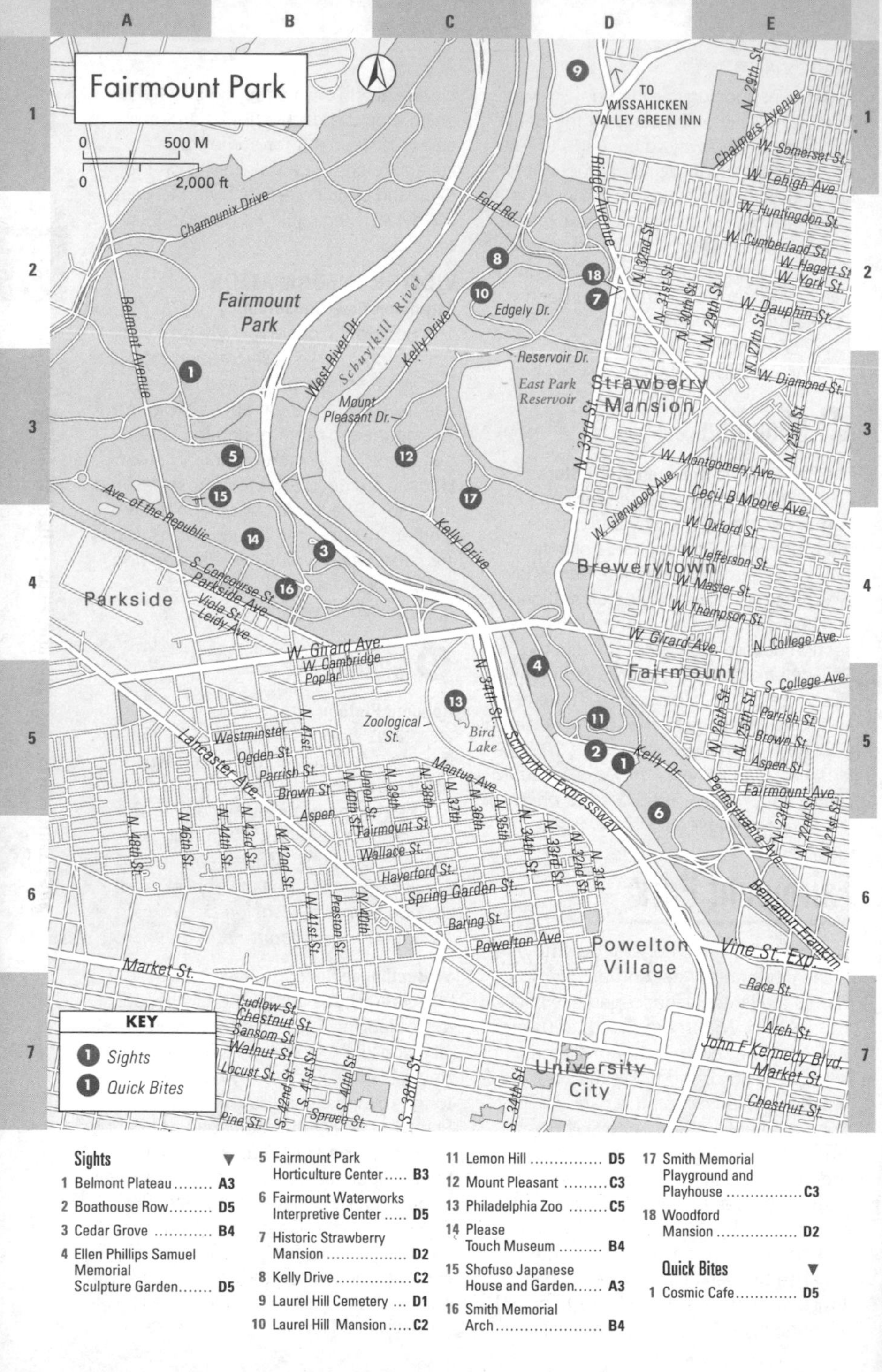

Sights

1 Belmont Plateau A3
2 Boathouse Row......... D5
3 Cedar Grove B4
4 Ellen Phillips Samuel Memorial Sculpture Garden....... D5
5 Fairmount Park Horticulture Center..... B3
6 Fairmount Waterworks Interpretive Center D5
7 Historic Strawberry Mansion D2
8 Kelly Drive C2
9 Laurel Hill Cemetery ... D1
10 Laurel Hill Mansion C2
11 Lemon Hill D5
12 Mount Pleasant C3
13 Philadelphia Zoo C5
14 Please Touch Museum B4
15 Shofuso Japanese House and Garden...... A3
16 Smith Memorial Arch....................... B4
17 Smith Memorial Playground and Playhouse C3
18 Woodford Mansion D2

Quick Bites

1 Cosmic Cafe............. D5

center with a gymnasium, bicycle rentals in season, and a café. ✉ *Kelly Dr. , near Sedgeley Dr., E. Fairmount Park, Fairmount Park* 🌐 *www.boathouserow.org.*

Cedar Grove

HOUSE | Five styles of furniture—Jacobean, William and Mary, Queen Anne, Chippendale, and Federal—reflect the accumulations of five generations of the Paschall-Morris family; additions and changes to the house itself, built 1748–50, reveal changing tastes. The stone house stood in Frankford, in northeastern Philadelphia, before being moved to this location in 1927. ✉ *1 Cedar Grove Dr., W. Fairmount Park, Fairmount Park* ☎ *215/763–8100* 🌐 *www.philamuseum.org* 🎫 *$8 (included in $25 2-day Philadelphia Museum of Art admission)* ⏲ *Closed Jan.–Mar. (except by appointment) and Mon. and Tues. Apr.–Dec.*

Ellen Phillips Samuel Memorial Sculpture Garden

PUBLIC ART | Seventeen bronze and granite sculptures stand in a series of tableaux and groupings on three riverside terraces. Portraying American themes and traits, they include *The Quaker,* by Harry Rosen; *Birth of a Nation,* by Henry Kreis; and *Spirit of Enterprise,* by Jacques Lipchitz. ✉ *Kelly Dr., E. Fairmount Park, Fairmount Park* ✣ *South of the Girard Ave. Bridge* 🌐 *associationforpublicart.org.*

Fairmount Park Horticulture Center

GARDEN | On the Horticulture Center's 27 wooded acres are an arboretum, a butterfly garden, a greenhouse, an exhibition hall (used for events), a reflecting pool, and the Pavilion in the Trees (by artist Martin Puryear) for bird-watching. The Shofuso Japanese House and Garden (fee) is nearby as well. See 🌐 *associationforpublicart.org for information about sculptures in this area.* The center is on the site of the 1876 Centennial Exposition's Horticultural Hall. ✉ *100 N. Horticultural Dr., Fairmount Park* ☎ *215/685–0096* 🌐 *www.phila.gov/departments/philadelphia-parks-recreation* 🎫 *Free.*

Fairmount Water Works Interpretive Center

BUILDING | FAMILY | Designed by Frederick Graff, this National Historic Landmark completed in 1815 was the first steam-pumping station of its kind in the country, and the notable assemblage of Greek Revival buildings is one of the city's most beautiful sights. The buildings, just behind the Philadelphia Museum of Art, include an interpretive center with some original features on display and kid-friendly exhibits about the region's water and the history of the water works; there's also a short film. Nearby paths provide good views of it and the Art Museum. ✉ *640 Waterworks Dr., E. Fairmount Park, off Kelly Dr., Fairmount Park* ☎ *215/685–0723* 🌐 *www.fairmountwaterworks.org* 🎫 *Free* ⏲ *Closed Mon.*

Historic Strawberry Mansion

HOUSE | Restorations and renovations have benefited the largest of the Fairmount Park Historic Houses, which has furniture and other antiques and art from the three main phases of its history: Federal, Regency, and Empire. In the parlor is a collection of rare Tucker and Hemphill porcelain; it also showcases a large collection of fine antique dolls and toys. The house was originally built around 1783–93 by Judge William Lewis. ✉ *2450 Strawberry Mansion Dr., near 33rd and Dauphin Sts., E. Fairmount Park, Fairmount Park* ☎ *215/228–8364* 🌐 *www.historicstrawberrymansion.org* 🎫 *$8* ⏲ *Closed Jan. (except by appointment), Sun.–Fri. Feb., and Mon. and Tues. Mar.–Dec.*

★ Kelly Drive

SCENIC DRIVE | One of the city's most scenic byways, woodsy Kelly Drive has a popular walking, running, and biking path that parallels the road as it stretches more than 4 miles along the eastern side of the Schuylkill River from behind the Philadelphia Museum of Art to City

The view of Boathouse Row from the west side of the Schuylkill River is marvelous—especially at night, when the buildings are outlined with hundreds of small lights.

Avenue. You can make an almost 9-mile loop on bike or foot by crossing Falls Bridge and returning on the path parallel to the west side's Martin Luther King, Jr. Drive (MLK Drive also closes to cars on weekends April–October and has great Boathouse Row views). Notable sights, as well as river views, can distract you as you head north from the museum: Boathouse Row (rent a bike at Wheel Fun Rentals); nearby historic houses like Lemon Hill; the Ellen Phillips Samuel Memorial Sculpture Garden (and other artworks; see 🌐 *associationforpublicart.org/tours*), and nearby Laurel Hill Cemetery. Kelly Drive is named for John B. Kelly, Jr., a city councilman and Olympic Rower who was the brother of actress Grace Kelly. ✉ *Kelly Dr., Fairmount Park.*

Laurel Hill Cemetery

CEMETERY | John Notman, architect of the Athenaeum and many other noted local buildings, designed Laurel Hill in 1836; it is an important example of an early rural burial ground and the first cemetery in America designed by an architect. Its hills overlooking the Schuylkill River, its rare trees, and its monuments and mausoleums sculpted by Alexander Milne Calder, Alexander Stirling Calder, William Strickland, and Thomas U. Walter made it a popular picnic spot in the 19th century; today it's a great place to stroll or bike, take a guided tour (fee), or download an app for a self-guided tour. Among the notables buried in this 78-acre necropolis are General George Meade and 39 other Civil War–era generals. Burials still take place here. ✉ *3822 Ridge Ave., Fairmount Park* ✣ *East side of Schuylkill River; also accessible off Kelly Dr. at Hunting Park Dr.* ☎ *215/228–8200* 🌐 *www.thelaurelhillcemetery.org* 🎫 *Free* Ⓜ *SEPTA bus rte. 61 from Center City.*

Laurel Hill Mansion

HOUSE | Built around 1767, this Georgian house on a laurel-covered hill overlooking the Schuylkill River once belonged to Dr. Philip Syng Physick (also owner of Society Hill's Physick House). The house furnishings are from a variety of periods. On some Sunday evenings in summer, Women for Greater Philadelphia sponsors candlelight chamber music concerts here; there are other events, too. Call before visiting. ✉ *7201 Randolph Dr., E. Fairmount Park, Fairmount Park* ☎ *215/235–1776* 🌐 *www.laurelhillmansion.org* 💵 *$8* ⏲ *Closed Mon.–Wed. and Jan.–late Apr.*

Lemon Hill

HOUSE | An impressive example of a Federal-style country house, Lemon Hill was built in 1800 on a 350-acre farm and has distinctive oval parlors with concave doors and an entrance hall with a checkerboard floor of Valley Forge marble. It was purchased by the city in 1844 and became part of Fairmount Park. The house is not fully furnished and needs some upkeep, but docents provide historical information. ✉*, 1 Lemon Hill Dr., off Sedgeley Dr., Fairmount Park* ☎ *215/232–4337* 🌐 *parkcharms.com* 💵 *$8* ⏲ *Closed Mon.–Wed.; also Jan.–Mar.*

Mount Pleasant

HOUSE | Built in 1761 by John Macpherson, a Scottish sea captain, Mount Pleasant is one of the finest examples of Georgian architecture in the country. The level of craftsmanship in the rooms, including architectural carvings, is high, and the historically accurate furnishings are culled from the Philadelphia Museum of Art's noted collection of Philadelphia Chippendale furniture. ✉ *3800 Mount Pleasant Dr., Fairmount Park* ☎ *215/763–8100* 🌐 *www.philamuseum.org* 💵 *$8; also included in $25 2-day Philadelphia Museum of Art admission* ⏲ *Closed Mon.–Tues. and Jan.–Mar.*

Philadelphia Zoo

ZOO | **FAMILY** | Opened in 1874, the 42 acres of America's first zoo are home to more than 2,000 animals representing six continents. It's small and well landscaped enough to feel pleasantly intimate, and the naturalistic habitats allow you to get close enough to hear the animals breathe. Some animals travel around the grounds via see-through mesh trails called Zoo360. The Reptile and Amphibian House houses 87 species, from 15-foot-long snakes to frogs the size of a dime. The 2½-acre Primate Reserve is home to 11 species from around the world. Notable attractions include Big Cat Falls, with leopards, jaguars, mountain lions, tigers, and lions; the McNeil Avian Center, the state-of-the-art nest for some 100 birds; and African Plains, stomping ground of giraffes and zebras. The children's zoo, KidZooU, has a goat bridge, where kids can test their climbing skills against live goats; a duck pond; an outdoor grooming area; and more. There's also WildWorks, a ropes course for kids and adults. ✉ *3400 W. Girard Ave., W. Fairmount Park, Fairmount Park* ☎ *215/243–1100* 🌐 *philadelphiazoo.org* 💵 *$16–$24; some attractions require additional fees/tickets; prepaid parking $16.*

Please Touch Museum

MUSEUM | **FAMILY** | Philadelphia's popular interactive children's museum, aimed at children ages nine and younger, instills a sense of wonder from the get-go with its marble-floored Hamilton Hall, which has an 80-foot-high ceiling and a 40-foot-tall sculpture of the torch of the Statue of Liberty as its centerpiece. The museum occupies a gorgeous beaux arts–style building constructed for the 1876 Centennial Exhibition, one of just two public buildings still standing from the event. Centennial Innovations, a permanent exhibit opening in spring 2020, examines the innovations of 1876 and encourages children to think about solutions to current problems. The facility is set up as a series of engaging exhibits, plus separate areas designed for toddlers, where kids can learn through hands-on play at a mock supermarket, a hospital area, a space gallery with a rocket-making station, Alice's Wonderland, and a theater with interactive performances. Children can discover the world of money or explore the Imagination Playground or the outdoor Please Touch Garden. Another highlight is a circa-1908 Dentzel

Built in 1896—1897 for the trolley, Strawberry Mansion Bridge, as seen from Kelly Drive, crosses the Schuylkill River. Today it can be crossed by foot or car.

Carousel ride with 52 colorful horses, pigs, cats, and rabbits that's in an adjacent, enclosed glass pavilion. A café serves lunch items and snacks. ✉ *4231 Ave. of the Republic, W. Fairmount Park, Fairmount Park* ☎ *215/581–3181* 🌐 *www.pleasetouchmuseum.org* 🎫 *$19.95; carousel ride $3 (unlimited rides $5); parking $16* Ⓜ *SEPTA bus 38 stops at Memorial Hall; buses 40, 43, and 64 stop nearby; PHLASH.*

★ Shofuso Japanese House and Garden

BUILDING | This exquisite replica of a 17th-century guesthouse, reassembled here in 1958 after being exhibited at the Museum of Modern Art in New York City, is set in a serene 1.2-acre garden with a teahouse, tiered waterfall, gardens, Japanese trees, and a koi pond. The house is called Shofu-So, which means "pine breeze villa," and its roof is made of the bark of the hinoki, a cypress that grows only in the mountains of Japan. There are also 20 murals by acclaimed Japanese contemporary artist Hiroshi Senju. Check the website for periodic tea ceremonies (reservations required) and other events like the Subaru Cherry Blossom Festival in the spring. Note: Shofuso is not wheelchair accessible. ✉ *N. Horticultural Dr. and Lansdowne Dr., W. Fairmount Park, Fairmount Park* ☎ *215/878–5097* 🌐 *www.japanphilly.org* 🎫 *$12* ⏲ *Closed mid-Dec.–late Mar.; Mon. and Tues. late Mar.–Oct; and weekdays Nov.–mid-Dec.* Ⓜ *SEPTA 38 bus, Please Touch Museum stop.*

Smith Memorial Arch

MEMORIAL | Built between 1897 and 1912 with funds donated by wealthy foundry owner Richard Smith, the memorial honors Pennsylvania heroes of the Civil War. Among those immortalized in bronze are Generals Meade and Hancock (both on horseback)—and Smith himself. At the base of each tower is a curved wall with a bench. If you sit at one end and listen to a person whispering at the other end, you can understand why they're called the Whispering Benches. ✉ *Ave. of the Republic, W. Fairmount Park, Fairmount Park.*

A Drive Around Fairmount Park

Follow Kelly Drive in East Fairmount Park to the end of Boathouse Row; turn right up the hill to a Federal-style country house, **Lemon Hill.** Head back to Kelly Drive, turn right, pass through the rock archway, and turn right again at the equestrian statue of Ulysses S. Grant. The first left takes you to **Mount Pleasant,** a Georgian house. Continue along the road that runs to the right of the house (as you face it) past Rockland, a Federal house in private use. At the road's end, turn left onto Reservoir Drive. You'll pass the redbrick Georgian-style Ormiston (open for rare special events). Take the next left, Randolph Drive, to another Georgian house, **Laurel Hill Mansion**; the street becomes Dauphin Street. Just about 10 feet before reaching 33rd Street, turn left on Greenland Drive, and you're at **Woodford,** which has an interesting collection of household goods. A quarter-mile northwest of Woodford stands the house that gave its name to the nearby section of Philadelphia, **Historic Strawberry Mansion.** It has furniture from three periods of its history.

Visit Laurel Hill Cemetery before you cross the river to West Fairmount Park. To get there, drive back down the driveway of Strawberry Mansion, turn left at the stop sign, and follow the narrow road as it winds right to the light. Turn left onto Ridge Avenue and follow it to the cemetery's entrance gate, which sits between eight Greek columns.

To skip the cemetery and continue your tour, proceed down the Strawberry Mansion driveway to the stop sign, turn left, and follow the road as it loops down and around to the Strawberry Mansion Bridge. Cross the river and follow the road; when it splits, stay left. You'll come to Chamounix Drive. Turn left and then left again on Belmont Mansion Drive for a fine view from **Belmont Plateau.** Follow Belmont Mansion Drive down the hill. Where it forks, stay to the left, cross Montgomery Drive, and bear left to reach the **Fairmount Park Horticulture Center** with its greenhouse and garden. Loop all the way around the Horticulture Center to visit the serene **Shofoso Japanese House and Garden** (closed in winter).

Drive back around the Horticulture Center and continue through the gates to Montgomery Drive. Turn left and then left again at the first light (Belmont Avenue). Turn left again on Avenue of the Republic. On your left is the **Please Touch Museum.** The two towers ahead are part of the **Smith Memorial Arch.** Turn left just past them to see **Cedar Grove,** a stone Colonial house. Head to Lansdowne Drive. Follow signs to the **Philadelphia Zoo** or head back toward the Art Museum and the Parkway.

You could do the drive (minus the walking section, which is 2 miles round-trip) in an hour or so with some brief time to explore, or you could check the open hours of different sights and spend a day exploring with your car.

Smith Memorial Playground and Playhouse
CITY PARK | **FAMILY** | Founded in 1899, this beloved facility has state-of-the-art, age-specific equipment; a favorite on the 6½-acre site is the Ann Newman Giant Wooden Slide, which measures 39 feet long, 12 feet wide, and 10 feet tall. The park, run by a nonprofit organization, includes the 16,000-square-foot Playhouse (for kids ages 10 and under), which is closed for renovations until September 2020. ✉ *3500 Reservoir Dr., E. Fairmount Park, Fairmount Park* ✣ *Near 33rd and Oxford Sts.* ☎ *215/765–4325* 🌐 *www.smithplayground.org* 🎫 *Free* ⏲ *Closed Mon.; slide closed Jan.–Mar.* Ⓜ *SEPTA bus 32, at 33rd and Oxford Sts.*

Woodford Mansion
HOUSE | The Naomi Wood collection of antique household goods, including Colonial furniture, unusual clocks, and English delftware, and designated her "colonial household gear" in her will, can be seen on guided tours in this fine Georgian mansion, a National Historic Landmark built about 1756. ✉ *2300 N. 33rd St., at Dauphin St., E. Fairmount Park, Fairmount Park* ☎ *215/229–6115* 🌐 *www.woodfordmansion.org* 🎫 *$8* ⏲ *Closed Mon. and Tues.*

Coffee and Quick Bites

Cosmic Cafe
$ | **CAFÉ** | "Good food, good karma" reads the banner outside this no-frills café in Fairmount Park that focuses on fresh local food produced sustainably and prepared on-site, and it delivers. Plenty of outdoor seating (there's some indoors, too) makes this a convenient, fun choice for coffee and fare including breakfast burritos and egg sandwiches; soups, wraps, and burgers; and cookies, desserts, and snacks. **Known for:** park views inside and out; all-day breakfast options; weekend music in summer and fall. $ *Average main: $12* ✉ *Lloyd Hall, 1 Boathouse Row, Fairmount Park* ☎ *215/978–0900* 🌐 *cafe.cosmicfoods.com* ⏲ *Closed Mon. and Tues. in winter. No dinner in winter.*

Performing Arts

★ **Mann Center for the Performing Arts**
ARTS CENTERS | Pop, jazz, contemporary music, Broadway theater, opera, dance, and movies are presented in an open-air amphitheater and the standing-room-only Skyline Stage in Fairmount Park from May through September. The site has great skyline views. In summer, the Philadelphia Orchestra has some performances here, along with noted soloists and guest conductors. ✉ *5201 Parkside Ave., W. Fairmount Park, Fairmount Park* ☎ *800/982–2787 ticketing* 🌐 *www.manncenter.org.*

Activities

BIKING

Wheel Fun Rentals
BICYCLING | **FAMILY** | From its space next to Lloyd Hall and the Cosmic Cafe (and the path near Kelly Drive), Wheel Fun rents bicycles from kids' bikes to cruisers to tandems. Surreys and deuce coupes, which hold adults and a couple of small children, are another option. Rental season is late March through mid-November. ✉ *1 Boathouse Row, W. Fairmount Park, Fairmount Park* ☎ *215/232–7778* 🌐 *wheelfunrentals.com* ☞ *From $10 an hour, $25 half day, $32 full day.*

ZIP LINE

Treetop Quest
ZIP LINING | **FAMILY** | Explore more than 60 obstacles and zip-lines in the trees at this aerial adventure park. Each participant is outfitted with a harness and gloves—helmets are available—and given a briefing on how things work. ✉ *51 Chamounix Dr., Fairmount Park* ☎ *267/901–4145* 🌐 *www.treetopquest.com.*

Chapter 8

SOUTH PHILADELPHIA AND EAST PASSYUNK

Updated by
Drew Lazor

Sights	Restaurants	Hotels	Shopping	Nightlife
★★★★☆	★★★★★	★★★☆☆	★★★★☆	★★★☆☆

NEIGHBORHOOD SNAPSHOT

TOP EXPERIENCES

■ **Italian Market:** Bring your appetite with you while you tour America's oldest continuously operating open-air market.

■ **Fleisher Art Memorial:** Take a brief eating break and fit in some culture at this historic community art space.

■ **Mummers Museum:** Get the real story behind the one New Year's Day tradition that's uniquely and gloriously Philly.

■ **Pat's and Geno's:** Scarf down cheesesteaks from both famed purveyors to declare which grill reigns supreme.

■ **Sports Complex:** Mingle with Philly's (in)famous sports fans on South Broad Street, home to the city's big four professional teams.

■ **Bella Vista and Queen Village:** Explore the best bars, restaurants, shops, and boutiques throughout these charming old neighborhoods.

GETTING HERE

You can reach the Italian Market and its South Philadelphia surrounds on foot from Center City, or you may take SEPTA bus route 47, which runs south on 8th Street and makes a return loop north on 7th Street. There is both free and metered parking available in the neighborhood, at the official Italian Market lot on Carpenter Street between 9th and 10th and in lots just off Washington Avenue between 8th and 9th Streets and 9th and 10th.

PLANNING YOUR TIME

It's best to visit the Italian Market Tuesday through Saturday, since many businesses close early on Sunday and take Monday off. Start early—vendors and shoppers tend to wind down by later afternoon—and allow three to four hours.

QUICK BITES

■ **East Passyunk Avenue.** For generations, East Passyunk was the primary commercial corridor for South Philly's Italian-Americans; it's more recently blossomed into an exciting and ever-changing shopping, dining, and nightlife district. ✉ *1904 E. Passyunk Ave., South Philadelphia* 🌐 *www.visiteastpassyunk.com*

■ **Italian Market.** Stroll up 9th Street to take in the tastes of South Philly as it once was—walk-up counters, cafés, and sit-down restaurants join cheese shops, fishmongers, produce peddlers, and old-school Italian groceries along the stretch. ✉ *919 S. 9th St., South Philadelphia* 🌐 *www.italianmarketphilly.org*

■ **Wing Phat Plaza.** A central gathering place for South Philly's "Little Saigon" community, this busy shopping center features a well-stocked Asian grocery store, plus Vietnamese, Indonesian, and Chinese restaurants. ✉ *1122-38 Washington Ave., South Philadelphia*

South Philadelphia is home to some of the city's most dynamic pockets: Queen Village, Bella Vista, and the neighborhoods around East Passyunk Avenue. Though they don't enjoy as much historical cachet as Old City or Society Hill, each played an invaluable role in the early rise of Philadelphia, nurturing industries and immigrant communities that define this great city. A contemporary influx of young professionals and the creative class has attracted interesting bars, restaurants, and shops to these traditionally residential areas.

Queen Village, stretching from Front to 6th Street and from South Street to Washington Avenue, was a hub of commercial activity in its earliest days, home to expert tradespeople, especially the shipbuilders active on the nearby Delaware River. Directly to the west, Bella Vista is a traditionally Italian hub, exemplified by the open-air market along 9th Street, still buzzing with charismatic produce hawkers and old-school butcher shops. Presidential candidates are fond of visiting the market on their swings through South Philly; it's a great photo op for them—and for you.

Further south, beyond Washington Avenue, you'll find an interesting mix of old- and new-school energy along East Passyunk Avenue, which cuts diagonally across the gridded streets. These are the neighborhoods that gave us Italian-American entertainers like Mario Lanza, Bobby Rydell, Frankie Avalon, and Fabian, but two other names in these parts might have even more renown—Pat's and Geno's. At the corner of 9th Street and East Passyunk Avenue, Pat's and Geno's are world-famous for their cheesesteaks, though locals tend to patronize smaller, lesser-known shops. Below Snyder Avenue stretches the rest of South Philadelphia to the south, east, and west, home to a diverse population, the city's flashy pro sports complexes, and myriad other gems.

South Philadelphia

Outside Bella Vista, Queen Village, and East Passyunk, dozens of mini-neighborhoods comprise the bulk of South Philadelphia, like historically Irish-American Pennsport, where 2nd Street is called "Two Sweet" and lined with Mummers clubhouses. Residential Newbold, a subsection of Point Breeze, is home to popular craft-beer bars like South Philadelphia Tap Room. Down by the Sports Complex, where fans catch the Phillies, Eagles, Sixers, and Flyers, the decommissioned Navy Yard has become an urban oasis of rolling lawns and slinky canals, home to more than 150 companies and organizations.

Sights

American Swedish Historical Museum

MUSEUM | This neoclassical building in FDR Park celebrates Swedish contributions to American history. The Swedes settled the Delaware Valley in the mid-1600s, and it was a pair of Swedish brothers who sold William Penn the land that became Philadelphia. Modeled after a 17th-century Swedish manor house, it features galleries and rooms that concentrate on specific eras and industrious characters. The John Ericsson Room honors the designer of the Civil War ship the USS *Monitor*; the Jenny Lind Room contains memorabilia from the P.T. Barnum–led American tour the soprano known as the "Swedish Nightingale" embarked upon in 1850. Other rooms display handmade dolls, crafts, paintings, and drawings, all in addition to rotating cultural exhibitions. It's not the most riveting place on paper, but the unconventional location, combined with its examination of overlooked history, make for an interesting visit. ✉ *1900 Pattison Ave., South Philadelphia* ✣ *Take the Orange Line subway south to its final stop (NRG Station); cross Broad Street and walk 5 blocks west through the park to the museum* ☎ *215/389–1776* 🌐 *www.americanswedish.org* 🎫 *$10.*

Citizens Bank Park

SPORTS VENUE | Since 2004, the Philadelphia Phillies have played in Citizens Bank Park, a 42,792-seat stadium that has a 13,000-square-foot interactive kids' baseball experience called The Yard. Ticketed tours are available all year long, and feature stops in the Phillies' dugout, the Diamond Club, the Hall of Fame Club, the broadcast booth, and the media room. ✉ *1 Citizens Bank Way, South Philadelphia* ☎ *215/463–1000* 🌐 *www.mlb.com/phillies* 🎫 *Tours $13.*

Franklin Delano Roosevelt Park

NATIONAL/STATE PARK | Frederick Law Olmsted is best known as the designer of New York's Central Park, and his sons followed in their father's footsteps in founding the Olmsted Brothers firm, which created this high-profile park in deep South Philly. Originally called League Island Park, when it was designed in the decade leading up to the 1926 Sesquicentennial Exposition, it's now colloquially known as "The Lakes" for its network of channels and lagoons. The park contains numerous historical structures, including a soaring granite gazebo ringed in Doric columns, the dramatically arched boathouse, and the castlelike American Swedish Historical Museum. ✉ *1500 Pattison Ave., South Philadelphia* ☎ *215/685–0060* 🌐 *www.fdrparkphilly.org.*

Lincoln Financial Field

SPORTS VENUE | The Linc, as it's called by locals, is a state-of-the-art facility with a grass playing field. It holds nearly 68,000 passionate Philadelphia Eagles fans, as well as supporters of the Temple Owls football team; the stadium also plays host to other sports, plus large-scale events and concerts. Tours are available. ✉ *1 Lincoln Financial Field Way, South Philadelphia* ☎ *267/570–4000* 🌐 *www.lincolnfinancialfield.com* 🎫 *tours $15.*

Mummers Museum

MUSEUM | FAMILY | Even if you aren't in Philadelphia on January 1, you can still get a feel for one of the city's most unique traditions by stopping by this museum. Famous for their extravagant sequin-and-feather costumes and boisterous behavior, the Mummers spend all year practicing for their New Year's Day parade down Broad Street, a tradition since 1901. With roots in old European folk performance traditions, today's Mummers clubs fall into several different categories, including satirical Comics, musical String Bands, and theatrical Fancies. All this and more is covered at the museum, which features family-friendly exhibits on Mummers culture; there are outdoor concerts in the summer. ✉ *1100 S. 2nd St., at Washington Ave., South Philadelphia* ☎ *215/336–3050* 🌐 *www.mummersmuseum.com* 🎫 *$5* 🕑 *Closed Sun.–Tues.*

South Street

NEIGHBORHOOD | "Where do all the hippies meet? South Street." So goes a 1963 song by Philadelphia R&B group the Orlons, helping this west-to-east strip of pavement develop a reputation as a gathering place for counterculture types. In its day, the immediate street was populated by artists and musicians and their left-of-center bars, galleries, and stores. Nowadays, this bohemian energy is far less palpable, but the section between Broad and Front Streets still hosts many gems amid duller holdings like chain pharmacies and cell-phone stores. Peruse the various antiques and vintage stores, clothing boutiques, bookstores, and record sellers between people-watching. There's a vast range of culinary options, too, from classic cheesesteak shops (Jim's, Ishkabibble's) to award-winning dining destinations like Serpico. ✉ *1400 South St., South Philadelphia* ☎ *215/413–3713* 🌐 *www.southstreet.com.*

Wells Fargo Center

SPORTS VENUE | The Wells Fargo Center is the home to the Flyers (NHL), 76ers (NBA), and Wings (NLL, pro lacrosse), and regularly hosts Villanova basketball (and other collegiate sports), big-name concerts, and high-profile arena entertainment of all kinds. Behind-the-scenes tours last 60 to 90 minutes and include a commemorative photo and frame for each guest. ✉ *3601 S. Broad St., South Philadelphia* ☎ *215/336–3600* 🌐 *www.wellsfargocenterphilly.com* 🎫 *tours $14.*

Restaurants

★ John's Roast Pork

$ | ITALIAN | FAMILY | Housed in humble digs next to a defunct railroad crossing, John's doesn't wow with curb appeal, but wise eaters know the close-to-centenarian grill spot turns out some of Philly's best sandwiches. Newbies and lifers alike line up in a zigzag along the counter, grabbing outdoor picnic tables after paying for their roast pork, roast beef, or cheesesteak. **Known for:** Italian roast pork sandwiches; highly praised cheesesteaks; friendly South Philly staff. [$] *Average main: $9* ✉ *14 E. Snyder Ave., South Philadelphia* ☎ *215/463–1951* 🌐 *www.johnsroastpork.com* 🕑 *Closed Sun. and Mon.*

Nam Phuong

$ | VIETNAMESE | Competition is fierce in South Philly's "Little Saigon," but Nam Phuong has managed to keep fans of Vietnamese cuisine happy for years, with its authentic and wide-spanning menu. Far more spacious than some of the spartan pho parlors around the neighborhood, the dining room is equipped with round tables that can fit the whole crew—and all your food, too. **Known for:** lengthy Vietnamese menu; room for big groups; ample family dinner options. [$] *Average main: $14* ✉ *1100-1120 Washington Ave., South Philadelphia* ☎ *215/468–0410* 🌐 *www.namphuongphilly.com.*

South Philadelphia
Schuylkill
Southwest Center City
Bella Vista
Grays Ferry
Hawthorne
Point Breeze
Girard Estate
Wharton
Whitman
Packer Park
Schuylkill Expressway
Delaware Expressway
Passyunk Ave.
East Passyunk Ave.
South Broad St.
W. Oregon Ave.
Pattison Ave.
Hartranft St.
Packer Ave.
Washington Ave.
Schuylkill River
0
1,000 M
0
2,000 ft

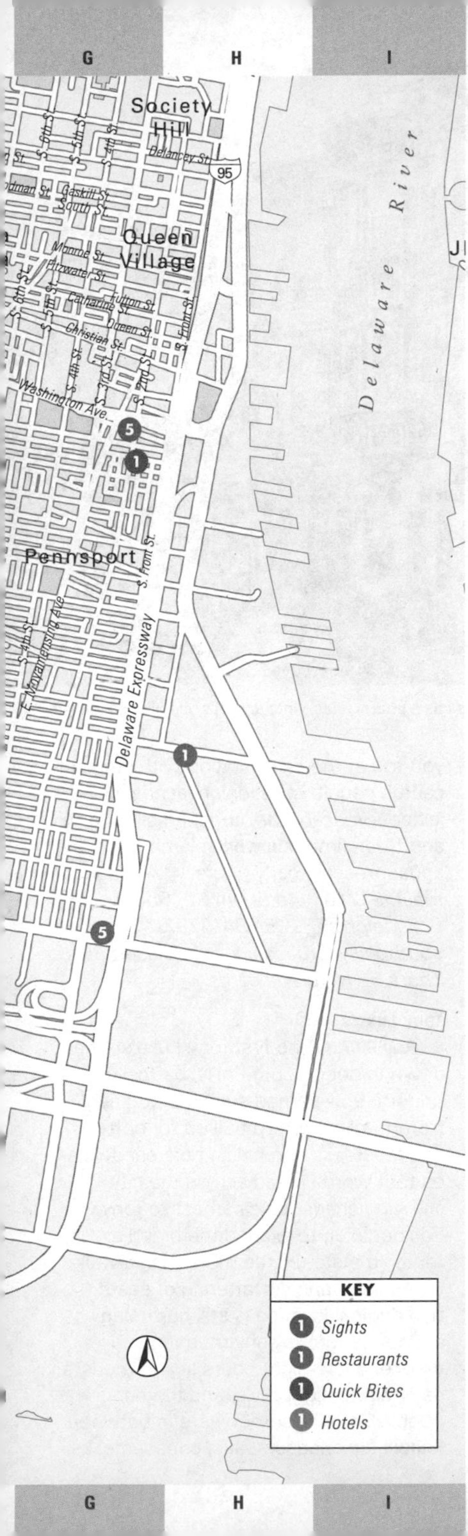

Sights

1 American Swedish Historical Museum C7
2 Citizens Bank Park....... E7
3 Franklin Delano Roosevelt Park.......... B8
4 Lincoln Financial Field E8
5 Mummers Museum G3
6 South Street............ D1
7 Wells Fargo Center..... D8

Restaurants

1 John's Roast Pork H5
2 Nam Phuong E2
3 South Philadelphia Tap Room D4
4 South Philly Barbacoa F3
5 Tony Luke's G6

Quick Bites

1 Federal Donuts.......... G3
2 Ultimo Coffee/Brew............ D4
3 Wing Phat Plaza E2

Hotels

1 Courtyard Philadelphia South at The Navy Yard........... D9
2 The Deacon D2
3 Fairfield Inn Philadelphia Airport.... A8

KEY
Sights
Restaurants
Quick Bites
Hotels

One of the city's most famous streets, South Street has chain pharmacies, vintage shops, clothing boutiques, and food options like cheesesteaks at Jim's Steaks.

★ South Philadelphia Tap Room

$$ | MODERN AMERICAN | FAMILY | Championing craft beer well before it was cool, this laid-back Newbold tavern set the bar for Philly's gastropub boom way back in 2003. SPTR's ever-rotating 14 tap selections, plus cask ales and a nice bottle selection, hit local, national, and international notes that nicely accompany a menu that reaches well beyond the expected pub grub with creative snacks, sandwiches, and seasonal specials conceived to celebrate local and organic products and produce. **Known for:** smart craft-beer program; local and seasonal menu items; relaxed atmosphere. *$ Average main: $15 ✉ 1509 Mifflin St., South Philadelphia ☎ 215/271–7787 ⊕ www.southphiladelphiataproom.com.*

★ South Philly Barbacoa

$ | MEXICAN | Cristina Martinez and Benjamin Miller specialize in *barbacoa,* the succulent, slow-cooked lamb of Martinez's Mexican homeland. The couple and their staff chop the meat with cleavers and pile it on fluffy corn tortillas, which you top at the salsa station with strips of cactus paddle *rajas*, onion-laced pickled jalapeno *escabeche*, chopped cilantro, and fresh lime. **Known for:** lamb tacos; aguas frescas; early hours. *$ Average main: $12 ✉ 1140 S. 9th St., South Philadelphia ☎ 215/694–3797 ⊕ www.southphillybarbacoa.com ⏲ Closed Tues.–Thurs. ▭ No credit cards.*

Tony Luke's

$ | AMERICAN | The first Tony Luke's—way down in deep South Philly, basically under I–95—earned such a reputation from truckers who'd pull off for hefty cheesesteaks and Italian pork sandwiches that word spread across the city, allowing charismatic namesake Tony Lucidonio Jr. to expand the brand to multiple states. Little more than a walk-up window and a scattering of seats, this original location is still humming, and its generous early-morning and weekend late-night hours accommodate early birds, night owls, and the hungry people who fall somewhere in between. **Known for:** cheesesteaks, cheesesteaks,

cheesesteaks; Italian roast pork sandwiches; accommodating breakfast and late-night hours. *Average main: $9* *39 E. Oregon Ave., South Philadelphia* *215/551–5725* *www.tonylukes.com.*

Coffee and Quick Bites

Federal Donuts

$ | **CAFÉ** | **FAMILY** | In 2011, the owners of the acclaimed Zahav partnered with a team of Philly food entrepreneurs to open the first Federal Donuts, and Philly quickly fell in love with the whimsical doughnut-and–fried chicken concept. The minichain now runs eight shops throughout the city, but this tiny flagship, on an unassuming corner in quiet Pennsport, is still going strong. **Known for:** unconventional doughnut flavors; creative fried-chicken styles; good coffee. *Average main: $10* *1219 S. 2nd St., South Philadelphia* *267/687–8258* *www.federaldonuts.com* *No dinner.*

Ultimo Coffee/Brew

$ | **CAFÉ** | Aaron and Elizabeth Ultimo launched Philadelphia's specialty coffee charge in 2009, offering expert espresso, pour-over brewing, and single-origin beans well before these were staples. The couple has since added three more shops, a bakery, and a roastery to the roster, while their relaxed Newbold flagship keeps on keeping on perhaps because of its shared real estate with bottle shop Brew, which allows guests to commingle coffee and craft beer. **Known for:** specialty coffee; outdoor seating; craft beer bottle shop. *Average main: $5* *1900 S. 15th St., South Philadelphia* *215/339–5177* *www.ultimocoffee.com.*

Wing Phat Plaza

$ | **ASIAN** | A central gathering place for South Philly's "Little Saigon" community, this busy shopping center features a well-stocked Asian grocery store, plus Vietnamese, Indonesian, and Chinese restaurants including the popular Nam Phuong. **Known for:** well-stocked Asian grocery store; home to Nam Phuong; great lunch spot. *Average main: $7* *1122-38 Washington Ave., South Philadelphia* *215/271–5866* *No credit cards.*

Hotels

Courtyard Philadelphia South at The Navy Yard

$$ | **HOTEL** | A welcome alternative to cookie-cutter accommodations down by Philadelphia International Airport, this LEED-certified Courtyard takes up residence in the Navy Yard, a 1,200-acre business campus in deep South Philly that is home to companies like GlaxoSmithKline and Urban Outfitters. **Pros:** close proximity to Sports Complex; quick ride to/from PHL Airport; better design than hotels in vicinity. **Cons:** far away from Center City; few walkable dining options outside hotel; isolated Navy Yard feels more like a college campus than a city. *Rooms from: $199* *1001 Intrepid Ave., South Philadelphia* *215/644–9200* *www.marriott.com/phlcs* *212 rooms* *No meals.*

The Deacon

$ | **HOTEL** | Built in 1906, this Gothic Revival building was long home to the influential First African Baptist Church, but structural concerns saw the congregation move to West Philly, allowing the Deacon to reimagine the address and pay respect to the past with the resulting thoughtful boutique hotel. **Pros:** one-of-a-kind setting; groups can book entire space; on-site classes and "experiences." **Cons:** no traditional concierge or turndown service; individual travelers share close quarters with group bookings; guest responsible for cooking or ordering all meals. *Rooms from: $125* *1600 Christian St., South Philadelphia* *347/868–2996* *www.thedeaconphl.com* *8 rooms* *No meals.*

Fairfield Inn Philadelphia Airport

$$$ | **HOTEL** | As far as airport hotels are concerned, this Fairfield Inn is standard, but its staff has a reputation for being quite accommodating. **Pros:** accommodating staff; 24-hour shuttle service to airport; 24-hour fitness center. **Cons:** isolated from Center City; limited dining options outside hotel; surroundings can be noisy. *Rooms from: $264* ✉ *8800 Bartram Ave., South Philadelphia* ☎ *215/365–2254* 🌐 *www.marriott.com/hotels/travel/phlfa-fairfield-inn-philadelphia-airport* *97 rooms* *Free breakfast.*

Nightlife

BARS AND LOUNGES

Dock Street South

BREWPUBS/BEER GARDENS | In extending its footprint, West Philly's long-running Dock Street introduces its craft-beer ethos to a new audience. The local brewery has converted a formerly nondescript warehouse into a welcoming all-day destination for South Philadelphians. Morning coffee and pastries lead into lunch, and one of the best deals around—a sandwich, a side salad or chips, and a beer or coffee, all for $10. For dinner, small plates, sandwiches, and specials pair up with the dozen beers on draft. With ample room to play, this is an ideal stop for large groups, and it's kid-friendly. ✉ *2118 Washington Ave., South Philadelphia* ☎ *215/337–3103* 🌐 *www.dockstreetbeer.com/dock-street-south-point-breeze* ☞ *Closed Mon.*

Sidecar Bar & Grille

BARS/PUBS | An anchor establishment south of Center City, the Sidecar delivers an approachable mix of craft beer on tap, creative but satisfying pub food, and positive vibes. The narrow but cozy street-level bar is complemented by a roomier second-floor hangout that can host events and get-togethers in addition to everyday hangs. Specialties of the kitchen include handmade pastas and charcuterie, hearty sandwiches, and Detroit-style pizzas. ✉ *2201 Christian St., South Philadelphia* ☎ *215/732–3429* 🌐 *www.thesidecarbar.com.*

MUSIC CLUBS

Boot & Saddle

MUSIC CLUBS | Though it's got a honky-tonky heart—the gigantic glowing boot-and-saddle sign is an iconic South Philly landmark—this small Broad Street tavern skews more rock and roll in its current iteration, providing a stage for smaller independent acts and the occasional big name nightly. The venue is also a reliable neighborhood bar, pouring local craft beers and serving up filling finger food, with plenty of vegan and vegetarian options. ✉ *1131 S. Broad St., South Philadelphia* ☎ *267/639–4528* 🌐 *bootandsaddlephilly.com.*

Warmdaddy's

MUSIC CLUBS | This comfortable, down-home blues club and restaurant right near the Delaware River serves up live blues and soulful Southern cuisine six nights a week. ✉ *1400 Columbus Blvd., at Reed St., South Philadelphia* ☎ *215/462–2000 reservations* 🌐 *www.warmdaddys.com.*

Shopping

South Philadelphia is made up of smaller neighborhoods and commercial corridors, including South Street, Queen Village (home to Fabric Row), and the Italian Market. The shopping options in each are as varied as the folks who live down here. South Street's street-wear specialists, old-fashioned record stores, and varying hippie holdovers give way to indie boutiques and thrift shops in the satellite streets. The Italian Market's specialty stores are the avid home cook's dream, if you know where to look. Excellent independent bookshops survive throughout South Philly, supported by their own.

Philly's Music History

Philly holds a special place in pop music history. *American Bandstand*, hosted by Dick Clark, began here as a local dance show. When it went national in 1957, it gave a boost to many hometown boys, including teen heartthrob Fabian, Bobby Rydell, Frankie Avalon, and Chubby Checker, of "Twist" fame. Sun Ra, the legendary jazz pianist, was from Philly, in keeping with the city's rich tradition of jazz luminaries such as saxophonists Grover Washington Jr., Stan Getz, and John Coltrane, drummer Philly Joe Jones, and vocalist Billie Holiday.

In the 1970s, the Philadelphia Sound—a polished blend of disco, pop, and R&B—came alive through producers Kenny Gamble and Leon Huff at the famed Philadelphia International Records studios for artists like The Ojays, Lou Rawls, Teddy Pendergrass, and Three Degrees, whose megahit "Love Train" helped to define the '70s era. That lush sound was kept alive by chart toppers such as Hall and Oates, Patti LaBelle, Boyz II Men, Will Smith, Jill Scott, The Roots (now the house band for *Late Night With Jimmy Fallon*, among other accomplishments), neo-soul stylist Musiq Soulchild, pop queen Pink, and R&B sensation Jazmine Sullivan. Meek Mill, Lil Uzi Vert, PnB Rock, and Tierra Whack are just a few of the Philadelphia hip-hop artists to find a national, and in some cases international, audience in recent years.

Contemporary rock acts from Philly that have gained national renown include Dr. Dog, Kurt Vile, Man Man, Hop Along, Circa Survive, and The War on Drugs. The local DJ scene is also potent, with stalwart spinners like King Britt, Rich Medina, and The Roots' Questlove paving the way for a new generation of party starters.

BOOKSTORES

Head House Books

BOOKS/STATIONERY | Sunlight streams into the front windows of this well-curated indie bookshop. It's the kind of place that attracts regulars who sit sipping tea and reading for hours with a dog curled at their feet. This inviting shop has become a meeting place for the local literary community—both the readers and the writers. ✉ *619 S. 2nd St., South Philadelphia* ☎ *215/923–9525* 🌐 *www.headhousebooks.com.*

FOOD

Italian Market

SHOPPING NEIGHBORHOODS | If you want local color, nothing compares with South Philadelphia's Italian Market. On both sides of 9th Street from Fitzwater Street to Wharton Street and spilling out onto the surrounding blocks, outdoor stalls and indoor stores sell spices, cheeses, pastas, fruits, vegetables, and freshly slaughtered poultry and beef, not to mention household items, clothing, shoes, and other goods. It's crowded and filled with the aromas of everything from fresh garlic to imported salami. Food shops include Grassia's Italian Market Spice Co., Di Bruno Bros. House of Cheese, Claudio's, and Talluto's Authentic Italian Food. Fante's is well known for cookware. The market's general hours are Tuesday–Saturday 9–5:30; some vendors open earlier, and others close around 3:30. Some shops are open Sundays and even Mondays; it's wise to call ahead to specific shops and check. ✉ *9th St., between Fitzwater St. and Wharton St., and the surrounding blocks, South Philadelphia.*

The East Passyunk neighborhood is full of community gardens, murals, Italian restaurants, and boutiques, as well as Pat's and Geno's cheesesteak shops.

East Passyunk

South of Bella Vista, East Passyunk technically comprises two neighborhoods: Passyunk Square and East Passyunk Crossing. Together, they stretch between Washington and Snyder Avenues, Broad Street and 8th Street. The Italian presence is also felt around Passyunk (pronounced pash-unk), but in recent years, an influx of new home buyers has changed the cultural complexion of the area, not unlike Bella Vista. Among the century-old pizza parlors and cheese shops are Spanish wine bars, artisanal butcher shops, hip baby boutiques, and restaurants helmed by *Top Chef* winners.

No trip to South Philly would be complete without a stop at the site of the city's best-known cheesesteak rivalry, Pat's King of Steaks (🌐 *www.patskingofsteaks.com*) and adjacent competitor Geno's Steaks (🌐 *www.genosteaks.com*). Both can be found at the intersection of 9th Street and Passyunk Avenue and are open 24 hours a day. Each has its loyal fans for what's essentially the same sandwich: thinly sliced rib-eye steak, grilled onions, cheese—provolone, American, or Cheez Whiz—all piled on a fresh-baked Italian roll.

 Restaurants

Over the past few years, East Passyunk Avenue (the main thoroughfare of the neighborhood of the same name) has emerged as one of the city's eminent dining strips; it seems there are more critically acclaimed restaurants along its central stretch than anywhere else in town.

Bing Bing Dim Sum

$$ | **ASIAN FUSION** | Funky, unorthodox dim sum gets all the cool kids in the door at Bing Bing, which proudly bills itself as inauthentic. But beyond the high-low appeal of cheesesteak bao buns and corned beef ribs with beet barbecue sauce, there's real finesse from chef Ben Puchowitz's kitchen here. **Known for:**

creative dim sum variations; shareable cocktails; young lively crowd. $ *Average main: $18* ✉ *1648 E. Passyunk Ave., East Passyunk* ☎ *215/279–7702* 🌐 *www.bingbingdimsum.com* ⏲ *No lunch Mon.–Thurs.*

Geno's Steaks

$ | **AMERICAN** | Geno's, open since 1966, is a fresh-faced upstart compared to neighboring rival Pat's, which has been slinging steaks since 1930. That gulf manifests itself visually in the contrast between Pat's understated aesthetic and Geno's over-the-top use of neon, which burns so brightly astronauts can probably see it from space, and the fact that Geno's meat is sliced, not chopped. **Known for:** 24-hour service; classic cheesesteaks; late-night scene. $ *Average main: $11* ✉ *1219 S. 9th St., East Passyunk* ☎ *215/389–0659* 🌐 *www.genosteaks.com* 💳 *No credit cards.*

★ Laurel

$$$$ | **MODERN AMERICAN** | Reservations at Laurel are typically a tough get, given its cozy 22-seat dining room and chef-owner's Nicholas Elmi's sterling reputation. But dinner at this intimate, candlelit hideaway is worth the effort for fans of the *Top Chef* season 11 winner's elegant, intelligent French-American food, presented in six- or nine-course tasting formats five nights a week. **Known for:** elegant French-American cuisine; tasting menus; romantic atmosphere. $ *Average main: $85* ✉ *1617 E. Passyunk Ave., East Passyunk* ☎ *215/271–8299* 🌐 *www.restaurantlaurel.com* ⏲ *Closed Sun. and Mon. No lunch.*

Le Virtù

$$$$ | **ITALIAN** | Sublime charcuterie, ethereal pastas, and interesting wines by the glass are just a few of the details that make Le Virtù one of the best Italian restaurants in town. The sun-washed space began with a fierce dedication to the underappreciated region of Abruzzo, where the owners run culinary tours; that focus has been sharpened under the direction of talented chef Damon Menapace. **Known for:** rare Abruzzese cuisine; excellent pastas; charming atmosphere. $ *Average main: $30* ✉ *1927 E. Passyunk Ave., East Passyunk* ☎ *215/271–5626* 🌐 *www.levirtu.com* ⏲ *No lunch.*

Pat's King of Steaks

$ | **AMERICAN** | New cheesesteak restaurants come and go, but two of the oldest—Pat's and Geno's, at 9th and Passyunk—have a long-standing feud worth weighing in on. It comes down to a matter of taste, as both serve equally generous portions of rib-eye steak, grilled onions, and melted provolone, American, or Cheez Whiz on freshly baked Italian rolls. **Known for:** 24-hour service; classic cheesesteak; late-night scene. $ *Average main: $11* ✉ *1237 E. Passyunk Ave., East Passyunk* ☎ *215/468–1546* 🌐 *patskingofsteaks.com* 💳 *No credit cards.*

Perla

$$$$ | **PHILIPPINE** | Lou Boquila brings his modern interpretations of Philippine cuisine to South Philly with this romantic BYOB. Thursday to Saturday, the chef-owner creates innovative fine-dining takes on humble staples like *pancit* (fried noodles), *kare-kare* (Philippine stew with a thick peanut sauce), and *pinakbet* (mixed vegetables steamed in fish or shrimp sauce), and on Wednesday and Sunday, the popular *kamayan* dinner (Filipino style of communal eating without plates or utensils) features loads of delicious food presented to the table on banana-leaf place mats. **Known for:** creative Filipino food; intimate dining room; communal kamayan dinners. $ *Average main: $27* ✉ *1535 S. 11th St., East Passyunk* ☎ *267/273–0008* 🌐 *www.perlaphilly.com* ⏲ *Closed Mon.-Tues. No lunch.*

East Passyunk, Bella Vista, and Queen Village
A
B
C
D
E
F
1
2
3
4
5
6
7
8
9
0
500 M
0
1,000 ft
Spruce St.
Clinton St.
Pine St.
Addison St.
Rodman St.
South St.
Rodman St.
Kater St.
Webster St.
Christian St.
Bella Vista
Catharine
Christian
Montrose St.
Carpenter St.
Hawthorne
Washington Ave.
Federal St.
Dickinson St.
East Passyunk Ave.
Pennsport
Wharton
McKean St.
Snyder Ave
W. Ritner St.
S. 18th St.
S. 17th St.
S. 16th St.
S. 15th St.
South Broad St.
S. 13th St.
S. 12th St.
S. 11th St.
S. 10th St.
S. 9th St.
S. 8th St.
S. 7th St.
S. 6th St.
S. 5th St.
S. 4th St.
S. Delhi St.
S. Hutchinson
S. Mildred St.
E. Moyamensing Ave.

Sights

1 Fleisher Art Memorial E3
2 Gloria Dei Old Swedes' Episcopal Church H5
3 Italian Market D4
4 Philadelphia's Magic Gardens D2

Restaurants

1 Beau Monde F2
2 Bibou E4
3 Bing Bing Dim Sum C7
4 Bistrot La Minette F2
5 Blue Corn D4
6 Cry Baby Pasta G3
7 Dante & Luigi's D3
8 Geno's Steaks D5
9 The Good King Tavern E2
10 Hungry Pigeon G3
11 Jim's Steaks G2
12 Kalaya Thai Kitchen D3
13 Laurel C6
14 Le Virtù B8
15 Pat's King of Steaks D5
16 Perla C6
17 Ralph's Italian Restaurant D3
18 Sabrina's Cafe D3
19 Saloon Restaurant E3
20 Sam's Morning Glory Diner D3
21 Scrpico F2
22 South Street Souvlaki F2

Quick Bites

1 Anthony's Italian Coffee House E3
2 D'Emilio's Old World Ice Treats B8
3 Essen Bakery D6
4 Termini Brothers Bakery E6

Philly Cheesesteaks

Philly's best-known culinary creation is simple in theory, but complex in the details of its execution. Begin with the basic roll, which should be slightly crusty with a good amount of chew—Amoroso's is a popular choice. Add to that thin-sliced strips of top round or rib eye, griddled until well browned, next to a simmering bed of chopped onions. If you want the full effect, order your sandwich "wiz wit," meaning with a ladle of Cheez Whiz and fried onions; if you want only Whiz, it's simply "wiz witout." American and provolone are other commonly requested cheeses. As befitting a cultural touchstone, there are many other homages on Philly menus, including chicken dumplings, cheesesteak egg rolls, and vegetarian versions. Even high-end restaurants pay their respects—including a famous $120 Wagyu rib eye/foie gras/truffled Whiz version at Stephen Starr's Barclay Prime in Rittenhouse Square (a half bottle of champagne is included in the price).

Coffee and Quick Bites

D'Emilio's Old World Ice Treats

$ | **AMERICAN** | **FAMILY** | After a few years of selling his ices from a freezer sidecar on his motorcycle, owner Chris D'Emilio went into business with Mike Strauss from nearby Mike's BBQ to create this ice cream and sandwich spot. Whipping up original flavors like blueberry pomegranate and cherry lemonade, using his grandmother's recipe, D'Emilio sells his "ice treats" aka water ice, plus soft serve ice cream, alongside a short lineup of excellent sandwiches, the recipes for which come from famed Philly chefs like Marc Vetri, Jeff Michaud, etc. **Known for:** ice cream-filled pretzel; selling ices from a freezer sidecar on his motorcycle; excellent sandwiches inspired by famed Philly chefs. *Average main: $10* *1928 E Passyunk Ave., East Passyunk* *215/514–3930* *Closed mid-Dec.–Feb.*

Essen Bakery

$ | **BAKERY** | Babka, bagels, rugelach, and challah are but a few of the specialties at Tova du Plessis's "little Jewish bakery," where everything's handmade in small batches. In addition to these tasty artisanal items, Essen doles out traditional neighborhood bakery options, like cookies, croissants, coffee, and simple sandwiches. **Known for:** homemade bagels; Jewish baked goods; quaint atmosphere. *Average main: $7* *1437 E. Passyunk Ave., East Passyunk* *215/271–2299* *www.essenbakery.com* *No dinner.*

Termini Brothers Bakery

$ | **BAKERY** | Churning out Italian pastries since 1921, this famed bakery is best known for their filled-to-order cannoli, but their counters are also packed with pizzelles, biscotti, cakes, and another traditional Italian sweet treats. It's the perfect spot to stop for some traditional edible souvenirs to bring home—think cookie trays and gift boxes—or ship to your favorite cousin in California. **Known for:** filled-to-order cannoli; ships gift boxes everywhere; additional locations in Reading Terminal Market and the Market and Shops at Comcast Center. *Average main: $10* *1523 S 8th St., East Passyunk* *215/334–1816* *www.termini.com.*

Nightlife

BARS AND LOUNGES

The Pub on Passyunk East

BARS/PUBS | Less concerned with the papacy than fine craft beer, the P.O.P.E., as it's called by locals, is a comfy neighborhood joint smack-dab in the middle of the drinking and dining enclave of East Passyunk Avenue. A bona fide neighborhood hangout that gets slammed on the weekends, the bar offers 14 beers on tap and loads more in bottles; the kitchen prepares straightforward fare, including burgers, nachos, and vegetarian options. ✉ *1501 E. Passyunk Ave., East Passyunk* ☎ *215/755–5125* 🌐 *www.pubonpassyunkeast.com.*

Triangle Tavern

BARS/PUBS | An old-school grandpa bar rejiggered by the owners of Khyber Pass Pub, Royal Tavern, and Cantina Los Caballitos, the Triangle is at once new and old. While the smart craft beer and spirit selections nod to nouveau drinkers, the bar's nostalgic menu, featuring pastas, roast pork sandwiches, and other hearty specialties, is as South Philly as it gets. ✉ *1338 S 10th St., East Passyunk* ☎ *215/800–1992* 🌐 *www.triangletavernphilly.com.*

Shopping

CLOTHING

Metro Mens Clothing

CLOTHING | Well-dressed gents populate this handsome menswear boutique on a high-profile East Passyunk corner. Shopkeeper Tom Longo stocks Scotch & Soda denim, Penguin polos, Parke & Ronen swimsuits, and more. The window displays are epic. ✉ *1600 E. Passyunk Ave., East Passyunk* ☎ *267/324–5172* 🌐 *www.metromensclothing.com.*

GIFTS AND SOUVENIRS

Analog Watch Co.

JEWELRY/ACCESSORIES | Chic unisex watches composed of natural materials like marble and bamboo are the get at this combo boutique-workshop tucked in along East Passyunk. The friendly craftsmen there can help you find the watch that fits your style. Note that the shop is open by appointment only; call ahead before visiting. ✉ *1737 E. Passyunk Ave., East Passyunk* ☎ *484/808–5831* 🌐 *www.analogwatchco.com.*

Occasionette

GIFTS/SOUVENIRS | Sara Villari got her start screen-printing tea towels and totes, but her business eventually grew enough to open a bricks-and-mortar shop on East Passyunk. The store is a cheerful menagerie of thoughtful gifts and trinkets, like indie greeting cards, eco-friendly water bottles, alluring candles, books, and cocktail mixers. Check the website for multiple special events and deals. ✉ *1825 E. Passyunk Ave., East Passyunk* ☎ *215/465–1704* 🌐 *www.occasionette.com.*

Bella Vista

Bella Vista nuzzles against Queen Village, running from 6th Street to Broad Street, though the exact boundary is a favorite topic of debate among locals. It's the historic heart of Italian-American Philadelphia, and its centerpiece is the outdoor Italian Market along 9th Street, packed with vendors, shops, and restaurants. In more recent years, Mexican immigrants have made spaces in the Market their own, so the drag is now also the place to pick up warm-from-the-press tortillas, dozens of different dried chilies, and even festive piñatas.

Sights

Fleisher Art Memorial

MUSEUM | The realization of founder Samuel S. Fleisher's open invitation "to come and learn art," this school and gallery has offered classes, some tuition-free, since 1898. Fleisher presents regular exhibits of contemporary art as well as works by faculty and students. The Memorial consists of several connected buildings, including the Sanctuary, a Romanesque Revival Episcopal church designed by the architectural firm of Frank Furness and featuring European art from the 13th to the 15th century. A satellite building at 705 Christian Street is dedicated to works on paper. ✉ *719 Catharine St., Bella Vista* ☎ *215/922–3456* 🌐 *www.fleisher.org* 🎫 *Free.*

Philadelphia's Magic Gardens

LOCAL INTEREST | Stroll around South Street and it won't be long before you come across the work of mosaic muralist Isaiah Zagar, recognizable by its intricate, irreverent mix of found materials and folk motifs. The Magic Gardens is home base for Zagar's eye-catching art, which he's been creating around here since he and wife, Julia, a fellow artist, moved there in the 1960s. Consisting of two indoor galleries and an outdoor sculpture garden, it's an impressive and immersive visual feat. It's a popular spot with tourists and groups, so it's best to purchase tickets in advance; they go on sale online for visits one month in advance. ✉ *1020 South St., Bella Vista* ☎ *215/733–0390* 🌐 *www.phillymagicgardens.org* 🎫 *$10* ⏲ *Closed Tues.*

Restaurants

Beau Monde

$$ | FRENCH | In this city, at least, this is the closest you'll find to the crepes of Brittany, where the owners of this casual bistro traveled to study; imported cast-iron griddles are the secret to this crêperie's paper-thin wrappers. The menu is split into savory crepes (made with buckwheat flour) and sweet crepes (made with wheat flour)—tried-and-true combos include coq au vin with Swiss cheese and smoked salmon with leeks and crème fraîche. **Known for:** sweet and savory crêpes; Francophile atmosphere; popular brunch. $ *Average main: $19* ✉ *624 S. 6th St., Bella Vista* ☎ *215/592–0656* 🌐 *www.creperie-beaumonde.com* ⏲ *Closed Mon.*

Bibou

$$$$ | FRENCH | Tiny Bibou is one of the city's best BYOBs, as evidenced by how many tables are occupied by French speakers who'd otherwise seem out of place in this tiny restaurant on a nondescript South Philly block. The other proof is in the intensely flavorful and ever-changing menu, which can feature anything from perfectly crisped scallops to pig's feet stuffed with foie gras. **Known for:** romantic room; elegant French cuisine; polished service. $ *Average main: $125* ✉ *1009 S. 8th St., Bella Vista* ☎ *215/965–8290* 🌐 *www.biboubyob.com* 💳 *No credit cards* ⏲ *Closed Sun.-Tues. No lunch.*

Bistrot La Minette

$$$$ | FRENCH | The cheery atmosphere inside this long, narrow bistro exudes warmth and attention to detail, from the flea-market knickknacks picked out by chef Peter Woolsey and his Burgundian wife, Peggy, to the ceramic pitchers of house wine delivered to your table. Woolsey studied at the Cordon Bleu, fell in love with French food culture (and Peggy), and came back to his native Philadelphia to share the experience with his city; regulars swear by the mustard-braised rabbit with housemade pasta; pork cheeks braised in Malbec; and the exemplary desserts that speak to Woolsey's extensive training as a pastry chef. **Known for:** romantic atmosphere; classic French bistro menu; authentic ingredients. $ *Average main: $27* ✉ *623 S. 6th St., Bella Vista* ☎ *215/925–8000*

Philadelphia's Magic Gardens is home base for mosaic muralist Isaiah Zagar, whose eye-catching art can also be seen all around South Street.

www.bistrotlaminette.com *No lunch weekdays.*

★ Blue Corn

$$$ | **MEXICAN** | The sheer volume of Mexican restaurants on South 9th Street can be daunting—many are excellent, but how do you pick? The family-run Blue Corn consistently delivers, serving Pueblan cuisine with personality like tacos *al pastor* (taco made with spit-grilled pork) and *queso fundido* (hot melted cheese with spicy chorizo) alongside harder-to-find specialties, like *huaraches* (crispy masa–pinto bean flatbreads) or whole fish stuffed with the corn truffle *huitlacoche*. Warm service and killer cocktails round out the experience. **Known for:** authentic Pueblan cooking; tequila and mezcal cocktails; friendly service. *Average main: $20* *940 S. 9th St., Bella Vista* *215/925–1010* *www.facebook.com/bluecornrestaurant* *No credit cards.*

Dante & Luigi's

$$ | **ITALIAN** | Established in 1899 in the heart of Philly's Italian Market, Dante & Luigi's is located in two gorgeously appointed converted townhouses. The menu features old-world Italian cuisine like red-sauce pasta, lasagna (some say its the best in Philly), and osso buco. **Known for:** old-world Italian cuisine; lasagne; reservations by phone only. *Average main: $18* *762 S 10th St., Bella Vista* *215/922–9501* *www.danteandluigis.com* *Closed Mon. No lunch Sat.-Sun.*

The Good King Tavern

$$$ | **FRENCH** | Specializing in French country cooking and expertly selected wines, the Good King offers casual Gallic flair at accessible neighborhood prices. Pair a *socca* (chickpea pancake) platter or steak frites with a glass or pitcher of house red or white, helpfully classified "Good," "Better" and "Best." The bar also makes up a mean cocktail, with daily changing specials. **Known for:** creative wine program; simple French cuisine; upstairs wine bar. *Average main: $20* *614 S. 7th St., Bella Vista* *215/625–3700*

⊕ *www.thegoodkingtavern.com* ⊙ *No lunch Mon.-Sat.*

Kalaya Thai Kitchen

$$$ | THAI | Chef Nok Suntaranon shares a wealth of Thai family recipes at Kalaya, the 9th Street BYOB named after her mother. Addressing Philadelphia's dearth of authentic Thai restaurants, she offers curries, soups, and noodle dishes that don't skimp one bit on real-deal fiery, fishy flavor. **Known for:** authentic Thai cooking; fiery flavors; warm service. *$ Average main: $24* ✉ *764 S. 9th St., Bella Vista* ☎ *215/385–3777* ⊕ *www.kalaya.net* ⊙ *Closed Mon. No lunch Tues.-Thurs.*

Ralph's Italian Restaurant

$$ | ITALIAN | Owned and operated by the fourth and fifth generation of the Dispigno/Rubino family, you can expect old world favorites like sausage and peppers, osso bucco, and braciole, as well as house specialities like lasagne and fettuccini alfredo. **Known for:** traditional Italian comfort dishes; warm vibes; South Philly staple. *$ Average main: $18* ✉ *760 S 9th St., Bella Vista* ☎ *215/627–6011* ⊕ *www.ralphsrestaurant.com.*

Sabrina's Cafe

$ | CAFÉ | FAMILY | If there's one thing you can count on, it's an hour wait for Sunday BYOB brunch at this cozy former bakery around the corner from the Italian Market; locals call ahead and wait it out with coffee and the paper at home, and you can, too. Here's what everyone is waiting for: Mediterranean omelets; stuffed challah French toast with bananas and vanilla-bean maple syrup; and a Mexican-inspired egg scramble served with black bean grits, cilantro pesto, corn chips, and avocado. **Known for:** brunch specials; large portions; long weekend waits. *$ Average main: $13* ✉ *910 Christian St., Bella Vista* ☎ *215/574–1599* ⊕ *www.sabrinascafe.com* ⊙ *No dinner.*

Sam's Morning Glory Diner

$ | AMERICAN | FAMILY | The Morning Glory bills itself as a "finer diner," and offers traditional touches such as big mugs of steaming coffee, but the "finer" comes in the updated, wholesome versions of diner fare such as homemade ketchup on every table, curried tofu scrambles, thick pecan waffles with whipped peach butter, and flaky buttermilk biscuits that accompany breakfast. Unless you're an early weekend riser, weekdays are a better bet, as the wait for weekend brunch can be epic. **Known for:** hearty breakfast; classic diner atmosphere; long weekend waits. *$ Average main: $11* ✉ *735 S. 10th St., Bella Vista* ☎ *215/413–3999* ⊕ *www.themorninggorydiner.com* ▭ *No credit cards* ⊙ *No dinner.*

★ Serpico

$$$$ | MODERN AMERICAN | After earning a James Beard Foundation Award for his work at Momofuku Ko in New York, Peter Serpico teamed up with restaurateur Stephen Starr and opened this slick, glass-and-onyx box on South Street. There's a slight Asian undercurrent to the menu, but Serpico's style is absolutely global, mixing textbook charcuterie and sumptuous vegetable preparations with more playful ideas, like deep-fried duck legs on Martin's Potato Rolls. **Known for:** creative global cooking; natural wine list; sleek dining room. *$ Average main: $28* ✉ *604 South St., Bella Vista* ☎ *215/925–3001* ⊕ *www.serpicoonsouth.com* ⊙ *Closed Mon.*

Coffee and Quick Bites

Anthony's Italian Coffee House

$ | CAFÉ | When you're ready for an atmospheric break, stop by Anthony's Italian Coffee House in the heart of the Italian Market. Here, to the strains of Frank Sinatra, you can sample a fresh panino with prosciutto and mozzarella or indulge in homemade cannoli or gelato imported from Italy. **Known for:** Italian espresso drinks; Italian desserts; outdoor seating. $ *Average main: $8* ✉ *903 S. 9th St., Bella Vista* ☎ *215/627–2586* 🌐 *www.italiancoffeehouse.com.*

Nightlife

BARS AND LOUNGES

L'etage

BARS/PUBS | Upstairs from parent restaurant Beau Monde, a fine French crêperie, this unique spot has a lovely selection of wines and liquors. They also offer up a slate of unique entertainment that ranges from specialty cabaret and comedy to DJs and live storytelling. ✉ *624 S. 6th St., 2nd fl., Bella Vista* ☎ *215/592–0656* 🌐 *www.creperie-beaumonde.com* ☞ *Closed Mon.*

Royal Tavern

BARS/PUBS | Newly renovated as of 2019, the stalwart Royal Tavern is as poised as ever to satisfy aspiring young barflies and entrenched locals with equal aplomb. Beer, whether poured from one of the eight taps or sipped from a bottle, is abundant, as is the crazy-hearty comfort-food menu, featuring one of the city's best burgers. ✉ *937 E. Passyunk Ave., Bella Vista* ☎ *215/389–6694* 🌐 *www.royaltavern.com.*

Shopping

FOOD

Cardenas Oil & Vinegar Taproom

FOOD/CANDY | You've seen shops like Cardenas Oil & Vinegar Taproom in small-town downtowns all across the country. At this Italian Market shop, they've got the requisite refillable oils and vinegars (in flavors that include blood orange and coconut), but distinguish themselves with a serious lineup of rare, unadulterated elixirs sourced from Italy, Spain, even South Africa. The team is generous with samples. ✉ *942 S. 9th St., Bella Vista* ☎ *267/928–3690* 🌐 *www.cardenastaproom.com.*

Di Bruno Bros.

FOOD/CANDY | The first location of the famed specialty cheese shop, this Di Bruno's looks laughably tiny compared to the enormous branches in Center City and the suburbs. Slight in size though it may be—it's long, narrow, and cavelike, with salamis hanging from the ceiling like stalactites—it's absolutely jam-packed with all the specialties you expect from *la famiglia*. Peruse all the cheeses, oils, antipasti, and charcuterie you want, comforted by the assurance that the gregarious employees behind the counter will always break you off samples. ✉ *930 S. 9th St., Bella Vista* ☎ *215/922–2876* 🌐 *www.dibruno.com.*

HOME DECOR

Fante's Kitchen Shop

HOUSEHOLD ITEMS/FURNITURE | One of the nation's oldest gourmet supply stores offers amateur and pro cooks alike an impressive selection of kitchen tools and equipment. Family owned since 1906, Fante's is famous for oddball kitchen gadgets such as truffle shavers and pineapple peelers; restaurants and bakeries all over the country and overseas order from the store. **■ TIP→ It's in the Italian Market, so you can conveniently combine a visit here with shopping for ingredients.** ✉ *1006 S. 9th St., Bella Vista* ☎ *215/922–5557, 800/443–2683* 🌐 *www.fantes.com* Ⓜ *Broad and Ellsworth.*

JEWELRY

Bario-Neal Jewelry

JEWELRY/ACCESSORIES | Stunningly simple earrings, bracelets, and necklaces are designed and handcrafted locally at this store-workshop by two women (Anna Bario and Page Neal) who create environmentally friendly jewelry. All materials are reclaimed, ethically sourced, or retrieved using low-impact practices. Even the packaging—reclaimed glass bottles with cork stoppers—is green. ✉ *700 S. 6th St., Bella Vista* ☎ *215/454–2164* ⏲ *Closed Mon.-Tues.* ☞ *Appointments preferred.*

Queen Village

North of South Street is Society Hill. South of South, Queen Village. Though there was a time when the former looked down its nose at its southern neighbor, Queen Village has been a mighty nice place to live for the last 20 years, home to some of the city's priciest historic homes. Queen Village is dense, residential, and prettiest on the streets closer to the Delaware River. Cafés and restaurants dot the corners, while Fabric Row on 4th Street is where budding designers go shopping for materials at decades-old cotton and silk houses.

Sights

Gloria Dei Old Swedes' Episcopal Church
RELIGIOUS SITE | One of the few remaining relics from the Swedes who settled Pennsylvania before William Penn, Gloria Dei, also known as Old Swedes' Church, has been active since 1700. It's the oldest church in Pennsylvania and second oldest in the entire country. Models of the ships that transported the first Swedish settlers hang from the ceiling in the center of the church; the baptismal font dates all the way back to 1731, while religious carvings on display are even older. Grouped around the house of worship are the parish hall, the sexton's house, the rectory, and the church offices. Sitting in the center of a graveyard, Old Swedes' is calming in its tranquility. *916 S. Swanson St., Queen Village 215/389–1513 www.old-swedes.com Free.*

Restaurants

Cry Baby Pasta
$$$ | **ITALIAN** | Queen Villagers shed tears of joy when longtime neighborhood restaurateur Bridget Foy introduced this easy-to-love restaurant, specializing in handmade pastas and wine priced to glug. You'll spot plenty of young families with kids in tow in the early dinner hours, while the crowd gets a little more grownup later in the evening. **Known for:** house-made pasta; family friendly; accessible wine list. *Average main: $21 627 S. 3rd St., Queen Village 267/534–3076 crybabypasta.com Closed Mon. No lunch.*

Hungry Pigeon
$$$$ | **AMERICAN** | Chefs Scott Schoeder and Pat O'Malley work with local farmers and purveyors to build the conscientious menu at this neighborhood restaurant that features large-format shareable entrées, like whole fried chickens or luscious lasagna. Scattered with lush plants, the exposed-brick dining room has a homey feel, whether you're hanging at the lengthy bar with a pour of natural wine or sharing the communal table in the rear. **Known for:** local and seasonal ingredients; baked goods; relaxed environs. *Average main: $28 743 S. 4th St., Queen Village 215/278–2736 www.hungrypigeon.com No lunch Mon.-Thurs.*

Jim's Steaks
$ | **AMERICAN** | **FAMILY** | You'll know you're nearing Jim's when the scent of frying onions overwhelms your senses—or when you see people lined up around the corner. Big, juicy cheesesteaks—shaved beef piled high on long crusty rolls—come off the grill with amazing speed when the counter workers hit their stride, whether it's lunchtime or late-night. **Known for:** cheesesteaks; long and lively lines; nostalgic environment. *Average main: $9 400 South St., Queen Village 215/928–1911 www.jimssouthstreet.com No credit cards.*

South Street Souvlaki
$ | **GREEK** | **FAMILY** | The first thing you'll see is the large rotisserie, trumpeting the ubiquitous gyro—tasty slices of meat are stuffed inside a large fresh pita, with tangy yogurt and some exemplary fresh veggies. Other Greek specialties, such as stuffed grape leaves, moussaka, and,

of course, souvlaki, round out the menu. **Known for:** simple and authentic Greek fare; group dining; value-driven menu. *Average main: $13* ✉ *509 South St., Queen Village* ☎ *215/925–3026* 🌐 *www.southstreetsouvlaki.com* 🕓 *Closed Mon.*

Nightlife

BARS AND LOUNGES

For Pete's Sake

BARS/PUBS | Pete's, in Queen Village, could easily be mistaken for just another neighborhood watering hole, but the menu is eclectic, featuring a regularly changing lineup of creative food alongside the requisite wings and burgers. ✉ *900 S. Front St., Queen Village* ☎ *215/462–2230* 🌐 *www.forpetessake-pub.com.*

New Wave Café

BARS/PUBS | To its devoted Queen Village clientele, the New Wave is more than just the place to wait for a table at a nearby restaurant. The regulars come to this welcoming neighborhood bar to unwind with a local craft brew, play a game of darts, watch the game, or enjoy the oft-changing gastropub menu. ✉ *784 S. 3rd St., Queen Village* ☎ *215/922–8484* 🌐 *newwavecafe.com.*

Performing Arts

THEATER

Theatre of Living Arts

MUSIC CLUBS | A former playhouse, mainstream movie theater, and art-house cinema, the TLA is a South Street institution that helped launch the careers of many indie filmmakers; it was known for hosting screenings of cult hits like *The Rocky Horror Picture Show.* Nowadays, it's a midsized live-music venue, hosting a range of rock, blues, hip-hop, and alternative acts. ✉ *334 South St., Queen Village* ☎ *215/922–1011* 🌐 *venue.tlaphilly.com.*

Shopping

BOOKSTORES

Brickbat Books

BOOKS/STATIONERY | The charming, worn-in feel of this store lined with wooden shelves befits the merchandise for sale: the focus is on rare, small-press used and new books, although it's not unheard-of to find a $4 Hardy Boys paperback next to a first-edition Edward Gorey. The store also acts as a venue for fringe musicians from near and far. **■ TIP→ Following Brickbat on Instagram (@brickbatphilly) is an easy way to stay abreast of the latest arrivals.** ✉ *709 S. 4th St., Queen Village* ☎ *215/592–1207* 🌐 *www.brickbatbooks.com* 🕓 *Closed Mon.*

Garland of Letters

BOOKS/STATIONERY | Open since 1972, this is the original New Age bookstore, hailing from the days when hippies arrived on South Street and established its reputation as an artsy enclave. Follow the aroma of incense and step inside to find books on astrology, tarot, shamanism, and world religions and cultures, plus a selection of jewelry, crystals, and candles. ✉ *527 South St., Queen Village* ☎ *215/923–5946* 🌐 *www.southstreet.com/business/garland-of-letters.*

CLOTHING

Fabric Row

SHOPPING NEIGHBORHOODS | In the early 1900s, 4th Street, today's Fabric Row, was teeming with pushcarts selling calico, notions, and trimming. It was known as "der Ferder," or "the Fourth" in Yiddish. Today, several century-old fabric stores still stand, like stalwarts Maxie's Daughter and Fleishman Fabrics and Supplies, but many of the storefronts are home to locals selling wares from European-label shoes to fair-trade coffee. There's also a resurgent restaurant scene. ✉ *400 Monroe St., Queen Village* ✣ *S. 4th St. between Monroe and Catharine Sts.* 🌐 *www.fabricrow.com.*

Passional Boutique & Sexploratorium

CLOTHING | Not everyone desires to be fit for a luxurious handcrafted corset—but this is definitely the place to go if you do. The work on these custom steel-boned pieces is stunning, and they're just one of many sex-positive, body-positive specialties of this boutique. A high-quality alternative to neighboring shops that hawk cheapo sexy nurse costumes and the like, Passional and its second-floor Sexploratorium offer a range of masculine and feminine apparel, costumes, toys, accessories, and educational materials. They also pride themselves on stocking a wide, inclusive range of sizes to accommodate all body types and genders. ✉ *317 South St., Queen Village* ☎ *215/829–4986* 🌐 *www.passionalboutique.com.*

GIFTS AND SOUVENIRS

Eye's Gallery

GIFTS/SOUVENIRS | This long-running shop has the feel of a folk art museum, its three floors stocked with vibrant handmade textiles and garments, Day of the Dead art, instruments, carvings, masks, jewelry, and decorative pieces sourced from all over Mexico and South America. From basement to skylight, the interior is adorned with the mosaic murals of Philadelphia artist Isaiah Zagar; he and his wife, Julia Zagar, a fellow artist, founded Eye's in 1968, directly shaping the artsy, bohemian reputation that's long been associated with South Street. ✉ *402 South St., Queen Village* ☎ *215/925–0193* 🌐 *www.eyesgallery.com.*

SHOES

Bus Stop Boutique

SHOES/LUGGAGE/LEATHER GOODS | Founded by Elena Brennan, a Londoner turned Philadelphian, Bus Stop stocks fashion-forward, cutting-edge shoes from European labels like Vagabond, All Black, P. Monjo and many more—kicks that are hard to find on this side of the pond. In addition, the Fabric Row shop is a showcase for Brennan's own BUS STOP X brand, limited-run collections that span the stylistic gamut from tie-dye booties to chunky sneakers. ✉ *727 S. 4th St., Queen Village* ☎ *215/627–2357* 🌐 *www.busstopboutique.com.*

Chapter 9

UNIVERSITY CITY AND WEST PHILADELPHIA

Updated by
Drew Lazor

 Sights
★★★★★

 Restaurants
★★★☆☆

 Hotels
★★★★☆

 Shopping
★★★☆☆

 Nightlife
★☆☆☆☆

NEIGHBORHOOD SNAPSHOT

TOP EXPERIENCES

■ **Institute of Contemporary Art:** Andy Warhol, Robert Mapplethorpe, and Laurie Anderson have all shown their work at this exhibition space.

■ **Penn Museum:** The largest ancient Egyptian sphinx in the Western Hemisphere is just the start at this world-class treasury of global antiquities.

■ **University of Pennsylvania:** This Ivy League school's leafy campus offers a bucolic contrast to its urban surroundings.

■ **Philadelphia Big 5:** Penn's venerated Palestra is the stage for one of the most storied rivalry series in collegiate basketball.

■ **World Café Live:** The broadcast home of FM radio station WXPN hosts live performances from an array of artists, including its "Free at Noon" daytime concert series.

■ **Lightbox Film Center:** International House Philadelphia is the home to dynamic repertory film programming celebrating lesser-known cinematic voices.

GETTING HERE

Unless you're a big walker or have access to a bike, you'll want to take either a SEPTA bus or underground Blue or Green Line to University City. If you're driving, street parking can be easier to find here than in Center City, although it can be tight near the Penn and Drexel campuses when school is in session.

PLANNING YOUR TIME

University City is at its best when school is in session; the students rushing to classes give this area its frenetic flavor. Allow half an hour each in the Arthur Ross Gallery and the Institute of Contemporary Art, two hours in the Penn Museum, and an hour exploring the campus. If your time is limited, skip all but the Penn Museum, a don't-miss for the archaeologically inclined.

QUICK BITES

■ **Dana Mandi.** Hidden in the rear of this unassuming Indian grocery store is a quick-serve restaurant dishing out soulful Punjabi home cooking. ✉ *4211 Chestnut St., University City*

■ **Pod.** For a Pan-Asian fix, grab a stool at the sushi bar at the futuristic Pod, where you can select your favorite raw fish from a conveyor belt. ✉ *3636 Sansom St., University City* 🌐 *www.podrestaurant.com*

■ **Wah-Gi-Wah.** This no-frills Pakistani eatery specializes in *lahore chargha*, a fiery fried-chicken dish. ✉ *4447 Chestnut St., University City* 🌐 *www.wahgiwah.com*

DID YOU KNOW?

■ Citywide, West Philadelphia has a progressive reputation, given its historical importance to the American civil rights movement, artistic leanings, and embrace of global influences, in the form of both the international student population and its many established immigrant enclaves. African, Caribbean, South Asian, and West Indian influences are palpable throughout the area, present in everything from the many languages spoken on the street to the diversity of authentic restaurants offering authentic cuisine.

Situated on the side of the Schuylkill River opposite Center City, West Philadelphia is rich in heritage and personality. Here you'll find University City, the academic heart of the region given the confluence of college campuses, as well as a collection of charming neighborhoods characterized by Victorian architecture and ample green space.

University City is the portion of West Philadelphia that includes the campuses of the University of Pennsylvania, Drexel University, the University of the Sciences, and several other institutions. It also has the University City Science Center (a leading think tank), the Annenberg Center for the Performing Arts, an impressive collection of Victorian houses, and a variety of moderately priced restaurants, movie theaters, stores, and lively bars catering to nearly 55,000 residents. The neighborhood stretches from the Schuylkill River west to 50th Street, and from Woodland Avenue north to Powelton Avenue and Market Street.

This area was once the city proper's western suburbs, where wealthy Philadelphians built estates and established summer villages. It officially became part of the city in 1854. In the 1870s, the University of Pennsylvania moved its main campus here from Center City. Though closely associated with academia, University City is also a fast-growing professional and residential hub, its diverse population working and living throughout distinct pockets like Cedar Park, Powelton Village, and Spruce Hill.

Sights

Anne & Jerome Fisher Fine Arts Library

LIBRARY | One of the finest examples of the work of Frank Furness, this was the most iconoclastic library building in America when it opened in 1891. The acclaimed Philadelphia architect ignored tradition, adorning the enormous reading room with Romanesque archways and skylights, and separating the soaring stairwell from study areas and stacks to minimize distractions. The unusual aesthetic extends to the exterior, with its terra-cotta panels, short heavy columns, and gargoyles on the north end. The mottoes inscribed on many of the original leaded-glass windows were chosen by Horace Howard Furness, Frank's older brother and a Shakespeare scholar on Penn's faculty. Energetic visitors should consider making the long climb up the main staircase to see the upper half of the tower. The less energetic can take the modern elevator to the fourth

University City and West Philadelphia
A
B
C
D
E
F
1
2
3
4
5
6
7
8
9
Parrish St.
Brown St.
Mantua Avenue
N. 40th St.
Union St.
Aspen St.
N. 38th
N. 37th
N. 36th
N. 35th
N. 39th
N. 44th St.
Fairmount St.
Wallace St.
Haverford St.
Spring Garden St.
Hamilton St.
Baring St.
N. 42nd St.
N. 41st St.
Preston St.
N. 40th
Powelton Ave.
Powelton Ave.
Warren St.
Lancaster Ave.
Race St.
Filbert Street
Market Street
Ludlow Street
Chestnut Street
Sansom Street
Walnut Street
South 40th Street
South 39th Street
South 38th Street
South 36th Street
Locust St.
S. 42nd St.
S. 41st St.
Hamilton Field
University City
College Green
Spruce Street
Delancey St.
Pine St.
Baltimore Ave.
S. University Ave.
Civic Center Boulevard
S. 45th St.
S. 46th St.
Woodland Ave.
Southwest Schuylkill
0
300 M
0
1,000 ft

KEY
1 Sights
1 Restaurants
1 Quick Bites
1 Hotels

Sights

1 A Love Letter For You.............. A4
2 Anne & Jerome Fisher Fine Arts Library F6
3 Arthur Ross Gallery.................. F6
4 Bartram's Garden F9
5 The Ellen Powell Tiberino Memorial Museum E3
6 Institute of Contemporary Art F5
7 Penn Museum G7
8 Penn Park.......................... H7
9 Simeone Foundation Automotive Museum............... F9
10 World Cafe Live.................... H6

Restaurants

1 Dahlak.............................. A7
2 Distrito D5
3 Dock Street West................. A7
4 Manakeesh Cafe A5
5 Vientiane Café A7
6 Walnut Street Café I6
7 White Dog Cafe F5

Quick Bites

1 Avril 50 .... F5
2 City Tap House D5
3 Dana Mandi B5
4 Franklin's Table..................... F6
5 Pod E5
6 ReAnimator Coffee A6
7 Wah-Gi-Wah A4

Hotels

1 AKA University City................. I6
2 Akwaaba Philadelphia E3
3 The Gables A8
4 The Inn at Penn, a Hilton Hotel.... F6
5 Sheraton Philadelphia University City....................... F5

floor. ✉ *220 S. 34th St., University City* ☎ *215/898–8325* 🌐 *www.library.upenn.edu/finearts* 🎫 *Free; need photo ID; admittance is more restricted in late evening, weekends, and during exam periods; check website for details* ☞ *Library may be closed or restricted to the public during exams and campus events* Ⓜ *34th and Market Sts. (SEPTA Market-Frankford Blue Line); 33rd and Market Sts. and 36th and Sansom Sts. (SEPTA subway-surface Green Lines, Rtes. 11, 13, 34, 36).*

Arthur Ross Gallery

MUSEUM | Penn's official art gallery contains treasures from the university's collections and traveling exhibitions. The gallery shares its historic-landmark building, designed by Frank Furness, with the **Fisher Fine Arts Library.** ✉ *220 S. 34th St., between Walnut and Spruce Sts., University City* ☎ *215/898–2083* 🌐 *www.arthurrossgallery.org* 🎫 *Free.*

Bartram's Garden

GARDEN | Established in 1728 by pioneering botanist John Bartram, this is America's oldest surviving botanical garden. Bartram, with his son William, collected and identified thousands of indigenous North American plants, showcasing them for both scientific and commercial purposes. Today, the 45-acre National Historic Landmark on the west bank of the Schuylkill River boasts a diversity of flora, from flowering shrubs and trees (azalea, rhododendron, magnolia) to rare specimens like the Franklinia, a tree that died out in its native Georgia, surviving today only because Bartram cultivated it. The best months to come are May and June, when the gardens are fragrant and filled with the lively chatter of birds. The original 18th-century farmhouse still stands, and you can tour its rooms and various exhibits, including Native American artifacts from the property dating back 3,000 years. **■ TIP→ Drive or take a cab, as the grounds are tucked down a driveway in an out-of-the-way part of Southwest Philadelphia.** ✉ *5400 Lindbergh Blvd., at 54th St., Southwest Philadelphia* ☎ *215/729–5281* 🌐 *www.bartramsgarden.org* 🎫 *Garden free to the public daily, dusk to dawn; house tour $12 available Apr. 1–Dec. 3, Thurs.–Sun.* Ⓜ *SEPTA Rte. 36 Trolley.*

The Ellen Powell Tiberino Memorial Museum

MUSEUM | The creative legacy of the Tiberinos, a dynamic family of artists sometimes referred to as "the West Philly Wyeths," is celebrated at this unconventional indoor-outdoor museum built out of the family's Powelton Village home. Though Ellen Powell and Joseph Tiberino, the matriarch and patriarch of this artistic clan, have passed away, their paintings, murals, and sculptures are preserved for future generations by their children, who incorporate their own original work, along with contributions from dozens of other artists, into the mix. ✉ *3819 Hamilton St., University City* ☎ *215/386–3784* 🌐 *www.tiberinomuseum.com* 🎫 *$10 suggested donation* ⏲ *Visits by appointment only.*

Institute of Contemporary Art

MUSEUM | This museum, part of the University of Pennsylvania, has established a reputation for identifying promising contemporary artists and championing them at critical points in their careers. Among the creators who have had exhibitions at ICA and later gone on to international prominence are Andy Warhol (his first-ever solo museum show, in 1965), Laurie Anderson, and Robert Mapplethorpe. ✉ *118 S. 36th St., at Sansom St., University City* ☎ *215/898–7108* 🌐 *www.icaphila.org* 🎫 *Free* Ⓜ *SEPTA Green Line Trolley stop at 36th St. (University of Pennsylvania).*

A Love Letter For You

PUBLIC ART | You don't have to walk far to encounter one of Philadelphia's 3,600-plus public murals. But the best way to take in a few of the most impressive

Penn Museum's vast collection includes priceless artifacts from Africa, Asia, Central and North America, and ancient Europe.

selections is by hopping on the Market-Frankford line. Artist and West Philly native Steve "ESPO" Powers's *A Love Letter For You,* a series of 50 works on buildings depicting the story of a budding romance, is best viewed via elevated train. The murals, which resemble old-fashioned ads, are both witty and touching, with messages like "This love is real, so dinner is on me" and "Miss you too often not to love you." You can download a guide for your own experience or join a Mural Arts Program tour, held at 10:30 am on Saturday and 1 pm on Sunday. ✉ *Market St., from 45th to 63rd, University City* ☎ *800/537–7676* 🌐 *www.muralarts.org* 🎫 *Free with SEPTA subway fare, or $23 for Mural Arts guided tour* Ⓜ *SEPTA Market-Frankford Subway Line.*

Penn Museum

MUSEUM | Overflowing with the rarest treasures of yore, this is one of the finest archaeological and anthropological museums out there. The vast collection includes the largest ancient Egyptian sphinx in the Western Hemisphere, a crystal ball once owned by China's dowager empress, some of the oldest writing known to humanity—Sumerian cuneiform clay tablets—and 4,600-year-old golden jewels from the royal tombs of Ur (modern-day Iraq). Other collections focus on priceless artifacts from Africa, Asia, Central and North America, ancient Europe, and more. Creative children's programming makes the museum especially appropriate for history-loving families. ✉ *3260 South St., University City* ☎ *215/898–4000* 🌐 *penn.museum* 🎫 *$16* 🕐 *Closed Mon.* Ⓜ *Market-Frankford Subway Line, 34th and Market Sts.; Blue and Green Line Trolley Rtes. 11, 13, 34, 36.*

Penn Park

CITY PARK | Unveiled in 2011, this 24-acre park stretches along the western side of the Schuylkill River and serves as a green-space conduit connecting Center City and the University of Pennsylvania

Collegiate Big 5 Basketball

There are plenty of storied rivalries in college sports, but none quite like Philadelphia's Big 5. Established in 1955, it's an in-season, intracity round-robin tournament that supersedes formalities like school size, national polls, or conference affiliation. Philly basketball bragging rights are the coveted prize. Each season, the men's and women's squads from five area schools—La Salle, Pennsylvania, St. Joseph's, Temple, and Villanova—face off against each other, with many of the matchups hosted at Penn's nearly century-old Palestra, the venerated arena known as "the Cathedral of College Basketball." The unique mix of public, Ivy League, and Catholic institutions produces fierce annual competition. A national powerhouse, Villanova has long dominated the men's Big 5, with 13 outright or shared titles over the last 20 years (Temple still holds a slight historic edge). As of 2018–19, the Wildcats are also the all-time winningest Big 5 team on the women's side, where there is more season-to-season parity. You can get tickets at *www.philadelphiabig5.org.*

campus. The park offers a natural-grass playing field and 12 tennis courts for public use, and extensive bike and walking trails, but its most striking feature is an elevated walk offering pedestrians panoramic views of the Philadelphia skyline. *3000 Walnut St., University City* *215/898–5986* *www.facilities.upenn.edu/maps/locations/penn-park* *Free.*

Simeone Foundation Automotive Museum

MUSEUM | A nondescript hangar five minutes from the Philadelphia International Airport is home to what's been dubbed the most impressive racing car collection on the planet. Dr. Fred Simeone spent half a century amassing a fleet of more than 75 vehicles that tell the sweeping story of racing history, and in 2019, the effort earned the retired neurosurgeon a number one ranking from Liechtenstein's prestigious Classic Car Trust. What separates Simeone from other gearheads is his staunch dedication to preservation as a means of education. All the museum's cars have their original parts and are in good running order. You can see them in action during regular "demo days," when staffers fire up the antique roadsters and take them out for some air. *6825 Norwitch Dr., Southwest Philadelphia* *215/365–7233* *www.simeonemuseum.org* *$12* *Closed Mon.*

Restaurants

In University City you can enjoy the many affordable, funky eateries geared toward Penn and Drexel students. West Philly features some of the city's best ethnic dining, from Ethiopian to Lebanese.

Dahlak

$ | **ETHIOPIAN** | A Baltimore Avenue institution, Dahlak is often credited with introducing the cuisines of Ethiopia and Eritrea to a wider Philadelphian audience. Family owned and operated, it serves signatures like *doro wat* (chicken stew spiced with zingy berbere) and *beg tibs* (stir-fried lamb with peppers and onions), accompanied by ample *injera,* the spongy bread traditionally used as a utensil. **Known for:** Ethiopian/Eritrean cuisine; vegetarian friendly; DJ nights. *Average main: $12* *4708 Baltimore Ave., University City* *215/726–6464* *www.dahlakrestaurant.com* *No lunch.*

Distrito

$$ | MODERN MEXICAN | Chef Jose Garces's Distrito is colorful, energetic, and enormous—just like Mexico City, its cultural and culinary muse. The menu features shareable small plates, tacos, enchiladas, and more, a celebration of Mexican street food with subtle fine-dining twists. **Known for:** creative tacos; lively crowd; kitschy decor. *Average main: $19* *3945 Chestnut St., University City* *215/222–1657* *philadelphia.distritorestaurant.com.*

Dock Street West

$$ | PIZZA | FAMILY | Housed in a handsome redbrick firehouse built in the early 1900s, Dock Street serves up wood-oven pizzas, fish-and-chips, vegan burgers, and seasonal salads to both residents and students in West Philly. The six taps and one cask spout house-brewed beers that range from approachable flagships (Bohemian Pilsner, Rye IPA) to experimental one-offs (a stout brewed with smoked goat brains; a barrel-aged saison whose yeasts were stimulated by the music of the Wu-Tang Clan). **Known for:** wood-fired pizzas; diverse crowd; creative craft brews. *Average main: $19* *701 S. 50th St., University City* *215/726–2337* *www.dockstreetbeer.com* *No lunch weekdays.*

★ Manakeesh Cafe

$ | LEBANESE | FAMILY | A Spruce Hill staple, Manakeesh specializes in the Lebanese flatbreads of the same name. Served warm from the oven, the puffy, round loaves come with both traditional toppings (za'atar, kafta) and unorthodox ones (turkey bacon-egg-cheese, cheesesteak), which speak to the diverse crowd that fills the comfortable café-style space. **Known for:** Lebanese/Middle Eastern cuisine; house-baked Middle Eastern pastries; coffee and fruit smoothies. *Average main: $7* *4420 Walnut St., University City* *215/921–2135* *www.manakeeshcafe.com* *Closed 1–2 pm Fri. for prayer.*

Vientiane Cafe

$$ | LAO | For more than 20 years, the Phanthavong family has served the soulful cuisine of its native Laos to the West Philly community, starting with a spartan street tent that blossomed into this homey, friendly BYOB restaurant. Three-course lunch specials, topping out at $14, are an excellent deal by day, and the options expand come evening—don't miss the house-made pork sausages and yellow curry fried rice. **Known for:** Lao cuisine; adventurous dishes; BYOB. *Average main: $18* *4728 Baltimore Ave., University City* *215 /726–1095* *www.vientiane-cafe.com* *Closed Sun.* *No credit cards.*

Walnut Street Café

$$$$ | AMERICAN | Taking up the ground floor of the FMC Tower, home to the AKA University City, the Walnut Street Café serves refined new American cuisine in a light-flooded, art deco–inspired space. Open for breakfast, lunch, and dinner, plus weekend brunch, the restaurant's edible highlights include house-baked bread and pastries, elegant raw seafood platters, and rotating handmade pastas. **Known for:** art deco decor; innovative wine list; open most of the day. *Average main: $30* *Cira Centre South, 2929 Walnut St., University City* *215/867–8067* *www.walnutstreetcafe.com* *No dinner Sun.-Tues.*

White Dog Cafe

$$$$ | AMERICAN | White Dog did farm to table long before the concept rose to national prominence. The Sansom Street stalwart specializes in sustainable foods ethically sourced from the region—think simple cooking that highlights the beauty of Kennett Square mushrooms, Lancaster beef, or Chester County goat cheese. **Known for:** farm-to-table cooking; local and seasonal ingredients; casual-chic decor. *Average main: $27* *3420 Sansom St., University City* *215/386–9224* *www.whitedog.com.*

Coffee and Quick Bites

Avril 50
$ | **CAFÉ** | They don't make shops like this University City mainstay anymore. Not only is it an international newsstand—there's a selection of foreign periodicals, postcards, and hip art publications—but it's also a café, offering high-end coffee, tea, and chocolate, and an old-school smoke shop, selling specialty tobacco products. **Known for:** great people-watching; a coffee (or tea) stop while exploring; all sorts of magazines. *Average main: $3* *3406 Sansom St., University City* *215/222–6108* *www.avril50.com* *No dinner.*

City Tap House
$$$ | **AMERICAN** | A popular hangout with the Penn crowd, this contemporary bar and grill pours a staggering six dozen draft options, with a heavy focus on American craft beer. This selection pairs well with an accessible gastropub menu offering a little of everything, from burgers and brick-oven pizzas to mussels and prime steaks. **Known for:** craft beer on tap; hearty pub grub; young and lively crowd. *Average main: $20* *The Radian, 3925 Walnut St., University City* *215/662–0105* *www.citytaphouseucity.com.*

Dana Mandi
$ | **INDIAN** | Hidden in the back of this unassuming Indian grocery store is a quick-serve restaurant dishing out soulful Punjabi home cooking. The cafeteria-style setup is nothing fancy, but the entrancing aromas of goat *biryani* (a rice dish), *shahi paneer* (a curry of cheese, cream, tomatoes, and spices), and garlicky naan bread will make you shrug off the spartan surroundings in an instant. **Known for:** authentic Punjabi cuisine; fresh naan and roti; Indian groceries. *Average main: $10* *4211 Chestnut St., University City* *215/387–5250.*

Franklin's Table
$ | **CONTEMPORARY** | At 8,000 square feet, with 175 indoor seats and even more room on an alfresco patio, this multi-concept food hall just steps from Penn's campus dishes out diverse quick-serve options for hungry students and faculty. Choose between Japanese (DK Sushi), Israeli falafel (Goldie), specialty sandwiches (High Street Provisions, KQ Burger), and artisanal pizza (Pitruco). **Known for:** lunch scene; vegan/vegetarian friendly; grab-and-go options. *Average main: $10* *3401 Walnut St., University City* *215/746–0123* *www.shopsatpenn.com/franklins-table.*

Pod
$$$ | **JAPANESE** | The sci-fi-style atmosphere of this restaurant (all-white tables and chairs; partially enclosed booths whose lighting changes color with the touch of a button) is a fitting setting for Pan-Asian cuisine that ultimately defies precise description. The conveyor belt along the bar is a novel touch, but the sushi chefs here boast serious skill with fish. **Known for:** futuristic atmosphere; specialty sushi; creative Asian cuisine. *Average main: $24* *3636 Sansom St., University City* *215/387–1803* *www.podrestaurant.com* *No lunch weekends.*

ReAnimator Coffee
$ | **CAFÉ** | Locally founded, owned, and operated, ReAnimator stands out in the Philadelphia coffee scene thanks to its dedicated sourcing of single-origin beans, dynamic roasting techniques, and smartly designed cafés. Tucked away in the tiny Garden Court area, slightly removed from the University City hubbub, this West Philadelphia outpost is a calming caffeinated oasis, a clean minimalist shop with a laid-back vibe. **Known for:** single-origin coffees; espresso drinks; relaxed atmosphere. *Average main: $5* *4705 Pine St., University City* *215/921–5953* *www.reanimatorcoffee.com.*

Wah-Gi-Wah

$ | PAKISTANI | This no-frills Pakistani eatery specializes in lahore chargha, a fiery fried-chicken dish. But that's not the only dish worth seeking out here—they also cook up a wide variety of flavorful halal meat skewers in the tandoor, along with hot-from-the-oven naan and roti breads, and a selection of vegetarian-friendly menu staples and specials. **Known for:** Pakistani fried chicken; fresh naan and roti; vegetarian options. *Average main: $11 4447 Chestnut St., University City 215/921-5597 www.wahgiwah.com.*

Hotels

★ AKA University City

$$$$ | HOTEL | This property undoubtedly has the best 360-degree views of the city and in an überluxury apartment-style setting. **Pros:** a Tesla model X town car and driver is available for guests (for a price); it's a two-minute walk to 30th Street Station; Philadelphia's highest and largest indoor infinity-style "pool in the sky". **Cons:** can feel more like a chic office building than a hotel; isolated in an area removed from the hearts of both Center City and University City; on-site Walnut Street Café can be a spendy dining option. *Rooms from: $395 Cira Centre South, 2929 Walnut St., University City 215/372-9000 www.stayaka.com 130 rooms Free breakfast.*

Akwaaba Philadelphia

$$ | B&B/INN | Akwaaba is a collective of five mid-Atlantic bed-and-breakfasts founded by Monique Greenwood, the former editor in chief of *Essence,* and her husband, Glenn Pogue; Philadelphia's outpost occupies a circa-1880s porched residence on a leafy residential block just north of the main University City drag. **Pros:** charming historic setting; hotel-style concierge service in a B&B; complimentary afternoon wine and refreshments. **Cons:** limited on-site parking; tight check-in window due to small size; not accommodating to children under 12. *Rooms from: $200 3709 Baring St., University City 866/466-3855 www.akwaaba.com/akwaaba-philadelphia 6 rooms Free breakfast.*

The Gables

$$ | B&B/INN | Built in 1889 by architect Willis Hale and first occupied by a prominent doctor and his family, this ornate mansion is a wonderful place for a B&B—the ground-floor parlor and entryway feature natural cherry and chestnut wood, and the guest rooms have oak floors with elaborate inlays of mahogany, ash, and cherry. **Pros:** off the beaten path; a dream for lovers of antiques; free parking. **Cons:** some may find it too far removed from central areas, attractions; the Victorian aesthetic can be overwhelming; not equipped to accommodate children under 10. *Rooms from: $195 4520 Chester Ave., University City 215/662-1918 www.gablesbb.com 10 rooms Free breakfast.*

The Inn at Penn, a Hilton Hotel

$$$ | HOTEL | Near the University of Pennsylvania, this hotel is a welcome sight for anyone needing to stay in the thick of the action. **Pros:** collegiate feel near major campuses; neat amenities such as in-room iPads; handsome and comfortable communal hangout areas. **Cons:** rates can fluctuate around collegiate events and gatherings; away from Center City; challenging to book during graduation season. *Rooms from: $259 3600 Sansom St., University City 215/222-0200, 800/445-8667 www.theinnatpenn.com 249 rooms No meals.*

Sheraton Philadelphia University City

$$$$ | HOTEL | With plush beds and 37-inch flat-screen televisions, spacious work areas, and complimentary Internet access, this hotel offers a nice balance of luxury and practicality. **Pros:** free Internet access; 24-hour gym; pet friendly. **Cons:** check-in during big weekends can be interminable; rates can get pricey; some

University City is home to radio station WXPN-FM, which does the popular NPR music program "World Café." If you like acoustic, independent, and world-beat music, try for tickets when you're in town.

structural and aesthetic updates needed. *Rooms from: $343* ✉ *3549 Chestnut St., University City* ☎ *215/387–8000, 877/459–1146* 🌐 *www.sheraton.com/universitycity* *332 rooms* *No meals.*

Nightlife

MUSIC CLUBS

★ World Cafe Live

MUSIC CLUBS | University City is home to radio station WXPN-FM, which specializes in acoustic, independent, and world-beat contemporary sounds. In addition to being the broadcast home for the popular NPR music program "World Cafe," the building features two restaurants and two live concert spaces, the larger of which, Downstairs Live, can pack in up to 650 concertgoers. If you can land gratis tickets via online pre-registration, XPN's "Free at Noon" is a wholly unique concert experience—notable artists break the routine, performing stripped-down lunchtime sets for an intimate crowd. Adele, John Legend, Kacey Musgraves, Pixies, and the Pretenders are just a few of the big names who have graced the daytime stage. ✉ *3025 Walnut St., University City* ☎ *215/222–1400* 🌐 *www.worldcafelive.com.*

Performing Arts

CONCERT HALLS

Annenberg Center for the Performing Arts

CONCERTS | The performing-arts complex on University of Pennsylvania's campus features multiple stages, from the 115-seat Bruce Montgomery Theatre to the 936-seat Zellerbach. Something's always going on—including productions of musical comedy, drama, dance, and children's theater. ✉ *3680 Walnut St., University City* ☎ *215/898–3900* 🌐 *www.annenbergcenter.org.*

MUSIC FESTIVALS

Clark Park Music and Arts Festival

FESTIVALS | Typically scheduled for the Saturday closest to the summer solstice, this annual celebration brings together live bands, performers, vendors, food, and kid-centric activities—a tradition that's been in place since 1970 in this 9-acre city park. It's an inviting introduction to the all-are-welcome, multicultural energy so closely associated with West Philadelphia. ✉ *Clark Park, 4300 Baltimore Ave., University City* ☎ *215/552–8186* 🌐 *clarkparkfest.wordpress.com.*

VENUES

Lightbox Film Center

FILM | University City's go-to venue for cinephiles, Lightbox screens some 500 titles a year with programming centered on art-house, experimental, and foreign films rarely given a chance on the big screen. Situated inside the International House, a residence for foreign students enrolled in city universities, the 360-capacity repertory theater also plays host to talks, live performances, exhibitions, film festivals, and more. Tickets can be purchased online, or at the box office Tuesday to Saturday from noon to 8; some programming, including family matinees of kid-friendly movies, is free to attend with RSVP. ✉ *International House, 3701 Chestnut St., University City* ☎ *215/895–6590* 🌐 *www.lightboxfilmcenter.org.*

Shopping

Most of the action in University City revolves around the universities, specifically the University of Pennsylvania and Drexel University. An active retail scene has sprouted around the U. of Penn campus to serve that huge population of students. A pocket of interesting, eclectic shops and restaurants has also sprung up farther west, in a residential area that's home to mostly grad students and professors on the other side of Clark Park.

ART GALLERIES

VIX Emporium

CRAFTS | Owned by married couple Sean and Emily Dorn—he's a graphic designer, she's a jewelry maker—this boutique stocks a curated array of one-of-a-kind items, many of them crafted by Philadelphia artists. At VIX (Roman numerals for the "5009" address), you'll find locally made soaps, prints, greeting cards, candles, shirts, and more. The quaint shop still features the original cabinetry and beveled-glass windowpanes from its former life as a millinery, nearly a century ago. ✉ *5009 Baltimore Ave., University City* ☎ *215/471–7700* 🌐 *www.vixemporium.com.*

BOOKSTORES

House of Our Own

BOOKS/STATIONERY | Despite its location in a brownstone flanked by University of Pennsylvania fraternity residences, there's nothing Animal House about this erudite bookstore. There are two floors of rambling rooms with shelves reaching up to the soaring ceilings, boasting an enormous mix of literature, course texts for students, and used books alike. Spend an hour perusing the stacks in a place that makes you feel like you're back in college. ✉ *3920 Spruce St., University City* ☎ *215/222–1576* 🌐 *www.shopsatpenn.com/house-our-own-books.*

Penn Bookstore

BOOKS/STATIONERY | At more than 50,000 square feet, this shop, operated by Barnes & Noble, is one of the largest academic bookstores in the United States. Renovated in 2018, it offers best sellers and tomes from the University of Pennsylvania faculty, loads of insignia clothing and memorabilia, a multimedia section, and space for regular author events. A Wi-Fi-enabled Starbucks café, as well as a convenient grab-and-go marketplace, can be found on the second floor. ✉ *3601 Walnut St., University City* ☎ *215/898–7595* 🌐 *www.upenn.edu/bookstore.*

HOME DECOR

Hello World

GIFTS/SOUVENIRS | A tastefully curated destination for unique gifts, this bright and airy lifestyle boutique sells artisan-crafted jewelry, whimsical housewares, kitchen accessories, and children's toys, as well as bigger-ticket items like customizable mid-century modern furniture. ✉ *3610 Sansom St., University City* ☎ *215/382-5207* 🌐 *www.shophelloworld.com.*

Chapter 10

NORTHERN LIBERTIES AND FISHTOWN

Updated by
Jill Wilson

Sights	Restaurants	Hotels	Shopping	Nightlife
★★★★★	★★★★★	★★★☆☆	★★★★★	★★★★★

NEIGHBORHOOD SNAPSHOT

TOP EXPERIENCES

■ **Food scene:** Fishtown and Northern Liberties are home to a diverse array of cuisines and some of Philadelphia's best restaurants.

■ **Breweries:** With major players like Yards, Philadelphia Brewing, Goose Island, and Evil Genius, beer fans have plenty of spots to enjoy a pint.

■ **Pizzeria Beddia:** With national accolades from *Bon Appetit*, *Time* magazine, and more, the trendy restaurant is a must-visit spot for best-in-your-life pizza.

■ **Schmidt's Commons:** While the businesses that inhabit the Schmidt's Commons are not always there for the long haul, the area has no shortage of energy, fueled by outdoor movie nights, summer festivals, delicious food, and cold drinks.

■ **Nightlife:** On any given night, but especially on weekends, the bars along 2nd Street, Frankford Avenue, and Girard Avenue welcome troves of people looking to party until last call.

GETTING HERE

SEPTA's Market-Frankford subway line makes stops in the heart of Fishtown via the Girard stop and a few blocks from the hustle and bustle of Northern Liberties at the Spring Garden stop. It's a quick, 10-minute subway ride from City Hall to both stops, which are just one apart from each other. As far as driving, street parking is available throughout both neighborhoods, along with a number of paid parking lots and a free parking lot at the Piazza.

PLANNING YOUR TIME

Depending on your interests, the time you visit these neighborhoods will vary. Night owls can enjoy plenty of late-night food and drink options, along with concerts and dance parties, those who enjoy daytime strolls can visit the neighborhoods for shopping, brunch, and festivals at set points throughout the year.

QUICK BITES

■ **Joe's Steaks and Soda Shop.** Open until 3 am on the weekends—and for lunch and dinner before that—Joe's is a go-to spot for all-day and all-night cheesesteaks, burgers, loaded fries, milk shakes, and sodas at the corner of Girard and Frankford Avenues. ✉ *1 W. Girard Ave., Fishtown* 🌐 *www.joessteaks.com* Ⓜ *Girard Station, Market-Frankford Line*

■ **One Shot Coffee.** Set away from the hustle and bustle of 2nd Street, this two-level cafe serves Stumptown coffee beverages, sweet lattes, herbal teas, and an assortment of brunch-ready food items. ✉ *217 W. George Street, Northern Liberties* 🌐 *1shotcoffee.wordpress.com/eats/* Ⓜ *Girard Station, Market-Frankford Line*

■ **Soup Kitchen Cafe.** With options like tomato-basil soup with a side of toasted baguette, simple coffees and teas, and a flavor-forward grilled cheese, it's no surprise that this café has a dedicated following of comfort-food-loving fans. ✉ *2146 E. Susquehanna Ave., Fishtown* 🌐 *www.soupkitchencafe.com*

As Philly has grown as a city in the metaphorical sense, so have the borders of Center City. Nowadays, it's a regular part of daily life for locals (and visitors) to spend time (sometimes most of their time) in outlying neighborhoods like Northern Liberties and Fishtown, that, among other things, offer a bevy of culinary distractions.

An influx of new residents and businesses has brought Northern Liberties and the nearby neighborhoods of Fishtown, Kensington, and Port Richmond into the zeitgeist. Specifically Northern Liberties and Fishtown have evolved into some of Philly's coolest neighborhoods, with restaurants by award-winning chefs, picture-ready bars, and concert venues that host some of the biggest musicians in the world. While they are beginning to expand, Kensington and Port Richmond are still largely residential and have a working-class feel, though much of the area's old industry—including printing, textiles, and metalworking—is long gone.

Northern Liberties

Once a postindustrial graveyard, Northern Liberties has been transformed over the last decade into a haven whose hipster edge has faded into a family-friendly neighborhood. At the northern end of the district, the Piazza at Schmidt's redevelopment of the former Schmidt's Brewery draws a postcollegiate crowd.

Sights

Edgar Allan Poe National Historic Site

HOUSE | One of America's most original writers, Edgar Allan Poe (1809–49), lived here from 1843 to 1844; it's the only one of his Philadelphia residences still standing. During that time some of his best-known short stories were published: "The Telltale Heart," "The Black Cat," and "The Gold Bug." You can tour the three-story brick house; to evoke the spirit of Poe, the National Park Service displays first-edition manuscripts and other rare books and offers interactive exhibits as well. An adjoining house has exhibits on Poe and his family, his work habits, and his literary contemporaries; there's also an eight-minute film and a small Poe library and reading room. A statue of a raven helps set the mood. The site is five blocks north of Market Street and just a stone's throw away from Spring Garden Street. SEPTA bus 47 travels on 7th Street to Green Street, where you should disembark. ✉ *532 N. 7th St., Northern Liberties* ☎ *215/597–8780* 🌐 *www.nps.gov/edal* 🎫 *Free* 🕒 *Closed Mon.-Thurs.*

Northern Liberties and Fishtown
A
B
C
D
E
F
1
2
3
4
5
6
7
8
9
Yorktown
Ludlow
Olde Kensington
Northern Liberties
W. Oxford St.
Jefferson St.
Master St.
N. Marshall St.
Germantown Ave.
N. American St.
N. 2nd St.
N. Hancock St.
N. Mascher St.
N. Howard St.
Frankford Ave.
E. Oxford St.
Marlborough St.
Crease St.
N. Hope St.
N. Front St.
N. Lee St.
W. Thompson St.
W. Girard Ave.
Poplar St.
N. Franklin St.
N. Lawrence St.
N. Orianna St.
Brown St.
Fairmount Ave.
Green St.
Richmond St.
N. 4th St.
N. 3rd St.
N. 2nd St.
Spring Garden St.
N. 8th St.
N. 7th St.
N. 6th St.
N. 5th St.
Delaware Expressway
95

Sights

1 Edgar Allan Poe National Historic Site.............. B8
2 Philadelphia Distilling.............. F7
3 Rowhouse Spirits Distillery....... H1
4 Yards Brewing Company.......... B9

Restaurants

1 Cadence.............................. E6
2 Elwood.............................. F7
3 Front Street Cafe..................... E5
4 Heritage.............................. D7
5 Las Cazuelas Restaurant.......... C6
6 Laser Wolf........................... E5
7 Martha.............................. H1
8 Memphis Taproom.................. I2
9 North Third.......................... D8
10 nunu.............................. F5
11 Pizzeria Beddia..................... F5
12 Sancho Pistola's.................... F6
13 Silk City Diner, Bar, and Lounge... C8
14 Standard Tap....................... D7
15 Stock.............................. G6
16 Sulimay's Restaurant.............. H5
17 Suraya............................ F4
18 Wm. Mulherin's Sons.............. F5

Quick Bites

1 Joe's Steaks + Soda Shop Fishtown............... F6
2 La Colombe.......................... F5
3 One Shot Coffee.............................. D6
4 Pizza Shackamaxon................ F6
5 Soup Kitchen Cafe................. G2
6 Weckerly's Ice Cream............. F6

Hotels

1 Lokal Hotel Fishtown............... F5
2 Wm. Mulherin's Sons.............. F5

A National Historic Site, American author Edgar Allan Poe lived here from 1843 to 1844; it's the only one of his Philadelphia residences still standing.

Yards Brewing Company

WINERY/DISTILLERY | Yards is the oldest continuously operating craft brewer in the city, and runs a sprawling brewery and taproom. 40-minute guided tours ($10) are offered daily for those 21 and over, and include a beer sample, a full "walk-about" beer, and a souvenir. The bar features 20 taps of their signature beers—Loyal Lager, Philadelphia Pale Ale, Love Stout, to name a few—as well as limited releases only available in the taproom. The taproom kitchen is lead by James Beard Award semifinalist, Chef Jim Burke, who menu includes classic pub fare as well as Philly favorites like the Yards IPA Pretzel and a Roast Pork sandwich. ✉ *500 Spring Garden St., Northern Liberties* ☎ *215/525–0175* 🌐 *yardsbrewing.com.*

Restaurants

★ Cadence

$$$$ | **AMERICAN** | Named *Food & Wine's* "Best New Restaurant in America" in 2019, Cadence lives up to its title with menus that are dictated by the season and by the high-quality food producers that the BYOB restaurant calls on for its ingredients. The tasting menu (the only option on weekends) features four courses of highly curated and expertly sourced options. **Known for:** BYOB format; local ingredients; vegan options. $ *Average main: $68* ✉ *161 W. Girard Ave., Northern Liberties* ☎ *215/419–7537* 🌐 *www.cadencerestaurant.com* ⏲ *Closed Sun. and Mon. No lunch.*

Heritage

$$$ | **MODERN AMERICAN** | A spacious neighborhood hangout on bustling 2nd Street, Heritage is an industrial-style restaurant where you'll find live music on the dining-room stage, live herbs creeping over the reclaimed ceiling beams, and lively cooking from chef Mackenzie Hilton. Regulars gravitate toward the hearty sandwiches served with crisp fries, the signature cocktails, which are largely named after classic songs, or one of the 30-plus draft-beer options. **Known for:** live music; seasonally focused menu;

extensive draft-beer list. $ *Average main: $20 ✉ 914 N. 2nd St., Northern Liberties ☎ 215/627–7500 🌐 heritage.life ⏲ No lunch weekdays.*

Las Cazuelas

$$ | **MEXICAN** | This authentically Mexican family-run place is an anomaly in sceney Northern Liberties. The colors, both inside and out, are warm and bright and the food is simple and rather gently spiced, apropos of the family's roots in the town of Puebla. **Known for:** hearty weekend brunch; BYOB margaritas; convenience for large groups. $ *Average main: $18 ✉ 426–28 W. Girard Ave., Northern Liberties ☎ 215/351–9144 🌐 lascazuelas.net ⏲ Closed Mon.*

North Third

$$ | **AMERICAN** | North Third is one of the first restaurants to settle in Northern Liberties at the infancy of the neighborhood's transformation. The menu hasn't changed much, mostly because locals love hits like the Moroccan-spiced lamb burger, mushroom flatbread, and house-made pierogies. **Known for:** late-night food; exciting craft-beer list; sought-after buffalo wings. $ *Average main: $16 ✉ 801 N. 3rd St., Northern Liberties ☎ 215/413–3666 🌐 www.norththird.com ⏲ No lunch weekdays.*

Silk City Diner, Bar, and Lounge

$$ | **AMERICAN** | Mark Bee, the local restaurateur behind favorite gastropub N. 3rd, bought the Silk City Diner in 2006, polished off its grease-coated, 1950s-era pink Formica counter, and started serving updated comfort food. Menu items include a fierce plate of buttermilk fried chicken, deep-fried veggie wings, the city's best bowl of mac and cheese (baked with a garlic-bread crust), and some lighter fare (salads and roasted veggies) should you want to go next door to the bar and lounge and dance 'til dawn beneath the disco ball. **Known for:** brunch every day; brightly colored outdoor dining space; late-night dancing. $ *Average main: $16 ✉ 435 Spring Garden St., Northern Liberties ☎ 215/592–8838 🌐 www.silkcityphilly.com.*

Standard Tap

$ | **AMERICAN** | This neighborhood gastropub is a Northern Liberties fixture, popular with the hipsters who populate this particular neighborhood, and for good reason. The frequently changing menu, presented unpretentiously on a chalkboard, is much more ambitious—and much tastier—than you'd expect from average bar food, and since you're in a bar, you can wash down the shellfish, terrines, local-veggie-forward salads, and wild game with one of the local microbrews on tap. **Known for:** local draft beers; multiple areas for hanging out throughout the multifloor, indoor-outdoor space; local produce. $ *Average main: $12 ✉ 901 N. 2nd St., Northern Liberties ☎ 215/238–0630 🌐 www.standardtap.com ⏲ No lunch weekdays.*

Coffee and Quick Bites

One Shot Coffee

$ | **CAFÉ** | Serving Stumptown coffee in a bi-level space, One Shot Coffee is a hidden spot for solid beverages and snacks, set a few blocks back from the hustle and bustle of the Piazza. The menu features café staples like cold brew, drip coffee, flavored lattes, hot tea and more, in addition to brunch-focused fare like breakfast burritos, egg sandwiches, croissants and more. **Known for:** seasonal lattes; upstairs library; vegetarian-friendly menu. $ *Average main: $5 ✉ 217 W. George St., Northern Liberties 🌐 1shot-coffee.wordpress.com ⏲ No lunch.*

Nightlife

BARS AND LOUNGES

The Abbaye

BARS/PUBS | NoLibs' reliable corner bar takes a Belgian approach, serving the appropriate beers (Chimay, Duvel) along with local crafts, in bottle and on draft. The hearty pub menu skews Euro, too, with some twists (vegan versions of wings and meatballs). ✉ *637 N. 3rd St., Northern Liberties* ☎ *215/627–6711* 🌐 *theabbaye.net/index.php.*

N. 3rd

BARS/PUBS | A dozen-plus-long beer list, snackable food, and a casual atmosphere draws crowds to owner Mark Bee's N. 3rd. One of the first places of its kind in NoLibs, the hangout is a bar and restaurant with a kitschy kitchen perspective. The worldly but accessible menu is right for this well-rounded neighborhood; outdoor seating along the titular street is a hot commodity in spring and summer. ✉ *801 N. 3rd St., Northern Liberties* ☎ *215/413–3666* 🌐 *www.norththird.com.*

North Bowl

BARS/PUBS | Cleverly located in the thick of Northern Liberties' 2nd Street scene, this boozing-friendly bowling alley delivers in the tenpin department. The large, colorful space serves a snacky menu, featuring a big selection of wackily topped tater tots. ✉ *909 N. 2nd St., Northern Liberties* ☎ *215/238–2695* 🌐 *www.northbowlphilly.com.*

★ Standard Tap

BARS/PUBS | A pioneering establishment in Philadelphia's pub culture, Standard Tap has been pairing local beer with thoughtful seasonal food since 1999. (The owners also have Johnny Brenda's close by.) The dimly light, multilevel interior, all beautiful dark wood and tucked-away nooks, endear it to locals as a gathering space, as does the consistent food and drink. ✉ *901 N. 2nd St., Northern Liberties* ☎ *215/238-0630* 🌐 *www.standardtap.com.*

DANCE CLUBS

The Barbary

DANCE CLUBS | While set away from the busy thoroughfare Frankford Avenue, the Barbary is a go-to for live shows and DJs. Between the dance-y, disco ball–adorned downstairs and the smaller "Barbarella" subconcept upstairs, the space draws diverse crowds tuned in to all sorts of different musical genres nearly every night of the week. ✉ *951 Frankford Ave., Northern Liberties* 🌐 *www.instagram.com/the_barbary.*

MUSIC CLUBS

Franklin Music Hall

MUSIC CLUBS | Hip-hop artists, singer-songwriters, rock bands, and more are regular performers at the Franklin Music Hall, formerly known as the Electric Factory. With room for 3,000 guests, the venue offers a not-too-big, not-too-small viewing experience within a historic venue to boot. ✉ *Franklin Music Hall, 421 N. 7th St., Northern Liberties* ☎ *215/627–1332.*

Ortlieb's Lounge

MUSIC CLUBS | This out-of-the-way, yet fan-favorite, venue in NoLibs has expanded its musical scope well beyond the traditional jazz. The vintage barroom, named after a defunct Philly brewery, now books indie rock, hip-hop, funk, and more. Hit up the bar for the cheap tacos, pretty close to the perfect drinking snacks. ✉ *847 N. 3rd St., Northern Liberties* ☎ *267/324–3348* 🌐 *www.ortliebsphilly.com.*

Union Transfer

MUSIC CLUBS | A former train station and restaurant converted into a haven for live music, Union Transfer might be Philly's best pound-for-pound place to catch a show. The spacious layout, impressive booking, and incredible sound make for an easygoing, one-of-a-kind concert experience. ✉ *1026 Spring Garden St., Northern Liberties* ☎ *215/232–2100* 🌐 *www.utphilly.com.*

Shopping

ANTIQUES

Architectural Antiques Exchange

ANTIQUES/COLLECTIBLES | Victorian embellishments from saloons and apothecary shops, stained and beveled glass, gargoyles, and advertising memorabilia entice shoppers at this expansive, warehouse-style antiques shop. ✉ *715 N. 2nd*

St., Northern Liberties ☎ 215/922–3669 ⊕ www.architecturalantiques.com ☞ Closed Sun. Ⓜ Spring Garden stop on the Market–Frankford Line.

ART GALLERIES

Art Star

ART GALLERIES | Two grads of the local Tyler School of Art run this retail shop and gallery that carries independent designers and artists with a crafty bent. You'll find everything from necklaces made with recycled bottle caps and silk-screened T-shirts to original art. The pair also host pop-up shopping events throughout the city. ✉ *623 N. 2nd St., Northern Liberties* ☎ *215/238–1557* ⊕ *www.artstarphilly.com* ⏲ *Closed Mon.*

Dane Fine Art

ART GALLERIES | The specialty here is contemporary paintings and prints by such artists as Salvador Dalí, Peter Max, Marc Chagall, Louis Icart, Erté, Andy Warhol, Pablo Picasso, and Roy Lichtenstein. ✉ *606 Spring Garden St., Northern Liberties* ☎ *267/687–8378* ⊕ *www.danefineart.com.*

Fleisher/Ollman Gallery

ART GALLERIES | Active since 1952, this gallery focuses on the creations of self-taught American artists with alternative and avant-garde origins, such as Sister Gertrude Morgan, Martín Ramírez, and Joseph Yoakum. ✉ *915 Spring Garden Street, Unit 215, Northern Liberties* ☎ *215/545–7562* ⊕ *www.fleisher-ollman-gallery.com.*

SHOPPING DISTRICTS AND MALLS

The Piazza

SHOPPING CENTERS/MALLS | This local developer's mixed-use interpretation of Rome's Piazza Navona was a long time coming, and was the cause of so much controversy over the years that locals were almost shocked to see it finally open in summer 2009. Restaurants, bars, and shops fill the ground-floor commercial spaces, which see high turnover due to the competition in the area, while apartments occupy the floors above. Nonetheless, the businesses ring a giant plaza that features a giant stage and screen with pavement scalloped in the same pattern as in Rome. Visitors can expect some sort of revelry or celebration going on in the Piazza no matter the time of year—concerts, shopping markets, movie nights, outdoor yoga and more. ✉ *2nd and Hancock Sts., Northern Liberties* ⊕ *livepiazza.com.*

Fishtown

One of Philly's hottest neighborhoods, Fishtown spent the better part of the last century as a working-class enclave for Irish- and Polish-Americans. Longtime residents still live in Fishtown, proud flags fluttering from their tidy row homes, but the area has gotten way more diverse as the creative class took refuge in the affordable real estate, and families and speculators followed. Great independent restaurants and funky boutiques make it a great place to spend a day.

★ Philadelphia Distilling

WINERY/DISTILLERY | A fairly recent move to a former warehouse in central Fishtown helped elevate Philadelphia Distilling's popularity and grow the following of its high-quality spirits. Today, its tasting room, shop, distillery—which is open for tours—and private-event space are all housed on East Allen Street mere steps away from the Fillmore and Punchline Philly. The bar is the focal point, with cocktails expertly made by experienced bartenders using Philadelphia Distilling's own Bluecoat American Dry Gin, Penn 1681 Vodka, Bluecoat Elderflower Gin, and more. The drink menu features cocktails rooted in ingredients like bitters and citrus, and elderflower and lavender. The food complements the inspired drink list with options like cheese boards, brisket grilled cheese, and snackable veggies. ✉ *25 E. Allen St., Fishtown* ☎ *215/671–0346* 🌐 *philadelphiadistilling.com* ⏲ *Closed Mon.–Wed.*

Rowhouse Spirits Distillery
WINERY/DISTILLERY | A Pennsylvania "Limited Distillery," Rowhouse distills and bottles all of their products in their East Kensington distillery—Roadhouse Gin, Drowned Devil Rum, Nordic Akvavit, and Bear Trap, an herbal liqueur. There's also specialty releases once or twice a year. Tastings are available Thursday through Saturday. ✉ *2430 Frankford Ave., Fishtown* ☎ *267/825–7332* 🌐 *www.rowhousespirits.us* ⏲ *Closed Sun.–Wed.*

Philadelphia Distillery Trail

While not an official tour or trail, this website (🌐 *www.phillydistillery-trail.com*) lists all the distilleries in the Philadelphia area—currently more than 15—including Rowhouse Spirits, Philadelphia Distilling, Red Brick Craft Distillery, and Federal Distilling in Philadelphia proper. Visit the website for more information and the location of more distilleries outside of the city.

Restaurants

Elwood
$$$ | **AMERICAN** | At Elwood, chef Adam Diltz's fine-dining homage to Philadelphia cuisine, the menu finds inspiration from the different eras of the city's history that's showcased in locally-sourced dishes like potato rolls, the Pennsylvania cheese plate, and Earl Keiser's guinea hen. Diners are presented with an amuse bouche of venison scrapple, dotted with harissa ketchup and spiked onto deer antlers to start the dining experience. **Known for:** venison scrapple; family-style dining; BYOB. 💲 *Average main: $25* ✉ *1007 Frankford Ave., Fishtown* ☎ *215/279–7427* 🌐 *www.elwoodrestaurant.com* ⏲ *Closed Mon. No lunch.*

Front Street Cafe
$ | **AMERICAN** | Beneath the Market-Frankford subway line lives this all-day dining destination suitable for guests seeking everything from smoothies to steak. The front door opens to the café section of the restaurant, which promises a menu of draft kombucha, hot teas, coffee, juices, and pastries. **Known for:** multiple areas for dining; healthy menu; weekend brunch. 💲 *Average main: $14* ✉ *1253 N. Front St., Fishtown* ☎ *215/515–3073* 🌐 *frontstreetcafe.net.*

Laser Wolf
$$ | **ISRAELI** | Like many of CookNSolo's places, Laser Wolf focuses on an aspect of Israeli cuisine, this time the grill or skewer house. Meals are prix-fixe so diners pick their protein to grill (beef, lamb, chicken) and the rest is taken care of—first comes the *salatim* (salads) and then the freshly baked pita and hummus followed by your grill choice. **Known for:** opened by James Beard Award winners Mike Solomonov and Steve Cook; a homemade ice cream sundae is included in the prix-fixe; Israeli grillhouse cuisine. 💲 *Average main: $35* ✉ *1301 N Howard St., corner of Howard and Thompson, Fishtown* ☎ *267/499–4660* 🌐 *www.laserwolfphilly.com* ⏲ *No lunch.*

★ **Martha**
$ | **AMERICAN** | Though technically right outside of Fishtown, Martha is the neighborhood bar that every neighborhood wants but only some are lucky enough to have. Large, with indoor and outdoor space, the bar-restaurant boasts one of the most impressive natural-wine programs in the city and some of the tastiest hoagies, too. **Known for:** hoagies; vegetarian-friendly options; charcuterie and cheeses. 💲 *Average main: $10* ✉ *2113 E. York St., Fishtown*

215/867–8881 marthakensington.com Closed Tues.

Memphis Taproom

$ | **AMERICAN** | Beer aficionado Brendan Hartranft and his wife, Leigh Maida, are the masterminds behind Fishtown's favorite gastropub. Hot wings, cheesesteak pierogies, and juicy burgers are addictively good options for soaking up the many tasty brews available, as are vegan options like a lentil-based meatball parm and jackfruit po' boy. **Known for:** vegetarian-friendly fare; curated beer list; beer-focused events. *Average main: $14 2331 E. Cumberland St., Fishtown 212/425–4460 www.memphistaproom.com.*

nunu

$ | **JAPANESE** | Once you spot the red lanterns set along Fishtown's Frankford Avenue, you've found nunu, a 30-seat Japanese bar and restaurant thats curated interior matches its inventive menu of sushi, meat- and veggie based skewers, and raw appetizers—the chicken *katsu sando* is one of the most ordered items on the menu. But nunu is known for being a bar first, with one of the city's best sake collections in addition to thoughtful cocktails, Japanese whiskeys, and *shochu*—a Japanese distilled drink. **Known for:** vegetarian and vegan options; weekend and weekday happy hour; chicken katsu sando (crispy Japanese chicken sandwich). *Average main: $11 1414 Frankford Ave., Fishtown 215/278–2804 www.nunuphilly.com No lunch.*

★ Pizzeria Beddia

$$$ | **PIZZA** | The most talked-about restaurant in Philadelphia is Pizzeria Beddia—*Bon Appétit* named it the best pizza place in America. This second iteration, just blocks away from Beddia's first spot, is a different world, with more than 100 seats, the ability to make reservations, and a larger menu that goes beyond pizza—think natural wines, flavorful salads, and creamier-than-you-can-ever-imagine soft serve. **Known for:** red-sauce pizzas; natural wines; private hoagie room. *Average main: $20 1313 N. Lee St., Fishtown 267/928–2256 www.pizzeriabeddia.com/ No lunch.*

Sancho Pistola's

$ | **MEXICAN** | An offshoot of Jose Pistola's in Center City, brother Sancho brought a bigger kitchen for chef Adan Trinidad to showcase his talents. Some of his food is ultra-traditional, like inky black bean soup seasoned with avocado leaf and zesty ceviche, while other plates (Korean rib tacos, spicy tuna guacamole) mash up his Mexican heritage with a global hipster aesthetic. **Known for:** late-night food menu; fruity margaritas; weekend brunch. *Average main: $12 19 W. Girard Ave., Fishtown 267/324–3530 www.sanchopistolas.com.*

Stock

$ | **VIETNAMESE** | Thanks to a robust Vietnamese population, Philly is practically drowning in pho. But pho made with high-quality ingredients—you have to head to Stock in Fishtown for that. **Known for:** numerous noodle soup options; BYOB policy; dine-in and take-out options. *Average main: $9 308 E. Girard Ave., Fishtown 215/425–5307 www.stockphilly.com.*

Sulimay's Restaurant

$ | **AMERICAN** | **FAMILY** | This old-school diner serves traditional breakfast and lunch fare that runs the gamut from overstuffed omelettes to pancakes and french toast and burgers. Don't miss Sulimay's take on scrapple, the traditional Pennsylvania Dutch breakfast meat, which is showcased in the Eggs Bensington, a breakfast sandwich that features runny eggs, thick toast, scrapple, and cheddar cheese. **Known for:** large portions of breakfast faves; good for families; large portions. *Average main: $10 632 E Girard Ave., Fishtown 215/423–1773 www.facebook.com/Sulimays No dinner.*

★ Suraya

$$$$ | **LEBANESE** | Fishtown's official turn into a foodie haven came in the form of Suraya, a Levant all-day café with an interior that sends any design buffs spinning. The 12,000-square-foot expanse is composed of a coffee shop slinging Lebanese chai tea topped with crushed pistachios and rose petals, drip coffee, pastries, and more; a sit-down area for lunch, dinner, and brunch; a bar overlooking the buzzing kitchen; and a picturesque outdoor garden. **Known for:** creamy hummus; brunch pastry basket; Arak cocktails. *Average main: $25 ✉ 1528 Frankford Ave., Fishtown ☎ 215/302–1900 ⊕ surayaphilly.com.*

★ Wm. Mulherin's Sons

$$$$ | **ITALIAN** | Wood-fired pizzas topped with creamy cheeses, striking meats, or in-season vegetables are the major draw at Wm. Mulherin's Sons, an elevated Italian restaurant—that sounds Irish—nestled in the midst of Fishtown. **Known for:** wood-fired pizza; weekend brunch; upstairs four-room hotel. *Average main: $25 ✉ 1355 N. Front St., Fishtown ☎ 215/291–1355 ⊕ wmmulherinssons.com ⏲ No lunch.*

Coffee and Quick Bites

Joe's Steaks + Soda Shop Fishtown

$ | **AMERICAN** | Open until 3 am on the weekends—and for lunch and dinner before that—Joe's is a go-to spot for all-day and all-night cheesesteaks, burgers, loaded fries, milk shakes, and sodas at the corner of Girard and Frankford Avenues. Its central location means it's often packed with Frankford Avenue barhoppers who are in need of a late-night snack. **Known for:** cheesesteaks; late-night hours; burgers. *Average main: $9 ✉ 1 W Girard Ave., Fishtown ☎ 215/423–5637 ⊕ joessteaks.com.*

★ La Colombe

$ | **CAFÉ** | A photo-ready interior invites guests to La Colombe's world headquarters, a sprawling space covered in artsy graffiti and crusty brick walls, that offers food, drinks, and ample space for hanging out. Communal tables stream down the center of the space, so grab your spot before you order at the counter: savory scones, sandwiches on excellent baguettes, sweet pastries, and coffee, of course. **Known for:** draft lattes; enticing sandwiches; picturesque space. *Average main: $8 ✉ 1335 Frankford Ave., Fishtown ☎ 267/479–1600 ⊕ www.lacolombe.com.*

★ Pizza Shackamaxon

$ | **PIZZA** | If good roots can make a pizza place, then Pizza Shackamaxon has it made. Housed in the original location of the best-pizza-in-America-winning Pizzeria Beddia, Shackamaxon slings pizza by the slice and by the pie. **Known for:** slice-first pizza shop; tomato pie; standing-room only. *Average main: $10 ✉ 115 E. Girard Ave., Fishtown ⊕ www.pizzashackamaxon.com.*

Soup Kitchen Cafe

$ | **AMERICAN** | **FAMILY** | With options like tomato basil soup with a side of toasted baguette, simple coffees and teas, and a flavor-forward grilled cheese, it's no wonder that this cozy eatery has a dedicated following of comfort-food-loving fans. Focused on creating simple yet elevated fare, Soup Kitchen Cafe serves more than its namesake with a solid lineup of craft beers, handcrafted cocktails, and elevated sandwiches. **Known for:** craft beer; soup and sandwich deal; brunch options. *Average main: $8 ✉ 2146 E Susquehanna Ave., Fishtown ☎ 215/427–1680 ⊕ www.soupkitchencafe.com.*

★ Weckerly's Ice Cream

$ | **CAFÉ** | The bright and cheerful one-room ice-cream shop matches the happy feelings that accompany a cup, cone, or ice-cream sandwich from Weckerly's Ice Cream. Local dairy, fruit, herbs, and eggs are the base for the shop's creamy and decadent flavors, which change to match the season (with the exception

Suraya in Fishtown serves Middle Eastern cuisine all day long; it's also a great place to pop in for coffee and pastries.

of a few staples). **Known for:** handmade ice-cream sandwiches; creamy custards; dairy-free sorbet options. *Average main: $5 9 W. Girard Ave., Fishtown 215/423–2000 www.weckerlys.com Closed Mon.*

Hotels

Lokal Hotel Fishtown

$$$ | **HOTEL** | Touting itself as Philadelphia's first "invisible service" boutique hotel, Lokal Hotel Fishtown offers its namesake: a local experience for all guests. **Pros:** truly local experience; curated rooms; high-quality amenities, including Sonos speakers and Apple TV. **Cons:** no front desk; no on-site staff unless requested; sells out quickly. *Rooms from: $250 1421 N. Front St., Fishtown 267/702–4345 staylokal.com 6 rooms No meals.*

Wm. Mulherin's Sons

$$$$ | **HOTEL** | Part restaurant, part boutique hotel, Wm. Mulherin's Sons is Fishtown's answer to an all-in-one space for visitors to the neighborhood. **Pros:** thoughtful design; proximity to Fishtown bars, restaurants, and attractions; local-inspired experience. **Cons:** no front desk; housekeeping for weeklong visitors only; can be loud. *Rooms from: $350 1355 N. Front St., Fishtown 215/291–1355 wmmulherinssons.com 4 rooms No meals.*

Nightlife

BARS AND LOUNGES

★ Evil Genius Beer

BREWPUBS/BEER GARDENS | The brews on the menu are as delicious as they are uniquely named. With options like Purple Monkey Dishwasher (a chocolate–peanut butter porter) and Ma! The Meatloaf (a Belgian white ale), the beers stick out, and for good reason. Within the Front Street brewpub, the beers are brewed and moved just a few steps to the often-busy bar. Guests can order flights, pints, and a selection of easy-to-eat food like grilled-cheese sandwiches, tacos, and dips. The brewpub is open for tours on

Saturday. ✉ *1727 Front St., Fishtown* ☎ *215/425–6820* 🌐 *evilgeniusbeer.com.*

Frankford Hall

BREWPUBS/BEER GARDENS | Stephen Starr's big, loud, and lively beer garden brings a bit of Bavaria to Fishtown's nightlife scene. You and your crew can sit outside at one of the large picnic tables, or hang indoors when it's too cold for the heat lamps. Draft beers, many of them German, come in half or full liters, accompanied by rib-sticking pretzels, wurst, and schnitzel. ✉ *1210 Frankford Ave., Fishtown* ☎ *215/634–3338* 🌐 *www.frankfordhall.com.*

Johnny Brenda's

BARS/PUBS | Fishtown's "cool kid" vibes are felt all throughout Johnny Brenda's, a neighborhood original that has grown with the neighborhood's evolution without losing its first-on-the-street edge. Part bar-restaurant, part music venue, the Frankford Avenue hangout offers visitors a space for drinking local beer and eating the better-than-regular-bar-food fare—think fresh oysters and solid burgers—as well as a space for playing billiards and listening to the diverse lineup of performers booked for the upstairs stage. ✉ *1201 N. Frankford Ave., Fishtown* ☎ *215/739–9684* 🌐 *www.johnnybrendas.com.*

MUSIC CLUBS

The Fillmore Philadelphia

MUSIC CLUBS | Since its opening in 2015, the 25,000-square-foot Fillmore has seen sold-out shows featuring everyone from local musicians to top-40 singers. The venue is the first of its kind in Fishtown, introducing a rock club experience for the 21st century. Three raised balconies provide solid sight lines for as many as 2,500 concertgoers, with a secondary club, the Foundry, holding about 450 for smaller concerts and late-night dance parties. ✉ *29 E. Allen St., Fishtown* ☎ *215/309–0150* 🌐 *www.thefillmorephilly.com.*

Kung Fu Necktie

MUSIC CLUBS | Depending on the night, the music rocking Kung Fu Necktie ranges from local bands to national bands, to DJs spinning dance-party-ready sets. A block removed from the major intersection of Frankford and Girard, KFN welcomes music-loving fans to its small, moody barroom hidden underneath the elevated tracks of SEPTA's Market-Frankford line. ✉ *1250 N. Front St., Fishtown* ☎ *215/291–4919* 🌐 *kungfunecktie.com.*

Chapter 11

MANAYUNK, GERMANTOWN, AND CHESTNUT HILL

Updated by
Josh McIlvain

Sights	Restaurants	Hotels	Shopping	Nightlife
★★★☆☆	★★★☆☆	★☆☆☆☆	★★★★☆	★★☆☆☆

NEIGHBORHOOD SNAPSHOT

TOP EXPERIENCES

■ **American history:** More than 70 buildings dating to the 1700s still stand in Germantown, including the Germantown White House, which for two summers was the seat of government.

■ **The Schmitter:** Head to Chestnut Hill's McNallly's Tavern for one of the great bar sandwiches of all time, the Schmitter—steak, cheese, and fried onions topped with fried salami and a special sauce, all on a kaiser roll.

■ **Mountain biking:** Believe it or not, there are serious mountain-bike trails along the steep wooded hillsides near Valley Green, as well as the Schuykill River Trail.

■ **Main Street Manayunk:** Spend a pleasant afternoon ambling along the tow path, window-shopping, and refueling in bars along the way.

■ **Walking Chestnut Hill:** Perfect if you like strolling around neighborhoods, looking at people's homes, and deciding which ones you'd like to live in.

GETTING HERE

Manayunk is a 10-minute drive from the Philadelphia Museum of Art, along Kelly Drive. Heading north along Germantown Avenue, Germantown becomes Mount Airy around Upsal Street and then becomes Chestnut Hill at Cresheim Valley Drive. Wissahickon Park (the section of Fairmount Park that runs from Lincoln Drive to Northwestern Avenue) divides Mount Airy and Chestnut Hill from the Roxborough, East Falls, and Manayunk neighborhoods.

A car is helpful to explore the area, though Manayunk can be a challenge to park in as its backstreets can be intimidating. Parking lots are accessible from Main Street. Chestnut Hill, Mount Airy, and Germantown have abundant street-side parking; Chestnut Hill also has cheap parking lots.

An Uber or Lyft from downtown to Chestnut Hill/Mount Airy/Germantown usually costs $15–$25, and Manayunk $15.

QUICK BITES

■ **High Point Cafe.** Coffee, crepes, and homemade pastries. ✉ *602 Carpenter La., and 7210 Cresheim Rd., Mount Airy* 🌐 *www.highpointcafe.us.com*

■ **Market at the Fareway.** Great variety of lunch-stand choices from Vietnamese noodle soups and Korean tacos to rustic pizza. ✉ *8221 Germantown Ave., Chestnut Hill* 🌐 *www.marketatthefareway.com*

■ **Uncle Bobbie's Coffee and Books.** Their tagline pretty much says it all: Cool People, Dope Books, Great Coffee. ✉ *5445 Germantown Ave, Germantown* 🌐 *www.unclebobbies.com*

PLANNING YOUR TIME

■ Northwest Philadelphia appeals to sporty people and strolling shoppers. Manayunk, Germantown, and Chestnut Hill can be visited in the same day, with Manayunk more of a late afternoon and evening destination. Manayunk is also the center of the bicycling community and sits along a bike path that runs from Center City to Valley Forge and beyond—though the best biking and light hiking trails in Wissahickon Park are accessed from Mount Airy and Chestnut Hill.

Northwest Philadelphia includes several interlocking neighborhoods between the banks of the Schuylkill River, across the upper forested borders of Fairmount Park, and to the city's border. Each has a distinct personality reflected in its dining scene. Manayunk has a young-professional vibe and dining options to match. Mount Airy has family-friendly bar-restaurants, while its tony neighbor, Chestnut Hill, has chichi brunch spots, bakeries, and historic pubs.

Main Street in Manayunk is like a vacation village, with boutiques, bars, and restaurants. The main commercial corridor runs along the Schuylkill River, while the rest of the neighborhood rises steeply up the hill with houses crammed together up twisting streets.

Chestnut Hill is Philadelphia's most relaxed neighborhood and one of its greenest. People gather here to eat and wander about the precious shops on Germantown Avenue. It's a great neighborhood for peering into people's homes as well. Mount Airy has seen an increase in dining, drinking, and shopping establishments. Although it has fewer options than Chestnut Hill, a number of hidden corners reveal charming cafés, and great beer and flatbread pizzas at Earth Bread and Brewery.

In 1683, at the founding of Germantown by German settlers, the county encompassed present-day Germantown, Mount Airy, and Chestnut Hill. It played an important role in the nation's founding: during the American Revolution, it was the site of the Battle of Germantown, which marked the first attack by American armed forces on the British. Originally intended as a farming community, the land turned out to be too rocky for anything but subsistence farming. Instead the Germans turned to making textiles, milling, and printing.

Mount Airy and Chestnut Hill came into their own in the 19th century, when they became desirable as the location for summer homes for Philadelphia business owners drawn to Germantown's booming textile industry. Indeed, Philadelphia University had been the Philadelphia College of Textiles from the late 1800s to 1999. Germantown township was incorporated into Philadelphia in 1854, when local trains were already servicing the area, making rail travel to the city convenient to this day.

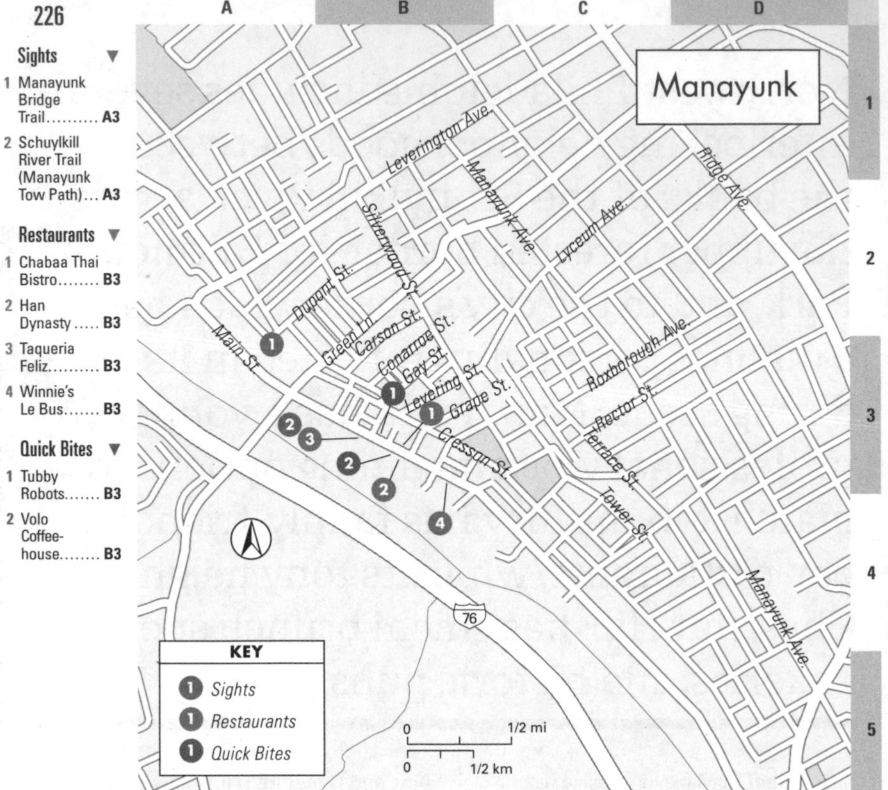

Aside from a number of B&Bs in the area, the only hotel is the Chestnut Hill Hotel, a functional but pleasant option in a great location about halfway up the hill in Chestnut Hill. If you are keen on staying at a B&B or Airbnb in Chestnut Hill, make sure it's in easy walking distance of Germantown Avenue—the whole charm of the area is to be able to walk out on the avenue and leave your car behind.

Manayunk

Manayunk has little of its history on display, unless you follow the tow path up the Schuylkill to see the last remnants of decaying mills. This predominantly Polish and Irish neighborhood renovated its Main Street in the 1980s into a quaint avenue with restaurants, funky shops, and a few good bars, evoking a small-town tourist destination like New Hope. It's perfect for a pleasant afternoon. It's also something of way station for bicyclists, as it sits on the Schuylkill River Trail that runs from Center City to Valley Forge and beyond—and serves as a point of departure for trails in Wissahickon Park. Up from Main Street the hill rises steeply and houses are jammed together along narrow, twisted streets—fun to walk on, but almost completely residential, don't expect to find hidden treasures. Though it is less pronounced these days, the blue-collar veneer of the rest of Manayunk—a mill town in the 1800s—still strikes a contrast to Main Street, and there's something Old World about the hill-town community.

GETTING HERE AND AROUND

If you're driving from Center City, follow I–76 west (the Schuylkill Expressway) to the Belmont Avenue exit. Turn right across the bridge and right again onto Main Street and park. On weekends you can be strolling with hundreds of visitors—and fighting with them for parking spaces. There are parking lots off Main Street toward the river. Participating stores offer validation stickers for reduced rates. From 6 pm on, valet parking is available for diners and shoppers for $10, but it's an easy Uber or Lyft ride from Center City. You can also take the SEPTA Norristown train from Market East, Suburban Station, or 30th Street Station to the Manayunk Station (on Cresson Street) and walk downhill to Main Street.

ESSENTIALS

BIKE RENTALS Cadence. ✉ *3740 Main St., Manayunk* 🌐 *www.cadencecycling.com.* **Trek Bicycle.** ✉ *4159 Main St., Manayunk* ☎ *215/487–7433* 🌐 *www.trekbikes.com.*

VISITOR INFORMATION Manayunk Development Corporation. ✉ *Manayunk* ☎ *215/482–9565* 🌐 *www.manayunk.org.*

Sights

Manayunk Bridge Trail

TRAIL | An old train trestle was revamped into a pedestrian- and bike-only bridge with pleasant views of Manayunk and the Schuylkill River Valley. It connects to the Cynwyd Heritage trail, an easy 2-mile "rail trail" for biking, jogging, and walking that leads past Laurel Hill Cemetery West and ends at Cynwyd Station and a small café. ✉ *Corner of Dupont and High Sts., Manayunk* ⏲ *Closed Apr.–Oct. 9 pm–8 am and Nov.–Mar. 6 pm–8 am.*

★ Schuylkill River Trail (Manayunk Tow Path)

TRAIL | This very popular bike and pedestrian trail follows the river all the way to Valley Forge National Park, or, in the other direction, to the Philadelphia Art Museum and beyond. It's very easy biking, but you'll want a hybrid or mountain bike because not all of it is paved. ✉ *Manayunk Tow Path, Main St. and Gay St., Manayunk* ✣ *There are many access points, but here a small park leads to the path* 🌐 *schuylkillrivertrail.com.*

Restaurants

Chabaa Thai Bistro

$$ | THAI | Known for the varieties of pad Thai—from crispy duck to peanut-crusted scallop—and delicious soups, this Thai bistro is a nice, calming escape from the noisy restaurant scene of Main Street. Enjoy authentic Thai flavors in your lime-infused Thai sausage, *po tek* (a spicy seafood hot pot with basil and lemongrass) portioned for two, or the various face-flushing curries. **Known for:** numerous versions of pad Thai; crazy noodles (stir-fried wide rice noodles with colorful veggies); consistently good Thai food. 💲 *Average main: $18* ✉ *4371 Main St., Manayunk* ☎ *215/483–1979* 🌐 *www.chabaathai.com* ⏲ *Closed Mon. No lunch Fri.*

Han Dynasty

$$ | CHINESE | The area's go-to for authentic Szechuan flavors—there are multiple locations around Philadelphia—features fan favorites like Dan Dan noodles, eggplant with garlic sauce, the popular (and fiery) dry pots and hot pots, and flavorful yet mild ginger duck. Pay attention to the spice levels listed in the menu (they are no joke) as you sit at wood tables under high ceilings with giant windows that overlook Main Street. **Known for:** bold Szechuan flavors; legions of local fans; bringing the heat. 💲 *Average main: $16* ✉ *4356 Main St., Manayunk* ☎ *215/508–2066* 🌐 *handynasty.net.*

Taqueria Feliz

$ | MEXICAN | This jumping joint is able to satisfy the margarita-and-nachos crowd as well as those seeking more authentic

The Schuylkill River Trail (a.k.a the Manayunk Tow Path) follows the river from the Philadelphia Art Museum to Valley Forge National Park.

Mexican flavors. A lively spot with colorfully painted walls, it's most fun to share the smaller bites—braised brisket tacos, mushroom quesadilla, tortilla soup—but the enchiladas are also excellent. **Known for:** great sharing plates; sidewalk tables; fresh ingredients. *Average main: $14 4410 Main St., Manayunk 267/331–5874 www.taqueriafeliz.com.*

Winnie's Le Bus

$$ | AMERICAN | FAMILY | Lively and upbeat, Le Bus is a solid choice for high-quality basics like burgers, tacos, and fish-and-chips. Winnie's also serves breakfast and baked goods. **Known for:** comfort foods; homemade chips; big open space. *Average main: $15 4266 Main St., Manayunk 215/487–2663 www.lebusmanayunk.com.*

Coffee and Quick Bites

Tubby Robot

$ | AMERICAN | Stop here for delicious ice cream served in small, pricey scoops—including many nondairy options. The fun part is playing video games on a system called Wall-O-Vision, which is two screens mounted on a wall across a narrow alley, while inside, four joysticks allow up to four players to go head-to-head on games that changed weekly. **Known for:** fun flavors that include non-dairy options; old-school arcade games; trendy vibe. *Average main: $5 4369 Main St., Manayunk 267/423–4376 www.tubbyrobot.com Closed Mon.-Tues.*

Volo Coffeehouse

$ | CAFÉ | A good place to camp out with a book or for a chat, the coffeehouse serves local La Colombe coffee, as well as tasty baked goods or simple sandwiches. **Known for:** a good cup of coffee; great location; no-fuss service. *Average main: $8 4360 Main St., Manayunk 215/483–4580 No dinner.*

Nightlife

BARS AND LOUNGES

The Goat's Beard

BARS/PUBS | Offering a bit more elegance than your average Main Street bar, the Goat's Beard specializes in hearty European bistro-style cooking, local beers, and smartly curated spirits (especially whiskey). ✉ *4201 Main St., Manayunk* ☎ *267/323–2495* 🌐 *www.thegoatsbeard-manayunk.com/.*

Lucky's Last Chance

BARS/PUBS | A down-to-earth pub, Lucky's is well known for (what some consider to be) the city's best burgers—we recommend the Pickle Monster. It's also a solid place to drink, with DJs, dance nights, and special events. ✉ *4421 Main St., Manayunk* ☎ *215/509–6005* 🌐 *www.luckyslastchance.com.*

BREWERIES AND BEER GARDENS

Conshohocken Brewing Company

BREWPUBS/BEER GARDENS | Located about 2 miles from Manayunk along the Schuylkill River Path, the best part of this brewery is the beer—core beers like Type A, an India Pale Ale, and User Friendly, a blonde ale, or seasonal beers like Philly Vice, a blueberry Berliner weisse, or Island in the Sun, a double IPA. The second-best part is that its back patio caters to bicyclists and people on the Schuylkill River Path, so it's the perfect pit stop before heading back to Manayunk. ✉ *739 East Elm St., Conshohocken* ✥ *If walking, follow the Manayunk Tow Path away from the city* ☎ *610/897–8962* 🌐 *www.conshohockenbrewing.com.*

Manayunk Brewery & Restaurant

BREWPUBS/BEER GARDENS | A long-running destination on the banks of the Schuylkill River, this brewpub offers a well-rounded selection of ales and lagers brewed on the premises. Check out the patio in the spring and summer—best for snacking. ✉ *4120 Main St., Manayunk* ☎ *215/482–8220* 🌐 *www.manayunkbrewery.com.*

Wissahickon Brewing Company

BREWPUBS/BEER GARDENS | In the adjacent neighborhood of East Falls, tucked partway down a hillside, you'll find this beer lovers' gem. They don't serve food, but often have food trucks—and yoga at 6:30 pm on Thursdays (no joke). ✉ *3705 W. School House La., Manayunk* ☎ *215/483–8833* 🌐 *wissahickonbrew.com* ☞ *Closed Mon.*

MUSIC CLUBS

Dawson's Street Pub

MUSIC CLUBS | Manayunk's best live-music venue features many of the most talented local bands curated for their crowd-pleasing aesthetics and musicianship. Expect excellent sound in a cozy, laid-back, and "local" bar setting that's tucked away in a residential area. ✉ *100 Dawson St., Manayunk* ☎ *215/482–5677* 🌐 *www.dawsonstreetpub.com.*

Performing Arts

Venice Island Performing Arts and Recreation Center

THEATER | This 250-seat theater between the canal and the river has a fairly steady supply of theater, comedy, and music shows. There is also an outdoor recreation area as part of the complex. ✉ *7 Lock St., Manayunk* ☎ *215/685–3583* 🌐 *www.veniceisland.org.*

Shopping

BOOKS

The Spiral Bookcase

BOOKS/STATIONERY | Just off Main Street, this charming bookstore features a book-savvy staff, a rich collection of often lesser-known authors, a cozy setting of plush chairs and crystals, and an affinity for the occult. ✉ *112 Cotton St., Manayunk* ☎ *215/482–0704* 🌐 *spiralbookcase.com* ⏲ *Closed Mon.*

CLOTHING

Nicole Miller

CLOTHING | This boutique-sized shop offers the latest from the stylish designer. ✉ *4249 Main St., Manayunk* ☎ *215/930–0307* 🌐 *www.marykdougherty.com.*

HOME DECOR

UrbanBurb Furniture

HOUSEHOLD ITEMS/FURNITURE | Featuring an array of modern furniture circa the 1950s, 1960s, and 1970s, this fun home-furnishings store has everything from bright yellow couches to old Coke machines, as well as funky lamps, random statuary, and giant slabs of wood. The store is full of kitschy charm, but the items are actually things you'd want to have. ✉ *4313 Main St., Manayunk* ☎ *215/298–9534* 🌐 *urbanburbfurniture.com.*

JEWELRY

Gary P. Mann Design

JEWELRY/ACCESSORIES | Noted local goldsmith Gary Mann creates elegant custom jewelry. The store is also known for its estate jewelry, carved jade and emerald pieces, stack rings, and Judaica. ✉ *4349 Main St., Manayunk* ☎ *215/482–7051* 🌐 *www.garymannjewelry.com* ⏲ *Closed Sun.-Mon.*

Germantown

Germantown, about 6 miles northwest of Center City, has been an integrated, progressive community since 13 German Quaker and Mennonite families moved here in 1683. They soon welcomed English, French, and other European settlers seeking religious freedom. The area has a tradition of free thinking—the first written protest against slavery in America came from its residents. It was also the seat of government for two summers during Washington's presidency, when yellow fever epidemics raged in the city. And the area became fashionable for wealthy Philadelphians wanting to escape the city's heat in the mid-1700s. Today the area houses a wealth of exceptionally well-preserved architectural masterpieces including more than 70 homes dating from the 1700s and some of the country's oldest mills. The business section of Germantown offers some quirky restaurants and shopping, but is still evolving.

GETTING HERE AND AROUND

The best way to tour the area is by car. From Center City follow Kelly Drive to Midvale Avenue and turn right. Follow Midvale all the way to Germantown Avenue. To get to Mount Airy and Chestnut Hill from Germantown, follow Germantown Avenue north. SEPTA's Regional Rail Chestnut Hill West and Chestnut Hill East trains service Germantown, but are a 10- to 15-minute walk to the avenue. The 23 bus runs along Germantown Avenue—use this bus only between Germantown and Chestnut Hill; it is a very long ride if you pick it up downtown.

Sights

Cliveden

HOUSE | The grounds take up an entire block, and its unique history, impressive architecture, and the guides who spin a good yarn combine to make Cliveden perhaps the best visiting experience of the historic Germantown homes. The elaborate country house was built in 1767 by Benjamin Chew (1722–1810), a Quaker and chief justice of the colonies, and something of a fence-straddler during the Revolution. Cliveden was at the center of the Battle of Germantown, occupied by British troops, and the walls still bear the marks of American cannon fire. An elaborate reenactment of the Battle of Germantown is held here annually on the first Saturday in October. Cliveden excels at its programming, much of which explores the experiences of slaves, servants and workers at Cliveden, and larger themes of Northern slavery, and slaveholders, like the Chew family, who owned plantations in the South.

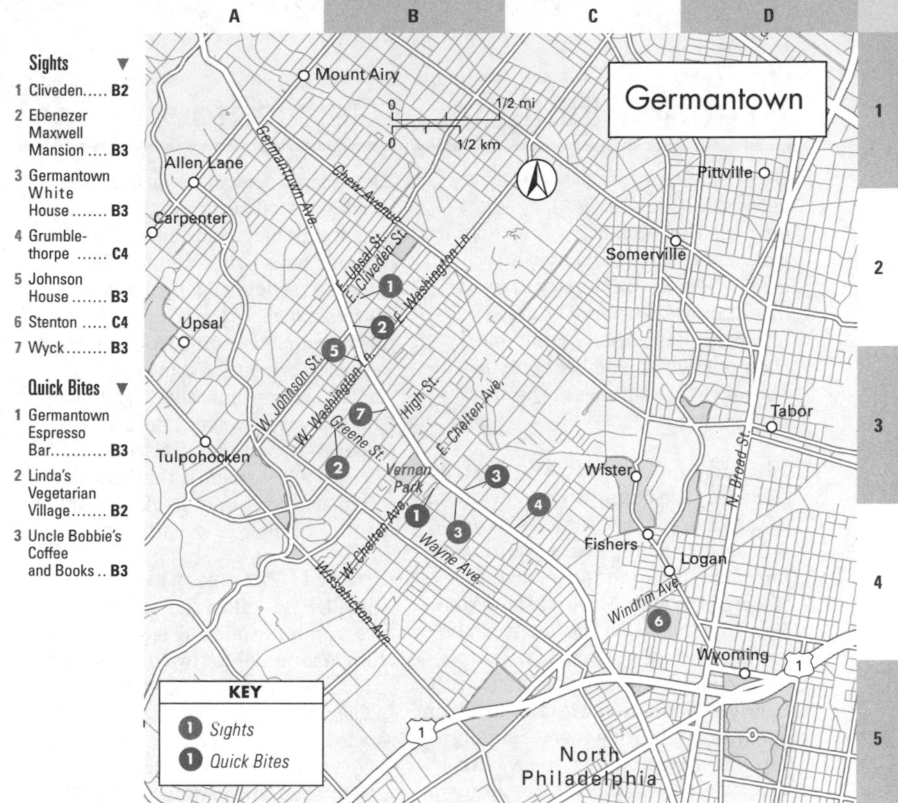

The house, on 6 acres, can be seen on a 45-minute guided tour. ✉ *6401 Germantown Ave., Germantown* ✥ *Entrance on E. Cliveden St.* ☎ *215/848–1777* 🌐 *www.cliveden.org* 🎟 *$10* 🕒 *Closed Mon.–Wed. and Dec.–Apr.; tours on the hr, last tour at 3 pm.*

Ebenezer Maxwell Mansion

HOUSE | Philadelphia's only mid-19th-century house-museum is a Victorian Gothic extravaganza of elongated windows and arches that's used to illustrate the way Victorian social mores were reflected through its decoration. The downstairs highlights the Rococo Revival (circa 1860), the upstairs is fashioned after the Renaissance Revival (1880s), and the difference is striking, especially the art deco–like wall details you may not associate with the time. Throughout the year there are a number of quality theater productions within the house—from Ibsen to Shakespeare to original work and lighter fare. The house is two blocks from the Tulpehocken stop on SEPTA's Chestnut Hill West line. ✉ *200 W. Tulpehocken St., at Greene St., Germantown* ☎ *215/438–1861* 🌐 *www.ebenezermaxwellmansion.org* 🎟 *$8* 🕒 *Closed Sun.–Wed.*

Germantown White House

HOUSE | Formerly called the Deshler-Morris House, the Germantown home was where President Washington lived and held cabinet meetings during the yellow fever epidemic of 1793–94, making it America's seat of government for a short time, and also the oldest "official" residence of an American president. A part of Independence National Historical Park, interpretive exhibits are displayed in the house next door, and the house itself

Historic Highlights of Germantown

Germantown was settled the same year as Philadelphia, 1683, by—you guessed it—Germans, so as its history was not chronicled in English, its story of pre-Revolutionary America life is not well known. The area still has more than 70 homes that date to the 1700s, with a number of historical houses that tell stories of the area's beginnings.

Planning Your House Tours

Generally speaking, you won't want to take in more than three sites, as you will become house-weary, but immersing yourself into the area's history is worth the visit. The first thing to keep in mind is that the hours can be wonky at these sites and it's best to double-check the hours before you go; nearly all the houses are closed during the winter—heating them is simply too expensive or nonexistent. With that said, Cliveden, Wyck, the Johnson House, Ebenezer Maxwell Mansion, and Stenton are the most consistent in their hours. The Germantown White House, Grumblethorpe, and the Historic Rittenhouse Town hours are almost absurdly fickle (though you can walk about Historic Rittenhouse at any time). The Germantown Historical Society (✉ *5501 Germantown Ave.*) has served in the past as a center to help guide visitors to the various houses, but Historic Germantown's Freedom's Backyard website (🌐 *freedomsbackyard.com*) has the most complete list of attractions and works to bring the various sights under a single umbrella. The houses themselves, however, operate very separately, and should be contacted directly. The upside is that you can often arrange a tour on off days by calling a couple of weeks in advance.

Special Programming

Cliveden has taken the lead in programming offering lectures and conversations—led by authors, historians, educators, and archivists—on subjects like slavery and slaveholders in the North, the lives of those who worked (paid and forced labor) at Cliveden, and various unexplored stories of the American Revolution era. Programs at Wyck and Stenton are also worthwhile, but the theatrical productions at Ebenezer Maxwell Mansion are excellent, as are the Victorian-themed events and the hosted teas, like Tea with Frederick Douglass.

has been restored to the time Washington was there. The emphasis has also shifted to telling the stories of the entire household, from the slaves who worked there to the president and his wife. In October 1777, during the Battle of Germantown, the house was the headquarters for British general Sir William Howe. As one of the many Germantown houses built flush with the road, it has enchanting side and back gardens. ✉ *5442 Germantown Ave., Germantown* ☎ *215/597–7130* 🌐 *freedomsbackyard.com/germantown-white-house/* 🎟 *Free* ⏲ *Closed Sept.–May.*

Grumblethorpe

HOUSE | The blood of General James Agnew, who died after being struck by musket balls during the Battle of Germantown, stains the floor in the parlor of this Georgian house. Built by Philadelphia merchant and wine importer John Wister in 1744, Grumblethorpe is one of Germantown's leading examples of early-18th-century

Pennsylvania-German architecture. The Wister family lived here for 160 years, and during the Revolution a teenage Sally Wister kept a diary that has become an important historical source for what that time was like. On display are period furnishings and family mementos, but the best part of the house is the large garden. Wisteria, the flowering vine, is named after Charles Wister (John's grandson), who was an avid botanist and amateur scientist, and there is plenty of it in the garden. There are also an enormous hundred-year-old rosebush, a peony alley, a two-story arbor with climbing clematis and a grapevine working its way across its base, and a number of tulips. **■ TIP→ Tours are offered May–Oct., on the second 2nd Saturday of the month; additional tours can be scheduled for Tuesday and Thursday.** ✉ *5267 Germantown Ave., Germantown* ☎ *215/843–4820* 🌐 *www.philalandmarks.org* 🎫 *$8 tours* ⏲ *Closed Nov.–Apr.*

Johnson House

HOUSE | After bringing visitors through the hidden back entrance of this 1768 home, guides retrace the experience of slaves who found a haven here when the Johnson House was a key station on the Underground Railroad. They weave the story of the Johnson family, Quakers who worked to abolish slavery, with that of Harriet Tubman, who was sheltered here with runaway slaves and later guided them to freedom. Visitors see hiding places, including the third-floor attic hatch that runaways used to hide on the roof when the sheriff came by, learn Underground Railroad code words, and view slavery artifacts, such as ankle shackles and collars. The home has contained the gamut of American history; in 1777 the house was in the line of fire during the Battle of Germantown; the shutters still show the impact of the musket rounds. In the early 1900s it was saved from demolition when it became a women's club. The house itself does not amaze, but hearing the stories of the home when you are standing within it is fascinating. **■ TIP→ Saturday tours are offered year-round and there are tours in the spring and fall on Thursday and Friday.** ✉ *6306 Germantown Ave., Germantown* ☎ *215/438–1768* 🌐 *www.johnsonhouse.org* 🎫 *$10* ⏲ *Closed Sun.–Wed.*

Stenton

HOUSE | James Logan may not be a household name, but he was a seminal figure in pre-Revolutionary America. Equal parts visionary, opportunist, and rogue, he was secretary to William Penn and managed the daily affairs of the colony. Logan, who went on to hold almost every important public office in the colonies, designed the 1730 Georgian manor himself and named it for his father's birthplace in Scotland. He used it to entertain local luminaries and Native American tribal delegates. It was also where he kept one of the area's first libraries, at a time when books were looked upon with suspicion. British General Howe claimed Stenton for his headquarters during the Battle of Germantown. The Stenton mansion is filled with family and period pieces; the site also includes a kitchen wing, barn, and Colonial-style garden. The guided 45-minute tour interprets the life of three generations of the Logan family and the life of the region from the 1720s through the American Revolution. This house has one of the best interiors of any of the Germantown homes. **■ TIP→ Tours are offered April to late December Tuesday–Saturday, noon–4.** ✉ *4601 18th St., Germantown* ☎ *215/329–7312* 🌐 *www.stenton.org* 🎫 *$8* ⏲ *Closed Jan.–Mar.*

Wyck

HOUSE | Between the 1690s and 1973, Wyck sheltered nine generations of the Wistar-Haines family. Their accumulated furnishings are on display, along with ceramics, children's needlework, dolls, and artifacts generally contemporary with the mid-1800s. On one side is the oldest rose garden in the United States, dating

Built in 1767 by the Chew family, Cliveden is perhaps the best visiting experience of the historic Germantown homes.

to the 1820s, which blooms in May, as well as a magnolia tree from that time. Out back are a large lawn, where you can picnic, and a vegetable garden—the land has been continuously farmed since 1690, and during the summer it hosts many kid-friendly garden-related events. Known as the oldest house in Germantown, Wyck was used as a British field hospital after the Battle of Germantown. Walk-in tours are offered April–November, Thursday–Saturday, noon–4 pm, and the grounds are open for wandering Friday afternoons. ■ **TIP→ There's a farmers' market May to November on Friday.** ✉ *6026 Germantown Ave., Germantown* ☎ *215/848–1690* 🌐 *www.wyck.org* 🎫 *$5* ⏲ *Closed Dec.–Mar.*

Coffee and Quick Bites

Germantown Espresso Bar

$ | **AMERICAN** | On a somewhat dilapidated pedestrian street, this narrow espresso bar combines sophisticated coffee prep with a laid-back vibe and good breakfast and lunch sandwiches. Upstairs, the Listening Room features the occasional concert. **Known for:** finely prepped espresso drinks; artsy vibe; community hang. $ *Average main: $7* ✉ *26 Maplewood Mall, Germantown* ☎ *267/331–8380* 🌐 *www.germantownespressobar.com* ⏲ *No dinner.*

Linda's Vegetarian Village

$ | **VEGETARIAN** | Across the street from Cliveden, this much-loved neighborhood joint is one of only a few Northwest spots that specializes in vegetarian, vegan, and raw foods. Lunch and afternoon crowds are satiated with sandwiches, salads, and smoothies, which are all available for take-out as well. **Known for:** mom-and-pop meets vegetarian joint; stir-fry hoagie; falafel burger. $ *Average main: $10* ✉ *6381 Germantown Ave., Germantown* ☎ *215/438–2500* 🌐 *lindasvegetarianvillage.com* ⏲ *Closed Sun.–Tues. No dinner.*

Uncle Bobbie's Coffee and Books

$ | **AMERICAN** | Besides its popularity for its great coffee and light fare, Uncle Bobbie's is the most literary salonlike coffee shop in the city, with numerous author and reading events. Focused squarely on African American literature and history, intellectual studies, as well as mainstream biographies and the like, the books, all new, are both for sale and displayed in a way that makes you wish you had a library so neat and shiny. **Known for:** friendly service; cultural hub; lively up front, quiet in the back. *Average main: $6 5445 Germantown Ave., Germantown 215/403–7058 www.unclebobbies.com.*

Chestnut Hill and Mount Airy

Northwest of Germantown are Mount Airy and then Chestnut Hill. Chestnut Hill is one of the farthest points you can go outside Center City while still being within the city limits. The enclave looks the part with fairy-tale woods, winding drives, and moneyed addresses, but the walkable, family-oriented downtown is true to its streetcar suburb history. Beyond cobblestone Germantown Avenue, lined with restaurants, galleries, and boutiques, you can find lovely examples of Colonial Revival and Queen Anne houses. Wissahickon Park runs adjacent to Chestnut Hill and Mount Airy.

Like adjacent Germantown and Chestnut Hill, Mount Airy got its start as a vacation village for wealthy Philadelphians in the 1800s. Today, the area is an ideal mix of its neighbors, a blend of Germantown's grit and Chestnut Hill's polish with the same staggeringly gorgeous stock of Victorian and Colonial Revival architecture. Mount Airy is also recognized as one of the first racially integrated neighborhoods in the country, a point of pride among businesses and residents there today.

Chestnut Hill and Mount Airy are very pleasant, predominantly residential neighborhoods. Travel to downtown Philadelphia is easy by car or train. Restaurants and shops run all along a mile of Germantown Avenue in Chestnut Hill. Mount Airy is a little more sprawling, but there are a number of good restaurants and bars as well.

GETTING HERE AND AROUND

To get to Mount Airy or Chestnut Hill by car, follow Kelly Drive to Lincoln Drive and take that road to its end, making a right on Allens Lane and then a left on Germantown Avenue. SEPTA's Regional Rail Chestnut Hill West and Chestnut Hill East trains are good options as well.

Sights

Historic RittenhouseTown

HISTORIC SITE | North America's first paper mill was built here in 1690 by Mennonite minister William Rittenhouse. Over the next 150 years, 10 generations of his family lived on the site and operated the mill. His most famous offspring, born in 1732, was David Rittenhouse, astronomer, statesman, and first president of the U.S. Mint. You can stroll any time through this National Historic District that consists of 30 picturesque acres along the Wissahickon and seven outbuildings. Special events include papermaking workshops, cooking demonstrations, and an annual 5K race. Public tours (summer only) are offered intermittently—private tours can be arranged by phone. *206 Lincoln Dr., Chestnut Hill Accessible from lots on Lincoln Drive and trails in Wissahickon Park. 215/438–5711 www.rittenhousetown.org Free.*

Morris Arboretum

GARDEN | **FAMILY** | This is one of the best arboretums in the country, and it's a great place to reward yourself on a sunny day with an afternoon stroll—and you can let your kids run free. With 3,500 trees and shrubs from around the world, this 92-acre arboretum was based on Victorian-era garden and landscape design, with romantic winding paths,

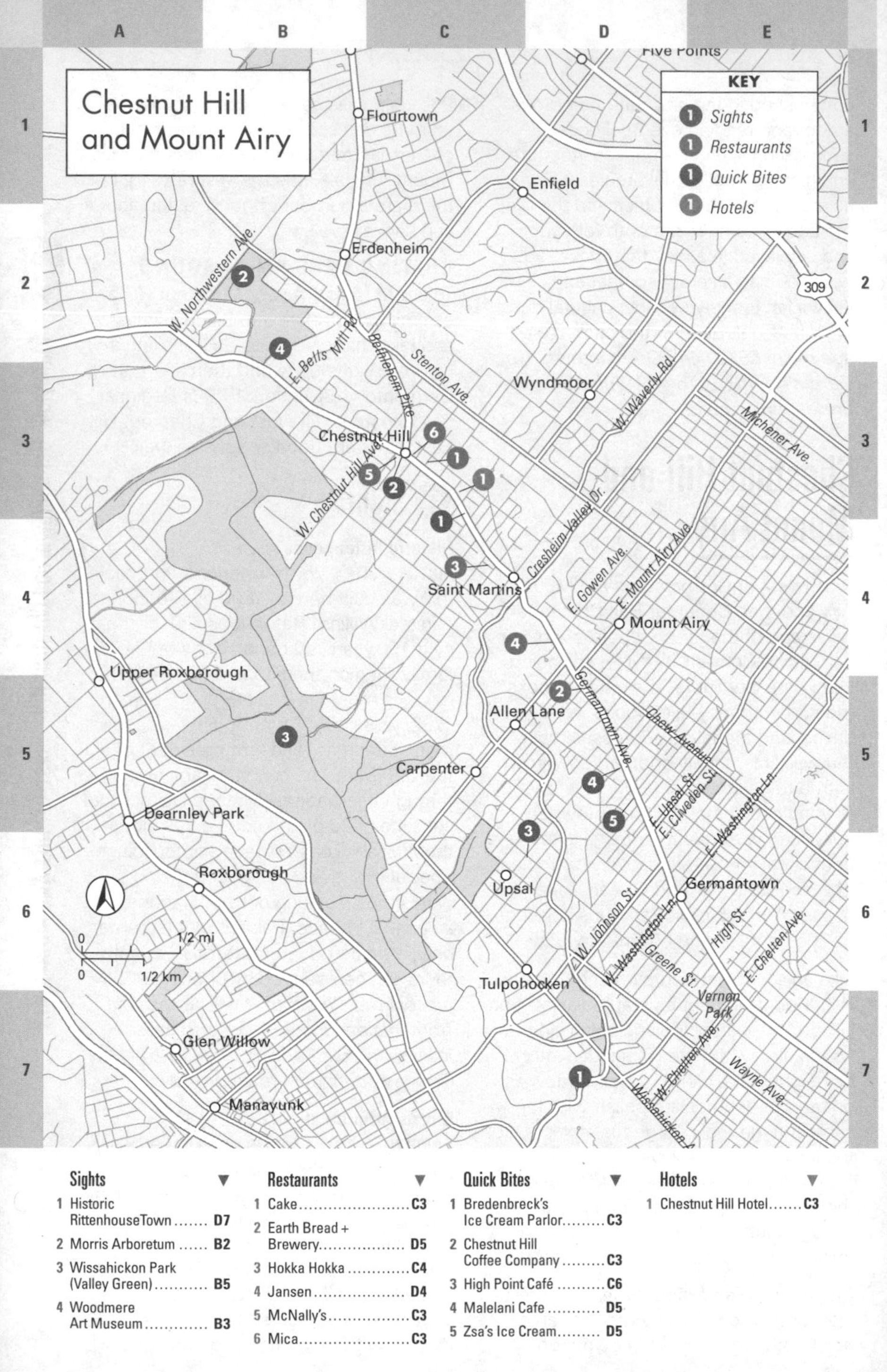

Sights

1 Historic RittenhouseTown D7
2 Morris Arboretum B2
3 Wissahickon Park (Valley Green) B5
4 Woodmere Art Museum B3

Restaurants

1 Cake C3
2 Earth Bread + Brewery D5
3 Hokka Hokka C4
4 Jansen D4
5 McNally's C3
6 Mica C3

Quick Bites

1 Bredenbreck's Ice Cream Parlor C3
2 Chestnut Hill Coffee Company C3
3 High Point Café C6
4 Malelani Cafe D5
5 Zsa's Ice Cream......... D5

Hotels

1 Chestnut Hill Hotel....... C3

a hidden grotto, a fernery, a koi pond, and natural woodland. The highlights are the spectacular rose garden, the swan pond, and "Out on a Limb," a 50-foot-high canopy where you can commune with the birds—and gleeful children. Large modern sculptures, some of which are spectacular, are sprinkled throughout the property, with outdoor sculptural exhibits during the year. Twice annually, the popular Garden Railway exhibit features an elaborate model railroad surrounded by miniature replicas of historic Philadelphia landmarks. You may want to drive, as it's a good hike from the top of Chestnut Hill. ✉ *100 E. Northwestern Ave., Chestnut Hill* ☎ *215/247–5777* 🌐 *www.morrisarboretum.org* 🎟 *$20.*

★ Wissahickon Park (Valley Green)

CITY PARK | There are many great sections of Fairmount Park, but the 1,800 acres around Valley Green known as Wissahickon Park may be the most stunning. Miles and miles of trails running along and above the river lead to covered bridges, a statue of a Lenape chief (rife with inaccuracies but created with good intentions), caves used by a 17th-century free-love cult, large boulders that drip water, and mallards quacking for bread bits. Forbidden Drive, on which cars are forbidden, runs from Northwestern Avenue (the westernmost part of Chestnut Hill) all the way to Lincoln Drive, where it connects to a bike and walking path that leads to Manayunk and Kelly Drive, where additional bike paths can take you to the city or out along the Schuylkill to Valley Forge. There are also many miles of surprisingly difficult mountain-bike trails. The Valley Green Inn is a decent restaurant at Forbidden Drive and Valley Green Road, and a refreshment stand is there as well. ✉ *Valley Green Rd., Chestnut Hill* ✥ *Follow Valley Green Rd down to the parking lots. There are many trails all over the area that also lead into the park* ☎ *215/247–0417* 🌐 *www.fow.org* 🎟 *Free.*

Woodmere Art Museum

MUSEUM | On the far side of Chestnut Hill, on the slope leading towards the suburbs, this Philly artist–centric museum focuses on 19th- and 20th-century eastern Pennsylvania art. The permanent collection features mid-1900s woodcuts and a number of 19th-century Pennsylvania landscapes. There are also worthwhile contemporary special exhibitions, along with live jazz and movie nights. ✉ *9201 Germantown Ave., Chestnut Hill* ☎ *215/247–0476* 🌐 *www.woodmereartmuseum.org* 🎟 *$10; Sun. free* ⏲ *Closed Mon.*

 Restaurants

Cake

$ | **AMERICAN** | Housed inside a former greenhouse, Cake is a refined spot for breakfast and lunch, though the sweets and pastries are still a highlight at this former bakery. The menu includes creative twists on lunchtime classics: try the Philly cheesesteak marsala or the croque monsieur brushed with apricot mustard. **Known for:** garden atmosphere; refined breakfast and lunch; buttery scones. Ⓢ *Average main: $13* ✉ *8501 Germantown Ave., Chestnut Hill* ☎ *215/247–6887* 🌐 *www.cakeofchestnuthill.com* ⏲ *Closed Mon. No dinner.*

Earth Bread + Brewery

$$ | **AMERICAN** | **FAMILY** | Although primarily a restaurant—families are ever-present—serving some of the city's best flatbread pizzas and salads, Earthbread is a beer lover's destination. A rotating selection of four specialty brews made on the premise is featured, while the rest of the taps are almost entirely local craft beers (like Victory, Stoudts, and Sly Fox). **Known for:** adventurous and accessible beers; flatbread pizzas; welcoming atmosphere. Ⓢ *Average main: $16* ✉ *7136 Germantown Ave., Chestnut Hill* ☎ *215/242–6666* 🌐 *www.earthbreadbrewery.com* ⏲ *No lunch weekdays.*

Located in Chestnut Hill, the 92-acre Morris Arboretum has 3,500 trees and shrubs from around the world and a 50-foot-high canopy where you can commune with the birds.

Hokka Hokka

$$$ | **JAPANESE** | This high-quality sushi joint has friendly service and particularly good rolls, including fun ones like the Hollywood—a massive creation with tempura shrimp, avocado, salmon, and eel sauce. Near the bottom of Chestnut Hill, Hokka Hokka also serves a variety of tempura and other Japanese dishes for the non-sushi eater. **Known for:** creative sushi rolls; cozy fireplace; good service. *Average main: $20 ✉ 7830 Germantown Ave., Chestnut Hill ☎ 215/242–4489 ⊕ www.restauranthokka.com ⏲ No lunch weekends.*

Jansen

$$$$ | **AMERICAN** | French cooking methods are married with refined takes on seasonal American comfort fare in the area's most classic fine-dining establishment. Set in an 18th-century "cottage" with a gorgeous back patio, the service is old-school in the care they take of diners, while a light touch—and seasonal ingredients—pervades their culinary concoctions. **Known for:** classic dishes expertly done; meticulous presentation; located in Cresheim Cottage, a building from the 1700s. *Average main: $30 ✉ 7402 Germantown Ave., Mount Airy ☎ 267/335–5041 ⊕ www.jansenmtairy.com ⏲ Closed Mon. and Tues. No lunch Wed.-Sat.*

McNally's

$ | **AMERICAN** | **FAMILY** | People come to McNally's more for the food than the beer (families are welcome), and generally order one of the six featured sandwiches. The Schmitter, a cheesesteak on a kaiser roll with fried salami, fried onions, and a special sauce, is insanely delicious. **Known for:** The Schmitter; family vibe; no-nonsense service. *Average main: $10 ✉ 8634 Germantown Ave., Chestnut Hill ☎ 215/247–9736 ⊕ www.mcnallys-tavern.com.*

★ Mica

$$$$ | **MODERN AMERICAN** | The area's best restaurant with the most adventurous flavors, Mica is a BYOB most known for its seven-course tasting menu (must be ordered by the whole table), but you can

also choose à la carte items that mix the locally sourced ingredients with international cooking. While heavily influenced by the seasons, such delicacies as crab beignets and tuna tartare—you could order a whole meal of just the tantalizing appetizers—are accompanied by hardier fare like hanger steak and pork shoulder. **Known for:** cozy elegance; themed tasting menus; artful presentation. *Average main: $30 ✉ 8609 Germantown Ave., Chestnut Hill ☎ 267/335–3912 🌐 micarestaurant.com ⏱ Closed Sun. and Mon. No lunch.*

Coffee and Quick Bites

Bredenbreck's Ice Cream Parlor
$ | **CAFÉ** | It's all about the ice cream, hot fudge, and homemade whipped cream. They scoop Bassetts ice cream and make fabulous sundaes, but the bakery is pretty standard. **Known for:** generous sundaes; tipping usually gets you bigger scoops; friendly vibe. *Average main:* $5 *✉ 8126 Germantown Ave., Chestnut Hill ☎ 215/247–7374 🌐 www.bredenbecks.com.*

Chestnut Hill Coffee Company
$ | **CAFÉ** | This trendy-for-Chestnut Hill spot roasts its own rich, delicious coffee, and fashions quite good mochas and frothy drinks with over-serious attention. The upstairs is a nice spot to chill for a while. **Known for:** its coffee-roasting pedigree; tasty mochas; hiring hip staff. *Average main: $5 ✉ 8620 Germantown Ave., Chestnut Hill ☎ 215/242–8600 🌐 chestnuthillcoffee.com ⏱ No dinner.*

High Point Café
$ | **CAFÉ** | Coffee shop, creperie, purveyor of baked goods, and local gathering spot, the High Point offers a convivial picture of Mount Airy life. A second café is at the Allens Lane train station, at Cresheim Street and Allens Lane. **Known for:** bustling atmosphere; sweet and savory crepes; orange-zest mocha. *Average main: $8 ✉ 602 Carpenter La., Mount Airy ☎ 215/992–2077 🌐 www.highpointcafe.us.com ⏱ No dinner.*

Malelani Cafe
$ | **GREEK** | Though the decor appears to be perpetually half finished, Malelani's serves up good Greek specialties, including a much-heralded moussaka. You can also come just for a coffee or the surprisingly good ice teas. **Known for:** a menu based on the whims of the chef; friendly welcome; homemade quality. *Average main: $14 ✉ 6734 Germantown Ave., Mount Airy ☎ 267/766–2396 ⏱ No dinner Sun.*

Zsa's Ice Cream
$ | **AMERICAN** | Be prepared to get your mind blown by the creamy insanity of Zsa's ice cream. The salted caramel, Black Magic (chocolate cake and coffee ice cream), and a chocolate sorbet—so rich you won't believe it's sorbet—vie with other specialty flavors that continue to conquer the artisanal-ice-cream wars. **Known for:** inventive flavors; ice-cream sandwiches; ultimate dessert decadence. *Average main: $5 ✉ 6616 Germantown Ave., Mount Airy 🌐 zsasicecream.com ⏱ Closed Mon.–Wed.; call ahead for summer hours.*

Hotels

Chestnut Hill Hotel
$ | **HOTEL** | This attractive, midsize hotel is the place to rest if you want to station yourself in Northwest Philadelphia; it's not fancy inside, but it's well run and offers a perfectly pleasant stay. **Pros:** multiple lunch and dinner options next door; convenient to shops; standard but attractive rooms. **Cons:** not a bells-and-whistles hotel. *Rooms from: $149 ✉ 8229 Germantown Ave., Chestnut Hill ☎ 215/242–5905 🌐 www.chestnuthillhotel.com 36 rooms Free breakfast.*

Nightlife

BARS AND LOUNGES

McMenamins

BARS/PUBS | This lively, family-friendly Mount Airy favorite has a fantastic choice of craft beer on tap, plus decent burgers, fish-and-chips, and dinner specials. ✉ *7170 Germantown Ave., Mount Airy* ☎ *215/247–9920.*

Mount Airy Tap Room

BARS/PUBS | A spacious spot if you want to stretch out your legs, there's a nice patio as well as a wood-burning stove, a stellar draft list, and decent pub fare. ✉ *300 W. Mount Pleasant Ave., Mount Airy* ☎ *267/766–6668* 🌐 *mountairytap-room.com.*

MUSIC CLUBS

The Jazz Café at Paris Bistro

MUSIC CLUBS | The coolest music venue in the area hosts excellent jazz combos in the bottom of the Paris Bistro in an intimate, subterranean music cave. ✉ *Paris Bistro, 8229 Germantown Ave., Chestnut Hill* ✥ *Enter the restaurant and head downstairs* ☎ *215/242–6200* 🌐 *www.parisbistro.net.*

Mermaid Inn

MUSIC CLUBS | If you head to the Mermaid, know the vibe is a little provincial, but you can hear good live music (folk, blues, rock, jazz) Thursday through Saturday. Cover charges range from $5 to $10. ✉ *7673 Winston Rd., at Mermaid La., Chestnut Hill* ☎ *215/247–9797* 🌐 *www.themermaidinn.net* ⏲ *Closed Sun.*

Performing Arts

Quintessence Theatre Group

THEATER | The area's only true professional theater, Quintessence mounts quality, and at times innovative, productions of classic plays. ✉ *7137 Germantown Ave., Mount Airy* ☎ *215/987–4450* 🌐 *www.quintessencetheatre.org.*

Shopping

FASHION

Greene Street

CLOTHING | Don't be surprised by the great finds here—this is the consignment shop for people who like to say, "Look, I got this $300 designer dress in perfect condition for only $60!" Greene Street Men's is a few stores down at 8518 Germantown Avenue. ✉ *8524 Germantown Ave., Chestnut Hill* ☎ *215/331–6725.*

Style Camp

CLOTHING | Very tasteful, well-made women's clothes and accessories by "under-the-radar" designers feature at this locally owned boutique. It's on the pricey side, but the high quality and appealing styles are worth it. ✉ *9 W. Highland Ave., Chestnut Hill* ✥ *Near the top of the hill, just off Germantown Ave.* ☎ *215/242–3108* 🌐 *style-camp.com* ☞ *Closed Mon.*

MARKETS

Market at the Fareway

OUTDOOR/FLEA/GREEN MARKETS | A mix of farmers' market, specialty-goods stands, and eateries with both indoor and outdoor seating, this is an excellent lunch or late-afternoon meal destination. The best options include Chestnut Hill Brewing Company (beer and pizza), Chicko Tako (Korean tacos), and the Saigon Noodle Bar. Plus, you can grab giant hoagies from Rancks, Persian dishes from Shundeez Market, and steamed dumplings from Momos of Tibet. Permanently housed behind the Chestnut Hill Hotel, the bulk of the market is only open Thursday through Saturday, but most of the take-out vendors are also open on Wednesday and Sunday. For more traditional fruits and vegetables, the Chestnut Hill Farmers' Market sets up shop outdoors on Winston Road between Germantown Avenue and Mermaid Lane on Saturday mornings from 9:30 to 1. ✉ *8221 Germantown Ave., Chestnut Hill* ☎ *215/242–5905* 🌐 *www.marketatthefareway.com.*

Chapter 12

SIDE TRIPS FROM PHILADELPHIA

Updated by
Linda Cabasin

Sights	Restaurants	Hotels	Shopping	Nightlife
★★★★★	★★★☆☆	★★★☆☆	★★★☆☆	★★☆☆☆

WELCOME TO SIDE TRIPS FROM PHILADELPHIA

TOP REASONS TO GO

★ **Brandywine River Museum of Art:** The work of iconic American artists Andrew Wyeth, N. C. Wyeth, and Jamie Wyeth are the focus.

★ **Longwood Gardens:** Internationally renowned gardens and conservatories are worth a visit any time of the year.

★ **American history lesson:** Valley Forge and Washington Crossing Historic Park are filled with historic structures and information.

★ **Winterthur:** The collection of American furniture and objects offer a window on the nation's past through design.

★ **Delaware River towns:** Historic riverfront towns like Bucks County's New Hope and Lambertville (across the river in New Jersey) attract day-trippers.

★ **Fun for kids:** Both LEGOLAND Discovery Center Philadelphia and Sesame Place are great spots for kids.

1 West Chester. Restaurants, shops, and some interesting sights.

2 Chadds Ford. The Brandywine Museum of Art is a top draw.

3 Centreville, Delaware. This tiny village has a great location near Brandywine sights.

4 Kennett Square. Strollable and filled with restaurants.

5 Wilmington, Delaware. Beyond the city's downtown are sights such as Nemours Mansion and Gardens.

6 Valley Forge. The historical park marking Washington's 1777–78 encampment and the King of Prussia mall.

7 Plymouth Meeting. Kids can get creative at LEGOLAND Discovery Center Philadelphia.

8 Sesame Place. Younger kids enjoy this Bucks County water and theme park.

9 Washington Crossing. A park marks the site where Washington crossed the Delaware in 1776.

10 New Hope. Delaware River views, indie shops, and lively restaurants.

11 Lambertville, New Jersey. This quaint town lures canal-path strollers and antiques shoppers.

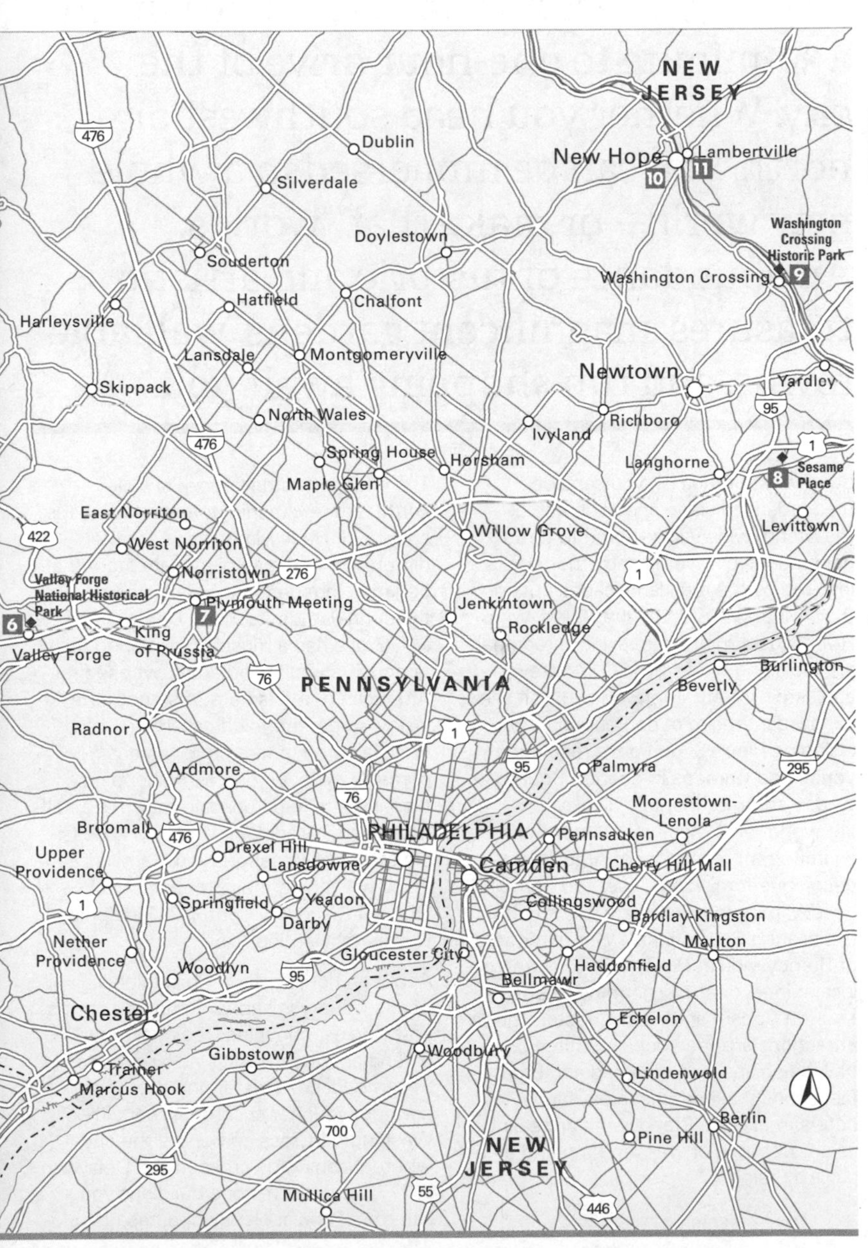
NEW JERSEY
476
Dublin
New Hope
Lambertville
10
11
Silverdale
Doylestown
Washington Crossing Historic Park
Souderton
Washington Crossing
9
Hatfield
Chalfont
Harleysville
Lansdale
Montgomeryville
Newtown
Yardley
Skippack
95
Richboro
North Wales
Ivyland
476
1
Spring House
Horsham
Langhorne
Sesame Place
8
Maple Glen
East Norriton
Levittown
422
Willow Grove
West Norriton
Norristown
276
1
Valley Forge National Historical Park
Plymouth Meeting
Jenkintown
6
7
Rockledge
King of Prussia
Valley Forge
Burlington
76
PENNSYLVANIA
Beverly
Radnor
1
95
Palmyra
Ardmore
295
76
Moorestown-Lenola
PHILADELPHIA
Pennsauken
Broomall
476
Drexel Hill
Upper Providence
Lansdowne
Camden
Cherry Hill Mall
Springfield
Yeadon
Collingswood
1
Darby
Barclay-Kingston
Nether Providence
Marlton
Gloucester City
Haddonfield
Woodlyn
95
Bellmawr
Chester
Echelon
Gibbstown
Woodbury
Trainer
Lindenwold
Marcus Hook
Berlin
700
Pine Hill
NEW JERSEY
295
55
Mullica Hill
446

It's easy to expand your view of the Philadelphia area by taking one or more day trips to destinations that are within a 30-minute to one-hour drive of the city. Whether you head southwest or north, you can be immersed in a whole new world—or make that "worlds." An abundance of historic and artistic treasures, magnificent gardens, walkable towns, and fun shopping await you.

Southwest of the city, you can see the verdant hills and ancient barns of the Brandywine Valley, home to three generations of Wyeths and other artists inspired by the rural landscapes outside their windows. Stop by the Brandywine River Museum of Art to explore regional art, including works by N.C., Andrew, and Jamie Wyeth. Then you can visit the extravagant realm of du Pont country, including Pierre S. du Pont's resplendent Longwood Gardens in Kennett Square, whose summer fountain displays are world-renowned, and Winterthur, an important repository of American decorative furnishings, over the border near Wilmington, Delaware. Or you can explore the Revolutionary War battlefield of Brandywine at Chadds Ford, taste local wines, or stroll charming towns like Kennett Square and West Chester. These attractions are year-round favorites of Philadelphians, and area bed-and-breakfasts and inns (and, these days, chain hotels) make the Brandywine appealing as an overnight or weekend trip and as a day excursion.

The national historical park at Valley Forge, where Washington and his troops spent a difficult winter, adds another dimension to the revolutionary story that began in Independence Hall. Nearby, the John James Audubon Center at Mill Grove has a museum exploring the famous naturalist and artist, whose first American home is here. Also not far from Valley Forge, the town called King of Prussia dates to that period, but is now primarily synonymous with shopping, thanks to its huge upscale mall. It's a half hour from Philadelphia and also accessible by public transportation. Families can enjoy expanding their creativity at LEGOLAND Discovery Center Philadelphia in Plymouth Meeting.

About an hour north of Philadelphia, Bucks County is known for quaint towns, art colonies, shopping, regional theater, and country inns. It's also home to Sesame Place, a water and theme park great for younger children. A park in Washington Crossing honors the site where Washington crossed the Delaware in 1776 and has historic buildings you can tour. Popular New Hope has historic sites as well as riverside walks, all kinds of shopping from crafts to clothing, and lively restaurants and bars. Pair a visit here with a stroll across the Delaware River to Lambertville, New Jersey, with its canal path and plenty of antiques and home-furnishing shops, galleries, and restaurants.

MAJOR REGIONS

With a strong legacy from two families, the artistic Wyeths and the industrialist du Ponts, the **Brandywine Valley,** an area southwest of Philadelphia, spans Pennsylvania and Delaware and offers many reasons to stay awhile, whether to take in vistas of the small river and tranquil landscapes, or explore top sights. **West Chester** and **Kennett Square** are both walkable towns with shops and restaurants; Kennett Square is near a major du Pont–related attraction, colorful Longwood Gardens. **Chadds Ford** has the excellent Brandywine River Museum of Art, with works by the Wyeths and regional artists, and a Revolutionary War battlefield. In Delaware, tiny **Centreville** is near major sights like Winterthur's American decorative arts collection, and the state's capital has good museums and another former du Pont home, Nemours Mansion and Gardens. Despite encroaching development, there are also still plenty of scenic back roads to explore around the Brandywine.

Several popular but very different attractions draw people to the area near suburban **Valley Forge,** northwest of the city. Serene **Valley Forge National Historical Park** commemorates and interprets the site of George Washington's 1777–78 winter encampment, a crucial point in the American Revolution. Nearby, sprawling **King of Prussia** mall has more than 450 shops and is a destination in itself. Twelve miles to the east, **LEGOLAND Discovery Center Philadelphia** provides plenty of engaging fun for kids who love the classic building toy.

About an hour north of Philadelphia by car, **Bucks County** was 622 square miles of sleepy, pretty countryside before being "discovered," first by artists and then by suburbanites and exurbanites. **Sesame Place,** in the more developed southern part of the county, is a favorite theme and water park for younger kids. **Washington Crossing,** by the Delaware River, recalls the American Revolution with a historic park and buildings. To the north, the river town of **New Hope** has long been popular with artists, craftspeople, and shoppers, or anyone seeking a fun day out. **Lambertville,** across the Delaware in New Jersey, shares the same vibe and has a canal path, antiques and home furnishings shops, and restaurants.

Planning

Getting Here and Around

While some of these attractions can be reached by public transportation, the only practical way to tour Bucks County and much of the Brandywine Valley is by car.

BUS

To get to Valley Forge, you can take SEPTA Bus 124 from 13th and Market Streets (it leaves twice an hour starting at 4:30 am) for King of Prussia mall. Bus 125 also goes to the mall and continues on to Valley Forge National Historical Park; the service (about once an hour) is limited to times the park is open.

CONTACTS SEPTA. ☎ *215/580–7800* 🌐 *www.septa.org.*

CAR

To reach the Brandywine Valley from Philadelphia, take I–95 south to U.S. 322 and then U.S. 1; it is about 25 miles away, and many attractions are on U.S. 1. To reach Wilmington, take I–95 south from Philadelphia; if you're on U.S. 1, pick up U.S. 202 south just past Concordville.

For Valley Forge, take the Schuylkill Expressway (I–76) west from Philadelphia to Exit 327 (Mall Boulevard). Make a right onto Mall Boulevard and a right onto North Gulph Road. Follow the road 1½ miles to Valley Forge National Historical Park. Mall Boulevard also provides easy access to the King of Prussia shopping mall.

The most direct route to Bucks Country is I–95 north, which takes you near sights in the southern part of the county. Before you cross into New Jersey, take the exit and continue on Route 32, which runs along the Delaware past Washington Crossing Historic Park. New Hope is about 40 miles northwest of Philadelphia.

TRAIN

Amtrak has frequent service from Philadelphia's 30th Street Station to Wilmington's station at 100 South French Street on the edge of downtown. It's a 20-minute ride. SEPTA's Wilmington/Newark commuter train has roughly hourly (less often on weekends) departures to Wilmington from Philadelphia's 30th Street, Suburban, and Jefferson train stations. The trip takes about 50 minutes.

CONTACTS Amtrak. ☎ *800/872–7245* 🌐 *www.amtrak.com.* **SEPTA.** ☎ *215/580–7800* 🌐 *www.septa.org.*

When to Go

Each season provides plenty of reasons to visit the Brandywine, which is about 45 minutes' to an hour's drive from Center City Philadelphia, and Bucks County, about an hour north of the city. Spring and summer bring a Technicolor display of flowers at Longwood Gardens and verdant green to the Brandywine Valley countryside, Valley Forge National Park, and Bucks County. The chance to witness some spectacular fall foliage and crisper weather is a compelling case for an autumnal visit, although the spectacular indoor and outdoor holiday light show at Longwood and the chance to relax by a cozy fire at a charming inn are reason enough to come during the cold-weather months. Christmas season brings holiday festivals to Bucks County as well, including the annual reenactment of Washington crossing the Delaware. You can easily make day trips to any of these regions from the city, but be sure to avoid traveling west on I–76, and to a lesser extent, north or south on I–95, during rush hour. Weekends, spring through fall, tend to be the busiest season for visitors; December brings crowds and traffic for Longwood's holiday light displays (timed tickets required).

Hotels

Many of the more charming, even historic, accommodations in these areas may be considered bed-and-breakfasts because of their intimate atmosphere, but they're far from the typical B&B—which is usually a room or two in a private home—and are more accurately characterized as inns or small hotels. These days, though, chain hotels are plentiful around the region. Although they have less atmosphere than inns, they are a family-friendly, good-value alternative to B&Bs, which may not accept very young children. *Hotel reviews have been shortened. For full information, visit Fodors.com.*

What It Costs In U.S. Dollars

$	$$	$$$	$$$$
RESTAURANTS			
under $15	$15–$19	$20–$24	over $24
HOTELS			
under $150	$150–$200	$201–$250	over $250

Restaurants

Many restaurants in both the Brandywine Valley and Bucks County serve American cuisine, with creative contemporary touches at the better establishments, but international cuisines also have a growing presence. You'll find both sophisticated restaurants and casual country spots, some with a focus on farm-to-table fare. Most also present local and regional specialties—fresh seafood from Chesapeake Bay and dishes made with Kennett Square mushrooms. *Restaurant reviews have been shortened. For full information, visit Fodors.com.*

Tours

May through October, you can explore the slow, gentle Brandywine River by kayak, canoe, or tube on a relaxing short or half-day self-guided trip with the family-run Northbrook Canoe Co. Check the website for periodic special trips, like a twilight canoe trip followed by dinner.

CONTACTS Northbrook Canoe Co. ✉ *1810 Beagle Rd., West Chester* ☎ *610/793–2279, 800/898–2279* 🌐 *www.northbrookcanoe.com.*

Visitor Information

Operated by the Chester County Conference and Visitors Bureau, the Brandywine Valley visitor center at the entrance to Longwood Gardens has helpful staff and plenty of brochures (on everything from the Underground Railroad to local wineries and breweries) and maps.

Bucks County maintains a visitor center in Bensalem, but the county website has information on all the region's sights, restaurants, and B&Bs.

CONTACTS Brandywine Valley Tourism and Information Center. ✉ *300 Greenwood Rd., Kennett Square* ☎ *484/770–8550* 🌐 *brandywinevalley.com.* **Bucks County Visitors Bureau.** ✉ *3207 Street Rd., Bensalem* ☎ *215/639–0300 Bucks County Visitor Center* 🌐 *visitbuckscounty.com.*

West Chester

35 miles west of Philadelphia via I–95.

The seat since 1786, this historic mile-square city holds distinctive 18th- and 19th-century architecture, with fine examples of Greek Revival and Victorian styles. A small but vital downtown has shopping possibilities as well as restaurants and bars serving everything from classic American fare to the latest microbrews. Fine examples of classical architecture, including the Historic Chester County Courthouse, can be found near the intersection of High and Gay Streets. The town is also home to West Chester University of Pennsylvania, which adds a lively student vibe to downtown, and to the QVC Studios, in an industrial park off U.S. 202.

GETTING HERE AND AROUND

From Philadelphia, West Chester is a 50-minute drive via I–76 west and U.S. 202 south. The town itself is highly walkable, but you will need a car to access QVC Studios and other nearby attractions.

Sights

American Helicopter Museum & Education Center

MUSEUM | FAMILY | Ever since Philadelphian Harold Pitcairn made the first rotorcraft flight in 1928, the southeastern Pennsylvania area has been considered the birthplace of the helicopter industry, and the aircraft on display here reflect this heritage. In fact, two of the three major U.S. helicopter manufacturers trace their roots to this region. You can view nearly three dozen vintage and modern aircraft, plus models, that reflect

Visiting the Brandywine Valley

The Brandywine Valley actually incorporates parts of three counties in two states: Chester and Delaware counties in Pennsylvania and New Castle County in Delaware. Winding through this scenic region (about 25 miles southwest of Philadelphia), the Brandywine River flows lazily from West Chester, Pennsylvania, to Wilmington, Delaware. Although in spots it's more a creek than a river, it has nourished many of the valley's economic and artistic endeavors. Today the Philadelphia (and Wilmington) suburbs continue to encroach: new housing developments continuously crop up, and the main highways, U.S. 1 and U.S. 202, bring with them shopping malls and traffic snarls. Yet, traveling down country roads, particularly those that intersect Route 52, makes you feel you have discovered a remote treasure: just be careful driving those curving back roads at night.

If you start early enough, and limit your time at each stop, you can tour the valley's top three attractions—the Brandywine River Museum of Art, Longwood Gardens, and Winterthur—in one day. If you have more time to spend in the valley, you can visit additional sites in Pennsylvania and then move on to those near Wilmington.

the copter's historic roles in war and rescue missions, in agriculture, and in police surveillance. Climb aboard four of these and also try the non-moving flight simulator to get a sense of the helicopter experience. Ask in advance about five-minute helicopter rides ($60 per person). ✉ *1220 American Blvd.* ☎ *610/436–9600* 🌐 *www.americanhelicopter.museum* 🎫 *$10* ⏲ *Closed Mon. and Tues.*

Chester County Historical Society

MUSEUM | Donated objects and acquisitions help tell the story of Chester County from the late 1600s to today. The society's architectural complex, known as the History Center, includes a former opera house where Buffalo Bill once performed. Galleries tell about the Delaware Valley's settlers and the decorative furniture they crafted; quilts, period clothing, and grandfather clocks are some key collections, as well as American cross-stitch samplers. A hands-on history lab lets kids churn butter and dress up in a hoop skirt. ✉ *225 N. High St.* ☎ *610/692–4800* 🌐 *www.chestercohistorical.org* 🎫 *$8* ⏲ *Closed Sun. and Mon.*

QVC Studio Park

FILM STUDIO | Though the large electronics retailer discontinued its studio tours in 2019, fans can still get free tickets to be part of a studio audience for a live broadcast. Visit the website for information about reserving a seat in the 130-person theater. There isn't a set schedule for live shows, so it's best to keep checking online. The studio is wheelchair accessible. ✉ *1200 Wilson Dr.* ☎ *800/600–9900* 🌐 *www.qvc.com/content/information/qvc-studio-live-events.html* 🎫 *Free.*

Restaurants

The Couch Tomato Café

$ | **AMERICAN** | **FAMILY** | College students, their parents, and locals all flock to this casual eatery for delicious soups, pizzas, sandwiches, and salad bowls that favor fresh, local, and organic ingredients and good vegan and gluten-free choices. Step up to the counter or use an iPad to order from the menu or build your own sandwich or pizza from generous ingredient lists, then grab a seat in a space

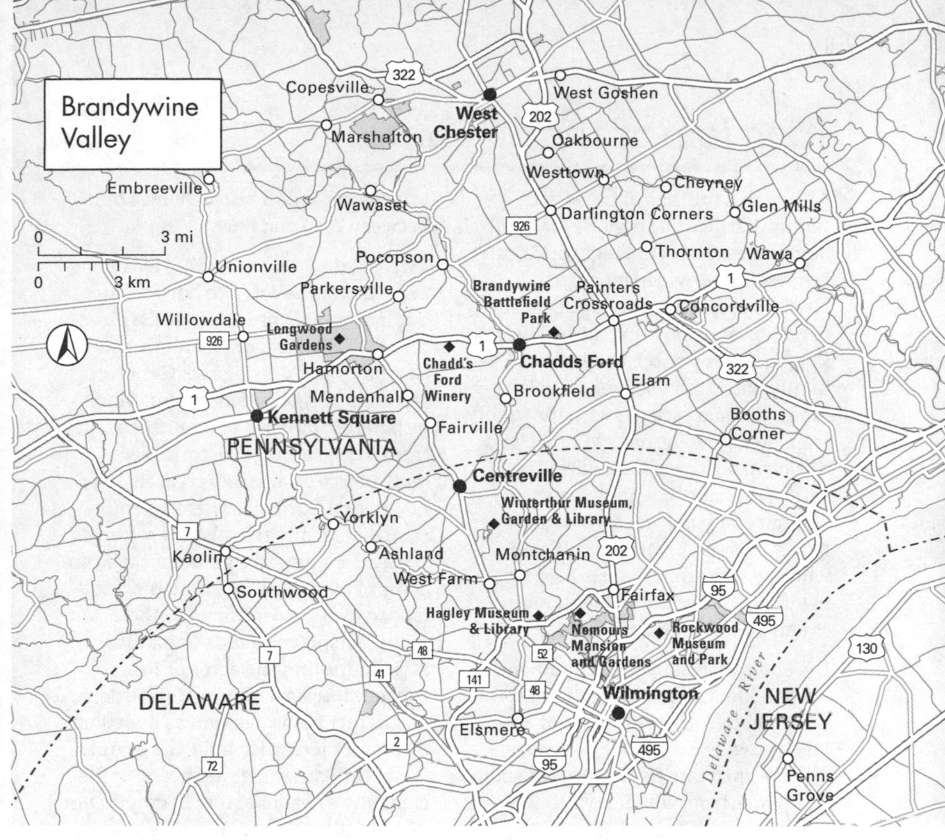

with exposed brick walls, tomato-colored (of course) banquettes, and simple wooden tables. **Known for:** multiple pizza crust options; grilled cheese and tomato bisque soup combo; rooftop deck for alfresco dining. *Average main: $11* *31 W. Gay St.* *484/887–0241* *the-couchtomato.com.*

High Street Caffe

$$$ | **SOUTHERN** | Silver beaded lighting fixtures create a fun and sexy vibe at this small, local-favorite café where everything is done up in the color purple—walls, tablecloths, and even the coffee mugs. The kitchen and waitstaff are attentive to details as they serve superior Cajun and Creole fare such as smoked alligator sausage, blackened crab cakes, jambalaya, étouffée, and other French Quarter favorites. **Known for:** specials with exotic meats such as ostrich and kangaroo; good-value prix-fixe option Sunday–Thursday; long, diverse beer list. *Average main: $23* *322 S. High St.* *610/696–7435* *highstreetcaffe.com* *No lunch Sat.–Mon.*

Iron Hill Brewery & Restaurant

$$ | **AMERICAN** | An old Woolworth's building with tin ceilings and maple floors is now this large, bustling restaurant and brewpub in the heart of downtown, one of a number of Iron Hill outposts in the state. The extensive menu lists everything from nachos and flatbreads to all kinds of burgers (meat and non-meat), steaks, and salads. **Known for:** seasonal beers on tap; good weekday happy hours; vegetarian, vegan, and gluten-free options. *Average main: $19* *3 W. Gay St.* *610/738–9600* *www.ironhillbrewery.com.*

Kingdom of the du Ponts

Although paintings of the Wyeth family distilled the region's tranquil landscapes, it was the regal du Pont family that provided more than a bit of its magnificence, adding grand gardens, mansions, and mills. Their kingdom was established by the family patriarch, Pierre-Samuel du Pont, who had escaped with his family from post-Revolutionary France and settled in northern Delaware. The earliest version of what is now the DuPont company was founded in 1802 by his son Éleuthère Irénée (E.I.), who made the family fortune, first in gunpowder and iron and later in chemicals and textiles.

E.I. and five generations of du Ponts lived in Eleutherian Mills, the stately family home on the grounds of a black-powder mill that has been transformed into the Hagley Museum. The home, from which Mrs. Henry du Pont was driven after accidental blasts at the powder works, was closed in 1921. Louise du Pont Crowninshield, a great-granddaughter of E.I., restored the house fully before opening it to the public. Louise's relatives were busy, too. Henry Francis du Pont was filling his country estate, Winterthur, with furniture by Duncan Phyfe, silver by Paul Revere, splendid decorative objects made or used in America, and entire interior woodwork fittings salvaged from American homes built between 1640 and 1860.

Pierre S. du Pont (cousin of Henry Francis) was devoted to horticulture, but he was also president and a director of E. I. du Pont de Nemours and Company and president of General Motors during his long career. In 1906, he bought 202 acres of an 18th-century farm to preserve its historic trees (now Peirce's Park) and created Longwood Gardens, where he entertained his many friends and relatives. Today the 1,100-acre gardens have 350 acres of meadows and meticulously landscaped gardens open to the public. Displays include Versailles-style fountains and acres of heated conservatories with tropical gardens and desert plants, as well as lush floral displays. Pierre also built the grand Hotel Du Pont in 1913, adjacent to the company's headquarters in downtown Wilmington. No expense was spared; more than 18 French and Italian craftspeople labored for two years, carving, gilding, and painting. Alfred I. du Pont's country estate, Nemours, was named after the family's ancestral home in north-central France. It encompasses 200 acres of grounds with formal French gardens and a grand but somehow homey mansion in Louis XVI style.

Shopping

Baldwin's Book Barn

BOOKS/STATIONERY | In the countryside 2 miles south of downtown West Chester, this book lover's refuge in a converted 1822 barn has nooks and crannies filled with more than 300,000 used and rare books on almost every subject, along with historic maps and prints. ✉ *865 Lenape Rd. (Rte. 52)* ☎ *610/696–0816* 🌐 *bookbarn.com*.

Malena's Vintage Boutique

CLOTHING | Well-organized, color-themed displays and helpful staff make this well-lighted vintage women's clothing and accessories shop downtown a delightful place to browse and buy.

Nicely displayed jewelry cases offer plenty of Bakelite, rhinestone, and other costume pieces. The reasonably priced clothing goes through the 1980s; for more options, make an appointment to see additional vintage, couture, and even antique items at the nearby showroom. ✉ *101 W. Gay St.* ☎ *610/738–9952* 🌐 *malenasboutique.com.*

Chadds Ford

11 miles south of West Chester, 30 miles southwest of Philadelphia via I–95 and U.S. 322.

Immortalized in Andrew Wyeth's serene landscapes, Chadds Ford was less bucolic in the 18th century, when one of the bloodiest battles of the Revolutionary War was fought here along Brandywine Creek. A battlefield park and the excellent Brandywine River Museum of Art, which celebrates American masters including Brandywine Valley residents, make this historic town appealing. Many businesses are spread out along U.S. 1, and developments make the town busier each year, but there are plenty of pretty side roads to explore as well.

GETTING HERE AND AROUND

From Philadelphia, take I–95 south to U.S. 322 toward West Chester and follow signs to U.S. 1. The latter is the major thoroughfare to visit attractions in Chadds Ford, and can get congested on weekends, so be prepared for some stop-and-go traffic.

Sights

Brandywine Battlefield Park

MILITARY SITE | The quiet park is near the site of the Battle of Brandywine, where British general William Howe and his troops defeated George Washington on September 11, 1777, after which the Continental Army fled to Chester, leaving Philadelphia vulnerable to British troops. The battle covered 10 square miles and played an important role in the larger war. The small visitor center has a film and displays about the battle that are a good introduction to the area's history. On the site are two restored Quaker farmhouses, one of which once sheltered Washington and General Lafayette; several guided tours of these are offered daily when the park is open. The 50-acre park is a fine place for a picnic. Ask for info about driving to see key battlefield sights like the Birmingham Friends Meeting house, where soldiers lie in a common grave, and Birmingham Hill. ✉ *1491 Baltimore Pike* ☎ *610/459–3342* 🌐 *www.brandywinebattlefield.org* 🎫 *Park and grounds free; house tours, museum, and film $8; museum admission and film only $3* ⏲ *Closed Jan.–mid-Mar.; Mon.–Thurs. mid-Mar.–May and Oct.–Dec.; Mon. June–Sept.*

★ **Brandywine River Museum of Art**

MUSEUM | In a beautifully converted Civil War–era gristmill, the museum contains the art of Chadds Ford native Andrew Wyeth (1917–2009), a major American realist painter, as well as works by his father, N. C. Wyeth, illustrator of many children's classics; and his son, Jamie. The collection also emphasizes still lifes, landscape paintings, and American illustration, with works by such artists as Howard Pyle and Horace Pippin. A glass-wall lobby on each of the three floors overlooks the river and countryside that inspired artists. Seasonal tours (daily, but a limited number) of three buildings enhance the museum experience; children under age six are not permitted. The N. C. Wyeth House and Studio, set on a hill, holds many props N. C. used in creating his illustrations. His daughter, Carolyn, lived and painted here until 1994. Andrew Wyeth's Studio, where the artist produced many notable works, is on view, too. You can also tour the Kuerner Farm; Andrew used the landscape, buildings, and animals as the subjects of many of his best-known paintings.

The Gideon Gilpin House is one of two restored Quaker farmhouses on the Brandywine Battlefield Park site; the other was Washington's headquarters.

A shuttle takes you from the museum to the buildings for an hour-long guided tour. A fine gift shop and the Millstone Café, both acessible without paying admission, round out the offerings. ✉ *1 Hoffman's Mill Rd.* ✣ *At U.S. 1 and Rte. 100* ☎ *610/388–2700* 🌐 *brandywine.org* 🎫 *$18 museum, free first Sun. of month Feb.–Nov.; $8 N. C. Wyeth House and Studio, $8 Andrew Wyeth Studio, $5 farm* 🕓 *No house or studio tours Dec.–Mar.*

Chaddsford Winery

WINERY/DISTILLERY | Pennsylvania's wine scene is growing: the Brandywine area has more than a dozen wineries, and at Chaddsford you can sample the vintages of one of the oldest (1982). Tastings, held in a woodsy restored barn, include your choice of seven pours from dry to sweeter; more expensive reserve tastings are also offered, along with sales of bottles. There's no sit-down restaurant, but food trucks come on weekends. The winery has concerts and special events (some require an extra fee) on its grounds. This place can get very busy on weekends; tastings are first come, first served. ✉ *632 Baltimore Pike/U.S. 1* ☎ *610/388–6221* 🌐 *chaddsford.com* 🎫 *Free. Wine tastings $12–$16, depending on tasting options.*

Penns Woods Winery

WINERY/DISTILLERY | A family-run business with more than 40 years experience, this winery produces award-winning wines from Pennsylvania-grown grapes that range from sweet and floral Moscato to bold Bordeaux-style wines. The 30-acre property is a great place to picnic with the family, and the outdoor wine bar is open April through October. Check the website as there's live music, food and wine pairings, and other events most weekends. ✉ *124 Beaver Valley Rd.* ☎ *610/459–0808* 🌐 *www.pennswoodsevents.com* 🕓 *Closed Mon. Jan.–Mar.*

Wyeth Country

You'll probably experience a strong sense of déjà vu during a journey to the Brandywine Valley. While creating some of the most beloved works in 20th-century American art, Andrew Wyeth made the valley's vistas instantly recognizable. Using colors quintessentially Brandywine—the earthen brown of its hills, the slate gray of its stone farmhouses, and the dark green of its spruce trees—the famous American realist captured its unostentatiously beautiful landscape. Andrew's father, N. C. Wyeth, moved to then-rural Chadds Ford in 1908, and others have come to fall in love with its peaceful byways.

Although Andrew Wyeth is the most famous local artist, the area's artistic tradition began long before, when artist-illustrator Howard Pyle started a school of illustration in Wilmington in 1900. He had more than 100 students, including the famous illustrator and artist N.C. Wyeth; Frank Schoonover; Jessie Willcox Smith; and Harvey Dunn. It was this tradition, as well as their famous father and grandfather, that inspired Andrew and his son Jamie.

In 1967 local residents formed the Brandywine Conservancy to prevent industrialization of the area and pollution of the river; their actions included significant land purchases. In 1971 the organization opened the Brandywine River Museum of Art in a preserved 19th-century gristmill. It celebrates the Brandywine School of artists in a setting much in tune with their world. The work of the conservancy continues today, focusing on protection of land and water, and may be more critical than ever as development continues around the Brandywine Valley.

Restaurants

Hank's Place

$ | **AMERICAN** | Locals and visitors flock to this cash-only wood-panel outpost, a cottagelike diner open since 1950, for hearty breakfast specials such as omelets with roasted Kennett Square mushrooms and corned beef hash with eggs. Hank's is also open for home-style lunches and dinners (come early, as it closes at 7 pm), serving old-fashioned favorites like French dip sandwiches, rainbow trout, and spaghetti and meatballs. **Known for:** apple dumplings and tasty pies, including strawberry; lines may be long on weekends but move fast; Andrew Wyeth was a patron back in the day. *Average main: $13 1625 Creek Rd. At intersection of U.S. 1 and Rte. 100 610/388–7061 hanksplacechaddsford.com No credit cards No dinner Sun. and Mon.*

Terrain Café

$$$ | **AMERICAN** | Part of the Terrain garden center and home furnishing store, this BYOB café and restaurant occupies a greenhouse space adorned with pieces of wood, party lights, and leafy plants. It's the perfect match for a lunch or dinner of fresh, seasonal regional fare such as artisanal cheeses, mushroom soup, vegetable-filled bowls and salads, and Pennsylvania beef burgers, or for La Colombe coffee and a pastry in the morning. **Known for:** bread served in a clay pot; extensive list of teas and flavored spritzers; decadent desserts offset the healthy fare. *Average main: $22 914 Baltimore Pike, U.S. 1, Glen Mills 610/459–6030 shopterrain.com No dinner Mon. and Tues.*

Hotels

Brandywine River Hotel

$$ | **B&B/INN** | Near the Brandywine River Museum of Art, this two-story hotel has traditional Queen Anne–style furnishings, classic English chintz, and floral fabrics that create a homey B&B feel. **Pros:** convenient to attractions and some restaurants; fitness room; friendly staff. **Cons:** uninspired decor could use some updating; close to busy U.S. 1; not as charming as a B&B. *Rooms from: $159* *1609 Baltimore Pike, U.S. 1* *610/388–1200* *brandywineriverhotel.com* *39 rooms* *Free breakfast.*

Fairville Inn

$$ | **B&B/INN** | Halfway between Longwood Gardens and Winterthur, this comfortable B&B has bright, airy rooms furnished with Queen Anne and Hepplewhite reproductions in three buildings: the 1823–37 main house and the more recently built carriage and springhouse. **Pros:** gracious, helpful hosts; central location for major Brandywine sights; delicious breakfast and afternoon tea. **Cons:** some street noise at times from busy Route 52; some bathrooms need updating; some rooms have small TVs. *Rooms from: $185* *506 Kennett Pike, Rte. 52* *610/388–5900, 877/285–7772* *www.fairvilleinn.com* *15 rooms* *Free breakfast.*

Hamanassett Bed & Breakfast

$$$ | **B&B/INN** | Innkeepers Ashley and Glenn Mon fill their hilltop country house with Southern hospitality and British style: breakfast in an elegant dining room, a pool table for entertainment, and a solarium for relaxing. **Pros:** lovely, expansive grounds; gourmet breakfast; personable, helpful hosts. **Cons:** some bathrooms are small; traditional look may not suit all tastes; two-night minimum on weekends. *Rooms from: $225* *115 Indian Springs Dr., Chester Heights* *610/459–3000, 877/836–8212* *www.hamanassett.com* *9 rooms* *Free breakfast.*

★ The Inn at Grace Winery

$$$ | **B&B/INN** | With a classic stone house at its center, this historic property—part of William Penn's land grant to the Hemphill family—carves out a tranquil 50 acres of Brandywine Valley countryside, including a winery. **Pros:** elegant decor in rooms and public areas; tasting room open Friday–Sunday; cottage rooms are child- and pet-friendly. **Cons:** walking in dark from cottages to main house; small free breakfast, though you can pay for additional items; somewhat farther from main Brandywine attractions. *Rooms from: $210* *50 Sweetwater Rd., Glen Mills* *610/459–4711, 800/793–3892* *gracewinery.com/accommodations* *15 rooms* *Free breakfast.*

Shopping

Terrain at Styer's

HOUSEHOLD ITEMS/FURNITURE | The Philly-based folks behind Anthropologie also created Terrain, a lively store that integrates the outdoors (a garden center) with the indoors (stylish home furnishings). Though this branch is set amid shopping centers, its barn- and greenhouse-like buildings (some from Styer's, the longtime nursery formerly in this location) create a small, enchanted world apart. Seasonal plants appear outdoors and inside, and terrariums, planters and pots, serving pieces and dishes, and soaps and lotions from around the world are all part of the mix; the holidays are particularly enchanting. Linger at the excellent café for a snack or dinner. *914 Baltimore Pike, U.S. 1, Glen Mills* *610/459–2400* *shopterrain.com.*

Centreville, Delaware

5 miles south of Chadds Ford via U.S. 1 and Rte. 52 (Kennett Pike).

The village is aptly named: Centreville, Delaware, founded in 1750 and listed in the National Register of Historic Places, was a midway point between the farms of Kennett Square and the markets of Wilmington. The tiny village, with a historical tavern and some art and antiques shops, is in the middle of the Brandywine Valley's attractions. Longwood Gardens, Winterthur, and the Brandywine River Museum of Art are all less than 5 miles away. Kennett Pike (Route 52) runs through the village; the surrounding two-lane roads take you through some of the still-bucolic parts of the valley.

GETTING HERE AND AROUND

Traffic on Kennett Pike picks up during rush hours; U.S. 1 gets busy on weekends, too.

Sights

Hagley Museum and Library

MUSEUM | **FAMILY** | A restored mid-19th-century mill community on 235 landscaped acres along the Brandywine River, the Hagley Museum and Library provides an enlightening look at the development of early industrial America and the du Pont family's role in it. This is the site of the first of the family's black-powder mills (founded 1802), family estate, and gardens. A visitor center provides historical context and some DuPont Company history, and live demonstrations depict the dangerous work of the early explosives industry. Admission includes a narrated bus tour through the powder yards with stops at Eleutherian Mills, the 1803 Georgian-style home furnished by five generations of du Ponts (guided tour of house included); Workers' Hill, where costumed interpreters describe the life of a typical mill worker; demonstrations in a machine shop and power yard; and a French Renaissance–style garden. **■ TIP→ Be prepared for some walking and allow a minimum of two hours for your visit, which can include tours and self-guided exploration.** ✉ *200 Hagley Creek Rd., Wilmington* ✥ *Off Rte. 141 between Rte. 100 and U.S. 202* ☎ *302/658–2400* 🌐 *www.hagley.org* 🎫 *$15.*

★ Winterthur Museum, Garden & Library

MUSEUM | Henry Francis du Pont (1880–1969) housed his nearly 90,000 objects of American decorative art in a sprawling country estate called Winterthur, and his collection, displayed in 175 rooms, is recognized as one of the nation's finest. Its objects, created or used in America between 1640 and 1860, include Chippendale furniture, silver tankards by Paul Revere, and Chinese porcelain made for George Washington. To view the collection, choose between an hour-long introductory tour, different one-hour theme discovery tours, and two-hour reserved tours that delve into ceramics, textiles, or furniture. The museum also has galleries with permanent and changing exhibitions (some timely, like costumes from *The Crown)* to study at your own pace. Children are welcome on introductory tours but must be eight years old for discovery tours. Surrounding the estate are 982 acres of landscaped lawns and naturalistic gardens, which you can visit on a narrated tram ride (weather permitting) or on your own. The Enchanted Woods is a fantasy-theme 3-acre children's garden with an 8-foot-wide bird's nest, a faerie cottage with a thatch roof, and a troll bridge. A gift shop and cafeteria are on the grounds. Winterthur suggests making tour reservations online in advance of your visit. ✉ *5105 Kennett Pike, Rte. 52, Winterhur* ✥ *5 miles south of U.S. 1* ☎ *302/888–4600, 800/448–3883* 🌐 *winterthur.org* 🎫 *$20 for house, garden, and introductory tour; $32 for house, garden, and 1-hr discovery tour; $42 for house, garden, and 2-hr reserved tour; all tickets good for 2 consecutive days* ⏲ *Closed early Jan.–Feb., and Mon. Mar.–late Nov. Library closed weekends.*

Restaurants

Buckley's Tavern

$$ | **AMERICAN** | Popular with locals, this casual roadside tavern in a building dating back to 1817 serves your typical burgers, classic comfort food, and salads, but the menu has a few surprises such as shrimp and grits and crab Cobb salad. Pick from the wine list and dine on the sunny porch, by the bar with its TV, or in a dining room with a fireplace. **Known for:** wear pajamas to Sunday brunch for big discount; rooftop bar and grill; beer flights from a good list of international and local brews. *Average main: $17* *5812 Kennett Pike, Centreville* *302/656–9776* *www.buckleystavern.com.*

Krazy Kat's

$$$$ | **MODERN AMERICAN** | Oil paintings of regal felines watch over diners at this plushly but wittily furnished restaurant, complete with animal-print chairs, in a former blacksmith shop at the Inn at Montchanin Village. The unique setting and creative modern American menu draw regulars from Wilmington, Philadelphia, and beyond, who come for a frequently changing seasonal menu that includes ample seafood and mushroom options as well as beef choices. **Known for:** romantic vibe; good breakfast and lunch options; interesting cheese choices. *Average main: $25* *Inn at Montchanin Village, 528 Montchanin Rd., Montchanin* *302/888–4200* *www.krazykatsrestaurant.net.*

Hotels

Inn at Montchanin Village and Spa

$$$ | **HOTEL** | This luxurious lodging, also home to Krazy Kat's restaurant, includes 11 painstakingly restored 19th-century cottages that once housed workers from the nearby du Pont powder mills. **Pros:** good mix of new amenities and period charm in rooms and suites; long list of treatments at spa; beautiful gardens. **Cons:** sprawling property with rooms in different buildings; some street noise; site for meetings and weddings. *Rooms from: $209* *528 Montchanin Rd., Montchanin* *Near intersection of Rte. 100 and Kirk Rd.* *302/888–2133* *montchanin.com* *28 rooms* *No meals.*

Kennett Square

7 miles northwest of Centreville via Rte. 52 and U.S. 1.

Just 3 miles west of popular Longwood Gardens, Kennett Square is also where mushroom cultivation began in the United States. By the mid-1920s, 90% of the nation's mushrooms were grown in southeastern Pennsylvania, and the area still produces 50% of the nation's mushrooms. The town celebrates its heritage with its annual Mushroom Festival in September, on the first weekend after Labor Day. With Victorian-era buildings and tree-lined streets, the small town is worth a visit; shops, galleries, and good restaurants fill East State Street between Broad and Union Streets.

Sights

★ Longwood Gardens

GARDEN | **FAMILY** | Today it has an international reputation for its immaculate, colorful gardens and conservatories full of flowers and themed displays, but the Longwood Gardens story began in 1906, when Pierre S. du Pont (1870–1945) bought part of a Quaker farm and turned it into the ultimate early-20th-century estate garden, with magnificent fountain displays. Seasonal attractions on the nearly 400 acres of the 1,100-acre property open to the public include magnolias and azaleas in spring; floral borders and water lilies in summer; chrysanthemums in fall; and the popular (timed tickets required) holiday light displays in winter. An 86-acre meadow garden includes wildflowers and a farmhouse. Spring through fall, displays in the 1,719-jet main fountain garden are a highlight (some feature fireworks at night) and may require reservations. Bad weather is no problem, as 4 acres of cacti, ferns, and changing floral displays are housed in heated conservatories. Besides children's gardens outside and in the conservatories, kids can explore three tree houses on the grounds. There are concerts and other performances (some requiring separate tickets) year-round. The cafeteria and 1906 restaurant (closed January and weekdays February–early March) serve reasonably priced meals; the seasonal Beer Garden is a fun option. ✉ *1001 Longwood Rd., 3 miles northeast of Kennett Square off U.S. 1* ☎ *610/388–1000* 🌐 *longwoodgardens.org* 🎟 *$20 off-peak; $30 peak season, including the winter holiday season.*

Restaurants

★ Talula's Table

$$$$ | AMERICAN | The pricey eight-course prix-fixe dinner at this cozy, cult-favorite market and eat-in spot in the heart of Kennett Square requires advance planning, but fortunately Talula's has its own artisanal cheeses, house-cured meats, and handmade breads and pastas throughout the day, along with a coffee bar and prepared meals for takeout. Breakfast and lunch at the communal table feature seasonal soups, salads, and sandwiches. **Known for:** dinner reservations required a year in advance; delicious baked goods and coffees; mini gourmet grocery. 💲 *Average main: $108* ✉ *102 W. State St.* ☎ *610/444–8255* 🌐 *www.talulastable.com.*

Shopping

The Woodlands at Phillips Mushroom Farms

FOOD/CANDY | Kennett Square is famous for mushrooms that appear on many local menus, and this shop in the old brick family farmhouse stocks all kinds of fresh and dried and marinated mushrooms, specialty mushroom products like soups and teas, and mushroom-theme items from aprons to guest towels. Visit the farm's mushroom-growing exhibit, too, and check the website for special events such as cooking demonstrations. It's 1½ miles south of downtown. ✉ *1020 Kaolin Rd.* ☎ *610/444–2192* 🌐 *thewoodlandsatphillips.com.*

Wilmington, Delaware

15 miles southeast of Kennett Square via Rte. 52.

Delaware's commercial hub and largest city has handsome architecture—with good examples of styles such as Federal, Greek Revival, Queen Anne, and Art Deco—and abundant cultural attractions. Wilmington began in 1638 as a Swedish settlement and later was populated by employees of various du Pont family businesses and nearby poultry ranches. The four-block area around Market Street, undergoing revitalization, marks the city center and has shops and restaurants as well as the Grand Opera House. The four-story theater, built by the Masonic Order in 1871, has a white cast-iron facade in French Second Empire style to mimic the old Paris Opera. The adjoining Giacco Building houses a smaller theater and art galleries. The city also has a 1¾-mile Rivertront Walk (🌐 *riverfrontwilm.com*) along the Delaware. It's near restaurants and sights such as a statue of Harriet Tubman and Thomas Garrett helping enslaved people as they fled to freedom along the Underground Railroad in the state. Outside Wilmington's compact city center are several outstanding museums, including some that are legacies of the du Ponts.

GETTING HERE AND AROUND

The city of Wilmington is less than 45 minutes by car via I–95 south from Philadelphia and is easily accessible by Amtrak and commuter rail. But since you won't want to miss visiting Longwood Gardens, Winterthur, or some of the other stately mansions in the area, you'll want to have a car. Typically, those driving south from Philadelphia to Wilmington during rush hours will encounter some traffic, but not gridlock, because the commute mostly runs the opposite way. Downtown Wilmington is compact and walkable, but it is somewhat quiet after business hours.

ESSENTIALS

The website for the Greater Wilmington Convention and Visitors Bureau has information about the seasonal (late May through early September) Brandywine Treasure Trail Passport, which entitles an individual or family to discounted admission at 12 attractions, including sights like Longwood Gardens in Pennsylvania. If you're staying awhile or making a couple of visits, it is a good value and can be purchased online.

VISITOR INFORMATION Greater Wilmington Convention and Visitors Bureau. ✉ *100 W. 10th St., Wilmington* ☎ *800/489–6664* 🌐 *visitwilmingtonde.com.*

Sights

Delaware Art Museum

MUSEUM | In an 85,000-square-foot building that includes the colorful *Persian Window* glass installation by Dale Chihuly at its north entrance, the Delaware Art Museum presents several notable American and international collections. Its holdings include a good selection of paintings by Howard Pyle (1853–1911), a Wilmington native known as the "father of American illustration," and works by his students N. C. Wyeth, Frank Schoonover, and Maxfield Parrish. Other American artists represented are Benjamin West, John Sloan, Winslow Homer, and Robert Motherwell. The museum is renowned for the largest American collection of 19th-century English pre-Raphaelite paintings and decorative arts, with works by Dante Gabriel Rossetti and Edward Burne-Jones, among others. These permanent collection galleries will be reinstalled on a rolling basis throughout 2020, but the museum will remain open. Other highlights are a children's interactive gallery and the 9-acre Copeland Sculpture Garden. ✉ *2301 Kentmere Pkwy., Wilmington* ☎ *302/571–9590, 866/232–3714* 🌐 *www.delart.org* 🎫 *$12, free all day Sun. and Thurs. 4–8* ⏲ *Closed Mon. and Tues.*

Nemours Mansion and Gardens

HOUSE | For a look at how the very wealthy lived in the early 20th century, visit Nemours Mansion and Gardens, a 300-acre, 47,000-square-foot country estate built for Alfred I. du Pont in 1910 by noted architectural firm Carrère and Hastings, who added the latest in technology. This modified Louis XVI château showcases more than 30 (of 77 in all) rooms of European and American furnishings, rare rugs, tapestries, and art dating to the 15th century. Despite its splendor, the mansion feels homey and personal. There are tours of certain rooms (first come, first served), but it's fun to explore on your own and ask the excellent staff questions. The formal French-style gardens, reminiscent of those at Versailles, are landscaped with fountains, pools, and statuary. Vintage cars are on display in the Chauffeur's Garage. The visitor center has an excellent film and exhibits about the house and Alfred I. du Pont (and his three wives). ■ **TIP→ There is no food on site.** ✉ *850 Alapocas Dr., between Rte. 141 and U.S. 202, Wilmington* ☎ *800/651–6912* 🌐 *nemoursestate.org* 🎫 *$18* ⏲ *Closed Mon. and Jan.–Apr.*

Rockwood Museum and Park

HOUSE | Rockwood, an elegant English-style country house and a fine example of rural Gothic architecture, stands in contrast to the opulent, French-inspired du Pont homes in the area. Built in 1851 by Joseph Shipley, a Quaker banker, and occupied by his descendants until 1972, the house is now a museum filled with ornate Victorian furnishings and decorative arts. Tours (required in the house) are given on the hour; there are some candlelight tours in December. Beyond the English landscape garden, the 72-acre public grounds feature 2½

Revolutionary War cannons sprinkle the fields at Valley Forge National Historical Park.

miles of paved, lighted trails. In summer Rockwood Park hosts one play in the Delaware Shakespeare Festival. ✉ *4651 Washington St. Extension, south of Shipley Rd., Wilmington* ☎ *302/761–4340* 🌐 *www.nccde.org* 🎟 *$10; free museum tours in Dec.* ⏲ *Museum closed Mon. and Tues.*

Hotels

Hotel Du Pont

$$$$ | **HOTEL** | Built in 1913 by Pierre S. du Pont, this luxury 12-story hotel in downtown Wilmington has hosted everyone from Charles Lindbergh to John F. Kennedy, and the elegant Italian Renaissance–style building still radiates an old-world feel. **Pros:** luxe historical ambience; large rooms and bathrooms; responsive service. **Cons:** small elevators; staff can be too formal; high extra charge for pets. 💲 *Rooms from: $440* ✉ *42 W. 11th St., Wilmington* ☎ *302/594–3100, 800/441–9019* 🌐 *www.hoteldupont.com* 🛏 *217 rooms* 🍽 *No meals.*

Valley Forge

20 miles northeast of downtown Philadelphia via I–76.

A major site of the Revolutionary War is near the suburban village of Valley Forge, named for an iron forge built in the 1740s. The monuments, markers, huts, and headquarters in Valley Forge National Historical Park illuminate a decisive period in U.S. history. The park, with its quiet beauty that seems to whisper of the past, preserves the area where George Washington's Continental Army endured the bitter winter of 1777–78.

Other nearby sights of interest include the mega-size King of Prussia mall and an Audubon center with the naturalist's first American home.

GETTING HERE AND AROUND

When traffic is flowing on I–76, the major east–west highway between Philadelphia and Valley Forge, the trip can take just 35 to 40 minutes. But gridlock, especially

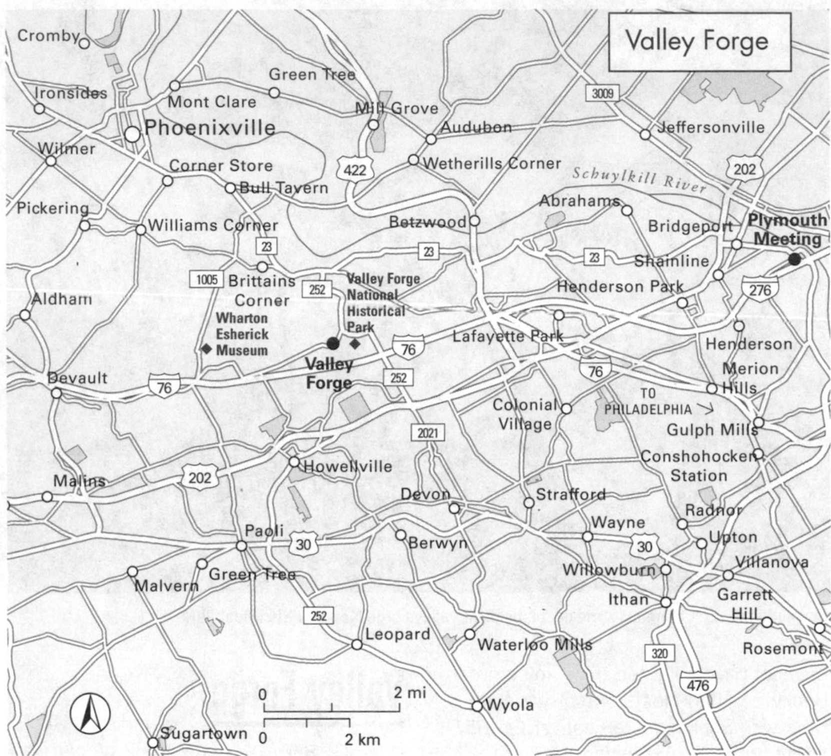

during rush hour, can stretch the trip to 90 minutes, so time your visit accordingly. If you arrive at the historical park without a car, you can pay to tour the park via a trolley. Other area attractions will require a car for access, however.

ESSENTIALS

VISITOR INFORMATION

The website of the Valley Forge Tourism & Convention Board lists attractions, events, and hotels and restaurants around Montgomery County, and also has special offers.

CONTACTS Valley Forge & Montgomery County, PA. ☎ *610/834–1550* 🌐 *valleyforge.org.*

Sights

John James Audubon Center at Mill Grove

MUSEUM | FAMILY | A small but lively museum, opened in 2019 on a site that holds the first American home of Haitian-born artist and naturalist John James Audubon (1785–1851), captures the wonders of the avian world as well as Audubon's life and his mission to paint all of North America's birds. Kid-friendly interactive exhibits explore nests, birdsongs, feathers, and more; galleries on Audubon's artistic process (with original prints and a copy of his massive *Birds of America*) will appeal more to older children and adults. There's also a bird-themed outdoor play space. Admission includes a tour (one tour daily, at 1 pm) of Mill Grove, Audubon's stone farmhouse home, built in 1762 and filled with displays relating to Audubon. Managed by the National Audubon Society, this site 2 miles north of Valley Forge National Historical Park is within the 175-acre Mill Grove estate, which has 5 miles of marked walking trails. ✉ *1201 Pawlings Rd., Audubon* ✣ *Follow sign on Pawlings Rd. for the center* ☎ *610/666–5593* 🌐 *johnjames.audubon.org* 🎫 *Museum $14, grounds and trails free.*

★ Valley Forge National Historical Park

NATIONAL/STATE PARK | The park is the location of the 1777–78 winter encampment of General George Washington and the Continental Army, where winter tested and proved the army's perseverance. Stop at the temporary Valley Forge Visitor Center for touring information; a renovated center is due to open in late 2020. The renovated center will have park and regional information, a new orientation film, and the Encampment Store, as well as displays of historical objects and engaging, immersive displays about the encampment. Take a driving tour (free cell phone guide) or buy a CD ($14.95); hire a guide for your car; or take a narrated trolley tour (limited times other than summer) for $17.50. Stops include reconstructed log huts of the Muhlenberg Brigade and the National Memorial Arch, which pay tribute to the soldiers, and Washington's headquarters.

In 1777 the army had just lost the nearby battles of Brandywine, White Horse, and Germantown. While the British occupied Philadelphia, Washington's soldiers endured horrid conditions—blizzards, inadequate food and clothing, and disease. Although no battle was fought at Valley Forge, 2,000 soldiers (of about 12,000) died here. The troops did win the war of will, regaining strength under the leadership of Prussian drillmaster Friedrich von Steuben. In June 1778 Washington led his troops away from Valley Forge in search of the British.

The park contains more than 8 miles of jogging and bicycling paths (bike rentals available in summer) and hiking trails, and you can picnic in designated areas. A leisurely visit takes about half a day. ✉ *1400 N. Outer Line Dr.* ✣ *Rte. 23 and N. Gulph Rd.* ☎ *610/783–1077* 🌐 *www.nps.gov/vafo* 🎫 *Free.*

Wharton Esherick Museum

MUSEUM | Preserving the former home and studio of the "Dean of American Craftsmen," the museum can be visited only by booking a tour in advance, although you can explore the visitor center and 12-acre grounds without a tour reservation. Best known for his sculptural furniture, Esherick (1887–1970) shaped a new aesthetic in decorative arts by bridging art with furniture. The museum, a National Historic Landmark, houses 200 examples of his work—paintings, woodcuts, furniture, and wood sculptures. The studio, in which everything from the light switches to the spiral staircase is hand-carved, is one of his monumental achievements. On weekdays a minimum of five people is required for a tour, so check online or call if your party is smaller; on the second Sunday of the month, you can explore on a self-directed tour. ✉ *1520 Horseshoe Trail, Malvern* ✣ *2 miles west of Valley Forge National Historical Park* ☎ *610/644–5822* 🌐 *www.whartonesherickmuseum.org* 🎫 *$15* ⏱ *Closed Mon.*

Performing Arts

★ Philadelphia Folk Festival

MUSIC FESTIVALS | First held in 1961, the oldest continuously running folk festival in the country takes place each year over three or four days in mid- to late August. Arlo Guthrie, Levon Helm, Trombone Shorty, Doc Watson, Taj Mahal, Joan Baez, and Judy Collins are just a few of the artists who have performed here. You can camp on-site. The festival site is 14 miles north of Valley Forge and 35 miles northwest of Philadelphia. ✉ *Old Pool Farm, 1323 Salford Station Rd., Philadelphia* ☎ *215/247–1300, 800/556–3655* 🌐 *pfs.org.*

Shopping

Chapel Cabin Shop

GIFTS/SOUVENIRS | In a log cabin behind the Washington Memorial Chapel parish on the grounds of the Valley Forge National Historical Park, this gift shop sells pewter, Colonial-style art, souvenirs related to the American Revolution, and toys and fun items for kids. Homemade cakes, candies, and jams are sold as well, and all proceeds support the privately owned chapel. The shop includes a small, handy luncheonette—there are also outdoor picnic tables—that dishes up hamburgers, tuna sandwiches, and similar fare. There is a secondhand bookstore directly behind the chapel, too. ✉ *Rte. 23* ✣ *Alongside Washington Memorial Chapel* ☎ *610/783–0576* 🌐 *wm-chapel.org/cabin-shop.*

King of Prussia

SHOPPING CENTERS/MALLS | One of the nation's largest shopping complexes is a tourist destination in itself, with more than 450 shops and over 30 restaurants. From department stores such as Nordstrom and Neiman Marcus to chain retailers both upscale (Jimmy Choo and Cartier) and more accessible (Club Monaco and Zara), there's plenty for different kinds of shoppers. Dining options include Morton's Steakhouse, Legal Sea Foods, Shake Shack, and abundant fast-food options on all levels. ✉ *160 N. Gulph Rd., King of Prussia* ✣ *U.S. 202 at I–76 (Schuylkill Expressway)* ☎ *610/265–5727* 🌐 *www.simon.com.*

Plymouth Meeting

15 miles northwest of downtown Philadelphia via I–76 west.

Founded in 1686 by Quakers, suburban Plymouth Meeting is home to the Plymouth Meeting Mall and LEGOLAND Discovery Center Philadelphia.

GETTING HERE AND AROUND

Plymouth Meeting is about 30 minutes west of central Philadelphia. Driving is your best bet as public transportation involves multiple transfers on numerous transportation types. An Uber will cost about $40 during non-peak hours.

CAR

From Center City, take I–76 west and I–476 north to West Germantown Pike in Plymouth Meeting. Take Exit 20 from I–476 north and follow signs for the Plymouth Meeting Mall and LEGOLAND Discovery Center.

Sights

LEGOLAND Discovery Center Philadelphia

AMUSEMENT PARK/WATER PARK | **FAMILY** | Opened in 2017, this 33,000-square-foot space, the ninth Discovery Center in the United States and the 17th in the world, is chock-full of all things LEGO, including a kid-sized race car that was made with more than 100,000 LEGO bricks. Miniland Philadelphia contains 50 of the city's iconic landmarks brought to life with nearly 1.5 million LEGO bricks—Independence Hall, Boathouse Row (with crew boats you can race), the Art Museum, and Lincoln Financial Field, just to name a few. Other highlights include the interactive LEGO Ninjago Training Camp; a LEGO 4-D Cinema; a LEGO-themed pirate ship play area called Pirate Adventure Island; and the LEGO Friends area where you can "meet" Olivia, Emma, Stephanie, Mia, and Andrea and build all of your favorite Heartlake City things. **■ TIP→ Note that adults must be accompanied by a child 17 or under to visit the attractions.** ✉ *Plymouth Meeting Mall, 500 W Germantown Pike, Plymouth Meeting* ☎ *267/245–9696* 🌐 *philadelphia.legolanddiscoverycenter.com* 🎟 *From $19.95 (ticket purchased online); admission varies by time and day.*

LEGOLAND Discovery Center Philadelphia's Miniland contains 50 of the city's iconic landmarks including Independence Hall, Boathouse Row, the Linc, and City Hall (pictured).

Sesame Place

25 miles northeast of Philadelphia via I–95 north.

Next to the Oxford Valley Mall, this park based on the popular children's show *Sesame Street* is a longtime favorite of families with young children.

GETTING HERE AND AROUND

Sesame Place is in Langhorne, about 25 miles northeast of Philadelphia. Driving is your best bet as public transportation involves multiple transfers on numerous transportation types.

CAR

From Center City, take I–95 north to 295 E to the Morrisville Exit 5A/Rt. 1 North to the Oxford Valley Exit and turn right onto Oxford Valley Road; follow the signs to Sesame Place.

Sights

Sesame Place

AMUSEMENT PARK/WATER PARK | FAMILY | Aimed squarely at young kids and their families, this water and theme park based on the popular children's show *Sesame Street* provides fun places for children to crawl, climb, and jump; float, slide, and splash; and meet, greet, and perhaps hug the ageless Big Bird and his friends. Though there are plenty of dry-land activities, the highlights of the park—especially on a hot summer day—are the water rides, including the popular Rambling River and Sky Splash, and the interactive Count's Splash Castle. (Keep in mind that water attractions are only open seasonally.) As befits a park for preteens, the rides in Elmo's World and the roller coasters—Vapor Trail and Oscar's Wacky Taxi—are modest by theme-park standards, but they've got more than enough excitement for young riders. Other kid favorites are the daily, and nightly, parades and shows; Sesame Neighborhood, a replica of the beloved

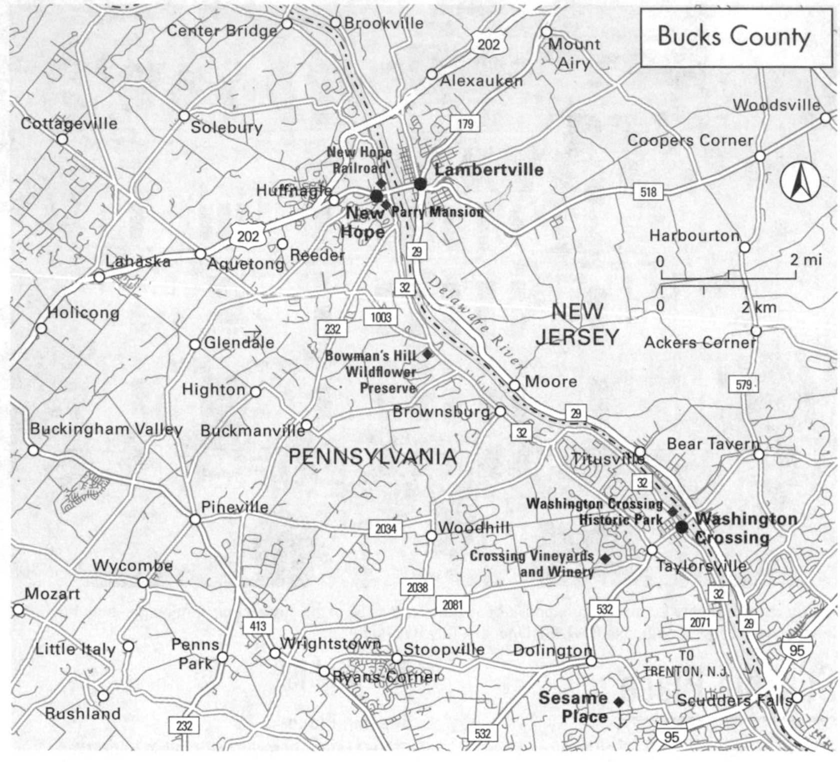

TV street; and meals with characters like Elmo and Grover. Sesame Place is the world's first theme park to be a Certified Autism Center; check the website for information. ✉ *100 Sesame Rd., Langhorne* ✣ *Off N. Oxford Valley Rd. near U.S. 1 at I–95* ☎ *215/702–3566* 🌐 *sesameplace.com* 🎟 *$69; parking $23–25; various packages available* 🕒 *Closed first 3 wks of Nov., Jan.–Mar., and weekdays Apr.–late May.*

Washington Crossing

35 miles northeast of Philadelphia via I–95 and I–295, Taylorsville Rd., and Rte. 532.

The small village of Washington Crossing on the Delaware River is home to basic services and residential areas as well as Washington Crossing Historic Park, which includes the site where Washington crossed the Delaware in December 1776 and then attacked Trenton. Where Route 532 crosses the old Delaware Canal, you'll find access to the towpath with parking.

GETTING HERE AND AROUND

Washington Crossing Historic Park stretches along River Road (Route 32). The Lower Park, or McConkey Ferry section, at the intersection with Route 532, is the site of both the actual crossing and the visitor center. There is a narrow bridge here, which makes crossing to New Jersey somewhat easier today. The Upper Park, or Thompson-Neely section, and a wildflower preserve are 5–6 miles north of the visitor center.

Sights

Bowman's Hill Tower

VIEWPOINT | On top of Bowman's Hill, this 125-foot fieldstone tower provides a spectacular view that extends up to 14 miles, weather permitting, taking in the Delaware River and countryside. It was built in 1929–31 to mark what might have been a lookout point for Washington's army, but historians have found no evidence of this. You can walk up, but an elevator will take you far enough that you have just 23 steps, via a narrow circular staircase, to get to the observation deck. ✉ *Washington Crossing Historic Park, 1 Tower Rd., New Hope* ☎ *215/493–4076 general park number* 🌐 *washingtoncrossingpark.org* 🎫 *$7* ⊙ *Tower closed Jan.–Feb. and weekdays Dec. and Mar.*

Bowman's Hill Wildflower Preserve

NATURE PRESERVE | The 134-acre preserve near the Thompson-Neely section of Washington Crossing Historic Park showcases hundreds of species of wildflowers as well as trees, shrubs, and ferns native to Pennsylvania. Stop at the visitor center and get a trail map, and then take the guided one-hour wildflower walk (included in admission and available in season at 2 pm, but call to check) or explore any of the short, well-marked trails (4½ miles in all) on your own. Wildflower blooms are seasonal, with mid-April through July a good period to visit, but fall brings colorful foliage; the website has bloom information. ✉ *1635 River Rd., New Hope* ☎ *215/862–2924* 🌐 *www.bhwp.org* 🎫 *$8* ⊙ *Closed Mon. July–Mar.*

Crossing Vineyards and Winery

WINERY/DISTILLERY | On a 200-year-old estate near where Washington crossed the Delaware, the family-run vineyard mixes vintage charm with modern wine-making techniques. Despite a nod to the rustic (a beam ceiling in the tasting room and gift shop), the old gambrel-roofed barn feels fresh and upscale. In a 45-minute tasting, the staff lets you know what to expect from 10 different types of wines. Look for Chardonnay, Riesling, Cabernet Franc, and Merlot, among other varieties. Concerts are offered throughout the year, and there are wine classes Thursday night and other public events. ✉ *1853 Wrightstown Rd., off Rte. 532, Newtown* ☎ *215/493–6500* 🌐 *www.crossingvineyards.com* 🎫 *Tasting $10 (with reservation), $15 for walk-ins.*

Washington Crossing Historic Park

NATIONAL/STATE PARK | It was from the site of what is now this park that on Christmas night in 1776 General Washington and 2,400 of his men crossed the ice-studded Delaware River, attacked the Hessian stronghold at Trenton, and secured a much-needed victory for the Continental Army. This crossing was immortalized in Emanuel Leutze's famous 1851 painting, which hangs in New York's Metropolitan Museum of Art. The park's historic houses and memorials are divided between the Lower Park (McConkey Ferry section) and Upper Park (Thompson-Neely section), about 5 miles apart.

In the Lower Park, the visitor center has park information and historic exhibits, and sells tickets for guided tours of two areas. The historic village tour includes McConkey Ferry Inn, where tradition has it that Washington had Christmas dinner. You can see replicas of the Durham boats used in the crossing.

In the Upper Park, 125-foot-tall Bowman's Hill Tower (open weather permitting) offers a commanding view of the Delaware River. An elevator takes you up the 1931 tower, but you walk the last 23 steps. The Thompson-Neely House offers tours that tell of life in Bucks County during the Revolution. The house was used as a hospital during the 1776–77 encampment of Washington's army; there's also a gristmill. The park's special events include a reenactment of the crossing in December. ✉ *1112 River Rd. (Rte. 32)* ☎ *215/493–4076* 🌐 *www.*

washingtoncrossingpark.org *Grounds free, 1 tour or tower $7, 2 tours and tower $15* *Tower and Thompson-Neely House closed Jan.–Feb. and weekdays Dec. and Mar. No historic village tours weekdays Jan.–Mar.*

Restaurants

Francisco's on the River

$$$ | **ITALIAN** | Cozy rooms, including an enclosed front porch, beamed ceiling, white tablecloths, and windows all around, give a refined but undeniably country feel to this river-view, BYOB Italian restaurant. Chef-owner Francisco Argueta breathes new life into old favorites like a thin-sliced, layered eggplant *parmigiano;* linguine *al frutti di mare fradiavolo;* and lasagna with a hint of smoked bacon—just keep in mind that portions can be large. **Known for:** whole-wheat garlic bread (worth the charge); wide variety of salads for appetizers; coconut cake. *Average main: $24* ⊠ *1251 River Rd.* ☏ *215/321–8789* 🌐 *www.franciscosontheriver.com* *Closed Mon. No lunch.*

It's Nutts

$$ | **AMERICAN** | **FAMILY** | If this place had been here in 1776, you can bet that George Washington and company would have stopped in for some lemon-chiffon pancakes, ice-cream treats, or tomato pie (a yummy thin-crust pizza native to the Trenton area) before heading off to stomp the Hessians. Don't let the drive-in facade fool you: there's more here than a good old-fashioned soda fountain, and the "little dive," as it calls itself, serves breakfast, lunch, and dinner. **Known for:** cash-only, comfort food classic; lengthy menu from salads to burgers to fried chicken; second location in Lambertville, NJ. *Average main: $15* ⊠ *1382 River Rd., Titusville* *Off NJ Rte. 29, ½ mile from Washington Crossing–Pennington Rd.* ☏ *609/737–0505* 🌐 *itsnuttsrestaurant.com* *No credit cards.*

Hotels

Inn at Bowman's Hill

$$$$ | **B&B/INN** | South of New Hope on the road leading to Bowman's Tower, this modern interpretation of country charm was built in the late 1970s as a private home and converted to a high-end B&B in the mid-2000s, with clean-lined traditionally furnished rooms with luxe amenities such as gas fireplaces. **Pros:** outdoor pool and hot tub; lovely countryside location close to New Hope; breakfast options include signature full English breakfast. **Cons:** quite expensive for area, especially some suites; some rooms are small; weddings can fill the inn. *Rooms from: $395* ⊠ *518 Lurgan Rd., New Hope* ☏ *215/862–8090* 🌐 *theinnatbowmanshill.com* *8 rooms* *Free breakfast.*

Nightlife

Bowman's Tavern

PIANO BARS/LOUNGES | The piano that once graced Odette's, the restaurant, bar, and cabaret that was a New Hope institution until it was flooded out one too many times, now resides at Bowman's Tavern, a quintessential tavern halfway between New Hope and Washington's Crossing. Many of those who loved Odette's have followed, too, making the piano lounge's seven-nights-a-week entertainment, with music from standards to jazz to roots, quite popular and gay-friendly. The hearty American fare has a strong following, too. ⊠ *1600 River Rd., New Hope* ☏ *215/862–2972* 🌐 *www.bowmanstavernrestaurant.com.*

New Hope

8 miles north of Washington Crossing via Rte. 32, 40 miles northeast of Philadelphia via I–95 and Rte. 32.

For a small town, New Hope is a mix of many things, with something for all kinds of travelers. A hodgepodge of old homes,

Bucks County Then and Now

Named after England's Buckinghamshire, Bucks County was opened to European settlement by William Penn in 1681 under a land grant from Charles II. The county's most celebrated town, New Hope, was settled in the early 1700s and, together with its neighbor across the river, Lambertville, New Jersey, was called Coryell's Ferry. One of the original gristmills was the home of what is now the Bucks County Playhouse. The town was the Pennsylvania terminal for stagecoach traffic and Delaware River ferry traffic. Barges hauled coal along the 60-mile Delaware Canal until 1931.

Commerce built up New Hope, but art helped sustain it. An art colony took root in the late 19th century, including the Pennsylvania impressionists and, later, the New Hope modernists. The area was revitalized beginning in the 1930s by theater and literary folk, such as lyricist Oscar Hammerstein II and playwright George S. Kaufman, and more recently with the arrival of galleries and artists from around the country. Writers James Michener (winner of the Pulitzer Prize) and Pearl S. Buck (winner of the Pulitzer and Nobel prizes) also left their marks on Bucks County, which the latter called, "a region where the landscapes were varied, where farm and industry lived side by side, where the sea was near at hand, mountains not far away, and city and countryside were not enemies."

Today suburbanites and exurbanites are attracted to the area, and housing developments have sprouted where grain once grew. It's not unusual to find suburban sprawl adjacent to an old clapboard farmhouse or ancient stone barn. Yet many areas of Bucks County (especially those farther north) remain as bucolic as ever—a feast of lyrical landscapes, with canal and river vistas, rolling hills, and fertile fields. Driving back roads is one of the county's pleasures, and making your way through quiet little towns, stopping at historic sites, checking out antiques shops, and staying overnight in an appealing inn make for a classic weekend getaway.

narrow streets and alleys, courtyards, busy restaurants and bars, and shops, it attracts artists, shoppers, and hordes of day-trippers, especially on summer and fall weekends. Festivals feature everything from classic cars to films to gay pride. In summer, First Friday–night fireworks over the river bring still more crowds. New Hope has had its ups and downs as businesses change, and it can look tired in places, but a fresh vibe is evident in the revival of the Bucks County Playhouse, new and renovated lodgings, and restaurant openings that include Stella by Philadelphia-favorite chef Jose Garces. Even the old stone building that housed the closed Odette's restaurant, now restored on the exterior, has a new location, moved from River Road (where the new River House hotel is taking its place) to the intersection of Route 32 and New Street.

The heart of town, listed on the National Register of Historic Places, is easy to explore on foot; the most interesting sights and stores are clustered along four blocks of Main Street and on the cross streets—Mechanic, Ferry, and Bridge Streets—which lead to the river. New Hope is also near the Delaware Canal and its walkable towpath. Some parts of town are older than others. As you might guess from their names, Ferry Street dates back to Colonial times; Bridge Street is Victorian.

GETTING HERE AND AROUND

Getting to New Hope by car is easy. U.S. 202, Route 179, and Route 32 run through it. Getting around New Hope on a busy weekend is harder. If you see cars backed up along Main Street, drive around the periphery instead, as it can take a fair amount of time to inch your way through town. Grab a parking spot either on the street or in a municipal or private lot— and walk where you want to go. A kiosk system for public parking takes cash, credit cards, and parking apps.

VISITOR INFORMATION

CONTACTS New Hope Visitors Center. ✉ *1 W. Mechanic St., at Main St.* ☎ *215/862–5030* 🌐 *visitbuckscounty.com.*

Sights

New Hope Railroad

TRANSPORTATION SITE (AIRPORT/BUS/FERRY/TRAIN) | **FAMILY** | Pulled by an authentic steam locomotive or vintage diesel, this heritage passenger train makes a 9-mile, 45-minute scenic round-trip between New Hope and Lahaska, and standard trips are narrated. The route crosses a trestle used in the rescue scenes in silent films like *The Perils of Pauline*. The New Hope depot is an 1891 Victorian gem. Special events include dinner trips on Saturday evenings and holiday excursions in December. Advance reservations are encouraged, and required for special events. ✉ *32 W. Bridge St.* ☎ *215/862–2332* 🌐 *newhoperailroad.com* 🎫 *Coach $22, first class $32; holiday and special excursion fares substantially higher.*

Parry Mansion

HOUSE | Built in 1784, and home of the New Hope Historical Society, this stone house is fascinating because the furnishings reflect decorative changes from 1775 (Colonial) to 1900 (Victorian)—including candles, whitewashed walls, oil lamps, and wallpaper. Wealthy Quaker lumber- and flour-mill owner and businessman Benjamin Parry, often called the "father of New Hope," built the house, which was occupied by five generations of his family. Guided tours, including a brief film, give you a good sense of New Hope history. ✉ *45 S. Main St.* ☎ *215/862–5652* 🌐 *www.newhope-hs.org* 🎫 *Free* ⏲ *Closed Dec.–Apr. and weekdays May–Nov.*

Restaurants

Karla's

$$ | **AMERICAN** | A casual hangout in the heart of New Hope, Karla's has been open since 1978, offering hearty American food (meat loaf, burgers, and sandwiches) enlivened with some interesting international ingredients. Dine on dishes like panko-crusted mac and cheese, Korean barbecue tacos, and short ribs in cozy rooms with an assemblage of mismatched tables under a corrugated-plastic ceiling, with plants in retro macramé hangers. **Known for:** Monday Locals' Night good-value prix fixe; hummus trio appetizer; creative martini list. 💲 *Average main: $19* ✉ *5 W. Mechanic St.* ☎ *215/862–2612* 🌐 *www.karlasnewhope.com.*

Sprig & Vine

$$$ | **VEGETARIAN** | Chic and BYO, this vegan restaurant known for fresh, sophisticated fare attracts plenty of non-vegetarians to its space in Union Square, an old-converted-warehouse-meets-new-construction complex. The menu is small—an assortment of small plates and salads, and a handful of large-plate dinner options such as a roasted radish and turnip curry—but offers interesting dishes with unusual, complex flavors, often made with ingredients from local farms. **Known for:** beet and ricotta ravioli; varied dessert options; green onion pancake roll. 💲 *Average main: $22* ✉ *450 Union Square Dr.* ☎ *215/693–1427*

The New Hope Railroad, whose depot was built in 1891, offers numerous special rides throughout the year including themed dinners and seasonal rides.

sprigandvine.com *Closed Mon. No dinner Sun. No lunch Tues.*

Stella

$$$$ | **MODERN AMERICAN** | Part of the Ghost Light Inn, Philadelphia star chef Jose Garces's restaurant has expansive river views from its indoor and outdoor seating, enhancing the relaxed charm of a modern, high-ceilinged space with wood-topped tables, a fireplace, and a bar with TVs. It's a stunning setting for shareable, generally delicious small plates that include spreads, like smoked eggplant, served with bread; vegetable- and grain-based options such as quinoa tabbouleh; and fish and meat options like chicken and dumplings. **Known for:** special chef's selection prix-fixe menu; welcoming vibe for drinks, casual meals, or special occasions; some mixed responses to the food as this new restaurant settles in. *Average main: $28* *50 S. Main St.* *267/740–7131* *stellanewhope.com* *Closed Mon.-Tues. No lunch Wed.–Sat.*

Coffee and Quick Bites

C'est la Vie

$ | **CAFÉ** | Get a cup of coffee and a yummy pastry or light meal at C'est la Vie, a French bakery down a little alley off Main Street that proves that excellent things come in small packages. Grab and go, eat inside in the cozily cramped space, or sit outside at a table overlooking the river. **Known for:** sandwiches in savory croissants; madeleines, palmiers, and macarons; excellent breads. *Average main:* $4 *20 S. Main St.* *215/862–1956* *Closed Mon. No dinner.*

Ferry Market

$ | **ECLECTIC** | New Hope's welcome contribution to the food market trend brings an eclectic dozen-plus vendors, some of them outposts of area spots, to an airy brick-fronted, renovated space with an industrial vibe. You can grab a coffee at SkyRoast or a craft beer at Weyerbacher, or taste Italian or Mediterranean fare here: keep in mind that some vendors close at 5 pm, and all close by 8 pm.

Known for: fun lunch options; Peruvian and Latin American fare at Lima Fusion; good spot for various sweet treats. *$ Average main: $11 ✉ 32 S. Main St. ☎ 🌐 theferrymarket.com ⏲ Closed Tues.; hours vary by vendor.*

Hotels

Ghost Light Inn

$$$$ | **HOTEL** | By the river in the heart of town, this luxe new rustic-chic boutique hotel seriously notches up New Hope's lodging scene with stunning rooms and a superior small-plates restaurant and bar from Philadelphia star chef Jose Garces. **Pros:** spectacular Delaware River views from restaurant and many rooms; steps from the Bucks County Playhouse via riverfront promenade; gorgeous rooms with plenty of amenities. **Cons:** events in ballroom may disturb quiet mood; no in-house breakfast, but many options nearby; price is high for those river views. *$ Rooms from: $375 ✉ 50 S. Main St. ☎ 267/740–7131 🌐 ghostlight-inn.com ⇨ 15 rooms 🍽 No meals.*

Logan Inn

$$ | **HOTEL** | Established in 1727, this inn once accommodated passengers riding the ferry to Lambertville, and today its old rooms have been renovated and the inn is expanding (at this writing) to a 100-room complex. **Pros:** free parking in the thick of New Hope; modern style with colorful touches updates historic inn; alfresco dining. **Cons:** continental breakfast not the best; expansion may make property less intimate; history of several ghosts. *$ Rooms from: $200 ✉ 10 W. Ferry St. ☎ 215/862–2300 🌐 www.logan-inn.com ⇨ 100 rooms 🍽 Free breakfast.*

River House at Odette's

$$$ | **HOTEL** | The luxurious, newly built River House raises the bar for New Hope lodgings, filling a storied New Hope site (Chez Odette, later Odette's restaurant) by the Delaware Canal and the Delaware River. **Pros:** amazing riverside location; plush, chic guest rooms, some with balconies; lovely restaurant and piano lounge. **Cons:** relatively large property may feel out of place on this site to some; members-only rooftop bar may irritate some guests; good-size wedding and meeting venue on site. *$ Rooms from: $289 ✉ 274 S. River Rd. ☎ 215/682–2022 🌐 riverhousenewhope.com ⇨ 38 rooms 🍽 No meals.*

Wedgwood Inn

$ | **B&B/INN** | **FAMILY** | Accommodations at this Victorian antiques–decorated B&B are in an 1870s-era "painted lady" a Federal-style manor house, and an 1890s carriage house; all have rooms that work equally well for families and romance. **Pros:** lovely grounds near, but set apart from, the middle of town; welcomes children and dogs; many gas fireplaces and some porches. **Cons:** tasteful rooms but not for those who dislike Victoriana and Wedgwood blue; third-floor rooms require climbing; different-size rooms, so check carefully when booking. *$ Rooms from: $130 ✉ 111 W. Bridge St. ☎ 215/862–2570 🌐 www.wedgwoodinn.com ⇨ 18 rooms 🍽 Free breakfast.*

Nightlife

Havana

MUSIC CLUBS | A longtime New Hope fixture, this bar and restaurant with tropical-theme decor has karaoke several Mondays each month and a variety of live music from jazz to tribute bands many nights. National acts leaning heavily toward classic rock are sprinkled in for good measure. The list of mojitos and martinis is long, and beer and wine choices are ample. *✉ 105 S. Main St. ☎ 215/862–5501 🌐 www.havananewhope.com.*

John & Peter's

MUSIC CLUBS | Since 1972, this classic dive bar has featured live, original music nightly, and the tradition continues even with new owners. All kinds of folks come to hear jazz musicians, singer-songwriters, and plenty of rockers take the stage, as well as the not-yet-famous on Monday's open-mic night. Wednesday's invitational jam with local musicians is also popular. The bar food includes notable tater tots with all kinds of toppings. ✉ *96 S. Main St.* ☎ *215/862–5981* 🌐 *www.johnandpeters.com.*

Triumph Brewing Company
BREWPUBS/BEER GARDENS | Shiny vats are the tip-off to what's on tap at Triumph Brewing Company, a large, bi-level brewpub whose exposed-brick walls, beams, and ductwork give it an industrial feel. Entertainment includes live music most Friday and Saturday nights; Texas Hold 'Em on Monday and Wednesday; open mic on Sunday; and trivia night on Thursday. Typically there are eight craft beers on tap, with seasonal specials. ✉ *400 Union Square Dr.* ☎ *215/862–8300* 🌐 *triumphbrewing.com.*

Performing Arts

Bucks County Playhouse
THEATER | Opened in 1939, this regional theater in an 18th-century mill by the Delaware continues a long tradition of staging musicals (Broadway revivals and new works, with top-quality performers) and plays. It also hosts a visiting artists series and community and educational events. Performances are year-round, with the main shows generally staged May through November, but check the website for what's on. The Deck Restaurant and Bar at the Playhouse (🌐 *playhousedeck.com for hours; closed Monday), with fabulous river views, is open whether or not a performance is scheduled.* ✉ *70 S. Main St.* ☎ *215/862–2121 box office* 🌐 *bcptheater.org.*

Shopping

New Hope's streets are lined with independent shops selling a tourist-focused mix of upscale and lowbrow. Very nice arts and crafts and handmade accessories, clothing, antiques, and jewelry (some quite expensive) are juxtaposed with campy vintage items, collectibles, and some storefronts with tarot readers, a reminder of the town's funky side. The shopping center at Peddler's Village in nearby Lahaska has additional gift-oriented choices (a few outlet stores, part of Penn's Purchase, are across the road).

BOOKS

Farley's Bookshop
BOOKS/STATIONERY | The crowded shelves at Farley's Bookshop, a New Hope institution, hold plenty of choices, including books about the region. Staff picks, signed copies of local writers' works, children's books, and small press favorites: it's all here for the browsing, with helpful staff ready to offer suggestions. ✉ *44 S. Main St.* ☎ *215/862–2452* 🌐 *www.farleysbookshop.com.*

CRAFTS

Heart of the Home
CRAFTS | Open since 1994, this American craft and gift shop with a range of prices has three floors of treasures to browse, from pottery and jewelry to wood pieces and special gifts for children. Accessories and cards round out the inventory, and the staff are extremely helpful. ✉ *28 S. Main St.* ☎ *215/862–1880* 🌐 *heartofthehome.com.*

Topeo Gallery
CRAFTS | You can find all kinds of high-quality, handcrafted art glass and jewelry at this well-regarded crafts gallery, along with art pottery and garden art. The price range is wide. ✉ *35 N. Main St.* ☎ *215/862–2750* 🌐 *www.topeo.com.*

FOOD

Pierre's Chocolates
FOOD/CANDY | For superior chocolate, including yummy truffles, turtles, and chocolate-covered pretzels, head a little outside the main business district to the delectable Pierre's Chocolates. Check out special small-batch and single-origin

treats as well. ✉ *360 W. Bridge St.* ☎ *215/862–0602* 🌐 *www.pierreschocolates.com* ☞ *Closed Sun.*

Suzies Hot Shoppe
FOOD/CANDY | This quirky specialty shop is a foodie favorite, with an array of hot sauces, wing sauces, barbecue sauces, and salsas from all over, besides its own line of items. Some seasonal and local products are featured as well. ✉ *110 S. Main St.* ☎ *215/862–1334* 🌐 *www.squareup.com/market/suzies-hot-shoppe.*

MALLS AND OUTLETS

Peddler's Village
SHOPPING CENTERS/MALLS | In the early 1960s, the late Earl Jamison moved local 18th-century houses to a 6-acre site and opened a collection of small, mostly locally owned specialty shops and restaurants that today caters strongly to tourists. Some 60 shops in the 42-acre villagelike setting peddle toys, clothing, jewelry, housewares, crafts, home decor, and more. The dozen or so on-site food and drink options include Free Will Brewing, and there's an inn, the Golden Plough. The 1922 Grand Carousel still works, and Giggleberry Fair offers indoor games for kids; admission is charged for these. The many seasonal events draw big crowds. Peddler's Village is 5 miles west of central New Hope via U.S. 202. ✉ *5800 Upper York Rd., at the intersection of U.S. 202 and Rte. 263, Lahaska* ☎ *215/794–4000* 🌐 *www.peddlersvillage.com.*

Activities

Bucks County River Country
WATER SPORTS | Join the more than 100,000 people a year who take to the water in inner tubes every summer. Bucks County River Country also rents rafts, canoes, and kayaks from mid-May through October. Even when the wide Delaware River is a mass of yellow and green tubes, it's still peaceful. Point Pleasant is 8 miles north of New Hope via Route 32. ✉ *2 Walters La., Point Pleasant* ☎ *215/297–5000* 🌐 *www.rivercountry.net* ☞ *Tubing from $25 per person, kayak rentals from $48 for 2 hrs.*

New Hope Cyclery
BICYCLING | The store sells all kinds of bikes and gear, and also rents hybrid bikes, with helmets and locks included in the rental price. You can also rent family-friendly trailers and tagalongs. The helpful staff can direct you to scenic bike routes. These may include parts of the 60-mile towpath of the Delaware Canal State Park, which runs through New Hope. ✉ *404 York Rd.* ☎ *215/862–6888* 🌐 *newhopecyclery.com* ☞ *From $30 for half-day rental, $40 for full day.*

Lambertville, New Jersey

Across the Delaware River from New Hope, 40 miles from Philadelphia via I–95 and Rte. 29.

If you're interested in New Hope's refrain but prefer it in a lower key, head directly across the Delaware River. You can find more charm, a bit more quiet, and even better antiques in this New Jersey village. There are dozens of antiques and collectibles dealers in the small town, though these days they are matched by trendy home-furnishing shops and a lively assemblage of boutiques, art galleries, and restaurants. Interesting buildings line the streets, a legacy of the days when Lambertville was a bustling canal town and then a manufacturing center for everything from wheels to hairpins, before it evolved into a day-tripper's favorite.

One of Lambertville's chief pleasures doesn't involve commerce at all: the towpath along the Delaware and Raritan Canal is a retreat for strolling, running, or biking. Heading 7 miles south takes you to the popular Washington Crossing State

Park, directly across from the similarly named Pennsylvania park.

GETTING HERE AND AROUND

If you're in New Hope, head to Bridge Street and drive or walk over the bridge; the walk is short but can be windy. It's easy to explore most of Lambertville on foot, and you can visit the two towns in one day if you just want a taste of each. From Philadelphia, take I–95 and I–295 and head up along the Delaware on Route 29.

Sights

Delaware and Raritan Canal State Park

TRAIL | Walkers and cyclists in Lambertville have easy access from downtown to part of the park's 70-mile-long, multiuse trail (the former canal towpath), which travels through 22 towns and five New Jersey counties. Built in the 1830s to connect the Delaware and Raritan rivers, the D&R, as it's known, includes a feeder canal along the Delaware that runs past towns such as Frenchtown, Stockton, and Lambertville down to New Jersey's Washington Crossing State Park. ✉ *Lambertville* ✣ *Accessed from downtown Lambertville along the riverfront* ☎ *609/924–5705 park superintendent's office* 🌐 *dandrcanal.com.*

Restaurants

Broadmoor

$$$$ | **ITALIAN** | Gray walls with a few large paintings, hanging globe lights, and chic but simple wood and marble tables create a lovely, soothing backdrop for delicious, mostly Italian fare at this intimate BYOB in a space that formerly housed an antiques store. The chef, from longtime Lambertville restaurant Rick's, offers a list of salads and seafood or pasta appetizers like short rib ravioli; mains might include shrimp linguine or a grilled veal chop. **Known for:** superior fresh pasta options; good-size menu of tempting desserts; creative special appetizers and mains mix up the Italian theme. $ *Average main: $30* ✉ *8 N. Union St., Lambertville* ☎ *609/397–1400* 🌐 *broadmoorrestaurant.com* ⏲ *Closed Tues. No lunch.*

El Tule

$$$ | **LATIN AMERICAN** | At this Mexican and Peruvian restaurant, the plain black-stucco building and small, colorfully decorated dining room are secondary to wonderfully fresh, flavorful dishes that hold to tradition (tacos and fajitas) and add creative touches (lunch bowls with ceviche). Bring your own wine or beer to pair with Peruvian lamb stew, Oaxacan mole with chicken, or the many kinds of ceviche, or try the delicious fruit drinks. **Known for:** tostones fusion, with guacamole and ceviche; good-value lunch options; pozole and other soups. $ *Average main: $21* ✉ *49 N. Main St., Lambertville* ☎ *609/773–0007* 🌐 *eltulerestaurant.com* ⏲ *Closed Mon.*

Full Moon

$ | **AMERICAN** | Decorated with pictures on the dark wall, funky mirrors, and narrow neon lights, this popular breakfast and lunch spot is always filled with the sounds of happy customers. Egg dishes, including assorted omelets, figure prominently on the breakfast menu, and good-size sandwiches, salads, and burgers make up the lunch options. **Known for:** dinner served once a month, on full moon; different kinds of eggs Benedict; Bridge Street omelet. $ *Average main: $12* ✉ *23 Bridge St., Lambertville* ☎ *609/397–1096* 🌐 *www.cafefullmoon.com* ⏲ *Closed Tues. No dinner.*

Manon

$$$$ | **FRENCH** | The mural of van Gogh's *Starry Night* on the ceiling transports you to a whimsical corner of Provence at this family-owned, farmhouse-cozy BYO French bistro. The short menu varies with the seasons but might include starters such as warm goat-cheese salad or country pâté, and mains like bouillabaisse or rack of lamb with a distinctive sauce.

Delaware and Raritan Canal State Park's 70-mile-long, multiuse trail (the former canal towpath), travels through 22 towns and five New Jersey counties.

Known for: cash-only dining; handmade pottery; good-value two-course prix-fixe option Wednesday and Thursday. *Average main: $26* *19 N. Union St., Lambertville* *609/397–2596* *No credit cards* *Closed Mon. and Tues. No lunch.*

More Than Q

$ | **BARBECUE** | The smell of Texas-style wood-smoked barbecue wafts from this casual spot that channels a modern industrial vibe with wooden tables and walls, metal shelving and seats, and chalkboard-paint walls. At the counter, order a sandwich or platter piled high with tasty, carefully prepared brisket, pulled beef or pork, or chicken, or go for the spare ribs; and take your pick of sides like collard greens or burnt-end baked beans. **Known for:** meat platter for two; closes by 7 or 8 many nights, so don't delay; meat sold by the pound if you want more. *Average main: $10* *13 Klines Ct., Lambertville* *609/773–0072* *www.morethanq.com* *Closed Mon.*

Coffee and Quick Bites

Lambertville Trading Company

$ | **CAFÉ** | Stop by the coffee bar at Lambertville Trading Company for a cappuccino and some homemade goodies including muffins and bagels, or to pick up gourmet treats or gifts to take home. There's some seating in the cozy space, where shelves are packed with mugs, chocolate, and more. **Known for:** calorie-worthy cookies; cash or checks only; open at night. *Average main: $5* *43 Bridge St., Lambertville* *609/397–2232* *No credit cards.*

Rojo's Roastery

$ | **CAFÉ** | Small batches of carefully sourced artisanal coffees from around the world are roasted on the premises here and served during the day in a small café with an industrial vibe. Pair it with a muffin or other snack. **Known for:** micro lots of some coffees; interesting special blends; pricey but good beans. *Average main: $3* *243 N. Union St.,*

Lambertville ☎ *609/397–0040* 🌐 *www.rojosroastery.com* ⏲ *No dinner.*

Hotels

Inn at Lambertville Station

$$ | HOTEL | The "station" in this riverside hotel's name refers to the restaurant, an adorable 1867 stone building, but the hotel itself, tucked away from the street, is modern, with a comfortably traditional vibe. **Pros:** modern rooms, most with river views, near the heart of town; pretty sunsets over the Delaware River; bike rentals available. **Cons:** no fitness room, but hotel partners with one nearby; continental breakfast is small; big enough for weddings and other events. *$ Rooms from: $169* ✉ *11 Bridge St., Lambertville* ☎ *609/397–4400, 800/524–1091* 🌐 *www.lambertvillestation.com* *46 rooms* *Free breakfast.*

Lambertville House

$$$ | HOTEL | This handsome stone-and-brick building on Lambertville's main drag, a former stagecoach stop dating to 1812, maintains a traditional ambience but has modern comforts in its updated rooms. **Pros:** robes in rooms; steps from shops, restaurants, and the bridge to New Hope; the hotel's porch, overlooking Bridge Street. **Cons:** bar can be taken over by the many business travelers who stay here; not for those who want a secluded location; no in-house breakfast, but restaurants are steps away. *$ Rooms from: $210* ✉ *32 Bridge St., Lambertville* ☎ *609/397–0200* 🌐 *www.lambertvillehouse.com* *26 rooms* *No meals.*

Nightlife

The Boat House

BARS/PUBS | Tucked down Coryell Street in the Porkyard alley, this small, two-story wood-framed building displays loads of vintage nautical memorabilia from its floors to the rafters and ceilings. Dark and cozy, it's an atmospheric place for a cocktail or other drink; just know that there's no food, and it can get crowded. You can sit outdoors in summer. ✉ *8½ Coryell St., Lambertville* ☎ *609/397–2244.*

Shopping

Antiques and collectibles shops, furniture and home-furnishing stores, and galleries line Union Street, heading north from Bridge Street, and the intersecting cross streets. This is where the serious antiques collectors shop, as well as those seeking fun vintage wares of all kinds and contemporary crafts. Specialty food and other indie shops enhance the mix.

ANTIQUES

Golden Nugget Antique Flea Market

OUTDOOR/FLEA/GREEN MARKETS | Vintage is in these days because it's green, and you may discover period treasures, toy trains, porcelain, jewelry, and memorabilia from the '60s and '70s in the more than 20 antiques shops and outdoor stalls at this market open Wednesdays and weekends. Sunday is the biggest day, with dozens of outdoor vendors also competing for your business. A small café is on site. ✉ *1850 River Rd., Lambertville* ☎ *609/397–0811* 🌐 *gnflea.com.*

The People's Store Antiques and Design Center

ANTIQUES/COLLECTIBLES | It's fun to wander the nooks and crannies of this four-story, converted 1839 building filled with more than 40 dealers whose wares include fine American and European antiques and more modern furnishings, art, funky collectibles, china, and textiles from tea towels to clothing. There's something for every budget. Don't miss the few studios up top with working artists; they'll happily talk to you. ✉ *28 N. Union St., Lambertville* ☎ *609/397–9808* 🌐 *www.peoplesstore.net.*

FOOD

Savour

FOOD/CANDY | Packed with tempting edibles, this petite gourmet grocery shop carries dozens of types of cheese, specialty jams and crackers, honeys and mustards, tasty breads, and other treats from local and international sources. You can put together supplies for a bread and cheese picnic, or just pick up some lovely gifts. ✉ *37 N. Union St., Lambertville* ☎ *609/397–1930* 🌐 *savourlambertvillecheeseshop.business.site.*

HOUSEWARES AND FURNITURE

A Mano Gallery

HOUSEHOLD ITEMS/FURNITURE | In an old five-and-dime building, A Mano stocks all kinds of colorful crafts and home products at a variety of prices. Look for jewelry, glass, kaleidoscopes, and wearable art, as well as some contemporary furniture and lighting. ✉ *42 N. Union St., Lambertville* ☎ *609/397–0063* 🌐 *www.amanogalleries.com.*

Bucks County Dry Goods

HOUSEHOLD ITEMS/FURNITURE | They've got the goods here—a varied, highly curated assortment of jewelry, mid-century modern furniture, housewares, design books, gifts (like leather items), and hip clothing. A location just around the corner on Bridge Street carries vintage men's and women's attire. There's another location in Princeton, NJ. ✉ *5 Klines Ct., Lambertville* ☎ *609/397–1288* 🌐 *www.bcdrygoods.com.*

Activities

Pure Energy Cycling

BICYCLING | This serious, high-end bike store rents hybrid bikes and cruisers. These come with locks and helmets. It's best to call ahead to reserve a bike for busy weekends, and note that the company has limited kids' bikes. You can get coffee and tea on site. ✉ *99 S. Main St., Lambertville* ☎ *609/397–7008* 🌐 *pureenergycycling.com* *From $12 per hour; $40 per day.*

13

Chapter 13

LANCASTER COUNTY

Updated by
Kim O'Donnel

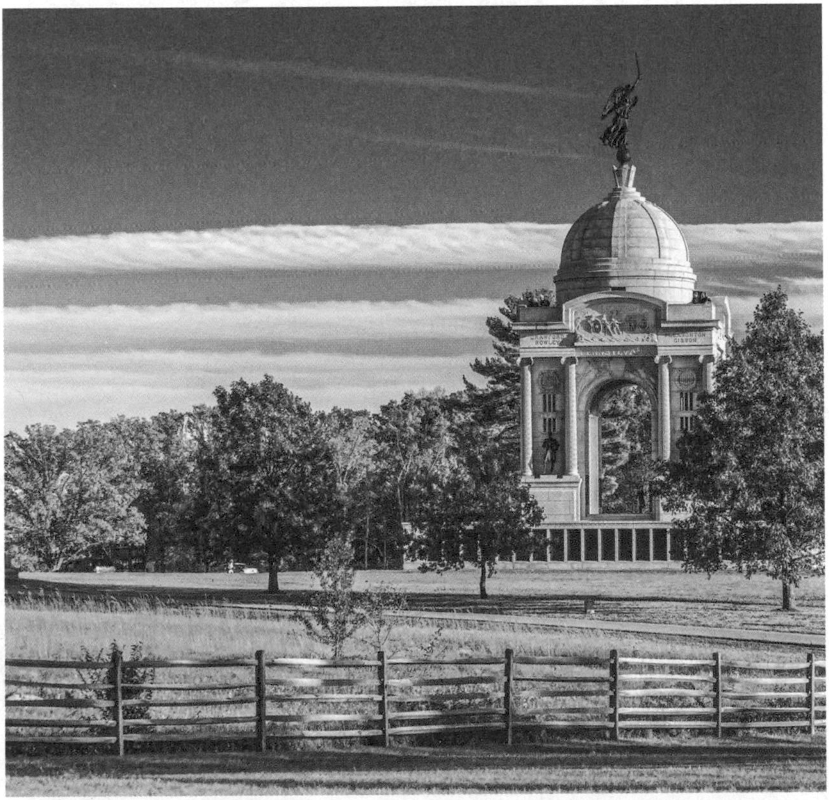

Sights	Restaurants	Hotels	Shopping	Nightlife
★★★★★	★★★★☆	★★★★☆	★★★☆☆	★★☆☆☆

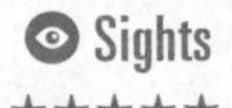

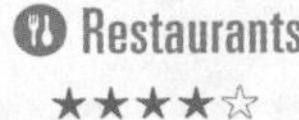

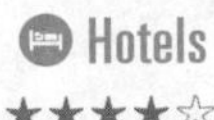

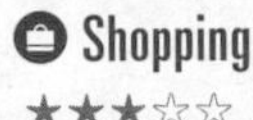

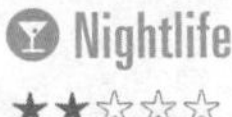

WELCOME TO LANCASTER COUNTY

TOP REASONS TO GO

★ **Green Acres.** There's breathtaking countryside and farmland everywhere you look.

★ **Dynamic food scene.** A growing food scene that includes craft coffee, beer, and cheese, global flavors, and farm-to-table dining.

★ **A hub of historical significance.** Spanning several centuries, from Native Americans to Colonial America, the Civil War, and the Industrial Revolution.

★ **Amish villages.** Learn about Amish culture via shops, crafts, restaurants, and on buggy rides.

★ **Family-friendly.** There are museums, theme parks, and more to entertain every family no matter the age range.

1 Lancaster. A walkable city full of restaurants, cafés, and small shops.

2 Bird-in-Hand. Working farms, horse-drawn buggies, and all facets of Amish culture.

3 Strasburg. A slow-paced village that doubles as a hot spot for railroad history.

4 Lititz. This 18th-century Moravian town has a charming downtown.

5 Ephrata. It's famously known for the Ephrata Cloister, a religious compound.

6 Adamstown. This is antiques heaven, home to the famous Renninger's antiques market.

7 Columbia. This town offers outdoor adventures, antiques shops, and historic tours.

8 Marietta. Marietta offers outdoors and antiques fun.

9 Manheim. An 18th-century town with a good estate winery and seasonal Renaissance fair.

10 Hershey. Expect chocolate, amusement rides, and world-class entertainment.

11 Gettyburg. There are dozens of sites to deepen your knowledge of the Civil War.

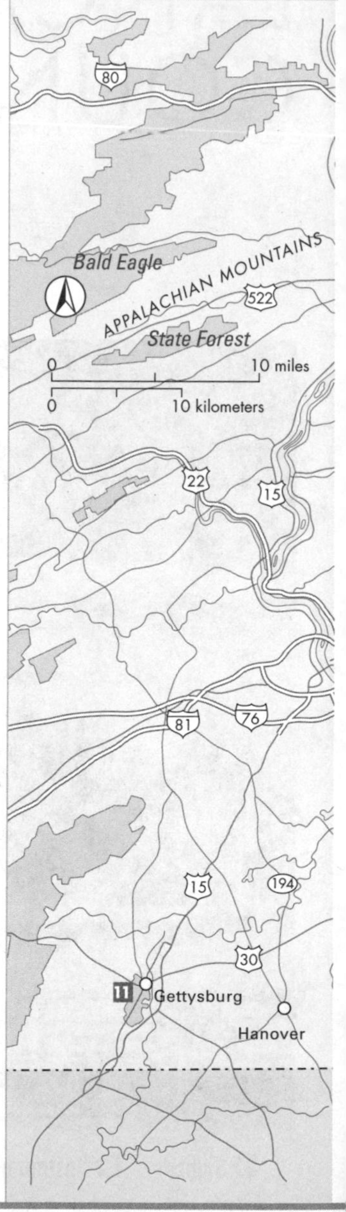

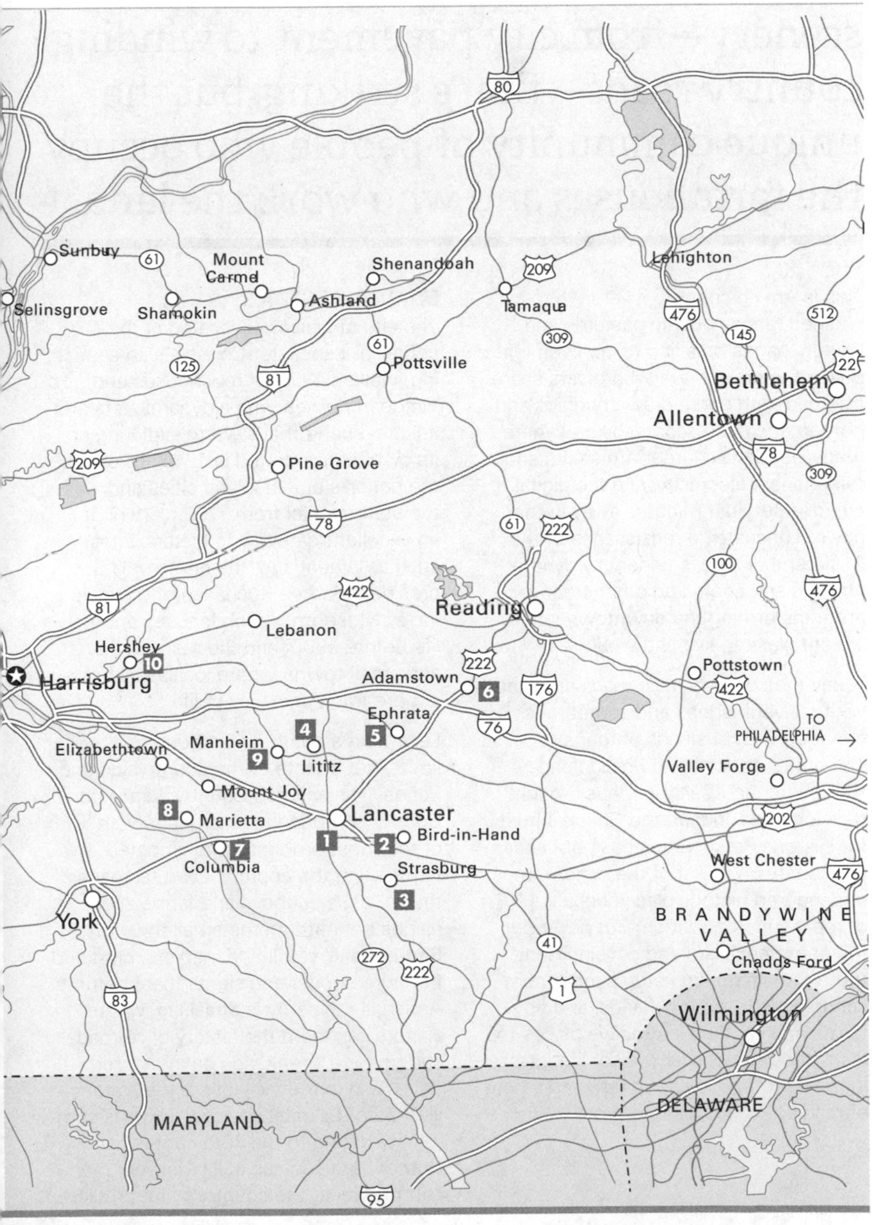

80
Sunbury
61
Mount Carmel
Shenandoah
209
Lehighton
Selinsgrove
Shamokin
Ashland
Tamaqua
476
512
145
309
61
Pottsville
125
81
22
Bethlehem
Allentown
78
209
Pine Grove
309
78
61
222
100
476
422
81
Reading
Lebanon
Hershey
10
Harrisburg
222
Pottstown
Adamstown
6
176
422
Ephrata
4
5
76
TO PHILADELPHIA →
Elizabethtown
Manheim
9
Lititz
Valley Forge
Mount Joy
8
Marietta
Lancaster
202
1
2
Bird-in-Hand
7
Columbia
Strasburg
West Chester
476
3
York
BRANDYWINE VALLEY
41
Chadds Ford
272
222
83
1
Wilmington
DELAWARE
MARYLAND
95

About 60 miles west of Philadelphia, a different world from a different time emerges. It's not just the change in scenery—from city pavement to winding country roads—that's striking, but the unique community of people who occupy the farmhouses and who work the land.

This is Amish country, where white-washed fences outline pastures and laundry hangs on a line to dry even in the dead of winter. This is where cars share the road with horse-drawn buggies and homemade push scooter-bikes. Where many, as the Old Order Amish do, shun telephones, electricity, and the digital culture. But, just minutes away in the city of Lancaster, a renaissance of the 21st-century kind is underway, where artisans and chefs and other creatives are transforming the downtown into a vibrant place to live and work.

Today the county's main roads are lined with souvenir shops and sometimes crowded with busloads of tourists. The area's proximity to Philadelphia, Harrisburg, and Baltimore has brought development. In fact, the National Trust for Historic Preservation has put Lancaster County on its list of the nation's most endangered historic places because of rapid suburbanization. But beyond the commercialism and development, there remain general stores, one-room schoolhouses, country lanes, and tidy farms. You can find instructive places to learn about the Amish way of life, pretzel factories to tour, quilts to buy, and a host of railroad museums to explore.

MAJOR REGIONS

The city of **Lancaster,** located at the center of Lancaster County, is an appealing, walkable city of row houses and Victorian homes with a dynamic arts and cultural scene that's worth exploring on its own. Incorporated in 1742, it's one of the nation's oldest inland cities and was the state capital from 1799 to 1812. It's an excellent gateway to historic sites, such as Wheatland, the home of U.S. president James Buchanan; the Landis Valley Museum, which focuses on rural life before 1900; and the many hamlets and small towns where locals still follow a more traditional way of life.

Less than a half hour outside the city limits, get a taste of the countryside and Pennsylvania Dutch Country. Lancaster County comprises the largest swath of the most productive nonirrigated farmland in the country. On rural roads, there's big sky above and farms and dairies beneath. In the small town of **Bird-in-Hand,** you'll find markets, craft and furniture shops, and sights that interpret Amish life. Nearby is **Strasburg,** where visitors can learn the history of railroads and go for a scenic ride on a restored train. Also in the vicinity are the historic villages of **Ephrata,** site of a religious community dating to the 18th century, and **Lititz,** where you can still twist your own soft pretzel at the country's first pretzel bakery. **Adamstown**, in the northeastern tip of the county, is a haven for collectibles, vintage and antique.

In Western Lancaster County, the Susquehanna River towns of **Columbia** and **Marietta** offer a mix of the great outdoors, quality antiquing, and a mellow vibe.

If you've brought your children as far as Lancaster, you may want to continue northwest to **Hershey,** the "Chocolate Town" founded in 1903 by Milton S. Hershey. Here the number one attraction is Hersheypark, a theme park with kiddie and thrill rides, theaters, and live shows. You may also wish to journey southwest to the Civil War battlefields and museums of **Gettysburg,** also within a short driving distance.

Planning

Getting Here and Around

CAR

From Philadelphia, it's about a 65-mile drive. From I–76 west (Schuylkill Expressway), there are two options: for the slower, more scenic, route, take U.S. 202 south to U.S. 30 west; quicker is I–276 (Pennsylvania Turnpike, with tolls). Lancaster County sights are accessible from Exits 266, 286, and 298.

A car is the easiest way to explore the many sights in the area; it also lets you get off the main roads and into the countryside. Lancaster County's main arteries are U.S. 30 (also known as the Lincoln Highway) and Route 340 (also called Old Philadelphia Pike). Some pleasant back roads can be found between Routes 23 and 340 through Smoketown and Bird-in-Hand as well as Route 896 through the village of Strasburg. You get a look at farms in the area, and Amish stores, schoolhouses, and the Amish themselves. **■TIP→ Remember to slow down for horse-drawn buggies when driving on country roads.**

TRAIN

Amtrak's Keystone line has frequent daily service between Philadelphia's 30th Street Station and its station in downtown Lancaster. The trip takes about 70 minutes.

CONTACTS Amtrak. ✉ *53 McGovern Ave.* ☎ *800/872–7245* 🌐 *www.amtrak.com.*

When to Go

Summer and autumn are busy times, when seasonal produce, county fairs and festivals, and fall foliage attract crowds. Farmers' markets and family-style restaurants overflow with visitors and locals alike. Crowds will likely be fewer in early spring and in September, when school is back in session. Although many Amish restaurants, shops, and farmers' markets are closed on Sundays, commercial attractions remain open.

Planning Your Time

The city of Lancaster, with its rich arts and cultural scene, can be used as a hub while visiting the surrounding countryside or as a jumping-off point before moving on to explore the area's more rural scenery. Consider spending a night at a bed-and-breakfast.

Lancaster County, with its working farms, offers a window into a traditional way of life.

Families will want to allocate at least a day or two for Hersheypark's rides and attractions, while history buffs should schedule one or two days to explore Gettysburg, site of one of the most important battles of the Civil War.

Hotels

Lancaster County lodging offers a wide range of options—stay at a historic inn, or indulge yourself at a luxurious resort. A good selection of moderately priced motels caters to families. Although hotels welcome guests year-round, rates are highest in summer. Some inns and B&Bs have minimum stays in high season.

Many working Amish and non-Amish farms throughout Lancaster County welcome guests to stay for a few days to observe and even participate in farm life. Operated as B&B establishments with a twist, the farms invite you to help milk the cows and feed the chickens, and afterwards share a hearty breakfast with the farmer and his family or help with other farm chores. Reservations must be made weeks in advance, as most farms are heavily booked in summer. Discover Lancaster has a listing of all area B&Bs and farms that welcome guests. Lancaster County Bed-and-Breakfast Association has information on several area B&Bs.

CONTACTS Lancaster County Bed-and-Breakfast Inns Association. ✉ *501 Greenfield Rd., Lancaster* ☎ *717/288–1700* 🌐 *www.padutchinns.com.*

Restaurants

Like the German cuisine that influenced it, Pennsylvania Dutch cooking is hearty and uses ingredients from local farms. Though their numbers are dwindling, traditional Pennsylvania Dutch restaurants do remain, many where you can dine family style. Lancaster County is home to numerous reasonably priced family restaurants, along with a growing number of eateries offering more globally inspired fare. Unless otherwise noted, liquor is served.

HOTEL AND RESTAURANT PRICES
Hotel prices in the reviews are the lowest cost of a standard double room in high season. Restaurant prices in the reviews are the average cost of a main course at dinner, or if dinner is not served, at lunch. Restaurant and hotel reviews have been shortened. For full information, visit Fodors.com.

What It Costs In US Dollars

$	$$	$$$	$$$$
RESTAURANTS			
under $15	$15–$19	$20–$24	over $24
HOTELS			
under $150	$150–$200	$201–$250	over $250

Tours

Although Lancaster County is easy to navigate on your own, tours can be helpful, particularly if you're interested in learning about the Amish and Mennonite ways of life. Local guides can offer cultural context you simply can't get from reading brochures.

TOUR CONTACTS Amish Country Tours. ✉ *3121 Old Philadelphia Pike, Rte. 340, Bird-in-Hand* ✣ *Most GPS systems use "Ronks" as the city.* ☎ *717/768–3600* 🌐 *www.amishexperience.com.* **Brunswick Tours.** ✉ *2076 Airy Hill Rd., Manheim* ☎ *717/879–9890, 800/979–8687* 🌐 *www.brunswicktours.com.* **Mennonite Information Center.** ✉ *2209 Millstream Rd., Lancaster* ☎ *717/299–0954, 800/858–8320* 🌐 *www.mennoinfocenter.org.* **Smoketown Helicopters.** ✉ *311 Airport Dr., off Rte. 340, Smoketown* ☎ *717/394–6476* 🌐 *www.smoketownhelicopters.com.*

Visitor Information

Discover Lancaster is the welcome center for Lancaster County, offering a selection of brochures, maps, and other resources, plus advice from its staff of travel consultants. You can check your email, get a free cup of coffee, and browse the gift shop's sampling of local crafts and souvenirs. The Mennonite Information Center provides information on local inns and Mennonite guest homes as well as a gift shop featuring local crafts.

CONTACTS Discover Lancaster. ✉ *501 Greenfield Rd., Lancaster* ☎ *800/723–8824* 🌐 *www.discoverlancaster.com.* **Mennonite Information Center.** ✉ *2209 Millstream Rd., Lancaster* ☎ *717/299–0954, 800/858–8320* 🌐 *www.mennoinfocenter.com.*

Lancaster

75 miles west of Philadelphia via I–76.

Just minutes from the countryside is Lancaster, a vibrant city with a population of 60,000 that combines Colonial and Pennsylvania Dutch influences. During the French and Indian War and the American Revolution, its craftsmen turned out fine guns, building the city's reputation as the arsenal of the colonies. On September 27, 1777, Lancaster became the nation's capital for just one day as Congress fled the British in Philadelphia. Today, markets and museums preserve the area's history in a stately downtown core whose red bricks and cobblestones will be familiar to anyone who's spent time in nearby cities like Philadelphia, Boston, and Baltimore. In recent years, Lancaster has upped its hipness quotient; you'll still find plenty of whoopie pies and rocking chairs, but also ramen and chia pudding, rehabbed row homes, and modern restaurants that have strengthened ties with the county's organic farmers.

Getting Here and Around

The most direct route from Philadelphia is to take I–76 to the Pennsylvania Turnpike. If you're staying near Penn Square, you can walk to the Central Market, the major museums, and cultural attractions. You'll need a car to access certain sightss within the city, including Wheatland, as well as the surrounding countryside. For lovely views of farms and unspoiled land, take a spin along the smaller roads between Routes 23 and 340.

Essentials

VISITOR INFORMATION The Lancaster City Visitor Center. ✉ *38 Penn Square* ✣ *For GPS, use 5 W. King St.* ☎ *717/517–5718* 🌐 *www.visitlancastercity.com.*

Sights

Demuth Museum

MUSEUM | This museum includes the restored 18th-century home, studio, and garden of Charles Demuth (1883–1935), one of America's first modernist artists, who lived in the city of Lancaster for most of his short life. A watercolorist, Demuth found inspiration in the geometric shapes of machines and modern technology, as well as the flowers in his mother's garden. Several of his works are on display. The gallery also features a changing exhibit of regional and national artists. The complex includes the former oldest operating tobacco shop in the country, which dates to 1770. ✉ *120 E. King St.* ☎ *717/299–9940* 🌐 *www.demuth.org* 🎫 *Donation requested* ⏲ *Closed Mon.*

Dutch Wonderland

AMUSEMENT PARK/WATER PARK | **FAMILY** | A self-proclaimed "Kingdom for Kids," this 44-acre amusement park features rides and activities suited for families with younger children. Most rides, such as the roller coaster, merry-go-round, and giant

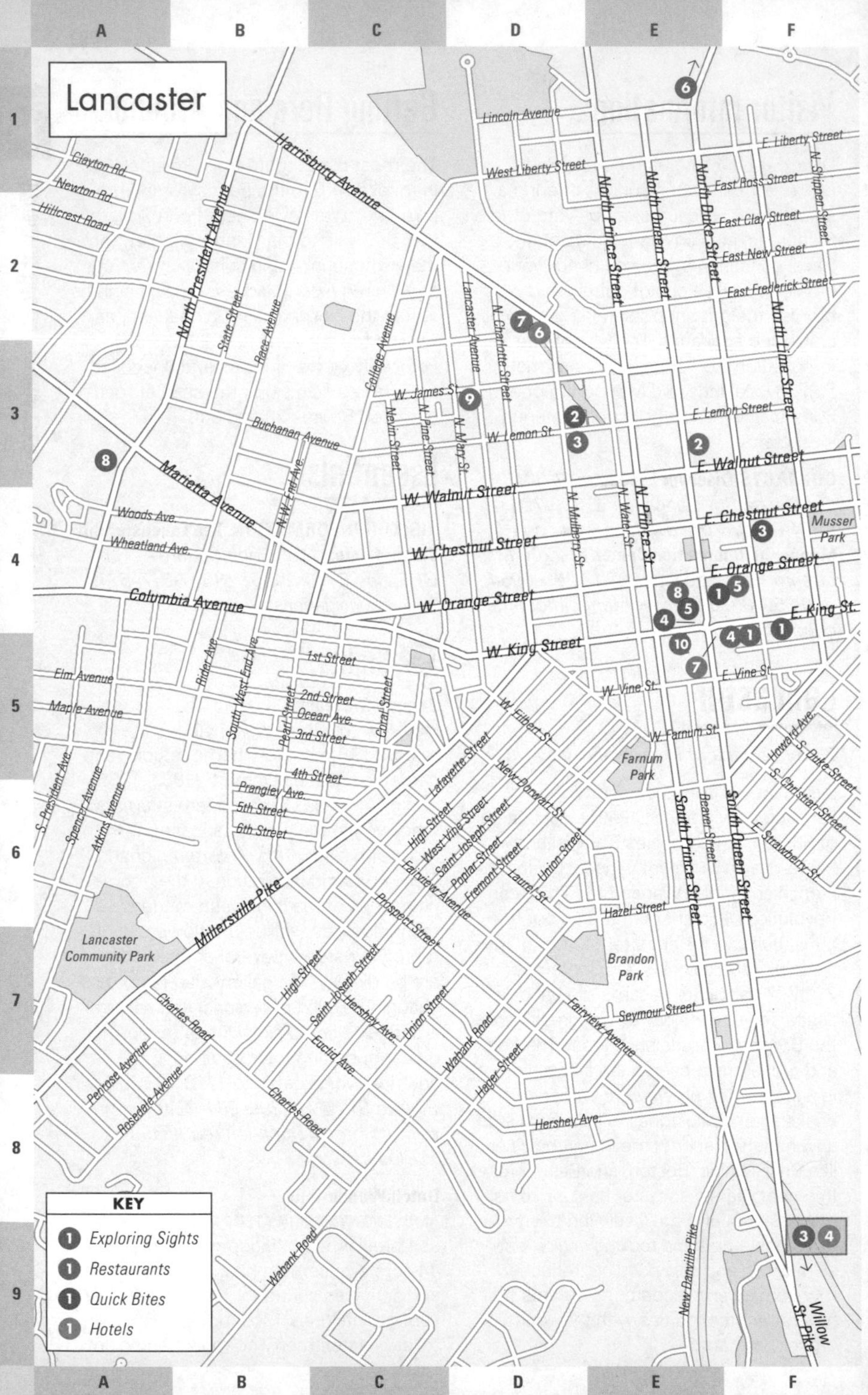

Lancaster
A
B
C
D
E
F
1
2
3
4
5
6
7
8
9
Lincoln Avenue
West Liberty Street
E. Liberty Street
East Ross Street
East Clay Street
East New Street
East Frederick Street
North Prince Street
North Queen Street
North Duke Street
North Lime Street
N. Shippen Street
Harrisburg Avenue
Clayton Rd.
Newton Rd.
Hillcrest Road
North President Avenue
State Street
Race Avenue
College Avenue
Lancaster Avenue
N. Charlotte Street
W. James St.
Nevin Street
N. Pine Street
N. Mary St.
W. Lemon St.
E. Lemon Street
Buchanan Avenue
E. Walnut Street
W. Walnut Street
Marietta Avenue
N.W. End Ave.
N. Mulberry St.
N. Water St.
N. Prince St.
E. Chestnut Street
Musser Park
Woods Ave.
Wheatland Ave.
W. Chestnut Street
E. Orange Street
Columbia Avenue
W. Orange Street
E. King St.
W. King Street
1st Street
Rider Ave.
South West End Ave.
E. Vine St.
W. Vine St.
Elm Avenue
2nd Street
Ocean Ave.
Maple Avenue
Pearl Street
Coral Street
3rd Street
W. Elbert St.
W. Farnum St.
Farnum Park
Lafayette Street
Howard Ave.
S. Duke Street
4th Street
New Dorwart St.
S. Christian Street
Prangley Ave.
5th Street
S. President Ave.
Spencer Avenue
Atkins Avenue
6th Street
High Street
West Vine Street
Saint Joseph Street
Poplar Street
Fremont Street
Union Street
South Prince Street
Beaver Street
South Queen Street
E. Strawberry St.
Laurel St.
Fairview Avenue
Prospect Street
Hazel Street
Millersville Pike
Lancaster Community Park
Brandon Park
High Street
Saint Joseph Street
Hershey Ave.
Union Street
Charles Road
Euclid Ave.
Wabank Road
Hager Street
Seymour Street
Fairview Avenue
Penrose Avenue
Rosedale Avenue
Charles Road
Hershey Ave.
KEY
Exploring Sights
Restaurants
Quick Bites
Hotels
Wabank Road
New Danville Pike
Willow St. Pike

Sights

1 Demuth Museum F5
2 Dutch Wonderland J4
3 Hans Herr House F9
4 Historic Lancaster Walking Tour E4
5 Lancaster Central Market E4
6 Landis Valley Village & Farm Museum.................... E1
7 Rock Ford Plantation I9
8 Wheatland.......................... A3

Restaurants

1 Annie Bailey's Irish Public House F5
2 Cabalar Meat Co.................... E3
3 Callaloo Trinidadian Kitchen...... D3
4 The Exchange....................... F5
5 Himalayan Curry and Grill E4
6 Horse Inn H4
7 John J. Jeffries D2
8 Lancaster Dispensing Co. E4
9 LUCA D3
10 The Pressroom...................... E5

Quick Bites

1 Harvest Moon Bagel Co E4
2 Lemon Street Market.............. D3
3 Square One Coffee Roasters..................... F4

Hotels

1 Cartoon Network Hotel J5
2 Cork Factory Hotel................ G3
3 Courtyard by Marriott Lancaster............................ J5
4 DoubleTree Resort by Hilton Hotel Lancaster..................... F9
5 King's Cottage Bed & Breakfast.................... J4
6 Lancaster Arts Hotel D2
7 Lancaster Marriott at Penn Square E5

slide, are quite tame. The adjacent water park (no separate admission), Duke's Lagoon, is open weekends, Memorial Day through Labor Day. From Thanksgiving to Christmas, the park is open for its "Dutch Winter Wonderland," with holiday-themed rides and a light show. ✉ *2249 Lincoln Highway East (U.S. 30)* ✣ *4 miles east of downtown Lancaster* ☎ *866/386–2839* 🌐 *www.dutchwonderland.com* 🎫 *$35.99 (purchased online)* 🕒 *Hrs can vary; call ahead or check the website.*

★ Hans Herr House

BUILDING | A registered historic landmark, the Hans Herr House is the oldest surviving homestead in Lancaster County and the oldest original (and remaining) Mennonite meeting house in the Western Hemisphere.

The subject of several paintings by Andrew Wyeth, it was the Colonial home of the Herr family, to whom the Wyeths were related. Today the house is owned by the Lancaster Mennonite Historical Society, which educates the public about the Mennonite religion. The 45-minute tour covers the grounds and the 1719 Mennonite meeting place. A separate 45-minute tour covers a reconstructed Native American longhouse. ✉ *1849 Hans Herr Dr., Willow Street* ✣ *5 miles south of downtown Lancaster, off U.S. 222.* ☎ *717/464–4438* 🌐 *www.hansherr.org* 🎫 *$15* 🕒 *Closed Sun. and Nov.–Apr.*

Historic Lancaster Walking Tour

TOUR—SIGHT | The Historic Lancaster Walking Tour is a two-hour stroll through the heart of this Colonial city by costumed guides who impart anecdotes about notable points of interest. Tours of the area depart daily at 1 pm from the downtown visitor center across from the Central Market; there's an additional tour at 10 am on market days (Tuesday, Friday, and Saturday). ✉ *38 Penn Sq.* ☎ *717/392–1776* 🌐 *historiclancasterwalkingtour.org* 🎫 *$8* 🕒 *Closed Nov.–Mar.*

★ Lancaster Central Market

MARKET | **FAMILY** | "Have you been to market?" is a question you'll likely hear from Lancaster locals. Built in 1889, this indoor farmers' market has been a city fixture since its days as an open-air market in 1742. The grand Romanesque building remains a pillar of the community, not only as a place to shop for fresh produce, meat, flowers and baked goods, but as a gathering place, where neighbors meet for coffee and talk about their week. In addition to Amish staples like Lebanon bologna and chowchow, there's a selection of globally inspired prepared foods, from Ugandan chicken patties to Puerto Rican empanadas. ✉ *23 N. Market St., off Penn Square* ☎ *717/735–6890* 🌐 *www.centralmarketlancaster.com* 🕒 *Closed Sun., Mon., Wed., Thurs.*

★ Landis Valley Village & Farm Museum

HOUSE | This open-air museum showcases Pennsylvania German rural life and folk culture between 1750 and 1940. Founded by brothers Henry and George Landis on their homestead in the 1920s, the farm and village are now operated by the Pennsylvania Historical and Museum Commission. You can visit more than 15 historical buildings, with costumed guides providing interesting bits of history. There are demonstrations of skills such as spinning and weaving, pottery making, and tinsmithing. Many of the crafts are for sale in the museum shop. ✉ *2451 Kissel Hill Rd., off Oregon Pike, Rte. 272* ☎ *717/569–0401* 🌐 *www.landisvalleymuseum.org* 🎫 *$12* 🕒 *Closed Mon. and Tues. Jan.–mid-Mar.*

Rock Ford Plantation

HOUSE | Set on 33 acres, the Historic Rock Ford Plantation is the restored homestead of General Edward Hand, a Revolutionary War commander, George Washington's confidant, and wealthy landowner. Period antiques and folk art are displayed in the 1794 Georgian-style mansion, which is on the National Register of Historic Places. In partnering

The Lancaster Central Market has been a city fixture since its days as an open-air market in 1742. Shop here for fresh produce, meat, flowers and baked goods.

with the African American Historical Society of South Central Pennsylvania, Historic Rock Ford's programs include the legacy and stories of the slaves who lived and worked on Hand's farm and in the household. *881 Rock Ford Rd.* *717/392–7223* *www.rockfordplantation.org* *$8* *Closed Nov.–Mar.*

Wheatland

HOUSE | Wheatland was the home of James Buchanan, the only U.S. president from Pennsylvania, who served from 1857 to 1861. A National Historic Landmark, the restored 1828 Federal-style mansion and outbuildings display the 15th president's furniture just as it was during his lifetime. A one-hour tour includes a profile of the only bachelor to occupy the White House, a movie, and access to historical artifacts and the arboretum on the grounds. There are holiday candlelight tours with costumed guides. *230 N. President Ave.* *Off Rte. 23, 1½ miles west of downtown Lancaster* *717/392–4633* *www.lancasterhistory.org* *$15* *Closed Sun.*

Restaurants

Annie Bailey's Irish Public House

$$ | AMERICAN | Located in a Victorian-era building in downtown Lancaster, Annie Bailey's is a traditional Irish pub, from the dark wooden bar and furnishings sourced in Ireland to classic menu staples like shepherd's pie and fish-and-chips. There are at least 10 rotating beers on tap and an impressive selection Irish whiskey. **Known for:** bangers and mash; good selection of Irish beer; vegetarian options; Irish curry. *Average main: $19* *28–30 E. King St.* *717/393–4000* *www.anniebaileys.com.*

Cabalar Meat Co.

$ | AMERICAN | This family-owned butcher shop locally sources pasture-raised beef, pork, and poultry, which is available for purchase in its meat case. It also doubles as a casual restaurant showcasing the meaty goods, with a simple menu of burgers, fries, sandwiches, and salads. **Known for:** beef-tallow fries; chicken wings; locally sourced pasture-raised meat. $ *Average main: $11* ✉ *Keppel Building, 325 N. Queen St.* ☎ *717/208–7344* 🌐 *www.cabalarmeatco.com* ⏲ *Closed Mon. and Tues.*

★ Callaloo Trinidadian Kitchen

$$ | **CARIBBEAN** | Chinese, Indian, and African cuisine meld together to create a beguiling melting pot of flavors and dishes on the Caribbean island of Trinidad. The resulting cuisine is front and center at this charming corner café, where you can have *buss-up shut*—a Trinidadian ode to *paratha* (flatbread) served with curried vegetables and chicken or beef—in a cast-iron skillet; or pineapple chow, a salsa of sorts that's good enough to eat with a spoon. **Known for:** huge portions; buss-up shut; shark and bake (fish and fried bread). $ *Average main: $17* ✉ *351 N. Mulberry St.* ☎ *717/824–3964* 🌐 *www.callalootrinidadiankitchen.com* ⏲ *Closed Sun. and Mon.*

The Exchange

$$ | **FUSION** | Perched atop the Marriott at Penn Square, this chic lounge and restaurant has the best views in town—the 3,500-square-foot space offers panoramic views of Lancaster and beyond. The menu offers globally inspired small plates, from Lebanon bologna sliders to crispy Halloumi cheese, along with a rotating selection of wood-fired pizzas. **Known for:** great sunset viewing; weekday happy hour food and drink specials; crowd is 21 and over only. $ *Average main: $15* ✉ *Marriott at Penn Square, 25 S. Queen St.* ☎ *717/207–4096* 🌐 *www.exchangeroof.com.*

★ Himalayan Curry and Grill

$$ | **INDIAN** | This family-owned Nepalese and Indian restaurant is a little gem in downtown Lancaster. The cozy dining room quickly gets packed on weekend nights, but the staff gracefully handles the constant flow, serving popular dishes such as *chana masala* (a chickpea-based curry) and veggie *pakoras* (pan-fried chickpea batter) as well as specialties from Nepal, where dry curries and steamed dumplings are common. **Known for:** dal palak (a spinach-and-lentil curry); vindaloo dishes; momo (Nepalese dumplings). $ *Average main: $17* ✉ *22 E. Orange St.* ☎ *717/393–2330* 🌐 *www.himalayanlancaster.com* ⏲ *Closed Sun.*

★ Horse Inn

$$$$ | **MODERN AMERICAN** | Husband-and-wife team Matt and Starla Russell run this seasonally driven gastropub that's located in a former inn and stable. The menu, posted on a chalkboard, is updated daily to reflect the "Farmers and Friends" list, its nod to its local ingredient sources. **Known for:** tips 'n toast (tenderloin tips on French bread); botanical craft cocktails; horse fries (sausage, cheese, and garlic heavy cream). $ *Average main: $25* ✉ *540 E. Fulton St.* ☎ *717/392–5528* 🌐 *www.horseinnlancaster.com* ⏲ *Closed Sun. and Mon.*

★ John J. Jeffries

$$$$ | **MODERN AMERICAN** | Named after a bygone tobacco inspector, John J. Jeffries is the dining anchor of the hip Lancaster Arts Hotel, which occupies a former tobacco factory in downtown Lancaster. Not only do the chefs here source produce, dairy, and eggs from local farms, but they also own and operate a grass-fed cattle ranch, abattoir, and nose-to-tail butcher shop in Chambersburg, Pennsylvania; in 2019, the restaurant received an EAT Real certification for its commitment to responsible sourcing and animal welfare. **Known for:** dry-aged steak from Lil' Ponderosa ranch; artisanal cheese plate from local creameries; using lesser-known cuts of meat, like beef cheeks or venison leg steak. $ *Average main: $28* ✉ *Lancaster Arts Hotel, 300 Harrisburg Ave.* ☎ *717/431–3307* 🌐 *www.johnjjeffries.com.*

Lancaster Dispensing Co.

$ | **AMERICAN** | Locally known as Dipco, this welcoming pub next to Central Market is a fun haunt for a nosh and a pint, especially when there's live music on the weekends. Sandwiches, house-made chili, burritos, as well as nightly specials, are among the many menu options. **Known for:** nachos platters; weekday happy hour; extensive selection of baked dips. *Average main: $10* *33–35 N. Market St.* *717/299–4602* *www.dispensingco.com.*

★ LUCA

$$$ | **ITALIAN** | A self-described "wood-burning Italian kitchen," LUCA serves up seasonally inspired pasta, Neapolitan-style pizza, and wood-roasted meats. Located in a residential neighborhood near the Franklin & Marshall campus, this sun-drenched space with roll-up garage doors is always busy, and for good reason—the food is consistently delicious and the dining room vibe is upbeat. **Known for:** wood-fired pizzas; house-made pasta; impressive selection of Italian spirits and craft cocktails. *Average main: $22* *436 W. James St.* *717/553–5770* *www.lucalancaster.com* *Closed Mon.*

The Pressroom

$$$ | **AMERICAN** | Originally a hardware store from the mid-1700s, this Victorian building in the center of town is now home to a casual bistro. It's owned by the company that also owns the local newspaper (hence the name) and is outfitted with a classic mahogany bar, tall leather booths, and an exposed baking hearth. **Known for:** tacos de asada; daily soup and quiche; friendly vibe. *Average main: $22* *26–28 W. King St.* *717/399–5400* *www.pressroomrestaurant.com* *Closed Mon.*

Coffee and Quick Bites

Harvest Moon Bagel Co.

$ | **BAKERY** | Hand-rolled bagels with organic flour are at the center of this small bakery located in downtown Lancaster. A husband-wife team is at the helm, producing a properly chewy bagel inspired by his Polish heritage, as well as a variety of bagel sandwiches and homemade babka. **Known for:** homemade babka; showcasing local ingredients and producers; many vegan options. *Average main: $7* *47 N. Queen St.* *717/984–6549* *www.harvestmoonbagels.com* *Closed Tues.*

★ Lemon Street Market

$ | **CAFÉ** | A locally owned full-service grocery store with a focus on sustainable and health-minded products, Lemon Street Market is a great spot to pick up snacks and fruit to take back to your hotel, or drop by for a smoothie or coffee break. It's within walking distance of many downtown Lancaster hotels. **Known for:** great selection of local products; delicious homemade soups (in cold weather); great take-away options. *Average main: $5* *241 W. Lemon St.* *717/826–0843* *www.lemonstreetmarket.com.*

Square One Coffee Roasters

$ | **CAFÉ** | One of two cafés owned by a Lancaster-based roaster (the other is in Center City Philadelphia), Square One (or SQ1, as it's locally known) serves exceptionally good brewed coffee and espresso. It's a favorite among locals who wander in for their first cup of the day, and a place where folks linger to read the local paper and catch up with neighbors while they munch on a selection of local pastries and grab-and-go lunch fare. **Known for:** garden courtyard when weather permits; rotating lineup of single-origin espresso; really good cold brew. *Average main: $3* *145 N. Duke St.* *717/392–3354* *www.squareonecoffee.com.*

Hotels

★ Cartoon Network Hotel

$$$$ | **HOTEL** | **FAMILY** | A first for the Cartoon Network, this one-of-a-kind hotel opened in 2020 next to the popular amusement park, Dutch Wonderland, and it's agenda is crystal clear—this place is all about the cartoons, and it's all about

kids. **Pros:** indoor pool and outdoor water park; rooms are expressly designed for families, with bunkbeds in most rooms; interior is hip, modern, and bright. **Cons:** no elevator for adjacent motel-style building where standard rooms are located; small bathroom in standard rooms; potential noise from U.S. 30 traffic. *Rooms from: $289 2285 Lincoln Hwy. E (U.S. 30) 717/740–2777, 833/TOONHTL www.cartoonnetworkhotel.com 159 rooms No meals.*

Cork Factory Hotel

$$ | HOTEL | The exposed-brick walls, vaulted wood ceilings, and ductwork of this boutique hotel take full advantage of its former life as the Armstrong Cork Company. **Pros:** sophisticated decor; atmospheric bar; friendly, unpretentious front desk vibe. **Cons:** lack of luxury amenities; located in a business park; rooms are a distance from the main lobby. *Rooms from: $169 480 New Holland Ave., Suite 3000 717/735–2075 www.corkfactoryhotel.com 75 rooms Free breakfast.*

Courtyard by Marriott Lancaster

$ | HOTEL | Located just minutes from U.S. 30, this Courtyard location is Marriott's first solar-powered property in the country. **Pros:** breakfast buffet (fee); refrigerator in room; pet friendly. **Cons:** few restaurants in immediate vicinity; indoor pool is small; a distance from attractions. *Rooms from: $149 1931 Hospitality Dr., off U.S. 30, 717/393–3600, 800/321–2211 www.marriott.com/hotels/travel/lnscy-courtyard-lancaster 138 rooms No meals.*

DoubleTree Resort by Hilton Hotel Lancaster

$ | HOTEL | FAMILY | About 4 miles south of downtown Lancaster, this Hilton property is well suited for families with a 9-hole golf course, an indoor pool, and large rooms surrounding a skylighted lobby. **Pros:** indoor pool; family-friendly; golf course and pro shop. **Cons:** feels a little large and corporate; indoor pool open to nonguests; off-site restaurants are a distance. *Rooms from: $125 2400 Willow St. Pike 717/464–2711, 800/444–1714 www.hilton.com/en/doubletree 185 rooms No meals.*

King's Cottage Bed & Breakfast

$$$ | B&B/INN | An elegant 1913 Spanish-style mansion on the National Register of Historic Places, this B&B's blend of architectural elements includes an art deco fireplace and stained-glass windows. **Pros:** gourmet breakfast and afternoon refreshments; convenient to Amish country; on-site massage. **Cons:** some rooms on small side; a few rooms have bathrooms that are private but not en suite; no elevator. *Rooms from: $205 1049 E. King St. 717/397–1017 www.kingscottagebb.com 7 rooms, 1 cottage Free breakfast.*

Lancaster Arts Hotel

$$ | HOTEL | This downtown boutique hotel—once a tobacco warehouse in the 1800s—offers sleek rooms furnished with executive desks, flat-screen TVs, iPod docking stations, and free Wi-Fi; there are also whirlpool tubs in the suites. **Pros:** hip rooms; high-end farm-to-table restaurant; more than 200 pieces of art displayed throughout the property. **Cons:** located a distance from downtown attractions; on a busy street; no pool. *Rooms from: $179 300 Harrisburg Ave. 717/299–3000, 866/720–2787 www.lancasterartshotel.com 63 rooms Free breakfast.*

Lancaster Marriott at Penn Square

$$ | HOTEL | Standing tall in the heart of downtown Lancaster, this Marriott property went through a major expansion in 2019 with the addition of a new 12-story tower that's topped with a rooftop lounge and restaurant that have panoramic views of the city and beyond and 110 rooms. **Pros:** prime location; upscale amenities; three on-site dining options. **Cons:** business-oriented focus; no period charm; as a convention hotel, can feel crowded. *Rooms from: $179 25 S. Queen St. 717/239–1600,*

800/228–9290 🌐 *www.marriott.com/hotels/travel/lnsmc* 🛏 *410 rooms* 🍴 *No meals.*

Performing Arts

American Music Theatre

THEATER | This 1,600-seat theater presents full-scale original musical productions, live concerts with national acts, and an annual Christmas show. ✉ *2425 Lincoln Hwy. East* ☎ *717/397–7700, 800/648–4102* 🌐 *www.amtshows.com.*

Dutch Apple Dinner Theatre

THEATER | At this 330-seat theater, it's all about dinner and a show. On stage, a mix of updated versions of classic musicals such as *Guys and Dolls* and *Annie Get Your Gun* join more contemporary productions such as *Legally Blonde* and *Sister Act,* plus regular children's productions. With the exception of a seated, full-service dinner on Thursdays, the theater offers a hearty buffet. ✉ *510 Centerville Rd., at U.S. 30* ☎ *717/898–1900* 🌐 *www.dutchapple.com.*

★ **Fulton Theatre** (*The Fulton*)

MUSIC | A National Historic Landmark, the 1852 Fulton Opera House is a crown jewel of performing arts for the region, showcasing world premieres of commissioned work, award-winning productions, and the Lancaster Symphony Orchestra. One-hour guided tours ($5) of the grand Victorian-era building are offered on Fridays during summer months. ✉ *12 N. Prince St.* ☎ *717/397–7425* 🌐 *www.thefulton.org.*

Sight & Sound Theatre

THEATER | FAMILY | Touted as the "Christian Broadway," Sight & Sound Theatre, located just 20 minutes from downtown Lancaster, produces shows based on the Bible. Musical productions in the 2,000-seat, state-of-the-art auditorium have included *Jonah, Samson, Joseph,* and *Noah.* As expected, these epic Biblical musicals attract a mostly Christian crowd, but the quality of the sets and performances are worth seeing even if you're not religious. ✉ *300 Hartman Bridge Rd., Ronks* ☎ *800/377–1277* 🌐 *www.sight-sound.com* 🎟 *$64.*

Shopping

CRAFTS

Landis Valley Museum Store

CRAFTS | Located on the grounds of the Landis Valley Village & Farm Museum, this shop is a destination in and of itself. You'll find a unique selection of artisan-crafted goods—many of which are made on the premises—that range from pottery to felt art, plus an extensive offering of Pennsylvania German arts and crafts. ✉ *Landis Valley Village & Farm Museum, 2451 Kissel Hill Rd.* ☎ *717/569–9312* 🌐 *www.landisvalleymuseum.org.*

Olde Mill House Shoppes

CRAFTS | Located in a restored barn and stone house, this family-owned business is a local must-visit for home decor, folk art, gifts, and country-style furniture. ✉ *105 Strasburg Pike* ☎ *717/299–0678* 🌐 *oldemillhouse.com.*

OUTLETS

The Shops @Rockvale

OUTLET/DISCOUNT STORES | More than 60 outlet brands—from Bass to West Elm, Coleman's to Puma—make up this outlet mall. A handful of fast-food restaurants are on site as well. ✉ *35 S. Willowdale Dr., U.S. 30 and Rte. 896* ✣ *Across the street from the American Music Theatre* ☎ *717/293–9292* 🌐 *www.shoprockvale.com.*

Tanger Outlets

OUTLET/DISCOUNT STORES | There are more than 60 outlet stores, including fashion brands like Ralph Lauren, J. Crew, New Balance, and North Face. A few fast-food restaurants are on-site as well. ■ **TIP→ Visit early, especially on weekends, when the stores are packed with road-tripping families.** ✉ *311 Stanley K.*

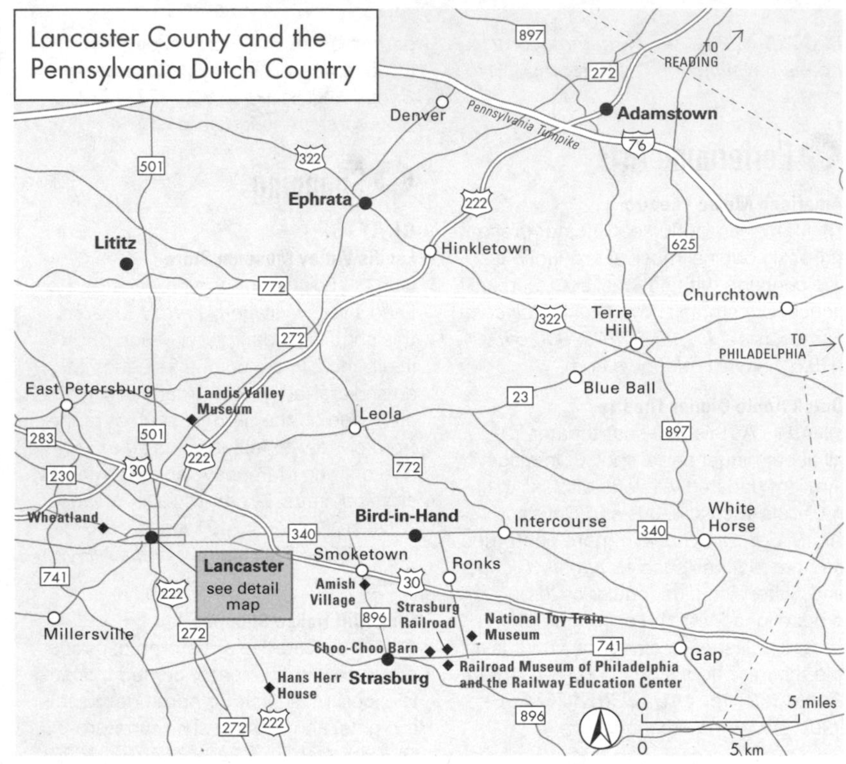

Tanger Blvd., U.S. 30 E ☎ *717/392–7260* 🌐 *www.tangeroutlet.com.*

Bird-in-Hand

6 miles east of downtown Lancaster via Rte. 462 and Rte. 340.

This village, which dates to 1734, remains a center for the Pennsylvania Dutch farming community. Its name, according to local lore, is attributed to two road surveyors, who had to decide whether to remain where they were or travel to Lancaster. They decided to stay, the story goes, when one said, "A bird in the hand is worth two in the bush." An early tavern began to be known as the Bird-in-Hand Inn and the name stuck.

Getting Here and Around

Bird-in-Hand is just a few minutes' drive from other Amish towns, including Ronks and Intercourse. Its attractions are clustered on Route 340 or nearby on U.S. 30.

TOURS

Aaron & Jessica's Buggy Rides

TOUR—SIGHT | FAMILY | Aaron & Jessica's Buggy Rides offers four guided tours of the Amish countryside, lasting between 30 and 60 minutes. Experience a taste of country life in an authentic Amish carriage with stops at farms, businesses, and of course, snacks. Rides depart from Plain & Fancy Farm. You can also book a private buggy ride. ✉ *3121 Old Philadelphia Pike, Rte. 340, between Bird-in-Hand and Intercourse* ✣ *GPS uses Ronks, PA* ☎ *717/768–8828* 🌐 *www.amishbuggyrides.com* 🎟 *From $10.*

Abe's Buggy Rides

TOUR—SIGHT | **FAMILY** | Abe's Buggy Rides offer tours ranging from 2- to 7-mile spins down country roads in an Amish buggy with an Amish driver at the reins. Visitors learn about Pennsylvania Dutch customs and the sights along the way. *2596 Old Philadelphia Pike, Rte. 340* *717/392–1794* *www.abesbuggyrides.com* *From $10.*

Sights

★ Amish Country Homestead

HOUSE | At this designated Lancaster County heritage site, take a guided tour of a replica nine-room Old Order Amish house, and attached one-room schoolhouse. Located on the Plain & Fancy Farm property, you'll learn about Amish culture, clothing, and day-to-day life. **■ TIP→ The Super-Saver Tour Package ($47.95) includes a 90-minute mini-shuttle tour; a guided tour of the homestead; and a ticket to see the film Jacob's Choice.** *3121 Old Philadelphia Pike ↔ Rte. 340, between Bird-in-Hand and Intercourse* *717/768–8400* *www.amishexperience.com* *$12.95.*

The Amish Farm and House

HOUSE | This family-owned property offers 40-minute tours through a 10-room circa-1805 house furnished in the Old Order Amish style. A map guides you to a waterwheel, lime kiln, as well as a traditional covered bridge. One of the older attractions in the area, it dates to 1955. **■ TIP→ The Neuber family also offers bus tours that include a farm visit.** *2395 Covered Bridge Dr., Lancaster* *717/394–6185* *www.amishfarmandhouse.com* *$9.50 farm and house tour; $22.95 combo farm, house, and 90-min bus tour.*

Restaurants

Good 'N Plenty

$$$$ | **AMERICAN** | **FAMILY** | If you don't mind sharing the table with a dozen or so others, you'll be treated to a family-style meal of hearty regional fare like baked country ham, chowchow (pickled relish), and traditional sweets and sours. More than 650 can be served at a time in this bustling family-style restaurant that's been around since 1969. **Known for:** daily specials; shoofly pie; fried chicken. *Average main: $25* *150 Eastbrook Rd., Smoketown ↔ Rte. 896, ½ mile north of U.S. 30* *717/394–7111* *www.goodnplenty.com* *Closed Jan. and Sun.*

Miller's Smorgasbord

$$$$ | **AMERICAN** | This buffet-style eatery has been a local institution since 1929, offering views of Amish farmland and enough food to satisfy any appetite. The spread here is lavish, with a good selection of Pennsylvania Dutch specialties at the daily smorgasbord. **Known for:** iced raisin bread; chicken corn soup; brown buttered noodles. *Average main: $26* *2811 Lincoln Hwy. E, Ronks ↔ U.S. 30, 2 miles east of Rte. 896* *800/669–3568* *www.millerssmorgasbord.com.*

Smokehouse BBQ and Brews at Plain & Fancy Farm

$$$ | **AMERICAN** | The newest dining option at the expansive Plain & Fancy Farm complex is catering to individual families and groups under 20. The menu is a variation on the traditional Amish theme, featuring various smoked meats, but still with many of the country sides like chowchow and pepper cabbage; the "Smokehouse Sampler," a fixed-price feast, is the heartiest offering. **Known for:** smoked brisket; the "Smokehouse Sampler," a fixed-price feast; a variety of barbecue sauces. *Average main: $22* *3121 Old Philadelphia Pike ↔ Rte. 340, between Bird-in-Hand and Intercourse* *717/768–4400* *www.plainandfancyfarm.com.*

Hotels

AmishView Inn & Suites
$$ | HOTEL | As part of the 10-acre Plain & Fancy Farm complex, this hotel offers exactly what its name implies: views overlooking Amish farmland as far as the eye can see. **Pros:** scenic views from almost every room; adult-only accommodations; indoor pool. **Cons:** no trace of Dutch Country decor in rooms; with many other attractions on property, it can get crowded; food options are not varied. *Rooms from: $174 ✉ 3125 Old Philadelphia Pike, Rte. 340 ☎ 866/735–1600 🌐 www.amishviewinn.com 90 rooms Free breakfast.*

Bird-in-Hand Family Inn
$ | HOTEL | Part of a mini-empire of hotels and Amish country attractions owned by the Smucker family, whose ancestors were Mennonites from Switzerland, this resort-style property has indoor and outdoor pools, and a variety of activities including a petting zoo, minigolf, a pond and walking path, and a family-style smorgasbord restaurant. **Pros:** free tour of Amish farm; two indoor pools, one outdoor pool; tennis and basketball courts. **Cons:** small bathrooms; some rooms need updating; can be crowded. *Rooms from: $118 ✉ 2740 Old Philadelphia Pike, Rte. 340 ☎ 717/768–8271, 800/537–2535 🌐 www.bird-in-hand.com/familyinn 125 rooms No meals.*

Shopping

Bird-in-Hand Farmers Market
FOOD/CANDY | This year-round indoor market has about 30 vendors selling a variety of Amish snacks, baked goods, and preserves, plus crafts and gifts. Fresh produce is in the minority. *✉ 2710 Old Philadelphia Pike ☎ 717/393–9674 🌐 www.birdinhandfarmersmarket.com.*

Kauffman's Fruit Farm & Market
FOOD/CANDY | This fifth-generation family has been growing fruit trees on 100 acres in Lancaster County for more than 100 years. The orchard produces apples, pears, and stone fruits, all of which are seasonally available for purchase in the country market, along with homespun "orchard foods," including cider, "schnitz" (air-dried apples), and a variety of jams and fruit butters. The market stocks a wonderfully quirky mix of fresh produce, an exceptional selection of bulk nuts, Pennsylvania honey and maple syrup, Amish meats, and household items. You won't leave empty-handed. *✉ 3097 Old Philadelphia Pike, Route 340 ☎ 717/768–7112 🌐 www.kauffmansfruitfarm.com/.*

Strasburg

5 miles south of Bird-in-Hand via U.S. 30.

Although settled by French Huguenots, the village of Strasburg is today a community of Pennsylvania Dutch. It's best known as the railroad center of eastern Pennsylvania; railroad buffs can easily spend a day here. You can also visit the Amish Village, which has buildings typical of the area.

Getting Here and Around

Strasburg is about a 15-minute drive from Bird-in-Hand and is a compact destination with many of the railroad exhibits and other attractions located within walking distance or short drive from the center of town.

Sights

Amish Village
MUSEUM VILLAGE | This 12-acre historic homestead offers guided tours of an authentically furnished house and one-room schoolhouse. The property includes a barn, blacksmith shop, smokehouse market, and outdoor picnic grounds when the weather permits. Mini-shuttle-bus tours of the area are also available.

✉ *199 Hartman Bridge Rd., Ronks* ☎ *717/687–8511* 🌐 *www.amishvillage.com* 🎫 *$10 house and village only; $23 Backroads bus tour; $29 combo bus, house, and grounds tour.*

Choo-Choo Barn, Traintown, USA

LOCAL INTEREST | **FAMILY** | What started as a family hobby in 1945 with a single model train chugging around the Groff family Christmas tree is now the Choo-Choo Barn, Traintown, USA. This 1,700-square-foot display of Lancaster County in miniature has 22 trains, mainly in O-gauge, with 150 animated figures, including an authentic Amish barn raising, a huge three-ring circus with animals and acrobats, and a blazing house fire with fire engines rushing to the disaster. Periodically, the overhead lights dim and the scene turns to night, with streetlights and locomotive headlights glowing in the darkness. ✉ *226 Gap Rd* ✣ *Rte. 741 E, near Fairview Rd.* ☎ *717/687–7911, 800/450–2920* 🌐 *www.choochoobarn.com* 🎫 *$8.50* 🕒 *Closed Jan. and Feb.*

National Toy Train Museum

MUSEUM | **FAMILY** | The showplace of the Train Collectors Association, this museum displays both antique and modern toy trains and is a must for toy train buffs. The museum has five huge train operating layouts, with toy trains from the 1800s to the present, plus nostalgic films and hundreds of locomotives and cars in display cases. ✉ *300 Paradise La., north of Rte. 741, Ronks* ☎ *717/687–8976* 🌐 *www.nttmuseum.org* 🎫 *$7.50* 🕒 *Closed Jan.–Mar.*

★ Railroad Museum of Pennsylvania and the Railway Education Center

MUSEUM | **FAMILY** | The first of its kind in North America, this Smithsonian-affiliated museum showcases a world-class collection of 100-plus locomotive and railroad cars made or operated in Pennsylvania. Located across the road from the historic Strasburg Rail Road, the 100,000-square-foot exhibit hall is a treasure trove of photos, artifacts, and memorabilia documenting the history of Pennsylvania railroading. There's an on-site gift shop. ✉ *300 Gap Rd., off Rte. 741, Ronks* ☎ *717/687–8628* 🌐 *www.rrmuseumpa.org* 🎫 *$10* 🕒 *Closed Mon. Nov.–Mar.*

Strasburg Rail Road

TRANSPORTATION SITE (AIRPORT/BUS/FERRY/TRAIN) | **FAMILY** | The Strasburg Rail Road marks more than 175 years of history, and visitors can step back in time to travel the rails on a scenic 45-minute round-trip excursion through Amish farm country from Strasburg to Paradise on a rolling antique chartered in 1832 to carry milk, mail, and coal. Called America's oldest short line, the Strasburg run has wooden coaches pulled by an iron steam locomotive. Eat lunch in the dining car or buy a box lunch in the restaurant at the station and have a picnic at Groff's Grove along the line. Visit the Reading Car No. 10, a restored business car that carried the top brass of the Philadelphia and Reading Railroad back in the early 1900s. Kids are crazy for the Thomas the Tank Engine shop and special events. Trains usually depart hourly. Dinner trains run April to December. ✉ *301 Gap Rd., Ronks* ✣ *Rte. 741, ½ mile east of Strasburg* ☎ *866/725–9666* 🌐 *www.strasburgrailroad.com* 🎫 *$16–$32* 🕒 *Closed Jan.–mid.-Mar.; some fall and winter trains may be canceled in inclement weather so call ahead.*

 Restaurants

★ Speckled Hen

$ | **CAFÉ** | Even on a rainy day, this homespun café always feels sunny. Owned by a young couple that grew up in Lancaster County, the menu showcases their commitment to use as many local ingredients as possible—the eggs are supplied by the family farm, the beef from a small farm about 10 miles away, the honey from an apiary down the road—you get the idea. **Known for:** eggs served multiple ways; lots of vegetarian options; baked oatmeal. 💲 *Average main: $9* ✉ *141 E.*

On the Strasburg Rail Road, visitors can travel on a scenic 45-minute round-trip excursion through Amish farm country from Strasburg to Paradise.

Main St. ☎ *717/288–3139* 🌐 *www.speckledhencoffee.com.*

Hotels

Carriage House at Strasburg

$ | **B&B/INN** | Recently given new life, this locally owned and managed property might entice you to stay awhile, especially for exploring Amish country, as the rooms have been nicely updated and the staff is welcoming. **Pros:** good value; shabby-chic look and feel; no carpet. **Cons:** front desk is not staffed 24/7; some rooms have window units for a/c; no common area or lobby to hang out. *Rooms from: $88* ✉ *144 E. Main St.* ☎ *717/687–7651* 🌐 *www.carriagehousestrasburg.com* *17 rooms* *Free breakfast.*

Clarion Inn Strasburg–Lancaster

$ | **HOTEL** | Located on 16 acres overlooking adjacent farms and woodlands, this hotel offers comfortable, albeit basic, quarters geared toward budget travelers and those traveling with pets. **Pros:** pet friendly; outdoor pool; scenic grounds. **Cons:** some rooms need updating; potential road noise from Rte. 896; lack of period ambience. *Rooms from: $114* ✉ *1400 Historic Dr., off Rte. 896* ☎ *717/687–7691* 🌐 *www.choicehotels.com* *100 rooms* *Free breakfast.*

Limestone Inn Bed and Breakfast

$ | **B&B/INN** | Rick and Denise Waller are the gracious hosts at this 1786 Georgian-style home listed on the National Register of Historic Places. **Pros:** old-world charm; fireplaces or electric heating stoves in rooms; home-style breakfast. **Cons:** no kids under 12; not all rooms have private baths; no TVs in rooms. *Rooms from: $129* ✉ *33 E. Main St.* ☎ *717/687–8392* 🌐 *www.thelimestoneinn.com* *6 rooms* *Free breakfast.*

Lititz

8 miles north of downtown Lancaster via U.S. 222 and Rte. 501.

Lititz was founded in 1756 by Moravian missionaries who settled in Pennsylvania and created their own private community. Lititz's historic character remains, with tree-shaded streets, 18th-century houses, and shops selling antiques, crafts, clothing, and gifts. This is a great town for walking; be sure to see the beautiful Moravian church, which dates back to 1787 and served as a hospital to treat the wounded during the Revolutionary War. In recent years, Lititz has upped its game with curated boutiques, Second Fridays (when the town stays open late), farm-to-table dining, a food hall, and two upscale hotels.

Getting Here and Around

Park the car and explore the town by foot; there are two major streets—Broad Street and Main Street.

Sights

Julius Sturgis Pretzel Bakery
STORE/MALL | **FAMILY** | In 1861, pretzel man Julius Sturgis opened the country's first pretzel bakery. These days, the original site, a stone house on the National Register of Historic Places, operates guided tours and a hands-on lesson in pretzel twisting. An on-site bakeshop has souvenirs and fresh pretzels. ✉ *219 E. Main St., Rte. 772* ☎ *717/626–4354* 🌐 *www.juliussturgis.com* 🎟 *$3.75* ⏲ *Closed 1st 2 wks of Jan.*

★ Lititz Farmers Market
MARKET | This seasonal outdoor farmers' market sets up shop in the center of town at historic Lititz Springs Park. Featuring small local growers, producers, and local restaurants with prepared food, the weekly market takes place on Thursday, starting at 4:30 pm, from May to October. It's a lovely way to end the day, especially when there's live music. ✉ *24 N. Broad St.* ☎ *717/626–6332* 🌐 *lititzfarmersmarket.com* ⏲ *Closed Nov.–Apr.*

Wilbur Chocolate Store
STORE/MALL | **FAMILY** | This is the new location for the locally beloved Wilbur Chocolate's retail store and museum, which moved across the street after its factory closed in early 2016. The shop carries an array of Wilbur confections, from the famous Wilbur Buds to chocolate-covered pretzels and tins of drinking cocoa. There is candy-related memorabilia displayed throughout, along with a collection of antique chocolate-drinking pots. Be sure to go to the back of the shop for a free Wilbur Bud sample. ✉ *45 N. Broad St.* ☎ *888/294–5287* 🌐 *www.wilburbuds.com* ⏲ *Closed Sun.*

Restaurants

★ Rooster Street Butcher
$$ | **MODERN AMERICAN** | This butcher shop turned restaurant and taproom focuses on pastured-raised meat from local farms, but there are also salads, sandwiches, and a good number of dishes designed for vegetarians. Diners order at the counter and find a seat, while the bar, where drinks are ordered separately, features Pennsylvania-only wine, beer, and spirits. **Known for:** steak frites; the all-pork bacon burger (not a beef burger with bacon on top); nightly specials. [$] *Average main: $15* ✉ *11 S Cedar St.* ☎ *717/625–0405* 🌐 *www.roosterst.com.*

Slate Cafe
$ | **CAFÉ** | Located in the heart of Lititz, this local fave is the perfect spot for fueling up on locally roasted coffee or grabbing something quick to nosh on. The kitchen serves up a variety of breakfast options, from baked oatmeal to an open-face egg sandwich on ciabatta, while lunch options include quesadillas, salads,

and soups. **Known for:** local kombucha and smoothies; many kids' choices; lots of variations on the egg sandwich. *Average main: $8* *43 E. Main St.* *717/568–2288* *www.slatelititz.com.*

Coffee and Quick Bites

Market at the Wilbur

$ | **CAFÉ** | This small food hall features six local businesses, making it the perfect spot to pop in for a coffee and a sandwich to go. The lineup includes Whiff coffee roaster; Rooster St. Butcher, for sandwiches and salads to order; Zig's bakery; Oola Bowls, serving acai bowls; Presto Pasteria for made-to-order pasta bowls; and a tasting room from Manheim-based Waltz Vineyards estate winery. **Known for:** indoor and outdoor seating; features local businesses; great take away options. *Average main: $5* *The Wilbur Lititz, 50 N. Broad St.* *www.facebook.com/marketatthewilbur/.*

Hotels

General Sutter Inn

$$ | **B&B/INN** | Located on the main square of Lititz, this three-story 1764 inn offers a mix of Victorian and modern decor. **Pros:** breakfast included; central location; beautiful Victorian-style lobby with fireplace. **Cons:** kitchenette for suites on third floor is shared; some rooms have sink in bedroom, not in bath; no elevator. *Rooms from: $150* *14 E. Main St., corner of Rtes. 501 and 772* *717/626–2115* *www.atthesutter.com* *17 rooms* *Free breakfast.*

★ **Hotel Rock Lititz**

$$ | **HOTEL** | Located at Rock Lititz, a unique 96-acre campus that caters to live-entertainment productions for big-name musical artists, this hotel is where many crews (and celebs) stay incognito while they rehearse before going on tour. **Pros:** unique design aesthetic; indoor pool; garment steamers in all rooms. **Cons:** other than fire-pit area, little outdoor lounging space; not walking distance to downtown Lititz; most rooms do not have tubs. *Rooms from: $159* *50 Rock Lititz Blvd.* *717/925–7625* *www.hotelrocklititz.com* *139 rooms* *Free breakfast.*

Swiss Woods

$$ | **B&B/INN** | Set on 35 acres about 5 miles north of downtown Lititz, this European-style B&B—with its light pine furnishings and contemporary country decor—has been a passion project for innkeepers Werner and Debrah Mosimann, who lived in Switzerland before moving to central Pennsylvania. **Pros:** bucolic, peaceful setting; delicious breakfast; great hospitality. **Cons:** small guest rooms; no restaurants within walking distance; young children are only welcome in the loft-style family suite, not the guest rooms within the main house. *Rooms from: $189* *500 Blantz Rd.* *717/627–3358* *www.swisswoods.com* *7 rooms* *Free breakfast.*

★ **The Wilbur Lititz, Tapestry Collection by Hilton**

$ | **HOTEL** | The former Wilbur Chocolate factory is now a beautifully repurposed boutique hotel property operated by the Hilton's Tapestry Collection. **Pros:** walking distance to everything in town; spacious and comfortable lobby-level lounge area; gym-quality fitness room. **Cons:** $10 self-parking; minimal outdoor space; no pool. *Rooms from: $147* *50 N. Broad St.* *717/625–1300* *www.hilton.com/en/tapestry* *74 rooms* *No meals.*

Ephrata

22 miles north of Strasburg via U.S. 222, 15 miles northeast of Lancaster via U.S. 222.

This is a classic American town, with a wide Main Street, a variety of shops selling locally made crafts, and an entertaining farmers' market. Except for the Ephrata Cloister, there's little to remind

This cemetery is located on the grounds of one of America's early religious communities, the Ephrata Cloister, which was founded in 1732 by a German immigrant.

you of the town's austere beginning as a religious commune.

Sights

★ Ephrata Cloister

RELIGIOUS SITE | A former and singular monastic community, Ephrata Cloister was founded in 1732 by German immigrant Conrad Beissel. Originally set on 250 acres of Native American wilderness, Beissel and his believers built 30 structures, including a monastery and a printing press and named their community "Ephrata." The monastic society of brothers and sisters were celibate and lived an austere life of work, study, and prayer. In the 1940s, the Commonwealth of Pennsylvania took over the property and has been running it as a museum, with 45-minute tours of three restored buildings, after which you can browse through several others, including the stable, printshop, and crafts shop. Self-guided cell-phone tours are also available. ✉ *632 W. Main St.* ✥ *Rtes. 272 and 322* ☎ *717/733–6600* 🌐 *www.ephratacloister.org* 🎫 *$10.*

Green Dragon Farmers Market and Auction

MARKET | This giant indoor-outdoor market, only open on Friday, is an oddball mashup of Amish snack bars, smoked meat and preserve purveyors, a small animal auction, bric-a-brac, tools, toys, and everything in between, including the kitchen sink. As the website states, there's a "carnival atmosphere" that is like no other. ✉ *955 N. State St., off Rte. 272* ☎ *717/738–1117* 🌐 *www.greendragonmarket.com* ⏲ *Closed Sat.–Thurs.*

Restaurants

Aromas del Sur

$$ | **SOUTH AMERICAN** | Colombian home cooking is on point in this welcoming café-style dining room, where the Buitrago family prepares and serves your meal. Don't worry if you're a first-timer, as the family goes to great lengths to describe the many classic dishes of their homeland on offer, from *lomo salteado* (a sirloin stir-fry) to *pollo a la plancha* (grilled chicken breast); tropical juices are also available, from passion fruit to soursop. **Known for:** empanadas; Colombian chorizo; lengua (cow's tongue). *Average main: $16* *548 S. State St.* *717/738–0101* *www.aromasdelsur.co* *Closed Mon. and Tues.*

Three Sisters Park

$ | **THAI** | Located along the main strip of Ephrata, this unassuming little space serves up a variety of Thai-Cambodian dishes. Grab a seat at the diner-style banquettes or small tables, and prepare yourself for the heat levels of the various curries and rice-noodle dishes, which are not dumbed down for Western palates; there is pad Thai on the menu for those seeking something familiar. **Known for:** panang curry; lunch specials; spicy grilled pork skewers. *Average main: $12* *119 East Main St.* *717/733–2386* *3sisterspark.com* *Closed Sun.*

Coffee and Quick Bites

Laura the Cookie Lady

$ | **BAKERY** | Laura Merkel is a self-taught baker who owns and operates this storefront cookie shop along the main strip of Ephrata. Known for her fanciful decorated cookies, Merkel has become a local celebrity after winning the "Christmas Cookie Challenge" on Food Network. **Known for:** Food Network Cookie Challenge winner; drop cookies like chocolate chip and molasses spice; cookie decorating classes. *Average main: $3* *30 E. Main St.* *717/466–6600* *www.lauracookielady.com* *Closed Sun.–Wed.*

Hotels

★ Historic Smithton Inn

$$ | **B&B/INN** | Hand-sewn quilts coexist comfortably with iPod docking stations and electric vehicle chargers at this B&B, a former tavern built in 1763. **Pros:** authentic period decor; electric vehicle chargers; wine bar on site. **Cons:** location is near busy intersection; no elevator to access second floor; children under 12 limited to the Taylor Cottage. *Rooms from: $159* *900 W. Main St., at Academy Dr.* *717/733–6094* *www.historicsmithtoninn.com* *8 rooms* *Free breakfast.*

Shopping

CRAFTS

Ten Thousand Villages

CRAFTS | Ten Thousand Villages is a network of fair-trade craft shops operated by the Mennonite Central Committee. Its store in Ephrata is the largest in North America, boasting an inventory of jewelry, textiles, clothing, and toys that benefit communities in developing countries. The Bunyaad Rug Room has an exceptional collection of hand-knotted rugs crafted by artisans who have been fairly paid. *240 N. Reading Rd.* *Rte. 272, north of Ephrata Cloister* *717/721–8400* *www.tenthousandvillages.com/ephrata.*

Adamstown

21 miles northeast of Lancaster via Rte. 222 and Rte. 272.

Known as the "Antiques Capital USA," Adamstown has dozens of shops, galleries, and markets selling goods from bygone eras. The bigger markets, such as Renninger's Antique Market and Stoudt's Black Angus Antiques Mall, have aisles and aisles of collectibles, including furniture, toys, jewelry, crystal, china, glassware, linens, and coins. For outdoor antiquing, there's nothing like Shupp's Grove, with acres of shady woods filled with an array of antiques and collectibles. There are many other smaller markets and galleries as well.

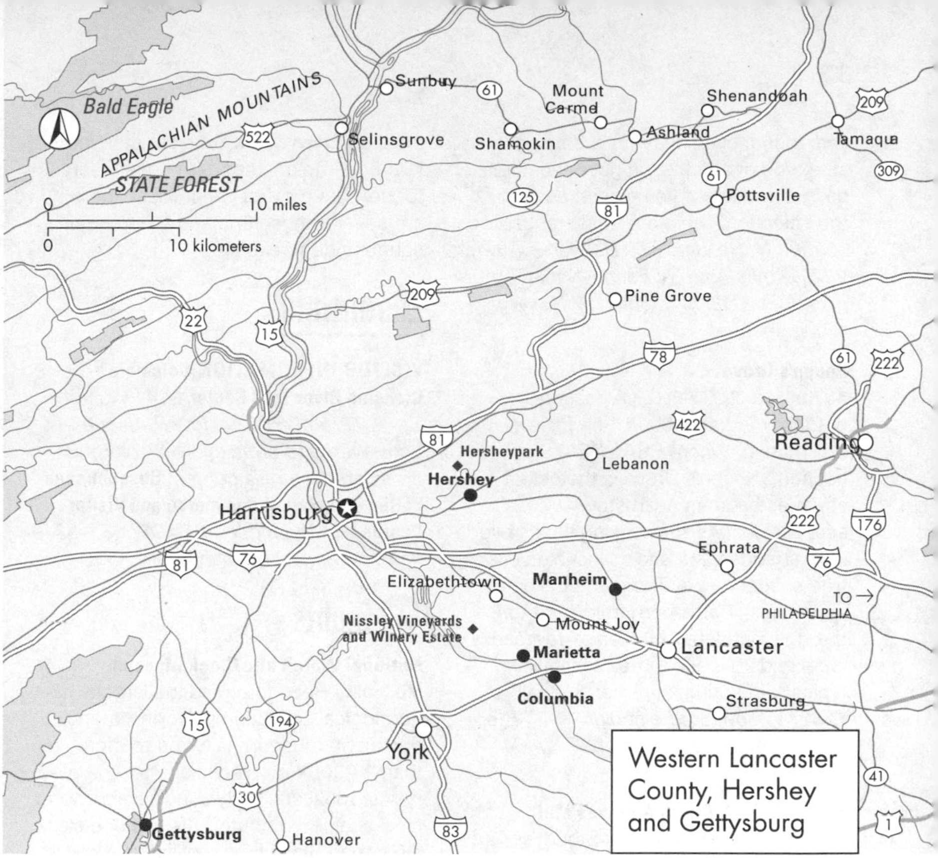

Western Lancaster County, Hershey and Gettysburg

Getting Here and Around

There's no real downtown in this small community, so you'll have to navigate the various markets and shopping areas by car.

Restaurants

Stoudt's Brewing Company

$$$ | STEAKHOUSE | Stoudt's Brewing Company is one of the pioneers of Pennsylvania's microbrewery scene, but this 50-year-old Victorian-style restaurant has stood twice as long. Founded by Carol Stoudt, the country's first female brewmaster, there are a selection of Stoudt's beers on tap, and the menu features Angus beef steaks and traditional favorites like schnitzel as well as an extensive menu of burgers and sandwiches; the bread and cheese plate features house-made goodies like artisanal bread and farmstead cheese that are also available at the adjacent Wonderful Good Market. **Known for:** house-made cheese plate; German-style soft pretzel with house-made beer mustard; smoked beef brisket grilled cheese. *$ Average main: $22 ✉ 2800 N. Reading Rd. ☎ 717/484-4386 🌐 www.stoudts.com ⏲ Closed Tues.*

Shopping

ANTIQUES

Renninger's Antique and Collector's Market

ANTIQUES/COLLECTIBLES | The huge Renninger's Antique and Collector's Market draws thousands of collectors and dealers on Sundays from 7:30 to 4 (5 am to 3 pm for outside vendors, weather permitting). Nearly 400 indoor stalls, open year-round, overflow with every conceivable type of antique; on good-weather days, the outdoor flea market adds to the selection. There are food stands, too ✉ *2500 N. Reading Rd., Denver* ✣ *Rte. 272, ½ mile north of Pennsylvania Turnpike, Exit 21* ☎ *717/336–2177* 🌐 *www.renningers.net.*

Shupp's Grove

ANTIQUES/COLLECTIBLES | A seasonal outdoor market dubbed "the Picker's market, where REAL DEALS still happen," Shupp's Grove is the oldest antiques haunt in Adamstown with acres of dealers showcasing tables piled with antiques, art, and collectibles in a tree-shaded grove. The market is open weekends, 7 am–4 pm from mid-April through October. Antiques extravaganza weekends happen three times a year, typically in spring, summer, and fall. ✉ *607 Willow St., Reinholds* ✣ *Off Rte. 897, south of Adamstown* ☎ *717/484–4115* 🌐 *www.shuppsgrove.com.*

Stoudt's Black Angus Antiques Mall

ANTIQUES/COLLECTIBLES | At Stoudt's Black Angus Antiques Mall, more than 300 dealers display old books and prints, estate jewelry, linens, china and glassware, coins, and plenty of furniture, inside and outside. The Stoudt's Brewing Company and Wonderful Good Market, featuring artisanal bread and cheese, are on the same site. Antiques Extravaganza Weekends occur in the spring, summer, and fall. Contact the property for details. ✉ *2800 N. Reading Rd.* ☎ *717/484–4386* 🌐 *stoudts.com/.*

Columbia

10 miles west of Lancaster via Rte. 462.

They're quiet towns now, but Columbia and other river communities were bustling in the days when boats were one of the easiest methods of transporting goods. Eighteenth-century Quaker missionary John Wright worked in this area, and two of his sons set up a ferry that became an important destination for settlers moving west. Today there are several museums and the tranquil countryside to explore.

Essentials

VISITOR INFORMATION Columbia Crossing River Trail Center. ✉ *41 Walnut St.* ☎ *717/449-5607* 🌐 *www.susquehannaheritage.org/explore-2/columbia-crossing-river-trails-center/.* **Susquehanna Valley Chamber of Commerce and Visitor Center.** ✉ *445 Linden St.* ☎ *717/684–5249* 🌐 *www.visitsusquehannavalley.com.*

Sights

National Watch and Clock Museum

MUSEUM | Recognized as the largest horological collection in North America, this niche museum is home to more than 12,000 timepieces and time-related items. You'll see early sundials and water clocks; a 19th-century Tiffany globe clock; a German Black Forest organ clock with 94 pipes; moon-phase wristwatches; and other timekeeping devices from around the world. ✉ *514 Poplar St.* ☎ *717/684–8261* 🌐 *www.nawcc.org/index.php/museum* 🎫 *$9* 🕒 *Closed Sun.–Tues. Dec.–Mar.; closed Mon. Apr.–Nov.*

Turkey Hill Experience

MUSEUM | FAMILY | Lancaster-based Turkey Hill Dairy, best known for its ice cream, is behind this indoor interactive exhibit with hands-on learning about dairy culture. Located in a restored mill, kids can milk a mechanical cow, climb aboard a vintage milk delivery truck, or even concoct a flavor, design its packaging, and shoot a commercial. Grown-ups may find the facts and figures about dairy farming and the family-owned Turkey Hill company interesting, but mostly this one is for the kids. **■ TIP → Reservations are required for the Taste Lab—the make-your-own-ice-cream portion of the experience.** ✉ *301*

Linden St. ↔ Off U.S. 30 ☎ 844/847–4884 🌐 www.turkeyhillexperience.com 🎫 $10.50 experience; $5.95 taste lab.

Wright's Ferry Mansion

HOUSE | Located just a few blocks from the waterfront, Wright's Ferry Mansion was the residence of English Quaker Susanna Wright, a silkworm breeder and intellectual who counted Benjamin Franklin among her friends. The 1738 stone house showcases period furniture in the William & Mary and Queen Anne styles as well as an extensive collection of English needlework, textiles, ceramics, and glass, all predating 1750. ✉ *38 S. 2nd St., 2nd and Cherry Sts.* ☎ *717/684–4325* 🌐 *www.lancastercountymuseums.org/wrights-ferry-mansion* 🎫 *$5* ⏲ *Closed Nov.–Apr.; closed Mon., Thurs., and Sun. May–Oct.*

Restaurants

John Wright Restaurant

$$$ | **AMERICAN** | At this waterfront spot in historic Wrightstown, you can enjoy a breathtaking view of the Susquehanna River while seated at the outdoor bar, eating wood-fired pizzas topped with ingredients grown on site. Directly across the river on the original ferry route from Columbia, this popular bar and restaurant also has a glass-walled dining room to enjoy the scenery year-round. **Known for:** seasonal pizza patio; farm-to-table focus; braised boar and gnocchi. 💲 *Average main: $23* ✉ *234 N. Front St.* ☎ *717/252–0416* 🌐 *www.jwrpa.com.*

Shopping

Burning Bridge Antiques Market

ANTIQUES/COLLECTIBLES | Three floors of antiques and collectibles are crammed into this former hardware store and sewing factory from the 1800s. With more than 200 booths to rummage through, Burning Bridge is a treasure trove of Americana, furniture, and artifacts great and small. ✉ *304 Walnut St.* ↔ *3 blocks south of U.S. 30* ☎ *717/684–7900* 🌐 *www.burningbridgeantiques.com.*

Marietta

5 miles northwest of Columbia via Rte. 441.

Almost half of the buildings in Marietta are listed on the National Register of Historic Places; the architecture ranges from rustic log cabins to elegant Federal and Victorian homes. This restored river town, now seeing new life as an artists' community, is perfect for a stroll past the well-preserved facades of art galleries and antiques shops.

Sights

Nissley Vineyards and Winery Estate

WINERY/DISTILLERY | Set on 300 acres in western Lancaster county, this family-owned winery grows 14 varieties of grapes and produces award-winning vintages. There are tours, tastings, and a shop with bottles for sale. You can picnic on the grounds, and in the summer there's a popular open-air concert series on the lawn. ✉ *140 Vintage Dr., Bainbridge* ↔ *7 miles northwest of Marietta, 1½ miles off Rte. 441* ☎ *717/426–3514, 800/522–2387* 🌐 *www.nissleywine.com* 🎫 *Free; $16 for concerts.*

Hotels

Olde Fogie Farm Bed and Breakfast

$ | **B&B/INN** | **FAMILY** | At this working farm, guests are awakened to the sound of a bell for "earning your keep" morning chores, which can include milking the goats and bottle-feeding the calves. **Pros:** welcoming hosts; great for children; seniors get 10% discount on stays September–March. **Cons:** no online booking or email contact info; credit cards accepted, but cash or check preferred; early hours of a working farm. 💲 *Rooms from: $110* ✉ *106 Stackstown Rd.* ☎ *717/426–3992,*

877/653–3644 ⊕ www.oldefogiefarm.com ⇨ 2 rooms, 2 apartments ⟠ Free breakfast.

Shopping

George's Furniture

CRAFTS | This family-owned business sells handcrafted, made-to-order furniture for every room in the house in walnut, oak, maple, and cherry. You can schedule a tour of the wood shop and then place an order. ✉ *9 Reichs Church Rd.* ☎ *800/799–1685* ⊕ *www.georgesfurniturepa.com.*

Manheim

10 miles west of Lititz via Rte. 772.

Baron Henry William Stiegel founded the small town of Manheim and manufactured Stiegel glassware here in the 18th century. Today the major draws are a winery and a renaissance fair a few miles north of town.

Sights

Pennsylvania Renaissance Faire

FESTIVAL | The seasonal Pennsylvania Renaissance Faire, on the grounds of the Mount Hope Estate and Winery, transforms the winery into an extensive 16th-century English village ruled by Her Majesty Queen Elizabeth I. The lively action includes street performers, human chess matches, jousting and fencing tournaments, knighthood ceremonies, street performances, craft demonstrations, battling pirates, jesters, medieval food, and Shakespearean plays performed on outdoor stages. Fun for all ages, but definitely more *A Kid in King Arthur's Court* than *Game of Thrones.* ✉ *2775 Lebanon Rd.* ☎ *717/665–7021* ⊕ *www.parenfaire.com* 🎟 *$33.95* ⏲ *Closed Nov.–July and weekdays Aug.–Oct.*

Waltz Vineyards

WINERY/DISTILLERY | To say that Pennsylvania wineries don't enjoy the greatest reputation would be an understatement. Jan and Kimberly Waltz coined the slogan "the wines that will change your mind," and there's actually a good chance they will. They offer local cheese and chocolate in the tasting room, but the refreshing Sauvignon Blanc or jammy Merlot stand on their own. ✉ *1599 Old Line Rd.* ☎ *717/664–9463* ⊕ *www.waltzvineyards.com/* 🎟 *$12 per person for a flight of 5 wines* ⏲ *Closed Sun.*

Restaurants

The Cat's Meow

$$$ | **AMERICAN** | In a restored 1869 railroad hotel, this eatery has the atmosphere of a speakeasy from the Roaring '20s with newspapers from the era and gangster portraits adding to the period flavor. Entrées include broiled crab cakes, seafood pasta, and tenderloin tips on toast, a Lancaster County tavern favorite that dates to Prohibition, as well as items with some cutesy, Prohibition-era names like machine gun linguine and a flapper salad. **Known for:** speakeasy vibe; huge menu with lots of options; tenderloin tips on toast. $ *Average main: $20* ✉ *215 S. Charlotte St.* ☎ *717/664–3370* ⊕ *www.thecatsmeowmanheim.com.*

Hershey

30 miles northwest of Lancaster.

Hershey is Chocolate Town, a community built around a chocolate factory and now home to Hersheypark, the Hershey Museum, and other diversions for children and adults.

Founded in 1903 by confectioner Milton S. Hershey, a Mennonite descendant, it celebrates chocolate without guilt, from streetlights shaped like foil-wrapped candies to avenues named Chocolate and Cocoa. Hershey is also known as a fine golf center.

Getting Here and Around

From Philadelphia, take I–76, the Pennsylvania Turnpike, west to the Lebanon-Lancaster exit, Exit 266. Proceed north on Route 72 to U.S. 322 to Hershey. Once there, you will need your car for some attractions. If you're staying at the Hotel Hershey or Hershey Lodge, a free shuttle bus is available to take you to Hersheypark.

Hershey Gardens

GARDEN | FAMILY | Hershey Gardens opened with a single 3½-acre plot of rosebushes at Milton Hershey's request and over eight decades has grown to include 11 theme gardens on 23 landscaped acres. Home to more than 3,000 roses and 28,000 tulips, the gardens come to life in spring as thousands of bulbs burst into bloom. Flowering displays last until fall, when late roses open. The year-round butterfly atrium hosts hundreds of pollinators from around the world. A gift shop is on site. ✉ *170 Hotel Rd.* ✥ *Across from the Hotel Hershey* ☎ *717/534–3492* 🌐 *www.hersheygardens.org* 🎟 *$13.50.*

The Hershey Story, The Museum on Chocolate Avenue

MUSEUM | FAMILY | Formerly known as the Hershey Museum, the Hershey Story is a multimedia experience that features the life and work of Milton S. Hershey, who founded the town bearing his name and just about everything in it. On display is a working Hershey Kiss wrapping machine plus other memorabilia from the company's long history. A highlight is the Chocolate Lab, which offers hands-on workshops. The Pantry Cafe offers light fare, snacks, desserts, and flights of hot chocolates from around the world. ✉ *63 W. Chocolate Ave.* ☎ *717/534–3439* 🌐 *www.hersheystory.org* 🎟 *$13.50 for museum only; $22 for museum and chocolate lab class.*

Hersheypark

AMUSEMENT PARK/WATER PARK | FAMILY | Billed as the "Sweetest Place on Earth," Hersheypark offers more than 65 rides and attractions, a boardwalk with a lazy river and wave pool, a wildlife park called ZooAmerica with hundreds of animals, as well as tons of live-entertainment options. Founded in 1907 as a town park for chocolate factory workers, Hersheypark, set on more than 100 acres, is prized as one of America's cleanest and greenest theme parks. Among its historical rides are the Comet, a 1946-vintage wooden roller coaster, and a carousel built in 1919 that has 66 hand-carved wooden horses. "Chocolatetown" is the latest park expansion that includes Candymonium, its tallest and longest roller coaster to date, a virtual-reality experience, a Hershey merch flagship store, and a full-service restaurant. ✉ *100 W. Hersheypark Dr., Rte. 743 and U.S. 422* ☎ *717/534–3900* 🌐 *www.hersheypark.com* 🎟 *One-day tickets $30.95* ⏲ *Closed Jan.–Mar.*

Hershey's Chocolate World

TOUR—SIGHT | FAMILY | This is a one-stop shop for exploring the history of chocolate and how it's made. The attractions are many, including a free 30-minute amusement-style ride with an overview of the steps for producing chocolate; a 4-D movie (separate admission); *Unwrapped,* an interactive theatrical performance (separate admission); and Create Your Own Candy Bar (additional fee). It's also the starting point for Hershey Trolley Works, which offers historical tours of the town and landmarks relevant to Milton Hershey. There's also an extensive chocolate-themed food court (think milk shakes and s'mores). ✉ *251 Park Blvd., 101 Chocolate World Way* ☎ *800/468–1714* 🌐 *www.hersheys.*

Hersheypark offers more than 65 rides and attractions, a boardwalk with a lazy river and wave pool, a wildlife park, and tons of live-entertainment.

com/chocolateworld 🎫 *Prices vary, check website; discount ticket bundles available* ⏲ *Hrs vary on weekends and holidays, check website.*

Restaurants

Hershey Pantry

$$$ | AMERICAN | FAMILY | This family-friendly restaurant is a beloved favorite among locals for its hearty breakfast lineup. Portions are generous, the menus are huge, and the food is unpretentious in a good-ole-diner sort of way. **Known for:** hearty breakfast; afternoon tea service; huge selection of in-house desserts. 💲 *Average main: $20* ✉ *801 E. Chocolate Ave.* ☎ *717/533–7505* 🌐 *www.hersheypantry.com* ⏲ *Closed Sun.*

Hotels

Hershey Lodge and Convention Center

$$ | RESORT | FAMILY | This bustling and sprawling resort caters to families as well as business and convention travelers. **Pros:** several dining options; free admission to Hershey Gardens and the Hershey Story; indoor pool with waterslides and games. **Cons:** ordinary guest rooms; sprawling layout not ideal for families with young children; leisure travelers may experience crowds during large conventions. 💲 *Rooms from: $159* ✉ *325 University Dr.* ☎ *717/533–3311, 800/437–7439* 🌐 *www.hersheylodge.com* 🛏 *683 rooms* 🍽 *No meals.*

★ Hotel Hershey

$$$$ | RESORT | This grand Mediterranean villa–style hotel is a sophisticated resort with plenty of options for recreation, starting with the golf course that wraps around the hotel, a pool complex, a ropes course and nature trails, as well as a falconry course and Segway tours. **Pros:** gourmet dining; indoor and outdoor swimming pools and lush grounds; full-service spa. **Cons:** some guest rooms are small; cancellations within 10 days of arrival date result in forfeit of first night's deposit; spa can be crowded.

Rooms from: $259 ✉ 100 Hotel Rd. ☎ 717/533–2171, 800/437–7439 🌐 www.thehotelhershey.com 276 rooms, 48 cottages No meals.

Shopping

Crossroads Antique Mall

ANTIQUES/COLLECTIBLES | For a break from chocolate adventures, there are antiques and collectibles to forage. Housed in a unique round-roofed parabolic barn, this antiques mall has two floors filled with goods from dozens of dealers. *✉ 825 Cocoa Ave., Rtes 743 and 322 ☎ 717/520–1600 🌐 www.crossroadsantiques.com.*

Activities

Hershey Country Club

GOLF | The Hershey Country Club maintains two private 18-hole courses, which are available exclusively to guests of the Hotel Hershey. The scenic East Course winds around three lakes and over 100 bunkers. The West Course has views of the town and a hole on the front lawn of Milton Hersey's estate. *✉ 1000 E. Derry Rd. ☎ 717/533–2464 🌐 www.hersheycountryclub.com West Course $170 including cart. East Course $1400 including cart; no caddies East Course: 18 holes, 7061 yards, par 71; West Course: 18 holes, 6860 yards, par 73.*

Spring Creek Golf

GOLF | A 9-hole course open to the public, Spring Creek is owned and operated by the Hershey Country Club. Designed in 1932, it is the country's first public golf course for youth. *✉ 450 E. Chocolate Ave. ☎ 717/533–2360 🌐 www.hersheycountryclub.com/golf/spring-creek $13–$15 walking, $9 extra for cart 9 holes, 2200 yards, par 33.*

Gettysburg

53 miles west of Lancaster on U.S. 30.

"The world will little note, nor long remember, what we say here, but it can never forget what they did here." These words from Abraham Lincoln's famous address were delivered in Gettysburg to mark the dedication of its national cemetery in November 1863. Four months earlier, from July 1 to 3, 51,000 Americans were killed, wounded, or counted as missing in the bloodiest battle of the Civil War. The events that took place in Gettysburg during those few days marked the turning point in the war. Although the struggle raged on for almost two more years, the Confederate forces never recovered from their losses.

Getting Here and Around

The most direct route from Philadelphia to Gettysburg from Lancaster is to take I–76, the Pennsylvania Turnpike, west to U.S. 15 South to U.S. 30, which takes you into downtown. From Lancaster, take Route 462 West to U.S. 30. Once in Gettysburg, you can park your car in town and walk to restaurants, shops, and some attractions, including the David Wills House and the Shriver House. But you will need to use your car to access the battlefield and visitor center.

Planning Your Time

The state-of-the-art visitor's center at the Gettysburg National Military Park is an essential stop to fully comprehend the significance of the battlefield and its impact on the outcome of the Civil War. Plan on spending at least three to four hours at the museum; the admission includes a documentary film and the "Battle of Gettysburg" cyclorama painting. Families with younger children who are concerned about short attention spans may wish to spend less time at the museum and opt instead for a free ranger talk. Rather than attempting to drive around the sprawling battlefield, you're better off hiring a certified guide for a two-hour tour. The guide not only will explain the events in compelling detail, but also drive your vehicle, so you don't have to worry about navigating the sprawling battlefield.

Essentials

VISITOR INFORMATION Destination Gettysburg. ✉ *571 W. Middle St.* ☎ *717/334–6274* 🌐 *www.destinationgettysburg.com.*

 Sights

David Wills House

HOUSE | The David Wills House is where Abraham Lincoln stayed and completed his Gettysburg Address on November 18, 1863. The restored building features seven galleries, including the bedroom where Lincoln slept and worked on the final versions of his speech, as well as the office of Wills, a prominent lawyer who helped direct the city's cleanup after the battle and was a leading force behind the creation of the national cemetery. ✉ *8 Lincoln Sq.* ☎ *717/334–2499, 866/874–2478* 🌐 *www.nps.gov/gett/planyourvisit/david-wills-house.htm* 🎫 *$7* 🕒 *Closed Jan.–mid-Feb.; Tues. in Mar., Apr., Sept., and Oct.; weekdays in Nov. and Dec.*

Eisenhower National Historic Site

HOUSE | The country-estate residence of President Dwight D. Eisenhower, who bought it in 1950, he and First Lady Mamie Eisenhower used it as a weekend retreat and a meeting place for world leaders. From 1961 until the president's death in 1969, it was the couple's full-time residence. The brick-and-stone farmhouse is preserved in 1950s style. The farm adjoins the battlefield and is administered by the National Park Service, which sells daily ticketed tours by way of shuttle bus on a first-come, first-served basis at the Gettysburg National Military Park Visitor Center. ✉ *250 Eisenhower Rd.* ☎ *717/338–9114* 🌐 *www.nps.gov/eise* 🎫 *$9.*

Gettysburg Battlefield Tours

TOUR—SIGHT | The Gettysburg Tour Center is the departure point for two-hour narrated tours of the battlefield. Dramatized audio guides are provided for open-air double-decker bus tours, while guided tours on enclosed buses depart more frequently. At night, costumed guides offer a ghost-themed walking tour. ✉ *778 Baltimore St.* ☎ *877/680–8687* 🌐 *www.gettysburgbattlefieldtours.com* 🎫 *$35.*

Gettysburg Heritage Center

MUSEUM | Renovated in recent years, the Gettysburg Heritage Center presents the story of the Civil War era and the Battle of Gettysburg through artifacts, a 20-minute film, 3-D programs, and interactive exhibits that include an educational scavenger hunt. There are several ways to tour the battlefield, including Victorian carriage, horseback, electric bike, and 90-minute walking tours (prices vary). Complimentary living-history camps that demonstrate what life was like for the Civil War soldiers are offered most weekends from May to November. ✉ *297 Steinwehr Ave.* ☎ *717/334–6245* 🌐 *www.gettysburgmuseum.com* 🎫 *$9* 🕒 *Closed weekdays Jan.–mid-Mar.*

Gettysburg National Military Park

NATIONAL/STATE PARK | There are few landmarks as touching as the Gettysburg National Military Park, where General Robert E. Lee and his Confederate troops encountered the Union forces of General George Meade. There are more than 1,300 markers and monuments honoring the casualties of the battle in the 6,000-acre park. More than 30 miles of marked roads lead through the park, highlighting key battle sites. In the first week of July, Civil War reenactors dress in period uniforms and costumes to commemorate the three-day battle. ■**TIP→ Self-guided tours as well as tour guides for hire are both available, as are tours on horseback.** *1195 Baltimore Pike 717/334–1124 www.nps.gov/gett Free.*

★ Gettysburg National Military Park Museum and Visitor Center
INFO CENTER | The museum and visitor center is an excellent starting point to understand the events leading up to the battle, its significance to the Civil War, and its impact on Gettysburg the town. The center includes a dozen interactive galleries, which feature a compelling mix of artifacts such as a wooden desk believed to have been used by General Robert E. Lee, paired with the latest in interactive video and audio displays. Each section takes its name from a phrase used in Lincoln's Gettysburg Address. It is also home to the 377-foot **"Battle of Gettysburg" cyclorama painting** from 1884, which has been completely restored including a 3-D foreground. The painting, a must-see in its colorful, lifelike depiction of Pickett's Charge, along with a documentary film, "A New Birth of Freedom," are packaged together as a 45-minute ticketed experience. There is a restaurant and a bookstore on-site. The National Park Service has a information desk with everything from battlefield walking tours to schedules of free ranger-conducted programs. Private, licensed guides may also be hired at the center. *1195 Baltimore Pike 717/334–2436, 877/874–2478 www.gettysburgfoundation.org $15 for museum, film, cyclorama; $9 for museum only; $75 for 2-hr guided auto tour for 1 to 6 people.*

Lincoln Train Museum
MUSEUM | The Lincoln Train Museum re-creates Abraham Lincoln's journey from Washington to Gettysburg in November 1863. A 12-minute ride simulates the sights and sounds and features actors portraying the reporters and officials on the train. You can also see the 1890 caboose, model train display, and military rail collection. *425 Steinwehr Ave. 717/334–5678 lincolntrain.com $8.50 Closed Mon.–Thurs. Dec.–Mar.*

Shriver House
HOUSE | The Shriver House was the home of George and Henrietta Shriver and their two children, and reveals what civilian life was like during the Civil War. After George joined the Union troops and his family fled to safety, the home was taken over by Confederate sharpshooters, two of whom were killed in the attic during the battle. Costumed guides give tours and share fascinating tales. A gift shop is on site. *309 Baltimore St. 717/337–2800 www.shriverhouse.org $9.50 Closed Jan. and Feb., except for President's weekend.*

Soldiers' National Cemetery
CEMETERY | Also known as Gettysburg National Cemetery, this is the final resting place for more than 3,500 Union soldiers who died on the battlefield. Dedicated by President Abraham Lincoln in his Gettysburg Address, the cemetery is where some 3,000 veterans of subsequent conflicts were also laid to rest. *Gettysburg ✥ Off Baltimore Pike, about a 15-min walk from visitor center www.nps.gov/nr/travel/national_cemeteries/pennsylvania/gettysburg_national_cemetery.html Free.*

Restaurants

Springhouse Tavern
$$ | AMERICAN | Built in 1776, the tavern is the oldest building in town. American and Colonial fare such as baked king's onion soup and duckling roasted with local apples are served in the tavern's six rooms with fireplaces and antiques. **Known for:** homemade colonial-era bread basket; menu written in 18th century English; time-travel experience. *Average main: $20 89 Steinwehr Ave. 717/334–2100 www.dobbinhouse.com.*

Coffee and Quick Bites

The Ragged Edge Coffee House

$ | **AMERICAN** | This homey café is a popular spot for locals to start their day with a cup of joe from locally roasted beans. The menu offers egg sandwiches and wraps for breakfast and a changing lineup of soups, sandwiches, and salads that are served all day. **Known for:** Locally roasted organic and fair trade coffee; housemade chai; great place to grab breakfast. *Average main: $7 110 Chambersburg St. 717/334–4464 www.facebook.com/raggededgecoffeehouse.*

Hotels

Baladerry Inn

$$ | **B&B/INN** | This 1812 farmstead property just south of downtown Gettsyburg offers 10 rooms among three 19th-century homes. **Pros:** bucolic grounds; convenient to National Park Visitor Center; hearty breakfast. **Cons:** TVs in some rooms only; private baths only in some rooms; street noise. *Rooms from: $158 40 Hospital Rd. 717/337–1342 www.baladerryinn.com 10 rooms Free breakfast.*

Gettysburg Hotel, Est.1797

$$ | **HOTEL** | Built before the Civil War, this six-story hotel is in the heart of the downtown historic district. **Pros:** walking distance to battlefield and other historic sites; seasonal rooftop pool; complimentary bike rentals. **Cons:** some street noise from traffic circle; some rooms need updating; parking not included. *Rooms from: $189 1 Lincoln Sq. 717/337–2000, 866/378–1797 www.hotelgettysburg.com 175 rooms No meals.*

Gettystown Inn-Dobbin House

$ | **B&B/INN** | Overlooking the spot where Lincoln gave his Gettysburg Address, this Civil War–era inn has both rooms and suites decorated in period furnishings, many with four-poster beds. **Pros:** convenient to shopping and attractions; period ambience; on-site dining. **Cons:** some street noise; window-unit air conditioners; limited grounds. *Rooms from: $130 89 Steinwehr Ave. 717/334–2100 www.dobbinhouse.com 4 rooms Free breakfast.*

Historic Farnsworth House Inn

$ | **B&B/INN** | This 1810 building has a rich history that includes sheltering Confederate soldiers during the Battle of Gettysburg—more than 100 bullet holes are forever part of the walls—and guest rooms are decorated with period antiques and Victorian furnishings including four-poster beds. **Pros:** close to battlefield and other historic sites; period atmosphere; ghost-tour experience. **Cons:** $50 cancellation fee regardless of date; children under 10 discouraged; said to be haunted. *Rooms from: $145 401 Baltimore St. 717/334–8838 www.farnsworthhouseinn.com 10 rooms Free breakfast.*

James Gettys Hotel

$$ | **HOTEL** | Located in the center of town, this four-story building, built in 1804, was originally operated as a tavern and roadhouse. **Pros:** convenient to downtown restaurants and shops; in-room breakfast basket; kitchenettes. **Cons:** some street noise; desk clerk not on duty 24/7; farther away from battlefield than some hotels. *Rooms from: $159 27 Chambersburg St. 717/337–1334, 888/900–5275 www.jamesgettyshotel.com 12 suites Free breakfast.*

Shopping

The Horse Soldier

ANTIQUES/COLLECTIBLES | The Horse Soldier carries one of the country's largest collections of military antiques—everything from bullets to discharge papers. Its **Soldier Genealogical Research Service** can help find your ancestors' war records prior to 1910. *219 Steinwehr Ave. 717/334–0347 www.horsesoldier.com.*

Index

A

B

C

W

Y

Z

Photo Credits

Front Cover: S. Greg Panosian [Description: Benjamin Franklin parkway leading to the Philadelphia skyline.]. **Back cover, from left to right:** f11photo/Shutterstock, f11photo/Shutterstock, Zack Frank/Shutterstock. **Spine:** F11photo/Dreamstime. **Interior, from left to right:** BrianEKushner/iStockphoto (1). Sean Pavone/iStockphoto (2). **Chapter 1: Experience Philadelphia:** Ultima_Gaina/iStockphoto (6-7). AevanStock/Shutterstock (8). Steve Weinik/Mural Arts Philadelphia (9). Pravada Photography (9). Matt Smith Photographer/Shutterstock (10). NPS (10). James McGuiness/Rails-to-Trails Conservancy (10). Reading Terminal Market Corporation (10). Albert Yee/Fairmount Park Conservancy (11). Jon Bilous/Shutterstock (11). James Kirkikis/Shutterstock (12). John Van Horn/Eastern State Penitentiary Historic Site (12). M*AR 2017 (12). The Franklin Institute (12). Fermentery Form (13). Lexy Pierce (13). D'Emilio's Old World Ice Treats (14). Woodrows sandwich shop (15). Darryl Moran Photography/Eastern State Penitentiary Historic Site (16). Smallbones (16). Jana Shea/Shutterstock (16). Sean Pavone/Shutterstock (16). Zrfphoto/Dreamstime (17). Jon Bilous/Dreamstime (17). Elfreth's Alley Association (17). Bluecadet/Museum of the American Revolution (17). J. Fusco for VISIT PHILADELPHIA® (18). Photo by A. Ricketts for VISIT PHILADELPHIA® (19). **Chapter 3: Old City and Historic Downtown:** littleny/iStockphoto (51). Sean Pavone/Shutterstock (52). Tupungato/Shutterstock (53). Zerothesignal/Shutterstock (53). Jon Bilous/Dreamstime (63). Dmitrii Sakharov/Dreamstime (68). Diego Grandi/Shutterstock (71). **Chapter 4: Society Hill and Penn's Landing:** Jon Bilous/Dreamstime (77). Jon Bilous/Shutterstock (81). Erix2005/Dreamstime (87). **Chapter 5: Center City East and Chinatown:** Steve Weinik/Mural Arts Philadelphia (93). WoodysPhotos/Istockphoto (94). Erin Alexis Randolph/Dreamstime (95). Sean Pavone/Shutterstock (95). MISHELLA/Shutterstock (103). Dmitry Br/shutterstock (105). fernandogarciaesteban/istockphoto (113). **Chapter 6: Center City West and Rittenhouse Square:** Fernando Garcia Esteban/Shutterstock (117). Joe Sohm/Dreamstime (123). Fernando Garcia Esteban/Shutterstock (127). Jon Bilous/Dreamstime (134). jpellgen (@1179_jp)/Flickr (139). **Chapter 7: Parkway Museums District and Fairmount Park:** f11photo/Shutterstock (147). Alexandre Fagundes De Fagundes/Dreamstime (148). Zachary Chung Pun/Shutterstock (149). littlenySTOCK/Shutterstock (149). L F File/Shutterstock (153). Marcorubino/Dreamstime (156). Vivvi Smak/Shutterstock (158). Mihai_Andritoiu/Shutterstock (166). Vishjag/Dreamstime (168). **Chapter 8: South Philadelphia and East Passyunk:** Brian Kushner/Dreamstime (171). Olga V Kulakova/Shutterstock (178). f11photo/Shutterstock (182). Scott Biales DitchTheMap/Shutterstock (189). **Chapter 9: University City and West Philadelphia:** Tyler Sprague/iStockphoto (195). PENN Museum (201). K. Ciappa for Visit Philadelphia (206). **Chapter 10: Northern Liberties and Fishtown:** J. Fusco for Visit Philadelphia (209). RTLibrary/Flickr (214). Wally Gobetz/Flickr (221). **Chapter 11: Manayunk, Germantown, and Chestnut Hill:** JanaShea/iStockphoto (223). Jana Shea/Shutterstock (228). chrisstorb/Flickr (234). Zack Frank/Shutterstock (238). **Chapter 12: Side Trips from Philadelphia:** Karen Grigoryan/Shutterstock (241). Lei Xu/ Dreamstime (252). Delmas Lehman/iStockphoto (259). Chris Kelleher/Dreamstime (263). Chris Kelleher/Dreamstime (269). CJ013/Shutterstock (274). **Chapter 13: Lancaster County:** Jon Bilous/Shutterstock (277). George Sheldon/Shutterstock (287). Robinchw/Dreamstime (296). fernandogarciaesteban/istockphoto (299). Lissandra Melo/Shutterstock (306). **About Our Writers:** All photos are courtesy of the writers.

**Every effort has been made to trace the copyright holders, and we apologize in advance for any accidental errors. We would be happy to apply the corrections in the following edition of this publication.*

Fodor's PHILADELPHIA

Publisher: Stephen Horowitz, *General Manager*

Editorial: Douglas Stallings, *Editorial Director*; Jill Fergus, Jacinta O'Halloran, Amanda Sadlowski, *Senior Editors*; Kayla Becker, Alexis Kelly, Rachael Roth, *Editors*

Design: Tina Malaney, *Director of Design and Production*; Jessica Gonzalez, *Graphic Designer;* Mariana Tabares, *Design & Production Intern*

Production: Jennifer DePrima, *Editorial Production Manager*; Elyse Rozelle, *Senior Production Editor;* Monica White, *Production Editor*

Maps: Rebecca Baer, *Senior Map Editor*; Mark Stroud (Moon Street Cartography), *Cartographers*

Photography: Viviane Teles, *Senior Photo Editor;* Namrata Aggarwal, Ashok Kumar, Carl Yu, *Photo Editors;* Rebecca Rimmer, *Photo Intern*

Business & Operations: Chuck Hoover, *Chief Marketing Officer*; Robert Ames, *Group General Manager*; Devin Duckworth, *Director of Print Publishing*; Victor Bernal, *Business Analyst*

Public Relations and Marketing: Joe Ewaskiw, *Senior Director Communications & Public Relations*

Fodors.com: Jeremy Tarr, *Editorial Director;* Rachael Levitt, *Managing Editor*

Technology: Jon Atkinson, *Director of Technology;* Rudresh Teotia, *Lead Developer*; Jacob Ashpis, *Content Operations Manager*

Writers: Linda Cabasin, Adam Erace, Drew Lazor, Josh McIlvain, Kim O'Donnel, Regan Stephens, Jillian Wilson

Editor: Alexis Kelly

Production Editor: Elyse Rozelle

2nd Edition

ISBN 978–1–64097–274–2

ISSN 2381–5302

SPECIAL SALES

This book is available at special discounts for bulk purchases for sales promotions or premiums. For more information, e-mail SpecialMarkets@fodors.com.

PRINTED IN CANADA

10 9 8 7 6 5 4 3 2 1

About Our Writers

Linda Cabasin worked on staff at Fodor's, including stints as Philadelphia editor, before becoming a freelance travel writer and editor. A contributing editor for Fathomaway.com, she lives in New Jersey and has been exploring Philly since her University of Pennsylvania days and marriage to a local boy. She updated the Side Trips and Parkway Museums District & Fairmount Park chapters. Find her at the Flower Show or on Instagram at @lcabasin.

An award-winning food and travel writer, **Adam Erace** contributes to more than 50 publications, including *Men's Journal, Fortune,* and *Travel + Leisure.* He's the co-author of *Laurel: Modern American Flavors in Philadelphia*and *Dinner at the Club: 100 Years of Stories and Recipes from South Philly's Palizzi Social Club.* He updated the Experience chapter. Follow him on Instagram and Twitter @adamerace or his website *adamerace.com.*

Drew Lazor is the co-author of *New German Cooking* (Chronicle Books, 2015); and the author of *How to Drink French Fluently* (Ten Speed Press, 2017) and *Session Cocktails* (Ten Speed Press, 2018). As a freelance journalist, he's contributed to *Bon Appétit, Condé Nast Traveler,* the *Philadelphia Inquirer, Saveur, Serious Eats, TASTE, TIME Out, The Wall Street Journal, Vice,* and more. For this guide he updated the Old City and Historic Downtown, Society Hill and Penn's Landing, Center City East and Chinatown, South Philadelphia & East Passyunk, and University City and West Philadelphia chapters. You can follow him on Instagram @drewlazor or his website *drewlazor.com.*

A former editor at Fodor's Travel Guides, **Josh McIlvain** is a writer and editor based in Philadelphia. He is also the artistic director of Automatic Arts, a performing arts company that creates and presents original work. He updated the Manayunk, Chestnut Hill, and Germantown chapter. You can follow his work at *AutomaticArtsCo.com.*

Kim O'Donnel is a 20-plus year veteran of the food world, as a chef, journalist, and teacher. Based in Lancaster, she writes about food for *LNP* and *Lancasteronline.com.* For this guide, she updated the Lancaster County chapter. Follow her on Instagram @ kimodonnel or at *kimodonnel.com.*

Regan Stephens is a Philadelphia-based freelance writer covering food and travel. She has been on staff at *Philadelphia* and *People* magazines, and now contributes to both regional and national digital and print outlets, including *Food & Wine, Fortune,* and *Edible Philly.* In her free time, Regan loves exploring Philly with her husband and three daughters. For this guide, she updated the Travel Smart chapter. Follow her on Instagram @Regan.Stephens.

Jillian Wilson is a writer and editor based in Philadelphia. She specializes in writing about a range of subjects: Philadelphia, travel, restaurants, festivals, self care—the fun stuff. Her work has appeared in *The Philadelphia Inquirer,* visitphilly.com, and more. She updated the Center City West and Rittenhouse Square and Northern Liberties and Fishtown chapters for this guide. See more of her work at *www.jillian-wilson.com.*

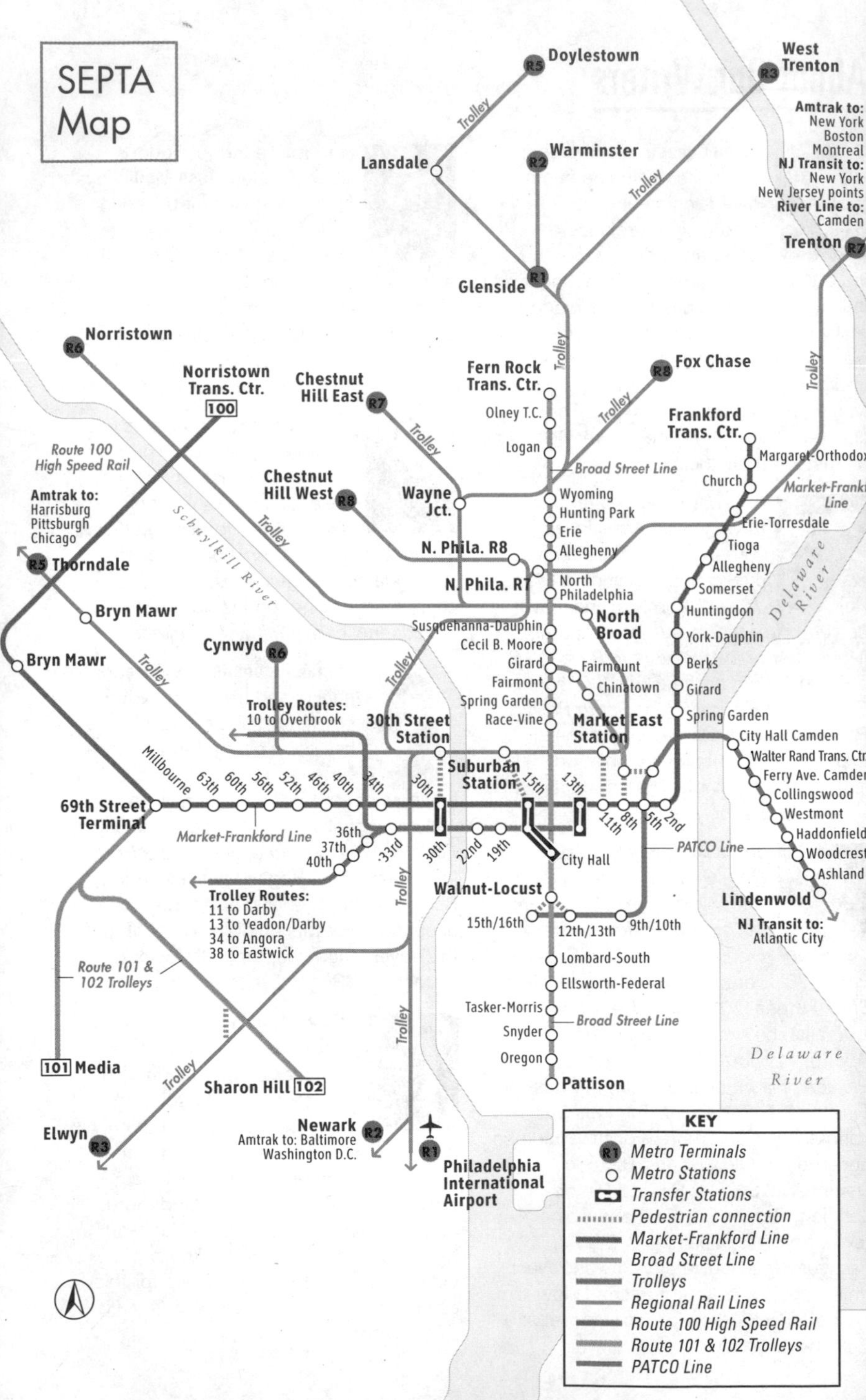

SEPTA Map
Doylestown
West Trenton
Amtrak to:
New York
Boston
Montreal
NJ Transit to:
New York
New Jersey points
River Line to:
Camden
Trenton
Warminster
Lansdale
Glenside
Norristown
Norristown Trans. Ctr.
100
Chestnut Hill East
Fern Rock Trans. Ctr.
Fox Chase
Olney T.C.
Logan
Broad Street Line
Frankford Trans. Ctr.
Margaret-Orthodox
Church
Erie-Torresdale
Tioga
Allegheny
Somerset
Huntingdon
York-Dauphin
Berks
Girard
Spring Garden
Route 100 High Speed Rail
Amtrak to:
Harrisburg
Pittsburgh
Chicago
Thorndale
Schuylkill River
Chestnut Hill West
Wayne Jct.
Wyoming
Hunting Park
Erie
Allegheny
N. Phila. R8
N. Phila. R7
North Philadelphia
North Broad
Delaware River
Bryn Mawr
Cynwyd
Susquehanna-Dauphin
Cecil B. Moore
Girard
Fairmount
Spring Garden
Race-Vine
Fairmount
Chinatown
Market East Station
Trolley Routes:
10 to Overbrook
30th Street Station
Suburban Station
City Hall Camden
Walter Rand Trans. Ctr.
Ferry Ave. Camden
Collingswood
Westmont
Haddonfield
Woodcrest
Ashland
Lindenwold
NJ Transit to:
Atlantic City
Millbourne
63rd
60th
56th
52nd
46th
40th
34th
30th
15th
13th
69th Street Terminal
Market-Frankford Line
36th
37th
40th
33rd
30th
22nd
19th
City Hall
11th
8th
5th
2nd
PATCO Line
Trolley Routes:
11 to Darby
13 to Yeadon/Darby
34 to Angora
38 to Eastwick
Walnut-Locust
15th/16th
12th/13th
9th/10th
Lombard-South
Ellsworth-Federal
Tasker-Morris
Snyder
Oregon
Pattison
Route 101 & 102 Trolleys
101 Media
Sharon Hill 102
Elwyn
Newark
Amtrak to: Baltimore
Washington D.C.
Philadelphia International Airport
Delaware River
Trolley
KEY
Metro Terminals
Metro Stations
Transfer Stations
Pedestrian connection
Market-Frankford Line
Broad Street Line
Trolleys
Regional Rail Lines
Route 100 High Speed Rail
Route 101 & 102 Trolleys
PATCO Line